PERSPECTIVES ON ENVIRONMENT AND BEHAVIOR

Theory, Research, and Applications

PERSPECTIVES ON ENVIRONMENT AND BEHAVIOR
Theory, Research, and Applications

Edited by

DANIEL STOKOLS
University of California, Irvine

PLENUM PRESS · NEW YORK AND LONDON

Library of Congress Cataloging in Publication Data

Main entry under title:

Perspectives on environment and behavior.

Includes bibliographical references and index.
1. Environmental psychology. 2. Psychological research. I. Stokols,
Daniel.
BF353.P44   155.9   76-45326
ISBN 0-306-30954-8

©1977 Plenum Press, New York
A Division of Plenum Publishing Corporation
227 West 17th Street, New York, N.Y. 10011

Printed in the United States of America

Contributors

Altman, Irwin, University of Utah, Salt Lake City, Utah

Baldassare, Mark, University of California at Los Angeles, California

Fischer, Claude S., University of California, Berkeley, California

Glass, David C., University of Texas, Austin, Texas

Kaplan, Rachel, University of Michigan, Ann Arbor, Michigan

Kaplan, Stephen, University of Michigan, Ann Arbor, Michigan

Kirmeyer, Sandra, Claremont Graduate School, Claremont, California

Krovetz, Martin L., Carmel High School, Carmel, California

Loo, Chalsa, University of California at Santa Cruz, California

McKechnie, George E., University of California, Berkeley, California

Michelson, William, University of Toronto, Toronto, Ontario, Canada

O'Hanlon, Timothy, Graduate School and University Center, City University of New York, New York

Patterson, Arthur H., Pennsylvania State University, University Park, Pennsylvania

Pennebaker, James W., University of Texas, Austin, Texas

Proshansky, Harold M., Graduate School and University Center, City University of New York

Singer, Jerome E., State University of New York at Stony Brook, Long Island, New York

Smith, M. Brewster, University of California at Santa Cruz, California

Sommer, Robert, University of California at Davis, California

Stokols, Daniel, University of California at Irvine, California

Wicker, Allan W., Claremont Graduate School, Claremont, California

Willems, Edwin P., University of Houston, Houston, Texas

Preface

The inception of this volume can be traced to a series of Environmental Psychology Colloquia presented at the University of California, Irvine, during the spring of 1974. These colloquia were held in conjunction with Social Ecology 252, a graduate seminar on Man and the Environment.

Although the eight colloquia covered a wide range of topics and exemplified a diversity of research techniques, they seemed to converge on some common theoretical and methodological assumptions about the nature of environment–behavioral research. The apparent continuities among these colloquia suggested the utility of developing a manuscript that would provide a historical overview of research on environment and behavior, a representation of its major concerns, and an analysis of its conceptual and empirical trends. Thus, expanded versions of the initial presentations were integrated with a supplemental set of invited manuscripts to yield the present volume of original contributions by leading researchers in the areas of ecological and environmental psychology.

I would like to thank several people whose assistance contributed to the development and improvement of this book. First, John Whiteley, Dean of Students at the University of California, Irvine, generously provided funding for the Environmental Psychology Colloquia held at Irvine in 1974. Also, Stacy Adams, Leonard Bickman, Gary Evans, Gilbert Geis, David Marrero, John Monahan, Rudolph Moos, Arthur Patterson, Peter Suedfeld, and Lawrence Wrightsman offered helpful comments on the manuscript. Pat Branovan provided able assistance in the preparation of the manuscript. Finally, I am grateful to my wife, Jeanne, for her critical readings of the manuscript and her encouragement throughout the editing process.

DANIEL STOKOLS
Irvine, California

Contents

SECTION I
Introduction ☐

During the late 1960's and early 1970's, the study of human behavior in relation to the physical–social environment emerged as one of the fastest-growing areas of psychological research. Collective interest among psychologists in this area first becme evident with the publication of a special issue of the *Journal of Social Issues* on "Man's Response to the Physical Environment" (Kates and Wohlwill, 1966) and the appearance of books by Hall (1966) and Sommer (1969) on human spatial behavior and by Barker (1968) on ecological psychology. Shortly thereafter the formalization of environment–behavioral studies as a new and vital research domain was signaled by the publication of programmatic articles and books on environmental psychology (cf. Craik, 1970, 1973; Proshansky, Ittelson, and Rivlin, 1970), the institution of graduate programs in "Man–environment relations," "architectural" and "environmental psychology," and more recently by the American Psychological Association's establishment of a Task Force on Environment and Behavior in January, 1974.

Numerous other articles, journals, and a stream of related conferences could be cited (cf. Proshansky and O'Hanlon, Chapter 4; Willems, Chapter 2), but the flurry of scholarly activity mentioned above should suffice to illustrate the recent surge of interest among psychologists in environment–behavioral research. Some observers both within and outside of psychology must find the sudden ascension of this research domain rather puzzling, considering that the study of behavior in relation to the physical and social environment seems to epitomize a major thrust of psychological research over the past 75 years. Learning theorists and engineering psychologists, for example, have conducted extensive research on the reinforcement properties and behavioral constraints of the physical environment, while clinical and social psychologists have studied the impact of the social environment on behavior. To what extent, then, do the newly emerging domains of ecological and environmental psychology differ from the more traditional areas of psychological research?

The present volume does not provide a final answer to this question. The "birthright" of the environment-and-behavior field will continue to be debated long after this book has been published (cf. Smith, Chapter 14). Nonetheless, it should be emphasized that the development of this volume was based on the assumption that the current concerns of research on environment and behavior are relatively novel to psychologists and can be differentiated from the foci of traditional subareas within psychology (cf. Stokols, Chapter 1). Thus, in the ensuing discussion, environment-behavioral research will be characterized as a "field," not in the sense of a consensually validated scientific paradigm (Kuhn, 1962) but rather as a set of interrelated areas of inquiry whose conceptual and methodological continuities are beginning to emerge. These continuities may eventually provide the foundation for a new, theoretically coherent discipline bridging the behavioral and design sciences.

The major goals of this book are (1) to provide a historical overview of environmentally oriented research in the field of psychology; (2) to present a characterization of the environment-and-behavior field in terms of its theoretical underpinnings and methodological strategies; and (3) to offer a set of original manuscripts that reviews empirical developments and assesses future trends within some of the major problem areas of the field.

The volume is organized into five main sections. The first portion of the book, Section I, incorporates a chapter that examines the development and convergence of two major lines of environment–behavioral research: ecological psychology and environmental psychology. An examination of the linkages between these areas provides the basis for presenting a characterization of the environment-and-behavior field and an analysis of its conceptual and methodological trends. A major purpose of this chapter is to offer an overview of the origins and the directions of the field that will serve as a framework within which the remaining chapters can be integrated.

The environment-and-behavior field, as described in the opening chapter, incorporates four major conceptual and procedural properties (see also Altman, 1975; Barker, 1968; Craik, 1970; Ittelson, Proshansky, Rivlin, and Winkel, 1974; Proshansky, Ittelson, and Rivlin, 1970; Willems, Chapter 2; Wohlwill, 1970). First, the study of behavior in relation to the man-made and the natural environment typically proceeds from an ecological perspective. This perspective combines a unique set of theoretical and methodological assumptions, which are discussed extensively in succeeding chapters (Wicker and Kirmeyer, Chapter 3; Willems, Chapter 2). Second, the role of psychological and social processes (such as perception, cognition, personality, social learning, and group dynamics) in mediating environment–behavioral transactions is emphasized. Third, the field is oriented toward the utilization of theories and research strategies in the development of solutions to community problems. Finally, research on environment and behavior tends to be interdisciplinary in nature because of the complexity of community problems and the necessity of approaching them from different perspectives and levels of analysis.

The remaining sections of the book elaborate upon each of the above-mentioned features of the environment-and-behavior field. Section II surveys the development of the ecological perspective within psychology. Recent research in the area of ecological psychology, which emphasizes group processes of adaptation to environmental constraints, is examined. Section III reviews research in the area of environmental psychology, which combines the perspective of ecological psychology with a greater emphasis on personal as well as social mediators of environment–behavioral transactions. Theoretical and empirical developments in research on such topics as human crowding, response to noise, environmental cognition, and environmental simulation and assessment are discussed. Section IV examines applications of behavioral research to the fields of architecture and community planning, with particular emphasis on the concept of behavior–environment congruence as a basis for environmental design. Finally, Section V provides an analysis of methodological developments and a projection of future trends in research on environment and behavior.

In summary, the chapters included in this volume do not exhaust the range of topics addressed by environment–behavioral researchers (cf. Craik, 1973). Hopefully, however, they are sufficiently representative to permit an accurate assessment of the field's origins, major concerns, and emergent directions at the end of its first decade.

References

Altman, I. *The environment and social behavior: Privacy, personal space, territory, and crowding.* Monterey, Calif.: Brooks/Cole, 1975.

Barker, R. *Ecological psychology: Concepts and methods for studying the environment of human behavior.* Stanford, Calif.: Stanford University Press, 1968.

Craik, K. Environmental psychology. In K. Craik, B. Kleinmuntz, R. Rosnow, R. Rosenthal, J. A. Cheyne, and R. H. Walters (Eds.), *New directions in psychology* (Vol. 4). New York: Holt, Rinehart, and Winston, 1970.

Craik, K. Environmental psychology. *Annual Review of Psychology,* 1973, *24,* 403–422.

Hall, E. *The hidden dimension.* New York: Doubleday, 1966.

Ittelson, W., Proshansky, H., Rivlin, L., and Winkel, G. *An introduction to environmental psychology.* New York: Holt, Rinehart, and Winston, 1974.

Kates, R., and Wohlwill, J. (Eds.). Man's response to the physical environment. *Journal of Social Issues,* 1966 22, 1–140.

Kuhn, T. *The structure of scientific revolutions.* Chicago: University of Chicago Press, 1962.

Proshansky, H., Ittelson, W., and Rivlin, L. (Eds.). *Environmental psychology: Man and his physical setting.* New York: Holt, Rinehart and Winston, 1970.

Sommer, R. *Personal space: The behavioral basis of design.* Englewood Cliffs, N.J.: Prentice-Hall, 1969.

Wohlwill, J. The emerging discipline of environmental psychology. *American Psychologist,* 1970, *25,* 303–312.

Origins and Directions of Environment–Behavioral Research

1

DANIEL STOKOLS

For several decades, experimental psychologists have characterized their discipline as the search for lawful relationships between dimensions of the environment and patterns of behavior (cf. Hull, 1943; Skinner, 1953; Spence, 1944; Tolman, 1938; Watson, 1913). This abbreviated view of psychology, though initially proposed by learning theorists, seems generally applicable today to several areas of psychological research. Thus it is not surprising that current mention of research on environment and behavior as an "emerging field" of scientific inquiry is met with some rather puzzled looks and hard questions from numerous psychologists. Most of these questions, of course, pertain to the alleged uniqueness of environment-behavioral research in relation to existing subareas of psychology.

The major purposes of this chapter are to identify some of the unique features of the environment-and-behavior field and to examine its relationship to more traditional areas of psychological research. To avoid pretension, we must make certain qualifications at this point concerning the characterization of environment-and-behavior research as a scientific field. At its loftiest level, the term *field* can refer to Kuhn's (1962) notion of a paradigm or "universally recognized scientific achievements that for a time provide model problems and solutions to a community of practitioners" (p. viii). On a more restricted level, it can refer to the operational definition of a particular research domain in terms of the unique concerns and activities of those scientists who identify with the area (cf. Proshansky, Ittelson, and Rivlin, 1970, p. 5). According to the latter definition, the concerns of a field

DANIEL STOKOLS ● University of California at Irvine.

should be distinguishable from those of existing areas of research, but no assumptions are made about the originality of the various approaches adopted by members of the field or about the relative utility of these approaches in providing solutions to problems of common concern.

The area of environment–behavioral research does not now qualify as a paradigm in its own right, for most of its theories and research strategies have been borrowed from several of the behavioral and design sciences. Moreover the diversity of interests reflected among researchers in the area and the recency of their collective identity preclude, for the time being, any identification of the "model problems and solutions" to which Kuhn refers.

Nonetheless it is currently possible to portray the environment-and-behavior field in terms of the unique concerns encompassed by two converging lines of research: *ecological psychology* (or behavioral ecology; cf. Barker, 1968; Wicker and Kirmeyer, Chapter 3; Willems, Chapter 2) and *environmental psychology* (cf. Craik, 1970; Proshansky, Ittelson, and Rivlin, 1970; Wohlwill, 1970). Both of these areas are directly concerned with the relationship between human behavior and elements of the architectural and the natural environment. While ecological psychology emphasizes the collective processes by which groups adapt to the physical and social resources available in the environment, environmental psychology focuses more upon intrapersonal processes, such as perception, cognition, and learning, that mediate the impact of the environment on the individual.

The remaining discussion is divided into two sections. The first provides a historical overview of major research developments within ecological and environmental psychology. This overview is not meant to be an exhaustive history of the environment-and-behavior field (for more complete historical treatments, see Altman, 1975; Proshansky and O'Hanlon, Chapter 4; Willems, Chapter 2). Rather, it is intended to provide a "topical map" or operational definition of the field in terms of its intellectual antecedents and substantive emphases.

The second portion of the chapter proceeds from an overview of ecological and environmental psychology to an integration of these areas in terms of their common theoretical and methodological trends. An analysis of these trends suggests several research questions whose eventual resolution may provide the basis for delineating an integrated paradigm of environment–behavioral research.

An Overview of Ecological and Environmental Psychology

The establishment of ecological and environmental psychology as definable areas of investigation can be traced to the recent programmatic writings of Altman (1973), Barker (1968), Craik (1970, 1973), Proshansky, Ittelson, and Rivlin (1970), and Wohlwill (1970). Yet the development of these areas is the product of both societal forces and intellectual trends within the behavioral sciences that began to emerge several decades ago.

At the societal level, mounting pressures from global problems such as overpopulation (cf. Ehrlich, 1968; Hauser and Duncan, 1959; Thompson, 1953), urban stress (cf. Jacobs, 1961; Levi and Andersson, 1975; Milgram, 1970; Simmel, 1950; Wirth, 1938), and environmental degradation (cf. Carson, 1962; Commoner, 1963; Harrington, 1962) have contributed to an increasing concern among policy makers and laymen about Man's relationship to the physical environment. At the same time, parallel research developments (e.g., Calhoun's 1962 report of the devastating impact of population concentration on laboratory animals) and an increasing theoretical emphasis on the relationship between human behavior and the molar environment have prompted a growing interest among psychologists in such problems as environmental perception (Downs and Stea, 1973; Ittelson, 1973; Lynch, 1960), spatial behavior (Altman, 1975; Hall, 1966; Sommer, 1969), and environmental design (Canter and Lee, 1974; Lang, Burnette, Moleski, and Vachon, 1974; Newman, 1973; Saarinen, 1976).

The overview presented below emphasizes the disciplinary rather than societal antecedents of ecological and environmental psychology. (Societal antecedents of environment–behavioral research are discussed more extensively by Proshansky and O'Hanlon, Chapter 4, and Smith, Chapter 14.) Specifically, the discussion will focus on the development of two major trends in psychological research: (1) the increasing elaboration and application of ecological approaches to the study of behavior; and (2) a growing awareness of the impact of the physical environment on human behavior and well-being.

Ecological Psychology

Ecology, in its simplest and most general terms, can be defined as the study of the interrelations between organisms and their environment (cf. Hawley, 1950). From an ecological perspective, *environment* subsumes all external forces to which organisms are actually or potentially responsive, whereas *behavior* is characterized as those responses made by organisms that either promote or impair their collective survival in the face of environmental fluctuations. Although these definitions are extremely broad, they do reflect two major emphases of ecology: (1) the behavioral relevance of the molar environment and (2) the survival value or adaptive nature of behavior.

To arrive at a more detailed account of ecology's specific concerns and those of ecological psychology in particular, we must trace the development and elaboration of the ecological perspective within the disciplines of biology, sociology, and psychology. In each of these areas, systematic attempts have been made to apply an ecological approach to the study of particular units of the environment in relation to different levels of behavior.

Ecological analyses of environment–behavior relationships first were articulated by biologists who emphasized the interdependence of plant and animal groups occupying the same habitat (cf. Clements, 1905; Darwin, 1859-1964; Taylor, 1936; Warming, 1909). According to the early bioecologists, the primary unit of environmental analysis was the *biome*, a spatially bounded area comprised of biotic (plant and animal species) and abiotic (climate and topography) elements. The concept of *ecosystem* (cf. Allee, Emerson, Park, Park, and Schmidt, 1949; Odum, 1959) later was introduced to emphasize the inherent interdependence of all elements within the biome and the dynamic processes by which plant and animal species survive through continual adaptation to environmental constraints.

Many of the key concepts and methods of modern bioecology can be traced to Darwin's now-classic work *The Origin of Species*, first published in 1859. In this volume, Darwin discussed four major classes of environmental constraints that are faced by all plant and animal species: (1) a limited supply of food, (2) the threat of predation, (3) abrupt geographical changes, and (4) the ravages of disease. At a behavioral level, the process of adaptation was viewed as the attempt of organisms to deal with these constraints.

Behavioral adaptation was analyzed by bioecologists from an aggregate or group level of analysis. The focus of investigation was on the manner in which groups of organisms, rather than individuals, collectively respond to environmental pressures. Individual behavior was viewed primarily as the reflection of a specialized function within a larger organizational structure. The ultimate criterion of successful adaptation was the continued survival of the species, which could be predicted largely in terms of the differentiation and the complexity of its internal organization.

Species survival has been studied in relation to both genetic and social organization. Several researchers, for example, have suggested that the diversity and complexity of characteristics present within the gene pool of a population places upper limits on the capacity of its members to survive environmental pressures and to propagate the species (cf. Dobzhansky, 1951; Stebbins, 1966). In regard to social organization, the adaptive value of such processes as the division of labor, territoriality, and the development of dominance hierarchies has been emphasized (cf. Wynne-Edwards, 1962). All of these processes contribute to the continued survival of the group by promoting a more efficient utilization of environmental resources and propagation by the strongest and fittest members of the community.

Bioecology contributed a unique set of conceptual and methodological assumptions to the study of environment and behavior. At a theoretical level, the environment was conceptualized as a dynamically organized system comprised of physical and biological components. Moreover, behavior was viewed as the vehicle of collective adaptation to multiple environmental factors, and specific adaptive mechanisms of biological and social organization were identified. At a methodological level, longitudinal and naturalistic approaches to the study of behavior were emphasized. Only through the extended observation of animals in their natural habitat could the functional aspects of individual and group behavior be understood.

The contributions of bioecology were elaborated upon by sociologists (e.g., McKenzie, 1925; Park and Burgess, 1921, 1925) seeking to develop a comprehensive model of human ecology or "the study of the form and development of the human community" (Hawley, 1950, p. 68). Like their biological cousins, human ecologists were concerned with the processes by which groups adapt to the vicissitudes of nature. The focus of their analysis, though, was on the human ecosystem comprised of the city and its surrounding agricultural area. The spatial and economic organization of the city was viewed as the primary index of human adaptation to the environment.

Several basic principles of bioecology were applied to an analysis of the human community. It was assumed, for example, that the spatial form and social structure of human communities become increasingly complex and differentiated over time and that those groups that achieve the highest levels of organization eventually succeed less organized groups and attain a position of dominance within their immediate geographical region.

According to the "Chicago school" human ecologists (e.g., Park, Burgess, and McKenzie), the economic base of a community, or its system of production and distribution, determines the degree of influence exercised by the community relative to that of other settlements within its geographical region. As the economic base of an area expands through technological advancements and the specialization of labor, the influx of people and resources into the community increases. On the other hand, a shrinkage of the economic base brought about by political or geographical difficulties results in an outflow of population and resources from the community. Thus the dominance of a community and its potential for continued survival can be measured in terms of the ratio of human and economic resources that enter the area to those that leave it.

Successful adaptation at the community level, however, creates a number of social, psychological, and health-related costs that are borne by certain segments of the population. Much of the early research in human ecology focused on the distribution of stress and pathology within communities as a function of shifts in the economic base and the related process of in- and out-migration (cf. Faris and Dunham, 1939; Thomas and Znaniecki, 1920). The findings from this correlational research suggested that the incidence of emotional and physical disorders was highest within the "transition zones" (Burgess, 1925/1961) of urban centers, where the newest and most transient members of the community resided.

Subsequent research elaborated upon the areal distribution of disease, crime, and poverty throughout the city in relation to socioeconomic factors (cf. Michelson, 1970; Shevky and Bell, 1955; Theodorson, 1961). The bulk of this work relied upon large-scale survey analyses in which the socioeconomic attributes of different census tracts were correlated with their respective rates of social disorganization and pathology. The inconclusive nature of these analyses has prompted contemporary researchers to adopt more reliable statistical procedures and quasi-experimental designs in an attempt to obtain a more adequate assessment of the relationship between economic cycles and community stress (cf. Brenner, 1973; Catalano, 1975).

The first major attempt to develop an ecological perspective within the discipline of psychology was presented by Roger Barker (1960, 1968). Barker's (1968) conceptualization of ecological psychology involved an extension of ecological principles from the macro or community level of analysis to a consideration of microsocial phenomena. This shift of emphasis was reflected in Barker's concept of the "behavior setting," an environment–behavioral unit characterized by cyclical patterns of activity that occur within specific time intervals and spatial boundaries. Examples of behavior settings are dormitory lounges, restaurants, and baseball games. Within Barker's framework, the ecology of the total community remained an important issue but was approached in terms of the dynamics of multiple behavioral settings that, together, comprised the larger environment.

The ecological analysis of behavior settings required certain theoretical and methodological departures from the research strategies of human ecology. First, behavior settings were, by definition, smaller in scale than the environmental units examined by human ecologists. One census tract, for example, would subsume a diversity of behavior settings. Second, behavior settings were defined not only in terms of their spatial boundaries but also of their social and temporal properties. Thus, a given area might serve as a behavior setting only when certain people gathered to perform particular activities at specified times. This conceptualization of environment was explicitly multidimensional, as compared to earlier ones that focused primarily on the physical attributes of a given area. Third, ecological psychologists were more concerned with the impact of the environment on small groups than on large-scale populations. Thus demographic methods of analysis were replaced by fine-grained observation of interpersonal behavior and the collection of individualized, subjective-report data.

Through a series of longitudinal, naturalistic comparisons among diverse behavior settings, Barker and his colleagues developed a theory of *undermanning* (cf. Barker, 1960; Barker and Gump, 1964; Barker and Wright, 1955). A central assumption of this theory is that all behavior settings have essential tasks or functions that are associated with specific personnel requirements. To the extent that a particular setting is understaffed, systemic pressures should arise that place demands on available personnel for more intensive participation in its activities. Thus for undermanned settings, where there are fewer participants than the number of available roles, maintenance pressures should induce members to take on a greater variety of tasks, work longer hours, and assume greater responsibility than they would under conditions of optimal manning (i.e., where the numbers of participants and of available roles are matched). These predictions received support in a variety of studies involving the comparison of large and small schools (cf. Baird, 1969; Barker and Gump, 1964; Wicker, 1968, 1969a; Willems, 1967), churches (Wicker, 1969b; Wicker and Mehler, 1971), and whole communities (cf. Barker and Schoggen, 1973).

As an extension of Barker's theory, Wicker, McGrath, and Armstrong (1972) developed the construct of *overmanning*. Overmanned settings were defined as those in which the number of eligible participants exceeds the personnel capacity of the system. As in the case of undermanning, overmanning was viewed as an unstable condition that generates forces toward adequate or optimal manning. These forces are manifested as pressures to increase the setting capacity or to decrease membership by raising eligibility standards and discouraging potential applicants. In support of these predictions, Hanson and Wicker (1973) found that members of overmanned groups felt significantly less needed, less important, and less valuable to the group than those working under adequate-manning conditions. Subsequently Wicker and Kirmeyer (Chapter 3) developed an extension of overmanning theory based on McGrath's (1970) model of stress and tested hypotheses derived from this extension within the context of a large-scale public setting.

In retrospect, the special significance of Barker's research is that it extended macroecological principles to an analysis of human behavior in small-group settings. The assumption that human communities respond collectively to environmental constraints, for example, is reflected in the group's adjustment of its personnel requirements so as to utilize the existing resources in the behavior setting most efficiently. The dynamic nature of adaptive processes is reflected in the sequential adjustment of group members to the pressures of under- and overmanning. Moreover the naturalistic and longitudinal emphases of earlier ecological research are clearly evident in the methodological strategies of behavior–setting analysis (cf. Barker and Schoggen, 1973; Wicker and Kirmeyer, Chapter 3; Willems, Chapter 2).

Despite its emphasis on small-group phenomena, however, ecological psychology provides a rather incomplete account of behavior at the micro level. For the most part, research in this area has focused on behavior as a function of group membership or the manner in which the average person would respond given specific social-structural and physical features of a setting. Although behavioral and subjective data are obtained on individuals, response profiles typically are aggregated over group members and tend to downplay the role of individual differences in mediating the rela-

tionship between the structure of the setting and the responses of its occupants.[1]

Through its neglect of dispositional factors and basic psychological
processes, ecological psychology has failed to address a variety of interesting and important questions: In what types of individuals will conditions of
under- or overmanning induce the most negative reactions? Under what
circumstances will conditions of inadequate manning be most salient to
setting members? Under what conditions and for which persons will perceived limitations of the environment (e.g., scarcity of social roles and physical resources) lead to maladaptive behavior? The resolution of these and
related questions requires explicit consideration of the relationship between
ecological and intrapersonal processes.

Environmental Psychology

The role of basic psychological processes—such as perception, cognition,
personality development, and social learning—in mediating the relationship between human behavior and the environment has been considered
more fully in the realm of environmental psychology. This line of research,
initially delimited by Proshansky, Ittelson, and Rivlin (1970; see also Ittelson, Proshansky, Rivlin, and Winkel, 1974; Craik, 1970, 1973; Wohlwill,
1970), was defined in terms of specific research commitments and methodological assumptions rather than a formal theoretical structure. Research in
environmental psychology, for example, has generally been organized
around a strong concern for the analysis and resolution of contemporary
community problems and has relied heavily on the use of naturalistic and
longitudinal techniques in the examination of the effects of the architectural and the natural environment on people. In this research, direct emphasis has been placed on the manner in which psychological and social
processes interact with features of the physical environment to yield varying patterns of behavior.

The formulation of environmental psychology was influenced to a
certain extent by early developments within ecological psychology (Barker,
1960, 1968). This influence is reflected in the current emphasis of environmental psychology on the importance of the molar physical environment as a determinant of behavior and on the use of naturalistic strategies
for studying the dynamic interchange between Man and his milieu.

Yet the intellectual origins of ecological psychology and environmental

---

[1]Two recent departures from this trend are the research programs of Willems (1973, 1974,
Chapter 2) and Wicker and Kirmeyer (Chapter 3). Willems's reformulation of ecological
psychology, under the heading of *behavioral ecology*, places a decidedly greater emphasis on
the assessment and modification of individual behavior than was reflected in Barker's (1968)
original conceptualization. Also, Wicker and Kirmeyer's analysis of overmanning departs
from traditional ecological perspectives through its emphasis on the importance of the individual's perceptions and cognitions.

psychology were essentially quite different. Whereas the former evolved from an extension of bioecological principles to the analysis of small-scale social systems, the latter emerged from conceptual developments within traditional areas of psychology that placed increasing emphasis on the interplay of personal and environmental determinants of behavior. The divergence of their origins accounts for the main dissimilarity between these two areas of research: the greater emphasis of environmental psychology on intrapersonal processes and on how the subjective, as well as the objective, environment affects individual and group behavior.

At least three major theoretical developments contributed to the emergence of an "interactionist" perspective (Bowers, 1973) within psychology, one that emphasizes the interaction of personal and environmental factors in determining behavior. These developments were (1) the advent of behaviorism (Watson, 1913); (2) the development of "field" theories in the areas of perceptual and social psychology (Brunswik, 1949; Lewin, 1936); and (3) the shift of focus in personality research from person-based (Allport, 1937; Freud, 1904/1938; Jung, 1925) to situation-oriented (Bowers, 1973; Mischel, 1968, 1973; Murray, 1938) explanations of behavior.

The dominant orientation within psychology during the late 1800's and early 1900's was that of *structuralism* (cf. Titchener, 1897/1948; Wundt, 1904) or the introspective analysis of the human mind. The focus of structuralist analysis was on the elements of mental experience and the connections between physiological conditions and states of the mind. This approach placed exclusive emphasis on intrapersonal explanations of human activity while ignoring the linkages among environmental conditions, mental processes, and overt behavior.

Watson's (1913) delineation of *behaviorism* represented a radical reaction against the assumptions and postulates of structuralism. According to Watson, the proper goals of psychology were the prediction and control of behavior, rather than the analysis of human consciousness. At a methodological level, Watson advocated the objective observation of environment–behavioral relationships as a substitute for the introspective analysis of mental states.

Watson's statement of behaviorism emphasized environmental antecedents of behavior while disavowing any reference to mental processes. This *stimulus–response* or radical behaviorist perspective was elaborated upon in the theories of Hull (1943), Spence (1948), and Skinner (1953). These theories conceptualized the environment as a complex set of stimuli, that is, events external to the person that directly elicit or alter behavior.

A number of post-Watsonian behaviorists, however, argued that the relationships between stimuli and responses could not be predicted accurately without reference to intervening cognitive processes (cf. Bandura, 1969; Rotter, 1954; Tolman, 1938). According to "mediational" models developed by these theorists, the functional significance of the environment and its impact on behavior were mediated largely by mental processes through which individuals construed the potential reinforcement properties of a setting. Rotter, for example, proposed that the perceived probability and subjective value of specific reinforcers determined the relationship between environmental stimuli and individual behavior. Thus, stimulus–response perspectives on human learning were succeeded by theoretical approaches that gave equal emphasis to personal and environmental determinants of behavior.

In the areas of cognitive and social psychology, an interactionist perspective was reflected in the work of Lewin (1935, 1936) and Brunswik (1949). Lewin's concept of *life space,* for example, emphasized the continual interaction of inner and outer forces, such as personal needs, values, and attitudes, as well as environmental conditions, which together determined an individual's behavior within a particular setting. In Lewin's formula, $B = f_i(PE)$, behavior was viewed as a joint function of personal factors (P) and the perceived environment (E). The concern of Lewin's *field theory* was not with the objective environment *per se* but rather with the individual's subjective interpretation of that environment and the manner in which environmental perception guides individual behavior. Many of the research areas in contemporary social psychology, including those relating to group dynamics (Cartwright and Zander, 1968), cognitive dissonance (Festinger, 1957)) and comparison level (Thibaut and Kelley, 1959), are derivatives of Lewin's field-theoretical perspective.

Brunswik's (1949) theory was concerned more specifically with the perceptual processes by which individuals come to know their environment. His orientation, like Lewin's, emphasized the importance of the subjective or perceived environment as a determinant of behavior. According to Brunswik, the individual's cognitive representation of the objective environment was determined through a combination of informational cues. The occurrence of perceptual differences among two or more observers of the same physical environment was explained in terms of the differential weighting of environmental cues by each person and the idiosyncratic strategies employed in combining such cues into an overall interpretation of the environment. Thus environmental perception was viewed as a highly subjective process, dependent on both external cues and individualized cognitive strategies.

In the area of personality research, initial theoretical work focused primarily on the identification and measurement of specific traits (cf. Allport, 1937). Personality traits were conceptualized as enduring attributes of individuals that exert generalized effects on their behavior across different situations. Person-based explanations of behavior were epitomized by psychoanalytic theories of personality (Freud, 1904/1938; Jung, 1925).

The limitations inherent in trait-centered perspectives prompted the development of Murray's (1938) theory of personality. In Murray's analysis, human behavior is determined not only by personal traits and underlying needs but also by *environmental presses* that either satisfy or frustrate these needs. This perspective emphasized the cross-situational variability of an individual's behavior, which is predictable in terms of the external presses confronted within each situation.

Increasing dissatisfaction with trait conceptualizations of personality was articulated by Mischel (1968, 1973). Mischel's contention, like Murray's, was that human behavior across situations is unpredictable in terms of personal factors alone and that if behavioral regularities within individuals are to be predicted, the functional properties of the settings they occupy must be considered. Mischel's (1973) notion of *behavior-contingency units* emphasized the close association between a person's behavior and the stimulus or cue properties of the setting in which it occurs. The strength of association between environment and behavior is reflected, according to Mischel, in numerous studies in which substantial proportions of behavioral variance are accounted for by situational variables.

The interactionist perspective in psychology has been stated most clearly and comprehensively by Bowers (1973; see also Bem and Allen, 1974). In Bowers's view, situations are as much a product of the person as the person's behavior is a function of the situation. The individual's capacity to shape the environment is evidenced quite clearly through behavioral processes such as art, architecture, and community planning. Yet cognitive processes also play an important role in structuring the environment. Cognitive schemas serve not only to filter and organize external stimuli but also exert a direct influence on the nature of one's social environment. The effect of cognitions on the environment is illustrated in Merton's (1957) notion of the *self-fulfilling prophecy,* or a person's expectations about other people that lead him to act in a way that brings out the traits he expects them to have. Thus the interactionist view of environment and behavior assumes a dynamic interchange between Man and the environment in which people affect, and are affected by, their settings.

Environmental psychology, which formally emerged in 1970, combines an interactionist view of environment and behavior with an explicit emphasis on the analysis and resolution of community problems. The community orientation of environmental psychology implies certain procedural assumptions that distinguish it from earlier, environmentally oriented research on human learning, cognition, and personality. One unique feature of environmental psychology is its focus on molar as well as molecular units of the environment. The effects of noise on people, for example, are studied not only in the context of controlled laboratory situations (e.g., Glass and Singer, 1972) but also at the neighborhood level (cf. Cohen, Glass, and Singer, 1972), where urban noise occurs in conjunction with numerous other physical and social factors. Moreover, environmental psychologists often conduct their research in collaboration with nonpsychologist professionals and policy makers who are directly involved in the processes of short-term and long-range community planning (cf. S. Kaplan, Chapter 10; Smith, Chapter 14; Sommer, Chapter 8).

Research in environmental psychology has expanded rapidly since the mid 1960's and today subsumes a variety of issues and methodologies. A brief summary of this research is presented below. The summary is intended to provide a representative sampling of those issues currently being studied by environmental psychologists rather than an exhaustive or detailed inventory of research in the area.

The various lines of research in environmental psychology can be categorized according to three basic kinds of human transactions with the environment: (1) *orientation*, (2) *operation*, and (3) *evaluation*. Orientation pertains to the processes by which people perceive where they are, predict what will happen there, and decide what to do. *Operation* refers to the processes by which people act upon, and are affected by, their surroundings. And *evaluation* involves the assessment of how effective one's actions in the environment have been in procuring certain goals and how adequate the environment is as a context for future activity and goal attainment.

Certain theorists have attempted to integrate the processes of orientation, operation, and evaluation into a sequential model of human interaction with the environment. Miller, Galanter, and Pribram (1960), for example, proposed a *TOTE* (i.e., "*test–operate–test–exit*") model of human behavior that assumes that the actions of a person are continuously guided by his images of the environment, his plans for attaining specific goals in the environment, and the outcomes of his operations or behavior. TOTE units are essentially feedback loops through which particular plans are enacted, tested, and terminated upon completion. Behavior patterns are comprised of hierarchically arranged TOTE units that occur in a cyclical fashion.

Similarly Kaplan (1973) developed a model of environmental perception that emphasizes four basic human needs: recognition, prediction, evaluation, and action. According to the model, the individual's cognitive representation of the environment is guided by these four perceptual biases or needs. In terms of the present discussion, these needs represent the motivational underpinnings of orientation, operation, and evaluation processes.

Most traditional areas of psychological research emphasize at least one of these human–environment processes. Studies of perception, cognition, and personality, for example, focus upon orientation processes; research on learning and socialization emphasizes processes of operation; and research pertaining to psychopathology, to a large extent, emphasizes dysfunctional evaluative processes. The major topics of inquiry within environmental psychology also can be classified in terms of their relative emphasis on orientation, operation, and evaluation processes.

An emphasis on orientation processes is reflected in recent research relating to environmental perception (cf. Ittelson, 1973) and cognitive mapping (Downs and Stea, 1973; Kaplan, 1973; Lynch, 1960). Work in these areas has focused on the ways in which individuals develop cognitive representations of the large-scale environment. In relation to this issue, Ittelson (1973) contributed an analysis of the differences between object perception and perception of the molar environment. Some of these differences relate to the fact that environments, unlike objects, surround the individual; provide multimodal and peripheral stimulation; have an aesthetic and social ambience; and cannot be perceived passively. Research on cognitive mapping was initiated by Lynch (1960), who proposed a taxonomy of environmental units, including paths, edges, districts, nodes, and landmarks. According to Lynch, the presence of these elements in an environment contributes to its "legibility" or "the ease with which its parts can be recognized and organized into a coherent pattern" (p. 2). And as noted earlier, Kaplan (1973) presented an analysis of the evolutionary and motivational bases of cognitive-mapping processes.

The assessment of personal dispositions toward the environment (cf. Craik, 1975; McKechnie, 1974) and the measurement of social climate within residential, work, and institutional environments (cf. Moos, 1973; Insel and Moos, 1974) represent two additional lines of research in environmental psychology that have emphasized orientation processes. The application of personality theory to the issue of environmental perception is exemplified by McKechnie's (1974) development of the Environmental Response Inventory, which measures personal orientations toward the environment along dimensions such as pastoralism, urbanism, and sensation seeking. A somewhat different application of personality perspectives to an analysis of environmental perception is reflected in the research of Moos, Insel, and their colleagues. A major contribution of these researchers was the development of standardized scales to measure the psychosocial attributes of different environments. From the use of these instruments in several settings, three categories of environmental attributes were delineated: relationship dimensions, personal-development dimensions, and system-maintenance dimensions. The degree to which environments fulfill individuals' needs along these dimensions is as important a determinant of environmental perception as the physical features of the settings.[2]

An emphasis on human–environment operations, or the ways in which people affect and are affected by their surroundings, is evident in at least two major areas of environmental psychology. First, a large number of studies have dealt with human spatial behavior (cf. Altman, 1975; Baum and Valins, 1976; Edney, 1976; Evans and Howard, 1973; Hall, 1966; Loo,

[2]Future extensions of the research by Moos (1973) and Insel and Moos (1974) may involve the development of criteria for creating social climates that are maximally congruent with the needs of particular user groups. This type of research, focusing not only on the perception and measurement of social climate but also on the assessment of human needs and the design of behaviorally supportive environments, would reflect an equal emphasis on the processes of orientation, operation, and evaluation.

Chapter 6; Sommer, 1969; Stokols, 1976; Sundstrom, 1977). These investigations have focused on the processes by which people appropriate and regulate space in their interactions with others. A second line of research has focused on the behavioral and psychological effects of environmental stressors, such as noise (Glass and Singer, 1972; Cohen, Glass, and Singer, 1973), high density (Booth, 1975; Freedman, 1975; Rapoport, 1975; Sherrod, 1974; Stokols, 1972a; Zlutnick and Altman, 1972), and pollution (Swan, 1970).

Proxemics, or the study of human spatial behavior, was launched by Hall (1966), an anthropologist. Hall's research focused on the manner in which people regulate the amount of space between themselves and others depending on the degree of intimacy and the cultural context of their social encounters. Four invisible zones of comfortable interaction were posited: intimate, personal, social, and public. The first two zones are reserved for interaction with intimates and close friends, whereas social and public distances are maintained in the presence of acquaintances and strangers. Moreover, the spatial boundaries of these zones vary considerably from culture to culture.

Sommer's (1969) research on personal space contributed to a further understanding of human spatial behavior by demonstrating the effects of specific situational variables (e.g., the type of activity being performed and the formality or informality of the setting) on the individual's spatial needs. Subsequent studies have focused on the relationship between personal space, privacy, territoriality, and crowding (cf. Altman, 1975; Edney, 1976; Proshansky, Ittelson, and Rivlin, 1970). Altman, for example, characterizes crowding as a situation in which an individual is unable to achieve desired levels of privacy. The maintenance of personal space through distancing behaviors and the establishment of personalized, defensible territories are viewed as responses aimed at maintaining the balance between achieved and desired levels of privacy.

Knowles (1973) has extended proxemic concepts to a consideration of the mechanisms by which groups establish and defend temporary territories. His notion of *group space,* an analogue of personal space, suggests that groups as well as individuals have characteristic needs for space that are governed by social and physical circumstances in the immediate situation. An interesting direction for future research is the possible integration of Knowles's notion of group space with the concepts of under- and overmanning (Barker, 1960; Wicker, McGrath, and Armstrong, 1972).

While research on spatial behavior has emphasized the ways in which people use the environment to attain their goals and fulfill certain needs, studies of human response to environmental stressors have focused on the reciprocal impact of the environment on people. The effects of stressors on people illustrate Wohlwill's (1970) contention that the environment not only elicits particular responses but also imposes constraints and exerts enduring effects on human behavior.

The research by Glass and Singer (1972) on human response to noise was particularly important in integrating Selye's (1956) work on physiological stress with Lazarus's (1966) conceptualization of psychological stress. Whereas the former concept refers to a state of the individual in which environmental demands exceed his capacity to cope with them, the latter pertains to a state in which *perceived* demands exceed *perceived* abilities to cope. The importance of psychological factors in regulating the emotional and behavioral effects of environmental stressors was demonstrated by Glass and Singer through a series of laboratory studies. The results of these studies indicated that the actual amplitude of noise, though it determines the intensity of certain immediate physiological responses, is less crucial than the predictability or perceived controllability of the noise in determining the debilitative aftereffects of noise on the individual.

Glass and Singer's analysis of the differential effects of controllable and uncontrollable stressors has received further empirical support in recent field investigations of the relationship between highway noise and reading ability among children living in urban areas (Cohen, Glass, and Singer, 1973); railroad commuting and levels of stress among urban workers (Singer, Lundberg, and Frankenhaeuser, 1977); and the magnitude of individuals' life changes and their susceptibility to coronary heart disease (Glass, Singer, and Pennebaker, Chapter 5).

With regard to the effects of high density on people, initial research in this area yielded a complex assortment of contradictory findings (cf. Freedman, Klevansky, and Ehrlich, 1971; Stokols, 1972b; Zlutnick and Altman, 1972). In an attempt to organize and understand these findings, subsequent work in the area of human crowding focused on a number of definitional and taxonomic issues (cf. Altman, 1977). Crowding was distinguished from physical density and defined as an experiential state of perceived spatial limitation (Stokols, 1972a, 1976), behavioral constraint (Proshansky, Ittelson, and Rivlin, 1970), or unwanted social interaction (Altman, 1975; Desor, 1972; Valins and Baum, 1973). In addition, further analyses of density in terms of its micro and macro elements (Galle, Gove, and McPherson, 1972; Zlutnick and Altman, 1972) and its objective and subjective components (Rapoport, 1975) were presented.

Recent research has attempted to specify the personal and environmental circumstances under which high density will induce either crowding stress or positive, affiliative reactions (Altman, 1975; Freedman, 1975; Stokols, 1976; Sundstrom, 1977). These analyses provide preliminary models of human crowding in terms of its sequential and situation-specific features. A common assumption underlying these models is that crowding stress can be avoided or reduced through an enhancement of the individual's perceived control over the environment. The importance of perceived control in reducing the stressful effects of high density was demonstrated in an experiment conducted by Sherrod (1974). Subjects in this study who were informed that they could leave a high-density situation if they so desired exhibited fewer post-density aftereffects on a measure of frustration tolerance than those who remained in the situation for the same amount of time but were instructed not to leave until told to do so.

Evaluation processes, or the ways in which people assess the effectiveness of their past behavior and the opportunities afforded by the environment for future goal-attainment, have been emphasized in research on environmental assessment and simulation (cf. Craik, 1971; McKechnie, Chapter 7; S. Kaplan, Chapter 10), landscape preference (cf. Craik, 1972; R. Kaplan, Chapter 11; Zube, 1976), and social impact assessment (cf. Catalano, Simmons, and Stokols, 1975; Wolf, 1974, 1975). An important assumption of research in these areas is that people evaluate and plan their surroundings in relation to specific needs and goals. The salient needs and goals of individuals provide the basis for establishing standards of environmental quality that are used to judge the adequacy of present or future environmental conditions.

Environmental-assessment research has attempted to identify the dimensions on which people evaluate the quality of existing settings. Criteria of environmental quality have been delineated in relation to both architectural and natural environments (see Craik, 1971, for a review of this literature). In the area of architectural assessment, Osmond (1957) presented a set of guidelines for psychiatric-ward design based on an analysis of the unique psychological and behavioral needs of schizophrenic patient groups. Among the needs emphasized in Osmond's analysis were privacy maintenance, the reduction of uncertainty, the preservation of choice, and the opportunity to form beneficial social relationships. In an attempt to develop criteria for the planning of suburban neighborhoods, Gans (1961) stressed the importance of spatial proximity and population homogeneity to the fulfillment of residents' needs for informal interaction with their neighbors. And, more recently, Wohlwill (1976) contributed an analysis of aesthetic criteria as a basis for environmental evaluation.

Research on the assessment of natural settings has examined the relationship between perceived environmental quality and users' recreational choices (Mercer, 1976), attitudes toward wilderness (Hendee and Harris, 1970), and landscape preferences (cf. Craik, 1972; R. Kaplan, Chapter 11; Zube, 1976). Shafer and Thompson (1968), for example, related the physical attributes of Adirondack campsites and their proximity to recreational areas (lake, hiking trails) to the frequency of their use. Recent research on the assessment of outdoor areas has focused on the development of models for the prediction of landscape preferences (cf. S. Kaplan, 1975; R. Kaplan, Chapter 11). These models emphasize human needs for spaciousness, orderliness, predictability, and complexity in the environment.

The anticipation of people's responses to future environments has been the focus of environmental-simulation research. McKechnie (Chapter 7) characterizes environmental simulations as a set of techniques used for previewing environments that have not yet been built or modified.

Appleyard and Craik (1974) pioneered in the development of a large-scale urban simulator, incorporating a mobile video camera, which permits the assessment of individuals' responses to simulated tours through a scale-modeled neighborhood. Also a theoretical analysis of cognitive-simulation processes and a method for assessing individual's architectural preferences through the use of scale-model buildings were developed by S. Kaplan (Chapter 10).

Closely related to environmental-simulation research is the area of social-impact assessment (cf. Catalano, Simmons, and Stokols, 1975; Wolf, 1974, 1975). Social-impact assessment involves the evaluation of proposed environmental changes in relation to their potential effects on the social and physical well-being of user groups. This area of study is a subspecialty of environmental-impact analysis that developed during the early 1970's as a result of legislation in several states requiring the evaluation of environmental designs in terms of their potential impact on the natural environment (e.g., on soil, air, and water quality). Research in the area of social-impact assessment has focused on the development of psychological, behavioral, and demographic criteria for forecasting the social and health consequences of environmental changes.

The above overview of research in relation to orientation, operation, and evaluation processes is, of course, selective and incomplete. Hopefully, though, it provides a representative survey of the major substantive concerns and methodological approaches within environmental psychology. The following section of the chapter examines the linkages between ecological and environmental psychology and provides a characterization of the environment-and-behavior field in terms of its theoretical and methodological trends.

Toward an Integrated Field of Environment and Behavior

Although ecological and environmental psychology emerged from different intellectual traditions, they currently appear to be converging toward some common substantive and methodological emphases. The *systems–theoretical emphasis of ecological psychology on adaptation and equilibrium processes*, for example, is becoming increasingly evident in environment–behavioral research. Recent analyses of the individual's response to environmental stressors rely heavily on homeostatic concepts (e.g., the sequential models of crowding proposed by Altman, 1975, Stokols, 1972b, and Sundstrom, 1977). Moreover, Altman's social-unit analysis (Chapter 15) offers a programmatic set of strategies for extending systems–theoretical principles to the analysis of person-by-environment and of group-by-environment interactions.

At the same time, the *concern of environmental psychology with intrapersonal processes* is receiving greater emphasis in several areas of environment–behavioral research, including ecological psychology. Willems's statement of behavioral ecology (Chapter 2), for example, reflects a more thorough consideration of the individual's adaptation to the environment than was evident in earlier, group-centered formulations of ecological psychology (Barker, 1968), while Wicker and Kirmeyer's extension of overmanning theory (Chapter 3) explicitly integrates concepts pertaining to the individual's perception of the environment with a behavior–setting perspective.

Two additional emphases of environment–behavioral research are its *concern with community problems* and *its incorporation of interdisciplinary strategies* for the analysis and resolution of these problems. The community-problems orientation of the field, which derives largely from its emphasis on human adaptation processes, is clearly evident in recent research on such topics as overmanning in public parks (Wicker and Kirmeyer, Chapter 3), the design of therapeutic environments for paraplegic patients (Willems, 1976), the behavioral consequences of environmental stressors (cf. Glass and Singer, 1972; Glass, Singer, and Pennebaker, Chapter 5), and social impact assessment (cf. Wolf, 1974, 1975). Moreover research pertaining to these and related topics typically has involved the collaboration of psychologists with other behavioral scientists and professionals in the fields of public health, architecture, and urban planning.

The substantive and procedural emphases, mentioned above, suggest a preliminary profile of the environment-and-behavior field. This profile is represented by the grid in Table 1. The categorization of columns in the grid as "Intrapersonal processes" and "Environmental dimensions" reflects the interactionist perspective of the field and elaborates upon Lewin's (1936) dictum that behavior is a joint product of personal and situational forces:

$$\text{Behavior} = f \left\{ \begin{array}{c} \overbrace{\text{physiological and}}^{\text{Intrapersonal processes}} \\ \text{psychological processes} \end{array} \right. \times \left. \begin{array}{c} \overbrace{\text{physical, social, and cultural}}^{\text{Environmental dimensions}} \\ \text{dimensions of the environment} \end{array} \right\}$$

Also the categories of behavioral antecedents included in Table 1 reveal the ecological orientation and the interdisciplinary scope of the field. The environment, for example, is portrayed as multidimensional and generally comprised of physical (topographical, climatic, architectural), social (interpersonal, organizational) and cultural (societal) components. These components receive equal emphasis in considerations of the overall relationship between environment and behavior.

The organization of rows in Table 1 also reflects the ecological and interdisciplinary nature of environment–behavioral research and indicates that this research proceeds from at least three different levels of analysis: from micro, intermediate, and macro levels. The first pertains to the relationship between individual behavior and molecular environmental units (e.g., ambient noise, room lighting, density, enclosure, and stimulus com-

Table 1. Substantive Emphases and Analytical Levels of Environment–Behavioral Research

Antecedents of behavior

Antecedents Levels	Intrapersonal processes		Environmental dimensions		
	Physiological processes	Psychological processes	Physical environment	Social environment	Cultural environment
Levels of behavioral analysis					
Micro		Environmental psychology			
Intermediate		Ecological psychology			
Macro		Environmental sociology, human ecology			

plexity). The second deals with individual and small-group behavior in the context of behavior settings and institutional environments (e.g., hospitals, shopping centers, and parks). And the third relates to the responses of communities in the context of large-scale environmental units (e.g., neighborhoods, cities, and geographically defined regions). These levels of analysis incorporate the full range of methodological strategies used to assess human adaptation processes (cf. Patterson, Chapter 16). As behavioral assessment moves from micro to macro levels, the research strategies emphasized generally shift from short-term, laboratory experiments to longitudinal, naturalistic investigations.

The cells of the matrix in Table 1 correspond to the foci of various disciplines that emphasize different determinants of behavior and are concerned with the assessment and the prediction of behavior at different levels of analysis. Research in environmental psychology, for example, generally has emphasized psychological, physical, and social determinants of behavior and has been conducted primarily at a micro level of analysis. Ecological psychology has focused on physical, social, and more recently, psychological determinants of behavior at an intermediate level of analysis. And areas such as human ecology and environmental sociology (cf. Gutman, 1975; Michelson, 1970; Zeisel, 1975) have emphasized physical and social as well as cultural determinants of behavior and, for the most part, have proceeded from a macro level of analysis.

There are obvious exceptions to this oversimplified categorization of research foci, as exemplified by environmental-simulation and impact-assessment studies that span micro, intermediate, and macro levels of analysis. Thus the cells of the matrix in Table 1 are separated by dotted rather than solid lines to reflect the decreasing rigidity of disciplinary boundaries within environment–behavioral research.

The grid presented in Table 1, of course, is an overly broad representation of the environment-and-behavior field. Its cells (most of which have been left unlabeled) encompass the concerns of several disciplines, including biology, psychology, architecture, sociology, and anthropology. Yet the environment-and-behavior field is more than a loosely defined aggregation of disciplines. Specifically, the field can be delineated in terms of core theoretical themes that distinguish it from alternative perspectives on human behavior. In the remaining discussion, an attempt is made to identify these themes, and priorities for future research are considered.

Core Themes of Environment–Behavioral Research

The columns and rows of Table 1 yield an operational outline of the environment-and-behavior field (cf. Proshansky, Ittelson, and Rivlin, 1970) in terms of its major independent (or predictor) variables and levels of analysis. To arrive at a more restrictive and theoretically focused characterization of the field, however, the behavioral side of Lewin's (1936) equation must be considered more fully. For the environment-and-behavior field focuses on a specific category of human behavior not typically emphasized by research in such disciplines as biology, psychology, architecture, sociology, and anthropology.

The major contention of this chapter is that the environment-and-behavior field is uniquely concerned with the processes of *human–environment optimization,* or the ways in which individuals and groups rationally guide their transactions with the environment in accord with specified goals and plans. Whereas the biological and social sciences generally are concerned with the relationship between organisms and their milieu, the focus on optimization processes distinguishes environment–behavioral research from traditional work in these disciplines.

The basic units of human–environment optimization are the processes of orientation, operation, and evaluation. As noted earlier, these processes reflect the active role taken by people in perceiving, shaping, and evaluating their surroundings according to their needs, as well as the reciprocal impact of the environment on people. Most areas of environment–behavioral research have focused on one, or at most two of these processes. The optimization theme, however, provides a basis for integrating the processes of orientation, operation, and evaluation into a dynamic and holistic model of human–environment transactions. The main assumption underlying this model is that individuals and groups strive to achieve *optimal environments,* or those which maximize the fulfillment of their needs and the accomplishment of their goals and plans.

The notion of human–environment optimization integrates two major emphases of ecological and environmental psychology mentioned earlier. On the one hand, the systems–theoretical perspective of ecological psychology is extended to the micro level of analysis in the sense that individual behaviors relating to orientation, operation, and evaluation are viewed as part of a systematic and sequential strategy of person-environment optimization. On the other hand, the emphasis of environmental psychology on orientation, operation, and evaluation processes is extended from a micro level of analysis to group and community levels. Specifically, it is assumed that social systems, like individuals, delineate hierarchical goals and plans that provide criteria for systematic assessment and modification of the environment. To the degree that social systems become more highly developed and differentiated, their transactions with the environment rely more heavily on rational strategies of design, evaluation, and long–range planning (cf. Hawley, 1973; Simon, 1962).

It should be noted that the optimization theme extends earlier conceptualizations of *behavior–environment fit,* or the association between particular patterns of behavior and specific environmental conditions (cf. Barker, 1968; Michelson, 1970, Chapter 9; Mischel, 1973; Wicker, 1972). Most of these formulations emphasize the role of environmental forces in shaping, eliciting, or constraining human behavior (cf. Wohlwill, 1970). For instance, Barker's (1968) notion of *behavior–milieu synomorphy* highlights the role of behavior–setting forces in generating standing (or typical) patterns of behavior. Similarly, Wicker's (1972) concept of *behavior–environment congruence* and Mischel's (1973) notion of *behavior–contingency units* emphasize situational processes such as under- and overmanning, reinforcement, and social learning, which account for the predictable correspondence between specific environmental conditions and associated response patterns. And Michelson's (1970) index of *intersystem congruence* concerns the degree to which the built environment facilitates or impairs the desired activities of its users.

Human–environment optimization, though closely related to these formulations, can be distinguished from them in several respects. First, optimization processes refer to sequential patterns of behavior rather than to actual or perceived states of environmental congruence. The assessment of behavior–environment fit, in effect, represents only one phase of the optimization process, that is, evaluation. Optimization also incorporates the orientation and operation phases of human–environment transactions. Only by orienting toward and acting upon the environment can people evaluate the degree of congruence between the environment and their needs and take steps, when necessary, to improve the quality of their settings. Thus in contrast with earlier notions of behavior–environment fit, which primarily stress the influence of situational forces on people, human–environment optimization gives relatively greater emphasis to the active role played by individuals and groups in shaping, symbolizing, and utilizing the environment.

Furthermore, optimization processes are explicitly value-laden and comparative in nature. The quality of a given setting is measured against predefined standards of environmental optimality. These standards reflect hierarchically organized goals and needs that become differentially salient under various personal and situational circumstances. By contrast, the processes that regulate behavior–environment congruence are not inherently evaluative or value-oriented (cf. Barker, 1968; Mischel, 1973; Wicker, 1972; Michelson's, 1970, intersystem-congruence notion, however, does emphasize the role of personal and cultural values as determinants of congruence).

The cyclical, directional, and design-oriented features of human–environment optimization further distinguish this concept from earlier formulations of behavior–environment congruence. Optimization processes are cyclical and directional in tht they involve successive attempts by individuals and groups to approximate standards of environmental quality. Optimization cycles are essentially sequences of orientation, operation, and evaluation processes. To the extent that optimality standards are not met through a single sequence of these processes, subsequent optimization cycles will occur. Moreover, the design orientation of optimization processes is reflected in the sequential environmental changes initiated by individuals and groups in an effort to meet prescribed standards of optimality. Whereas behavior–environment congruence is portrayed by Barker (1968) and Wicker (1972) as a dynamic, homeostatic process, it is not typically viewed as a cognitive or rational strategy directed toward environmental optimization. In the Barker and Wicker formulations, the correspondence between behavior settings and specific patterns of group activity reflects a "quasi-stationary" equilibrium (cf. Wicker, McGrath, and Armstrong, 1972) between environmental resources and the personnel requirements of the group rather than a goal-directed and design-oriented process.

While some of the differences between human–environment optimization and earlier notions of behavior–environment congruence have been discussed above, a broader and more important issue that remains to be considered is the extent to which the former concept provides a basis for distinguishing the environment-and-behavior field from other areas of behavioral research. Certainly it can be argued that much of the research in such areas as social and cognitive psychology is concerned with the ways in which people evaluate and attempt to optimize their situations in accord with hierarchically organized needs. Rotter's (1954; Rotter, Chance, and Phares, 1972) social-learning theory, for example, is based on the assumption that people behave in ways that maximize the perceived probability of personal fulfillment along a variety of need dimensions (e.g., physical comfort, independence, love and affection, and recognition–status). Similarly social-evaluation theory (Pettigrew, 1967; Thibaut and Kelley, 1959) emphasizes the subjective standards or comparison levels by which individuals judge the quality of their relationships with others. To the degree that the quality of one's social situation falls below the level of quality expected or felt to be deserved, the individual will take steps to improve the situation or if such actions are precluded, to lower expectations and thereby reduce dissatisfaction.

The goal-directed nature of human activity also is emphasized by attribution theory (Bem, 1967; Heider, 1958; Jones, Kanouse, Kelley, Nisbett, Valins, and Weiner, 1971; Kelley, 1967). According to the theory, people are motivated to predict and control their environment and, in service of this need, attempt to establish causal connections between environmental entities. A direct implication of attribution theory is that individuals strive to arrange their surroundings in ways that facilitate the formation of stable attributions about other people and the environment in general. Finally, the cyclical and directional features of optimization processes noted earlier are articulated clearly in Miller, Galanter, and Pribram's (1960) feedback model of human behavior, from which the present formulation of human–environment optimization is derived.

There are at least two important differences, however, between the proposed conceptualization of human–environment optimization and the above-mentioned theories of behavior (as well as several other theories of human motivation that were not discussed, e.g., Chein, 1954; Kelly, 1955/ 1963; Maslow, 1954). First, human–environment optimization refers in the present discussion to processes enacted not only by individuals but also by small groups, by organizations, and by whole communities. By contrast, most theories of motivation that are concerned with optimization processes focus exclusively on the behavior of individuals. Second, the proposed cycles of human–environment optimization are oriented toward improvement of the molar physical environment as well as its more molecular components. This broader focus of optimization processes, then, extends beyond the purview of the theories mentioned earlier, which typically emphasize the individual's attempts to optimize his immediate social environment.

Although the concept of human–environment optimization can be distinguished from several existing models of motivation and behavior, it does not now provide the basis for a theoretical conceptualization of the environment-and-behavior field. At this point in time, human–environment optimization is simply a unifying theme reflected in many areas of environment–behavioral research rather than a full-fledged theory of man–environment transactions. Numerous issues, such as those relating to the identification of relevant dimensions, levels, and criteria of human–environment optimization, must be clarified before the *theme* of optimization can be elevated to the status of a *theory*. In the discussion below, a number of questions that pertain to these issues are considered for future research. Their eventual resolution may contribute to the development of an integrative and theoretically focused characterization of the environment-and-behavior field.

Directions for Future Research and Theoretical Development

The concept of human–environment optimization poses at least three major questions for future research: (1) Along what dimensions do people attempt to optimize their environments? (2) What kinds of assessment criteria are appropriate for measuring optimization processes and their outcomes? (3) In what ways can empirical information concerning human–environment optimization be translated into guidelines for environmental design?

Relevant Dimensions of Environmental Optimization. The task of identifying key dimensions of environmental optimization requires an extensive analysis of human needs and the ways in which these needs are either satisfied or thwarted by features of the molar environment. As noted earlier, a considerable amount of research has been conducted on human needs in relation to the social environment but very little theoretical or empirical work has focused on the relationship between motivational processes and the large-scale physical environment.

At a very general level of analysis, it seems reasonable to assume that molar units of the built and natural environment can play either a supportive or an inhibitory role in relation to physiological, psychological, and behavioral needs (cf. Lang, Burnette, Moleski, and Vachon, 1974). Yet this rather general categorization of key optimization dimensions gives rise to several subsidiary questions. For instance, which categories of human needs will be most salient to people in different types of settings? And under what conditions will the needs of individuals be coordinated with the long-range goals of groups and communities in a manner that promotes environmental optimization at all three levels of analysis?

It may be possible through future research to identify situational determinants of need salience. In relation to this issue, Stokols (1976) has proposed a distinction between primary and secondary environments to account for some of the varying effects of environmental stressors within different types of settings. Primary settings are those in which people spend a substantial amount of their time, perform activities that are of importance to them, and relate to others on a personal rather than an anonymous level. Secondary settings are experienced on a more transitory basis and are associated with less important activities and more impersonal encounters with others. The analysis suggests that crowding and related forms of stress will be experienced more intensely in primary than in secondary settings because of the association of the former settings with higher expectations for environmental control over a wider range of personally important needs. In effect, crowding will interfere with a greater number of personal goals in the former settings than in the latter.

Perhaps the development of more refined environmental taxonomies will facilitate a more detailed prediction of need hierarchies in relation to the functional features of different settings. Analyses of this type could yield setting-specific guidelines for the design of environments that are maximally congruent with the needs of their users. (See also the discussions of Altman, 1975, Insel and Moos, 1974, and Price and Blashfield, 1975, regarding the development of environment–behavioral typologies.)

Effective strategies of environmental optimization will depend not only on situation-specific analyses of individual's needs but also on the delineation of relevant goal dimensions at intermediate (group) and macro (community) levels. Moreover, maximization of individual needs in conjunction with group and community goals will require a coordination of optimization processes among all three levels of analysis. Platt's (1973) analysis of "social traps," which result from conflicts between short-term, personal interests and long-term, societal goals, depicts some of the problems that arise from ineffective coordination of optimization processes and provides a useful framework for research on the resolution of these problems.

Criteria for the Assessment of Optimization Processes. The development of assessment strategies for measuring optimization processes and their outcomes poses several questions for future research. A crucial issue that has been mentioned already concerns the specification of key optimization dimensions for the individuals, groups, and communities occupying a particular environment. Shall the effectiveness of optimization processes be measured in terms of physical health, mental well-being, expressed satisfaction with the environment, or some combination of these dimensions? Furthermore, how shall the selected measurement criteria be weighted and compared across micro, intermediate, and macro levels of analysis? And an additional set of questions concerns the appropriate measurement intervals for evaluating the effectiveness of optimization processes at different levels of analysis.

The present formulation of human–environment optimization does not provide even preliminary answers to these complex questions. It does, however, emphasize certain points that may be pertinent to the development of suitable strategies for the assessment of optimization processes. Specifically the evaluative and cyclical features of optimization processes suggest that the effectiveness of these processes must be measured in terms of the deviation between actual or perceived levels of environmental quality and prescribed standards of optimality. Moreover, the periodic assessment of environmental-quality deviation scores should correspond to designated intervals of environmental assessment (orientation), intervention (operation), and evaluation, as established by individuals, groups, or whole communities. In relation to these issues, Campbell's (1969) analysis of "reforms as experiments" provides a persuasive argument for the systematic assessment of optimization processes at the societal level and suggests a set of research strategies for developing standardized evaluation procedures (see also Wortman, 1975).

Development of Guidelines for Environmental Design.   Ideally the development of guidelines for designing future environments should be based on the outcome of completed optimization cycles in which specific environmental interventions were implemented and evaluated. The availability of standardized data pertaining to previous optimization cycles, of course, presupposes the existence of criteria for specifying and measuring relevant optimization dimensions within different settings.

In the absence of standardized evaluation procedures and because of the urgency of contemporary community problems (e.g., urban congestion, pollution, and substandard housing), it often has been necessary to enact environmental changes without reference to data on the impact of prior interventions. While modifications of the large-scale physical environment typically have been implemented in an arbitrary and nonsystematic fashion, there have been an increasing number of attempts to develop guidelines for environmental planning on the basis of behavioral-science theory and research (cf. Altman, 1975; Canter and Lee, 1974; Lang *et al.*, 1974; Newman, 1973; Saarinen, 1976; Sommer, 1974; Zeisel, 1975). A major task for future research will be to assess the utility of these guidelines through a series of planned interventions and accompanying assessments of environmental impact at the individual, group, and community levels of analysis.

Summary

In the initial portion of this discussion, the intellectual origins of ecological and environmental psychology were traced, and the major concerns of these areas were identified. Subsequently two characterizations of the environment-and-behavior field were developed. The first was basically an operational outline of the field in terms of its substantive and procedural emphases. The second was a more elaborated view of the field based on the concept of human–environment optimization, a core theoretical theme reflected in several areas of environment–behavioral research.

Although at present the diverse concerns of this research domain are more appropriately represented in operational rather than in theoretical terms (cf. Proshansky and O'Hanlon, Chapter 4; Smith, Chapter 14), it is hoped that a systematic analysis of the research questions outlined above eventually will provide the basis for developing a theoretically focused conceptualization of the environment-and-behavior field.

References

Allee, W. C., Emerson, A. E., Park, O., Park, T., and Schmidt, K. P. *Principles of animal ecology.* Philadelphia: W. B. Saunders, 1949.

Allport, G. *Personality: A psychological interpretation.* New York: Holt, 1937.

Altman, I. Some perspectives on the study of man–environment phenomena. *Representative Research in Social Psychology,* 1973, *4,* 109–126.

Altman, I. *The environment and social behavior: Privacy, personal space, territory and crowding.* Monterey, Calif.: Brooks/Cole, 1975.

Altman, I. Crowding: Historical and contemporary trends in crowding research. In A. Baum and Y. Epstein (Eds.), *Human response to crowding.* Hillsdale, N.J.: Lawrence Erlbaum Associates, 1977.

Appleyard, D., and Craik, K. H. The Berkeley Environmental Simulation Project: Its use in environmental impact assessment. In T. G. Dickert and K. R. Domeny (Eds.), *Environmental impact assessment: Guidelines and commentary.* Berkeley: University Extension, University of California, 1974.

Baird, L. Big school, small school: A critical examination of the hypothesis. *Journal of Educational Psychology,* 1969, *60,* 253–260.

Bandura, A. *Principles of behavior modification.* New York: Holt, Rinehart and Winston, 1969.

Barker, R. Ecology and motivation. *Nebraska Symposium on Motivation,* 1960, *8,* 1–50.

Barker, R. *Ecological psychology: Concepts and methods for studying the environment of human behavior.* Stanford, Calif.: Stanford University Press, 1968.

Barker, R., and Gump, P. *Big school, small school.* Stanford, Calif.: Stanford University Press, 1964.

Barker, R., and Schoggen, P. *Qualities of community life*. San Francisco: Jossey-Bass, 1973.

Barker, R., and Wright, H. *Midwest and its children: The psychological ecology of an American town*. New York: Row, Peterson, 1955.

Baum, A., and Valins, S. *The social psychology of crowding: Studies of the effects of residential group size*. Hillsdale, N.J.: Lawrence Erlbaum Associates, 1976.

Bem, D. J. Self perception: An alternative interpretation of cognitive dissonance phenomena. *Psychological Review*, 1967, *74*, 183–200.

Bem, D. J., and Allen, A. On predicting some of the people some of the time: The search for cross-situational consistencies in behavior. *Psychological Review*, 1974, *81*, 506–520.

Booth, A. Final report: Urban Crowding Project. Paper presented to the Ministry of State for Urban Affairs, Government of Canada, Toronto, 1975.

Bowers, K. S. Situationism in psychology: An analysis and a critique. *Psychological Review*, 1973, *80*, 307–336.

Brenner, M. H. *Mental illness and the economy*. Cambridge, Mass.: Harvard University Press, 1973.

Brunswik, E. *Systematic and representative design of psychology experiments*. Berkeley: University of California Press, 1949.

Burgess, E. W. The growth of the city: An introduction to a research project. In G. A. Theodorson (Ed.), *Studies in human ecology*. Evanston, Ill.: Row, Peterson, 1961 (First published, 1925.)

Calhoun, J. Population density and social pathology. *Scientific American*, 1962, *206*, 139–148.

Campbell, D. T. Reforms as experiments. *American Psychologist*, 1969, *24*, 409–429.

Canter, D., and Lee, T. (Eds.). *Psychology and the built environment*. New York: Halstead Press, 1974.

Carson, R. *The silent spring*. Boston: Houghton Mifflin, 1962.

Cartwright, D., and Zander, A. (Eds.). *Group dynamics* (3rd ed.). New York: Harper and Row, 1968.

Catalano, R. Community stress: A preliminary conceptualization. *Man–Environment Systems*, 1975, *5*, 307–310.

Catalano, R., Simmons, S., and Stokols, D. Adding social science knowledge to environmental decision making. *Natural Resources Lawyer*, 1975, *8*, 41–59.

Chein, I. The environment as a determinant of behavior. *The Journal of Social Psychology*, 1954, *39*, 115–127.

Clements, F. *Research methods in ecology*. Lincoln: The University of Nebraska Press, 1905.

Cohen, S., Glass, D., and Singer, J. Apartment noise, auditory discrimination and reading ability in children. *Journal of Experimental Social Psychology*, 1973, *9*, 407–422.

Commoner, B. *Science and survival*. New York: Viking, 1963.

Craik, K. Environmental psychology. In K. Craik, B. Kleinmuntz, R. Rosnow, R. Rosenthal, J. A. Cheyne, and R. H. Walters (Eds.), *New directions in psychology* (vol. 4). New York: Holt, Rinehart, and Winston, 1970.

Craik, K. The assessment of places. In P. McReynolds (Ed.), *Advances in Psychological Assessment*. Palo Alto, Calif.: Science and Behavior Books, 1971.

Craik, K. Psychological factors in landscape appraisal. *Environment and Behavior*, 1972, *4*, 255–266.

Craik, K. Environmental psychology. *Annual Review of Psychology*, 1973, *24*, 403–422.

Craik, K. The personality research paradigm in environmental psychology. In S. Wapner, S. Cohen, and B. Kaplan (Eds.), *Experiencing environments*. New York: Plenum Press, 1976.

Darwin, C. *The origin of species*. Facsimilie with introduction and bibliography by Ernst Mayr, Cambridge: Harvard University Press, 1964. (First London edition, 1859.)

Desor, J. Toward a psychological theory of crowding. *Journal of Personality and Social Psychology*, 1972, *21*, 79–83.

Dobzhansky, T. *Genetics and the origin of species* (3rd ed.). New York: Columbia University Press, 1951.

Downs, R., and Stea, D. *Image and environment: Cognitive mapping and spatial behavior*. Chicago: Aldine, 1973.

Edney, J. J. Human territories: Comment on functional properties. *Environment and Behavior,* 1976, *8,* 31–48.

Ehrlich, P. *The population bomb.* New York: Ballantine, 1968.

Evans, G., and Howard, R. Personal space. *Psychological Bulletin,* 1973, *80,* 334–344.

Faris, R., and Dunham, H. W. *Mental disorders in urban areas.* Chicago: University of Chicago Press, 1939.

Festinger, L. *A theory of cognitive dissonance.* Evanston, Ill.: Row, Peterson, 1957.

Freedman, J. *Crowding and behavior.* San Francisco: W. H. Freeman, 1975.

Freedman, J., Klevansky, S., and Ehrlich, P. The effect of crowding on human task performance. *Journal of Applied Social Psychology,* 1971, *1,* 7–25.

Freud, S. The psychopathology of everyday life. In *The basic writings of Sigmund Freud.* New York: Random House, 1938. (First German edition, 1904.)

Galle, O., Gove, W., and McPherson, J. Population density and social pathology: What are the relationships for man? *Science,* 1972, *176,* 23–30.

Gans, H. Planning and social life: Friendship and neighbor relations in suburban communities. *Journal of the American Institute of Planners,* 1961, *27,* 134–140.

Glass, D., and Singer, J. *Urban Stress.* New York: Academic Press, 1972.

Gutman, R. Architecture and sociology. *The American Sociologist,* 1975, *10,* 219–228.

Hall, E. *The hidden dimension.* New York: Doubleday, 1966.

Hanson, L., and Wicker, A. Effects of overmanning on group experience and task performance. Paper presented at Western Psychological Association Convention, Anaheim, Calif., April, 1973.

Harrington, M. *The other America.* New York: Macmillan, 1962.

Hauser, P., and Duncan, O. *The study of population: An inventory and appraisal.* Chicago: University of Chicago Press, 1959.

Hawley, A. *Human ecology: A theory of community structure.* New York: Ronald Press, 1950.

Hawley, A. Ecology and population. *Science,* 1973, *179,* 1196–1201.

Heider, F. *The psychology of interpersonal relations.* New York: Wiley, 1958.

Hendee, J., and Harris, R. Foresters' perception of wilderness-user attitudes and preferences. *Journal of Forestry,* 1970, *68,* 759–762.

Hull, C. The problem of intervening variables in molar behavior theory. *Psychological Review,* 1943, *50,* 273–291.

Insel, P., and Moos, R. Psychological environments: Expanding the scope of human ecology. *American Psychologist,* 1974, *29,* 179–188.

Ittelson, W. *Environment and cognition.* New York: Seminar Press, 1973.

Ittelson, W., Proshansky, H., Rivlin, L., and Winkel, G. *An introduction to environmental psychology.* New York: Holt, Rinehart, and Winston, 1974.

Jacobs, J. *The death and life of great American cities.* New York: Random House, 1961.

Jones, E., Kanouse, D., Kelley, H., Nisbett, R., Valins, S., and Weiner, B. *Attribution: Perceiving the causes of behavior.* Morristown, N.J.: General Learning Press, 1971.

Jung, C. G. *Psychology of the unconscious.* New York: Dodd, 1925.

Kaplan, S. Cognitive maps, human needs and the designed environment. In W. F. E. Preiser (Ed.), *Environmental design research.* Stroudsburg, Pa.: Dowden, Hutchinson, and Ross, 1973.

Kaplan, S. An informal model for the prediction of preference. In E. H. Zube, R. O. Brush, and J. G. Fabos (Eds.), *Landscape assessment.* Stroudsburg, Pa.: Dowden, Hutchinson, and Ross, 1975.

Kelley, H. Attribution theory in social psychology. In D. Levine (Ed.), *Nebraska Symposium on Motivation, 1967.* Lincoln: University of Nebraska Press, 1967.

Kelly, G. A. *A theory of personality: The psychology of personal constructs.* New York: W. W. Norton, 1963. (First published, 1955.)

Knowles, E. S. Boundaries around group interaction: The effects of group size and member status on boundary permeability. *Journal of Personality and Social Psychology,* 1975, *26,* 327–331.

Kuhn, T. *The structure of scientific revolutions.* Chicago: University of Chicago Press, 1962.

Lang, J., Burnette, C., Moleski, W., and Vachon, D. *Designing for human behavior: Architecture and the behavioral sciences.* Stroudsburg, Pa.: Dowden, Hutchinson, and Ross, 1974.

Lazarus, R. *Psychological stress and the coping process.* New York: McGraw-Hill, 1966.

Levi, L., and Andersson, L. *Psychological stress: Population, environment and quality of life.* New York: Spectrum, 1975.

Lewin, K. *A dynamic theory of personality.* New York: McGraw-Hill, 1935.

Lewin, K. *Principles of topological psychology* (F. and G. Heider, trans.). New York: McGraw-Hill, 1936.

Lynch, K. *The image of the city.* Cambridge, Mass.: M.I.T. Press, 1960.

Maslow, A. H. *Motivation and personality.* New York: Harper, 1954.

McGrath, J. E. A conceptual formulation for research on stress. In J. E. McGrath (Ed.), *Social and psychological factors in stress.* New York: Holt, Rinehart and Winston, 1970.

McKechnie, G. E. *Manual for the Environmental Response Inventory.* Palo Alto, Calif.: Consulting Psychologists Press, 1974.

McKenzie, R. The ecological approach to the study of the human community. In R. Park and E. Burgess (Eds.), *The city.* Chicago: University of Chicago Press, 1925.

Mercer, D. C. Motivational and social aspects of recreational behavior. In I. Altman and J. Wohlwill (Eds.), *Human behavior and environment: Advances in theory and research* (vol. 1). New York: Plenum Press, 1976.

Merton, R. K. *Social theory and social structure.* Glencoe, Ill.: The Free Press, 1957.

Michelson, W. *Man and his urban environment: A sociological approach.* Reading, Mass.: Addison-Wesley, 1970.

Milgram, S. The experience of living in cities. *Science,* 1970, *167,* 1461–1468.

Miller, G., Galanter, E., and Pribram, K. *Plans and the structure of behavior.* New York: Holt, Rinehart and Winston, 1960.

Mischel, W. *Personality and assessment.* New York: Wiley, 1968.

Mischel, W. Toward a cognitive social learning reconceptualization of personality. *Psychological Review,* 1973, *80,* 252–283.

Moos, R. Conceptualizations of human environments. *American Psychologist,* 1973, *28,* 652–665.

Murray, H. *Explorations in personality.* New York: Oxford University Press, 1938.

Newman, O. *Defensible space.* New York: Macmillan, 1973.

Odum, E. P. *Fundamentals of ecology.* Philadelphia: W. B. Saunders, 1959.

Osmond, H. Function as the basis of psychiatric ward design. *Mental Hospitals,* 1957, *8,* 23–30.

Park, R., and Burgess, E. *An introduction to the science of sociology.* Chicago: University of Chicago Press, 1921.

Park, R., and Burgess, E. (Eds.). *The city.* Chicago: University of Chicago Press, 1925.

Pettigrew, T. F. Social evaluation theory: Convergences and applications. In D. Levine (Ed.), *Nebraska Symposium on Motivation, 1967.* Lincoln: University of Nebraska Press, 1967.

Platt, J. Social traps. *American Psychologist,* 1973, *28,* 641–651.

Price, R., and Blashfield, R. Explorations in the taxonomy of behavior settings: Analysis of dimensions and classification of settings. *American Journal of Community Psychology,* 1975, *3,* 335–351.

Proshansky, H., Ittelson, W., and Rivlin, L. (Eds.). *Environmental psychology: Man and his physical setting.* New York: Holt, Rinehart and Winston, 1970.

Rapoport, A. Toward a redefinition of density. *Environment and Behavior,* 1975, *7,* 133.

Rotter, J. B. *Social learning and clinical psychology.* Englewood Cliffs, N.J.: Prentice-Hall, 1954.

Rotter, J. B., Chance, J., and Phares, E. *Applications of a social learning theory of personality.* New York: Holt, Rinehart and Winston, 1972.

Saarinen, T. *Environmental planning perception and behavior.* Boston: Houghton Mifflin, 1976.

Selye, H. *The stress of life.* New York: McGraw-Hill, 1956.

Shafer, E., and Thompson, R. Models that describe use of Adirondack campgrounds. *Forest Science,* 1968, *14,* 383–391.

Sherrod, D. Crowding, perceived control and behavioral aftereffects. *Journal of Applied Social Psychology*, 1974, *4*, 171–186.

Shevky, E., and Bell, W. *Social area analysis*. Stanford, Calif.: Stanford University Press, 1955.

Simmel, G. The metropolis and mental life. In K. Wolff (trans. and Ed.), *The sociology of Georg Simmel*. New York: The Free Press, 1950, 409–424.

Simon, H. The architecture of complexity. *Proceedings of the American Philosophical Society*, 1962, *106*, 467–482.

Singer, J., Lundberg, U., and Frankenhaeuser, M. Stress on the train: A study of urban commuting. In A. Baum and S. Valins (Eds.), *Advances in environmental psychology*. Hillsdale, N.J.: Lawrence Erlbaum Associates, 1977.

Skinner, B. *Science and human behavior*. New York: Macmillan, 1953.

Sommer, R. *Personal space: The behavioral basis of design*. Englewood Cliffs, N.J.: Prentice-Hall, 1969.

Sommer, R. *Tight spaces: Hard architecture and how to humanize it*. Englewood Cliffs, N.J.: Prentice-Hall, 1974.

Spence, K. W. The nature of theory construction in contemporary psychology. *Psychological Review*, 1944, *41*, 47–68.

Spence, K. W. The postulates and methods of "behaviorism." *Psychological Review*, 1948, *55*, 67–78.

Stebbins, G. L. *Processes of organic evolution*. Englewood Cliffs, N.J.: Prentice-Hall, 1966.

Stokols, D. On the distinction between density and crowding: Some implications for future research. *Psychological Review*, 1972, *79*, 275–277. (a)

Stokols, D. A social-psychological model of human crowding phenomena. *Journal of the American Institute of Planners*, 1972, *38*, 72–84. (b)

Stokols, D. The experience of crowding in primary and secondary environments. *Environment and Behavior*, 1976, *8*, 49–86.

Sundstrom, E. Crowding as a sequential process: Review of research on the effects of population density on humans. In A. Baum and Y. Epstein (Eds.), *Human response to crowding*. Hillsdale, N.J.: Lawrence Erlbaum Associates, 1977.

Swan, J. Response to air pollution: A study of attitudes and coping strategies of high school youths. *Environment and Behavior*, 1970, *2*, 127–153.

Taylor, W. P. What is ecology and what good is it? *Ecology*, 1936, *17*, 333–346.

Theodorson, G. A. (Ed.). *Studies in human ecology*. Evanston, Ill.: Row, Peterson, 1961.

Thibaut, J., and Kelley, H. *The social psychology of groups*. New York: Wiley, 1959.

Thomas, W., and Znaniecki, F. *The Polish peasant in Europe and America*. New York: A. A. Knopf, 1920.

Thompson, W. *Population problems* (4th ed.). New York: McGraw-Hill, 1953.

Titchener, E. B. The postulates of a structural psychology. *Philosophical Review*, 1898, *7*, 449–465. As reported by W. Dennis (Ed.). *Readings in the history of psychology*. New York: Appleton-Century-Crofts, 1948.

Tolman, E. The determiners of behavior at a choice point. *Psychological Review*, 1938, *45*, 1–41.

Valins, S., and Baum, A. Residential group size, social interaction, and crowding. *Environment and Behavior*, 1973, *5*, 421–439.

Warming, E. *Oecology of plants: An introduction to the study of plant communities*. Oxford: Claredon Press, 1909.

Watson, J. B. Psychology as the behaviorist views it. *Psychological Review*, 1913, *20*, 159–177.

Wicker, A. Undermanning, performances, and students' subjective experiences in behavior settings of large and small high schools. *Journal of Personality and Social Psychology*, 1968, *10*, 255–261.

Wicker, A. Cognitive complexity, school size, and participation in school behavior settings: A test of the frequency of interaction hypothesis. *Journal of Educational Psycology*, 1969, *60*, 200–203. (a)

Wicker, A. Size of church membership and members' support of church behavior settings. *Journal of Personality and Social Psychology*, 1969, *13*, 278–288. (b)

Wicker, A. Processes which mediate behavior–environment congruence. *Behavioral Science,* 1972, *17,* 265–277.

Wicker, A., McGrath, J. E., and Armstrong, G. Organization size and behavior setting capacity as determinants of member participation. *Behavioral Science,* 1972, *17,* 499–513.

Wicker, A., and Mehler, A. Assimilation of new members in a large and small church. *Journal of Applied Psychology,* 1971, *55,* 151–156.

Willems, E. Sense of obligation to high school activities as related to school size and marginality of student. *Child Development,* 1967, *38,* 1247–1260.

Willems, E. Behavioral ecology, health status and health care: Applications to the rehabilitation setting. In I. Altman and J. Wohlwill (Eds.), *Human behavior and environment: Advances in theory and research* (vol. 1). New York: Plenum Press, 1976.

Wirth, L. Urbanism as a way of life. *The American Journal of Sociology,* 1938, *44,* 1–24.

Wohlwill, J. The emerging discipline of environmental psychology. *American Psychologist,* 1970, *25,* 303–312.

Wohlwill, J. Environmental aesthetics: The environment as a source of affect. In I. Altman and J. Wohlwill (Eds.), *Human behavior and environment: Advances in theory and research* (vol. 1). New York: Plenum Press, 1976.

Wolf, C. (Ed.). Social impact assessment. In D. Carson (Ed.), *Man–environment interactions: Evaluation and applications* (vol. 2). Milwaukee, Wis.: Environmental Design Research Association, 1974.

Wolf, C. Editorial preface to special issue on social impact assessment. *Environment and Behavior,* 1975, *7,* 259–263.

Wortman, P. M. Evaluation research: A psychological perspective. *American Psychologist,* 1975, *30,* 562–575.

Wundt, W. *Principles of physiological psychology* (vols. 1–10). New York: Macmillan, 1904.

Wynne-Edwards, V. C. Self-regulating systems in populations of animals. *Science,* 1962, *147,* 1543–1548.

Zeisel, J. *Sociology and architectural design.* New York: Russel Sage Foundation, 1975.

Zlutnick, S., and Altman, I. Crowding and human behavior. In J. Wohlwill and D. Carson (Eds.), *Environment and the social sciences: Perspectives and applications.* Washington, D.C.: American Psychological Association, 1972.

Zube, E. H. Perception of landscape and land use. In I. Altman and J. Wohlwill (Eds.), *Human behavior and the environment: Advances in theory and research* (Vol. 1). New York: Plenum Press, 1976.

SECTION II
Ecological Psychology   □

The environment-and-behavior field, as portrayed in the preceding section, emphasizes the unique concerns of two major research areas: ecological and environmental psychology. The present section examines the first of these areas in terms of its early development, its theoretical and methodological assumptions, and its current empirical trends.

The opening chapter, by Edwin P. Willems, traces the development of the ecological perspective within psychology and offers an in-depth analysis of the major conceptual and procedural earmarks of behavioral ecology (or ecological psychology). Whereas the ecological perspective is sometimes mistakenly characterized as simply a methodological orientation, Willems offers a systematic delineation of the theoretical underpinnings of this perspective as well as a discussion of its procedural properties. The conceptual thrust of behavioral ecology is conveyed, for example, through an analysis of the multidimensional and interdependent features of the molar environment and a discussion of systems concepts pertaining to human–environment equilibrium and adaptation processes. And at a procedural level, the emphasis of behavioral ecology on naturalistic and longitudinal strategies of research is discussed.

The succeeding chapter, by Allan W. Wicker and Sandra Kirmeyer, nicely illustrates the translation of ecological concepts and methods into a systematic program of behavioral research. The reported research is based on a reformulation of Barker's (1960, 1968) behavior–setting theory. Specifically Barker's notion of undermanning is extended through the development of a continuum of manning levels ranging from undermanned, poorly manned, adequately manned, richly manned, and overmanned settings (cf. Wicker, McGrath, and Armstrong, 1972; Wicker, 1973). Hypotheses regarding the effects of various manning conditions on the behavior and subjective experiences of setting occupants (e.g., "performers" and "nonperformers") are examined in relation to the findings from two laboratory experiments and a field study conducted at Yosemite National Park.

Together the chapters by Willems and by Wicker and Kirmeyer provide not only a comprehensive overview of the origins and assumptions of

37

ecological psychology but also a summary of its empirical developments and emerging trends. A potentially significant trend reflected in these chapters is an increasing emphasis on the interaction between ecological and intrapersonal determinants of behavior. This trend is particularly evident in Wicker and Kirmeyer's integration of manning notions with McGrath's (1970) theory of psychological stress. As noted earlier, the continuing convergence of ecological and intrapersonal perspectives on behavior should contribute to the development of a more integrated and theoretically focused field of environment and behavior than now exists.

References

Barker, R. Ecology and motivation. *Nebraska Symposium on Motivation*, 1960, *8*, 1–50.

Barker, R. *Ecological Psychology: Concepts and methods for studying the environment of human behavior*. Stanford, Calif.: Stanford University Press, 1968.

McGrath, J. E. A conceptual formulation for research on stress. In J. E. McGrath (Ed.), *Social and psychological factors in stress*. New York: Holt, Rinehart, and Winston, 1970.

Wicker, A. Undermanning theory and research: Implications for the study of psychological and behavioral effects of excess populations. *Representative Research in Social Psychology*, 1973, *4*, 185–206.

Wicker, A., McGrath, J. E., and Armstrong, G. Organization size and behavior setting capacity as determinants of member participation. *Behavioral Science*, 1972, *17*, 499–513.

Behavioral Ecology　　　　　　　　　　2

EDWIN P. WILLEMS

In recent years, much has been written about the need for new psychological perspectives on the environment and about new environmental perspectives in psychology. This burst of activity has arisen partly from pressures within psychology to make its theories and methods more commensurate with the problems of everyday human behavior and partly from outside of psychology, where many planners, designers, architects, and agents of environmental change stand in need of theories and methods that will provide them with more human, more behaviorally based principles on which to base their work. Within that context, one purpose of this chapter is to provide a synopsis of *behavioral ecology,* an emerging perspective on man-environment relations.

The sequence of presentation will be as follows: (1) a brief discussion of some antecedents and historical developments; (2) an overview of some general implications and themes; and (3) the presentation of some defining and distinguishing features of behavioral ecology. A second purpose is to provide a counterpoint to some of the other recent attempts to mark out the domain of environmental psychology (e.g., Altman, 1975; Ittelson, Proshansky, Rivlin, and Winkel, 1974).

Some Background

One of the major lines of development toward behavioral ecology came from within psychology. Roger Barker, one of the pioneers of the movement, summarized the guiding questions as follows:

EDWIN P. WILLEMS ● University of Houston, Houston, Texas. Work on this paper was supported in part by Research and Training Center No. 4 (RT-4), Baylor College of Medicine and Texas Institute for Rehabilitation and Research, funded by Rehabilitation Services Administration, USDHEW.

in varied and changing environments, the contribution of environmental input to the variance of behavior is enhanced. In a restless world, the nature of the environment is the intriguing scientific problem. And the applied fields and neighboring sciences ask: What are environments like? . . . it does not seem likely that our own curiosities and the demands of engineers, economists, educators, and political leaders will allow us to be content with a psychology of people to the neglect of a psychology of the environment of people. (1965, p. 13)

The present methods, concepts, and theories of the psychological sciences *cannot* answer the new questions . . . a new science is required to deal with them. (1969, p. 31)

The phrase *ecological psychology* has been circulating around American psychology for about 25 years, with a positively accelerating curve of visibility and acclaim. During the first 10 or 15 of those years, the major authors and agents of ecological psychology were Roger Barker and Herbert Wright, who, in turn, were co-workers and intellectual descendents of Kurt Lewin (Barker, 1960, 1963a,b, 1965, 1968, 1969; Barker and Schoggen, 1973; Barker and Wright, 1955; Wright, 1967, 1969–1970). Lewin (e.g., 1951) had developed his field theory around the well-known dictum that behavior is a joint function of person and environment. However, *environment* in Lewin's formula was the environment as perceived by the person. Thus, Lewin's psychology was a postperceptual psychology as far as the environment was concerned. Lewin recognized this problem and he coined the phrase "foreign hull" to represent the outside, preperceptual world of the environment. He even suggested the phrase "ecological psychology" to denote the attempt to study influences from the foreign hull on the person, but he never pursued the development of ecological psychology to any sophisticated extent.

To a large degree, ecological psychology in the hands of Barker and Wright was the formal, systematic attempt to (1) include the preperceptual environment (foreign hull) in a field-theoretical analysis of human behavior and (2) apply the approach of the naturalist to psychology. The results are clear. Suddenly, after their lonely pioneering, ecological concepts are now *in*. A few years ago, persons who stated interests in ecological psychology received quizzical and patronizing looks, but they now receive knowing and appreciative nods, and the number of requests for reprints, comments, and consultation has gone up at a remarkable rate. The pioneers made remarkable advances in developing methods of research, in understanding the naturally occurring structure and pattern of behavior, in documenting and measuring units of the environment, and in developing some models of the ways in which behavior and environment come to terms with each other.

However, something else happened at the same time that was not as positive, that is, the tendency to define ecological psychology primarily in terms of research techniques. It is my hypothesis that within the professional atmosphere of the 1950's and early 1960's, what struck the prime movers of ecological psychology was a twofold phenomeonon: (1) their work was evaluated (usually criticized) on methodological grounds, and (2) they found little justification and rationale for their naturalistic procedures in the existing literature. The prevailing values within scientific psychology during those years favored the controlled experiment, and the literature describing the rationale, merits, and advantages of the experiment was extensive and detailed. So it was that the authors of ecological psychology devoted many of their arguments and examples to buttressing the case for naturalistic research and nonexperimental methods.

As I shall argue later, behavioral ecology is a perspective, an orientation, or a set of theoretical principles in terms of which the investigator formulates questions about behavior and its habitat and context in particular ways. However, perhaps because it is easier and more efficient to demarcate a new and complicated position in terms of research techniques than by its substantive and theoretical thrust, the major authors and devotees of ecological psychology fell into the trap of defining and justifying it primarily in terms of naturalistic, nonexperimental strategies for gathering data (Barker, 1964, 1965, 1968; Willems, 1965; Wright, 1967). It is probably true that those psychologists who most eagerly describe their work as ecological have preferred naturalistic, nonexperimental methods in their work, and it is true that a great many ecological questions lend themselves best to field research. However, the tendency to identify behavioral ecology with naturalistic methods has led to the unfortunate error of involving behavioral ecology in arguments, claims, and counterclaims about the relative merits and tenabilities of experimental and naturalistic methods.

Thus, depending on how those arguments are proceeding at any particular time, the behavioral–ecology baby is thrown out or reinstated with the methodological bath water. To be sure, behavioral ecology has important implications for methodology, but it is first and foremost a substantive view of the nature of human behavior and the environment. One must keep this important distinction in mind in order to gain proper historical perspective on some landmark literature (e.g., Barker, 1960, 1963a, 1968; Barker and Barker, 1961; Barker and Schoggen, 1973).

The second major line of development into the present formulation of behavioral ecology comes from a convergence of forces outside of psychology. Ecology has its origin in the biological sciences and it refers traditionally to the study of relationships between living things and their habitats and the formalization of the natural rules by which those interactions are governed. Complex interdependencies that implicate organisms and their environments in exchanges of energy over time are the scientific coinage of the ecologist, and dramatic advances have been made in the understanding of such interdependencies in areas outside of psychology (Benarde, 1970; Chase, 1971; Colinvaux, 1973; Dubos, 1965, 1968; Margalef, 1968; McHale, 1970; Shepard and McKinley, 1969; Smith, 1966; Wallace, 1972; Watt, 1966, 1968).

These advances are important, but the formulation of the ecological perspective is still very spotty. This spottiness is most evident in the arena of human *behavior*. Much is known about the ways in which man's biological functioning and well-being are caught up in the complex webs of the environments he inhabits. However, very little is known about the laws of human use of environmental systems, the interrelations of those systems and behavior, and the paths by which behavioral problems emerge in those systems. Human behavior—what persons *do*—is inextricably bound up in the larger context. It could be argued that the most pressing need in ecological science is to develop *behavioral* ecology in a systematic way.

As just one example of these needs, consider ecological problems of community mental health or community psychology. Professionals in this area operate on at least two basic assumptions: (1) that human development and performance are shaped profoundly by the settings and institutions people inhabit; and (2) that it is legitimate for mental-health professionals to promote sound development and prevent maladaptive development by influencing such settings and institutions (Cowen, 1973). However, if we simply ask the question, "How *do* settings and institutions affect human development?" then we immediately see the dim outlines of a large domain of needed research in social and behavioral ecology. We need systematic frameworks for describing and classifying settings, institutions, and their involvements. We need to understand the mechanisms and processes by which they function, as well as the principles of organization and articulation they display. We need to understand the ways in which behavior is linked to them. And we need to develop new methods for extensive and long-term monitoring so that we can assess their effectiveness.

In recent years, an ecological approach to human behavior has been urged with increasing frequency and urgency. Among the central themes of behavioral ecology are:

1. Human behavior must be viewed and studied at levels of complexity that are quite atypical in behavioral science.
2. The complexity lies in systems of relationships linking person, behavior, social environment, and physical environment.
3. Such systems cannot be understood piecemeal.
4. Such behavior–environment systems have important properties that change, unfold, and become clear only over long periods of time.
5. Tampering with any part of such a system will probably affect the other parts and alter the whole.
6. We must develop an ecological awareness of the many ways in which simple intrusions can produce unintended effects and the many ways in which long-term harm may follow from short-term good.
7. The focal challenge is to achieve enough understanding of such

systems so that the effects of interventions and planned changes can be anticipated in comprehensive fashion.

In other contexts, the implications of behavioral ecology have been discussed for research and theory in psychology (Barker, 1965, 1968, 1969; Moos, 1973, 1974; Willems, 1973b, in press a,b), technologies of behavior change (Willems, 1973d, 1974), humanistic approaches to behavior (Alexander, Dreher, and Willems, 1976), environmental design (Willems, 1973a,c; Wicker, 1972), and problems of health status and health care (Insel and Moos, 1974; Moss, 1973; Willems, 1976; Willems and Campbell, 1975).

Some General Implications

At many levels of analysis, behavior is implicated in very complex organism–environment–behavior systems: "The significant feature is that the social, physical, and biological components function as an integrated system, and any tampering with any part of the system will affect each of the other parts and alter the whole" (Benarde, 1970, p. 24). Agents of change, including economic planners, housing authorities, architects, psychotherapists, social workers, industrial consultants, community psychologists, educational planners, psychopharmacologists, and operant-behavior modifiers have at their disposal various means of affecting behavior–environment systems. The questions of larger and unintended effects within interpersonal and environmental contexts and over long periods of time beg for evaluation and research, because lessons learned in other areas suggest that we should always be sensitive to "other" effects of both small and large intrusions. It is hard to think in terms of systems and we eagerly warp our language to protect ourselves and our favorite approaches from the necessity of thinking in terms of interdependent systems. It is quite foreign to psychologists to think of the physical and behavioral environment as inextricable parts of the behavioral processes of organisms and as relating to them in ways that are extremely complex. Two results that follow are (1) relatively splintered, bitlike attempts to understand large-scale, complex phenomena and (2) blithe forms of bitlike tinkering in complex, interdependent systems.

For the student of behavior, there is much to be learned from this emerging ecological orientation and there is an immediate and pervasive need for expansion of perspective. Until a few years ago, technologists believed that most, if not all, of their developments would be useful in a rather direct and simple sense. We know now that this is not necessarily true—feasibility and even intrinsic success are not sufficient grounds for immediate application (see Eisenberg, 1972). This widening awareness— the ecological perspective—suggests that many things that *can* be done either should not be done or should be done most judiciously and that more technology will not provide solutions to many technologically induced problems (Dubos, 1968, 1970–1971). Before we can be truly effective in designing and affecting human living conditions and alleviating human suffering, we must know much more about the principles that characterize and govern the systems into which such designs and alleviating efforts must, of necessity, intrude. Seeking that knowledge raises a host of theoretical, metatheoretical, and methodological problems.

This line of argument may well lead to a conservatism with regard to intervention in behavior–environment systems and the clear hint that the most adaptive form of action may sometimes be *in*action. The problem is that we know little as yet about the circumstances under which the price for a particular action outweighs the price of inaction and vice versa. We need a great deal more basic research and theoretical understanding that takes account of the ecological, systemlike principles that permeate the phenomena of behavior and environment. There is immediate need for a systematic, scientific basis in the planning of environmental designs, behavioral interventions, and technologies in such a way that they will not produce unanticipated negative costs in behavior–environment systems.

These arguments may appear pessimistic in suggesting that psychologists have scarcely begun to recognize and assimilate the complexities and interdependencies in which the phenomena of behavior are embedded. We might protest that science is supposed to be the search for unifying and *simplifying* principles. However, it just may be that in the long run the most direct and efficient path toward scientific understanding of behavior will involve the timely recognition and acceptance of complexity within an ecological perspective.

Defining Attributes of Behavioral Ecology

Behavioral ecology is a perspective—a point of view—on how the world of human behavior functions and it points to a number of issues that must be understood. Thus, it is not a single theory, a single model, or a single set of methods. Despite this apparent imprecision and despite the metatheoretical flavor of behavioral ecology, some of its defining attributes, orienting principles, and programmatic implications can be spelled out. The purpose of this section is to present 14 such major earmarks.

Naturalism in Methodology

The ecological perspective on behavior stresses complex and systemlike regularities and interdependencies among organisms, behaviors, and everyday environments, often over long periods of time. Behavioral ecology is not primarily a methodological orientation, but it has many implications for methodology, as has been suggested here and elsewhere (Barker, 1965, 1968; Willems, 1973b, in press a,b; Alexander, Dreher, and Willems, 1976). Thus, behavioral ecology is largely naturalistic in its methodological orientation; "largely" because it is not defined by any particular methodology and because this is an emphasis rather than a necessary condition (Willems, 1973b). Pluralism of methods is crucial to behavioral ecology, but the ecologist's methodological statement of faith has two parts. First, with Keller and Marian Breland (1966), the ecologist says, "you cannot understand the behavior of the animal in the laboratory unless you understand his behavior in the wild" (p. 20). Second, contrary to widely held canons in psychology, the ecologist believes that the investigator should manipulate and control only as much as is absolutely necessary to answer his questions clearly, an argument that has been made by many writers (Barker, 1965, 1969; Brandt, 1972; Chapanis, 1967; Gump and Kounin, 1959–1960; Menzel, 1969; Willems, 1965, 1969).

For many students of behavior, experimental manipulation is the highest and most fruitful form of activity to which they can aspire. Some professionals qualify their enthusiasm for the experimental method by recognizing the complexity of behavior. However, even though a great deal of human activity does not lend itself at present to experimental analysis, many psychologists believe that the most important issues in complex behavior will one day be solved through experimental procedures. Despite the qualifiers and doubts that have been raised about this set of beliefs (Chapanis, 1967; Willems and Raush, 1969), experimental analysis still resides at the top of our procedural pecking order, and many psychologists seem to believe that one should always do an experiment if one possibly can.

The ecologist works with the continual reminder that holding experimental conditions constant while varying a limited phenomenon is a figment of the experimental laboratory that may result in the untimely attenuation of both findings and theories. Since the complexities of everyday behavior are the targets to be understood, the ecologist probably would recommend that one never do an experimental manipulation unless one absolutely has to. The ecologist recommends more dependence on direct, sustained, naturalistic observation of human behavior and less on shortcut methods based upon verbal expression and the handiest investigative location, which so often is the experimental laboratory. Questionnaires, interviews, tests, and experiments all have one important characteristic in common: They require the subject to interrupt what he is doing in his natural context and perform a special task for the investigator.

Two recent reports illustrate these principles. Bakeman and Helmreich (1975) analyzed task performance and group cohesiveness from videotapes of persons functioning in the undersea environment of the Tektite 2 project and found that high cohesiveness followed from good performance rather than causing it. The classic assumption in social psychology, stemming from studies of groups in experimental laboratories, had been that high cohesiveness causes good performance by the group. Second, following Desor's (1972) conclusions from a role-playing experiment, Stokols, Smith, and Prostor (1975) conducted a field study and expected to find that partitioning of a waiting area would lessen behavioral tension and feelings of crowding. In the field setting, Stokols *et al.* found just the opposite; that is, partitioning of the environment produced higher levels of tension and stronger feelings of crowding.

Distributions of Phenomena

Behavioral ecology concerns itself with documenting the distribution of phenomena in nature; that is, the range, intensity, and frequency of behavior-environment relations in the everyday, investigator-free environment. Somehow this basic issue is poorly understood by psychologists and such research is not yet widely accepted, valued, or promoted (Barker, 1965, 1969; Elms, 1975; McGuire, 1969; Willems, 1969). Perhaps this is so because the model of experimental and analytical science and the development of technology is so appealing. By and large, psychologists favor manipulations, demonstrations, standard tests, and experiments that tell us little about natural distributions, and we smile condescendingly at those few behavioral scientists who engage in what we call "only observational research; only descriptive research."

Ecosystems seem to function according to laws of conservation and succession, by which events in the systems become distributed and redistributed over time (Margalef, 1968). In the United States, only one of the top three causes of death in 1900 appeared among the top *10* causes of death in 1967 (Chase, 1971), and cancer and heart disease now kill proportionately five times as many persons as they killed in 1900. Disturbing forms of interpersonal violence are changing in distribution, sometimes in ways that can be predicted according to type of neighborhood and dwelling complex (Newman, 1972). Not only are distributional aspects of behavior important to the basic ecological understanding of behavior, but if we are to continue our attempts to influence, change, and accommodate human behavior, then we must begin taking account (1) of the much larger organism–behavior–environment systems within which our activities take place; (2) of distributions of behavior within those systems; and (3) of optimal proportions and combinations of behaviors across populations and subpopulations.

Despite the relatively low status of such research, significant steps have been taken. Some important anthropological, sociological, and ethological studies have gathered distributional data. Closer to a direct focus on human behavior, Ebbesen and Haney (1973) made more than 13,600 observations of drivers at intersections and the environmental conditions under which the drivers took the risk of turning in front of oncoming traffic. The resulting tables of frequencies are full of implications for understanding the everyday behaviors of drivers and the factors that affect such risk taking. The pioneering descriptive work of Barker and Wright and their associates on behaviors of persons in their home communities is so rich and diverse that it defies a brief characterization (see Barker, 1963b, 1965, 1968; Barker and Schoggen, 1973; Barker and Wright, 1955; Wright, 1967, 1969–1970).

In addition to providing descriptive characterizations of ecological systems, distributional data can also suggest where scientific straw men are. Many early theories of child development placed singular importance on the concept of frustration. Fawl (1963) analyzed records representing over 200 hours of observation of children. Occurrences of blocked goals (frustration) were relatively few. When they did occur, the child usually did not appear disturbed, and the few disturbances were of a mild intensity. In another area, it has often been assumed that disfigurement of the face produces widespread negative effects in a person's life because of the social stigma surrounding the face as a crucial social stimulus. After 56 days of monitoring the everyday social and behavioral lives of children and adolescents with grotesque facial disfigurements resulting from burns (as well as matched control children), Schmitt (1971) and Ronnebeck (1972) found that facial disfigurement produced almost no disruptions of the subjects' daily social lives. Stuart (1973) conducted a similar study of wheelchair-bound college students for 7 days and found that the overall frequencies of various types of behavior, participation in various settings, and time spent in various activities and places for wheelchair-bound students was almost indistinguishable from the behavioral topographies of matched, nondisabled students.

Behavioral Focus

Traditionally, psychologists have studied many aspects of human functioning: thoughts, feelings, moods, structures of personality, habits, motives, judgments, cognitions, self-concepts, beliefs, attitudes, perceptions, sensory processes, ego strengths, and a host of other traits and dispositions. The anchoring point for the behavioral ecologist is individual and collective behavior, the molar performances of persons vis-à-vis the environment and their molar responses to it—where persons go, what they do with their time, how they use resources, how they interact with each other. This emphasis has emerged for several reasons. First, the great strides made in animal ecology and ethology have had an influence. In those areas, investigators have been forced to focus on overt behavior because the subjects cannot report feelings and subjective states.

Second, not only do attempts to measure subjective and dispositional variables often evolve into endless psychometric jungles of checking, cross-checking, and validation, but more distressingly, they often yield very weak correlations to behavior (Mischel, 1968; Wicker, 1969, 1971; Willems, 1967). On the basis of his review of the attitude–behavior field, Wicker (1969) concluded that there is

> little evidence to support the postulated existence of stable, underlying attitudes within the individual which influence both his verbal expressions and his actions. . . . Most socially significant questions involve overt behavior, rather than people's feelings, and the assumption that feelings are directly translated into actions has not been demonstrated. (p. 75)

Third, with a shift in emphasis to problems of everyday life and to naturalistic research, psychologists have begun to question some old, dearly held assumptions, one of which asserts that affective, attitudinal, and cognitive variables affect behavioral variables in a simple and unidirectional way. Bakeman and Helmreich (1975) argue:

> Much of the laboratory research of the last two decades in fact has viewed cognitive variables as affecting behavioral ones. Perhaps it is worthwhile to speculate why this is so. The experimentalist . . . manipulates what he can most effectively manipulate, and cognitions are far easier to manipulate than actual behavior. Perhaps feasibility comes to bias views of causality, and then theorists working from laboratory data are likely to become convinced that cognitive variables determine behavioral ones. (p. 488)

Fourth, behavioral performance and response are the major means by which person–environment adaptations are actually mediated. The ecologist does not argue against the reality of subjective phenomena. Rather his position is a matter of emphasis in his seeking to understand human functioning in relation to the environment. Nor does the relative emphasis on behavior imply a simplistic advocacy of behaviorism. To the ecologist, overt behavior simply is more important than many other psychological phenomena. For him it is more important to know how parents *treat* their children than how they feel about being parents; more important to observe whether or not passersby *help* someone in need than what their beliefs are about altruism and kindness; more important to note that a person *harms* someone else when given an opportunity than to know whether his self-concept is that of a considerate person; more important to know what persons *do* with trash than to measure their attitudes about waste disposal; more important to know what one *does* in the way of consuming alcohol or hiring women than to infer community beliefs regarding alcohol or women. To the behavioral ecologist, person–environment–*behavior* systems represent problems to be understood and solved that are simply more important than person–environment–*cognition* systems or person–environment–*attitude* systems.

Despite these developments, measures of cognitive and affective response to the environment remain popular, or even dominant, in the burgeoning field of environmental psychology (Altman, 1975; Downs and Stea, 1973; Ittelson, Proshansky, Rivlin, and Winkel, 1974). In fact, Ittelson *et al.* assert that "The single human psychological process most critical for man/environment interaction, and the one that underlies all the response characteristics that we have described, is that of cognition" (p. 98). The behavioral ecologist would disagree because behavior, in the sense of *doing* things overtly, is the principal means by which persons make long-range adaptations to the environment and it is the means by which they modify the environment. It is not readily apparent how all of the data on how-it-looks, how-it-feels, and what-people-think-they-want will become translated into an understanding of these problems of long-term environmental adaptation and adjustment (see Danford and Willems, 1975).

Environment and Behavior

Behavioral ecology places a great deal of emphasis upon the mutual and interdependent relations among organism, behavior, and environment (Alexander, Dreher, and Willems, 1976; Craik, 1970; Barker, 1963a, 1965, 1968, 1969; Gump, 1969). In their discussion of techniques for measuring behavior–environment relations, Ittelson, Rivlin, and Proshansky (1970) presented a truism that is also a poorly understood principle of man–environment relations: "Behavior always occurs someplace, within the limits of some physical surroundings" (p. 658). One of the central conceptual issues of behavioral ecology is the transactional character of organism–environment systems. Studying behavior by itself is always shortsighted because behavior points two ways or relates in two directions—organism and environment—and to mediating processes between them. Behavior represents the coming-to-terms that occurs in organism–environment systems. Organism and environment are part of the same system, with behavior being the major interface between them. Thus, the behavioral ecologist would argue, we must study *behavior–environment* units rather than just behavior units.

From this perspective, bits of behavior or bits of environment taken independently (as in an S–R model); the "independent" and "dependent" variables of most experiments; and the bits and pieces of behavior with which we tinker so blithely in psychotherapy, counseling, operant behavior modification, and behavioral pharmacology are all abstractions that have lost much of their scientific and practical meaning because they are separated from the larger, contextual interdependencies in which they occur. What is worse, when changing such abstracted bits of behavior, we may create unintended effects in the ecological systems with which the behaviors are linked (Willems, 1973d, 1974). As Rhodes (1972) argued, the credo of behavioral ecology is that, in both its positive and negative manifestations, behavior is a property of ecological systems rather than an attribute of the individual:

> The ecosystem, within the ecological perspective, is an active, energetic composite. . . . It is not only the individual members of the system who act and react, but the total ecosystem "behaves" as a whole. In this sense, behavior is not

only a function of an individual, it is also a function of the ecosystem or its
subsystems. Therefore, territory is not merely an inert geographical mass. It is
also a set of forces which encompasses the behavioral forces of the individual.
Together, they form living patterns which have their own, inbuilt self-sustaining
behavior-selecting regularity. (pp. 558–559)

Some of these principles are illustrated in a program of research on
rehabilitation for persons with spinal-cord injuries (Willems and Campbell,
1975; Willems, 1976). For such persons, where restoration of functional
performances is the central issue, we believe that diagnostic and prognostic
judgments based on behavior rates alone (e.g., how often the patient does
things) will be less complete, less accurate, and less effective than judgments based on changes in behavior–environment units (e.g., the number
of new *combinations* of behavior and situation).

Site Specificity and Place Dependencies

Closely related to the issue of understanding human functioning in terms
of behavior–environment units is the issue of predictability from place, or
setting, to behavior. To the behavioral ecologist, *where* organisms are located is never unimportant or accidental because behavior and place con-
catenate into lawful, functioning systems (Barker, 1963a; Moos, 1973;
Wicker, 1972; Willems, 1965): "The correlation between site and activity is
often so high that an experienced ecological psychologist can direct a person to a particular site in order to observe an animal exhibiting a given
pattern of behavior" (King, 1970, p. 4). Discussing intellectual development, Bruner (1965) noted, "I am still struck by Roger Barker's ironic
truism that the best way to predict the behavior of a human being is to
know where he is: In a post office he behaves post office, at church he
behaves church" (p. 1016). In the conduct of everyday affairs, not only do
we depend upon location specificity in behavior for predictability and social
order, but we often use departures from such correlations to label and
diagnose persons as being sick, crazy, deviant, hyperactive, depressed, etc.,
and in need of help or control.

In their discussion of basic assumptions regarding the influence of the
physical environment on behavior, Proshansky, Ittelson, and Rivlin (1970b)
argued that observed patterns of molar behavior in response to a physical
setting persist regardless of the individuals involved. From their studies of
persons in mental hospitals, the same investigators conclude that such in-
trasetting continuity of behavior often occurs even though inhabitants are
cognitively unaware of the structural aspects of the settings. Barker (1963a,
1968) has also pointed out that place–behavior systems have such strong
principles of organization and constraint that their standing patterns of
behavior remain essentially the same though individuals come and go.
Wicker (1972) called this "behavior–environment congruence." Barker
(1968) called it "behavior–milieu synomorphy" and argued that the appro-

priate units of analysis for studying such synomorphic relationships are *behavior settings,* whose defining attributes and properties he has spelled out in detail (1963a, 1968). One of the attractive aspects of the behavior setting as a unit of analysis for psychology is that it is defined and measured in terms of both place and the standing patterns of behavior correlated with it and, therefore, represents a building block in documenting environmental structure in studies of behavioral ecology. Barker has formulated a cybernetic model of behavior settings to account for their stability and for the behavior–environment congruence they produce.

A clear example of the importance of place dependencies is found in the work of Raush and his colleagues in their studies of normal children and children diagnosed as hyperaggressive or disturbed (Raush, 1969; Raush, Dittmann, and Taylor, 1959a,b; Raush, Farbman, and Llewellyn, 1960). By observing the children for extended periods of time in various settings and then examining the frequencies of various kinds of behavior by the children toward peers and adults, the investigators were able to demonstrate several aspects of place dependency. First, the interpersonal behavior of all the children varied strongly from one setting to another. Second, and perhaps most revealing, the place dependence of behavior was much stronger for normal children than for disturbed children; that is, the influence of the setting was greater for normal children. Finally, as the disturbed children progressed in treatment, the place dependence of their behavior came to approximate that of the normal children more and more.

Wahler (1975) observed two troubled boys periodically for 3 years in home and school settings. He found (1) that behaviors clustered differently in home and school settings; (2) that the clusters within each setting were very stable over time; and (3) that different patterns of deviant behaviors occurred in stable fashion in the two settings.

From the evolutionary standpoint, it makes sense to argue that behavioral responsiveness to settings is selected for, because location appropriateness of behaviors is crucial to adaptation in many settings (Sells, 1969). The implications of such phenomena are widespread. Two that have become part of the behavioral ecologist's credo are, first, that behavior is largely controlled by the environmental setting in which it occurs and, second, that changing the environmental setting will result in changes in behavior. The third implication is related to methodology. This is the investigative problem of describing and classifying the types and patterns of congruence between behavior and environment and formulating principles that account for the congruence. This effort is important because it promises to contribute much to programs of environmental design. To accomplish this goal, investigators must become more persistent in addiing descriptions and codes for locations and context to their measures and descriptions of behavior.

These principles are illustrated and elaborated by our program of research on persons with spinal-cord injuries mentioned above (Willems,

1976). First, when we look at distributions of patient behavior within different settings, we find that these profiles of behavior vary dramatically from one setting to another (LeCompte and Willems, 1970; Willems, 1972a,b). Some behaviors occurring in one setting do not occur at all in others, and the relative frequencies and percentage weights of behavior show strong variation between settings. *What* patients do varies systematically from one setting to another.

Second, in addition to these topographical dependencies on settings, we find dependencies in the more dynamic aspects of patient behavior. From the observations, we extract behavioral measures of *independence* (i.e., the proportion of performances that patients initiate and execute alone) and zest (i.e., the proportion of performances that patients initiate and carry out actively). Because increases from very low rates in these measures reflect a relative normalizing of the patients' behavior repertoires, both relate closely to important goals of the hospital's treatment system. Many traditional, person-based theories of human behavior in psychology would assume that independence and zest are largely a matter of individual motivation and thus should reflect a high degree of personal constancy across situations. What we find instead is that behavioral independence varies dramatically when patients move from one hospital setting to another.

Third, we find in many cases that differences between settings account for more variance in patient performance (e.g., zest) than do differences between patients.

Fourth, and most interestingly, there are powerful variations among settings in the rate of growth and behavioral development displayed by patients. That is, patients show much more change of behavior in some hospital settings than in others.

In summary, not only do we find that persons perform differently in different settings when we make simple comparisons between settings, but we find that persons change in different ways and at different rates in different settings. When these central principles of behavioral ecology really soak in, they will affect human behavioral science in profound ways. One area that will be affected strongly is the area of human assessment. It will no longer be as tenable or defensible to assess *a person's* performance. Rather, we will have to assess performance-by-settings, because variations in settings produce variations in performance.

Ecological Diagnosis

Diagnosis is a process that begins with careful scrutiny of a set of indicators and ends with a judgment, a statement, regarding the events to which those indicators point. For example, a certain pattern among indicators such as fever, respiratory congestion, joint pain, and malaise can lead to a judgment that influenza is occurring. In psychology and psychiatry, judgments of what is wrong—that is, diagnoses—are often highly constrained by prior theoretical commitments that lead one to look for the underlying problems inside the person. It is important to recognize this tradition because diagnostic judgments usually carry with them either implicit or explicit strategies of intervention. If the underlying problem is seen to lie inside the person, then remedial steps will usually be focused on the person and we are entrapped in what Caplan and Nelson (1973) and Ryan (1971) have called "person blaming" or "victim blaming." The problem lies in our models, theories, and research, which are preoccupied with the unity and integrity of persons taken one at a time and are preoccupied with what goes on inside them, rather than with behavior–environment systems. After all, it is the *person* who behaves, whose behavior we must understand, or who misbehaves, and it is the *person* who comes or is referred for help because of some serious internal disturbance, isn't it? This is the way it has been in psychology, but psychology must adopt a more holistic perspective if it is to deal effectively with human problems.

The classical mode of diagnosis, in which the person is seen as the repository of the problems, can lead to results that are too facile and too quick-and-dirty in their execution. The ease with which this can happen is illustrated by the work of Rosenhan (1973), who asked eight sane persons to gain admission to 12 different mental hospitals over a period of time. With only fleeting reference to hearing voices in otherwise straightforward presentations, all except one were admitted with diagnoses of "schizophrenia." The investigators who arranged the study told each pseudopatient that he would have to get out of the hospital by his own devices. The average length of stay was 19 days, with a range from 7 to 52 days. Even though several of the hospitals had excellent reputations, other patients—never staff members—were the ones who spotted the pseudopatients as pretenders. Furthermore, each of the pseudopatients was discharged with a diagnosis of "schizophrenia in remission." Note that they were not judged never to have been sick; they were judged to have been sick and somehow remitted. In other words, the original label stuck.

Rosenhan reported other data and his study certainly has far-reaching implications. The important point for present purposes is to note how simplistic and facile the classical mode of diagnosis can be. Under the assumption that the person carries around the roots of his problems inside him, the classical mode often involves only a few logical steps to respond to a simple set of verbal signals about what is presumably going on inside the person and to conclude, diagnostically, that his life is fouled up. What such a process disregards about the person's behavioral life and his functioning beyond the simple verbal, inward-pointing signals should give us all pause.

As Calhoun has argued (1967), the ecosystem and its members can collude in processes that are systematically or ecologically disharmonious and destructive; that is, they can become involved reciprocally in "ecological traps." The fact that some persons manifest the problems while others do not and that the disturbance process has varying concentrations and is not necessarily distributed equally throughout the ecological system should not divert us from the principle that we "cannot speak only of the disturbance of the individual, but . . . must speak of the disturbance of the system" (Rhodes, 1972, p. 559). Our traditional models lead us to focus on persons. The points in the ecological system in which we sample determine where we locate the behavioral problem. When our pet models lead us to attach our disturbance detectors to the individual, we will detect disturbance in the individual and we will make him our target of intervention and change. In the process, we disregard the fact that the problem or the disturbance may lie at the level of an ecological system of which the individual is only one component and that our scientific understanding of behavior, our principles of diagnosis, and our interventions must be adjusted to that level of complexity. One of the most important steps toward credibility and long-range impact that behavioral scientists can take is to develop sound procedures for new forms of contextual, ecological diagnosis (Alexander, Dreher, and Willems, 1976).

Systems Concepts and Analogies

It is common for the ecologist to couch much of what he does and thinks about in the terminology and concepts of systems. This happens for several reasons. Sometimes it is because of the extensiveness of the phenomena under study, sometimes because of their complexity or because of emphasis on the interdependence of many variables at many levels, sometimes because systems theory brings to bear an appropriate and powerful set of formal principles, and sometimes simply because *system* is the best metaphor or image the ecologist can conjure up to communicate what he is trying to say. As science and technology have grown in complexity, the use of systems theory and terminology has become more widespread. Thus, it is only reasonable that ecologists would turn to this discipline for tools of conceptual representation and analysis. There is a growing awareness that we need new and sophisticated forms of analysis and synthesis that are not amenable to the traditional, either–or methodology that permeates Western scientific thinking. Systems theory and its various derivatives offer promising tools for representing *interdependence* and simultaneous, time-related complexity (Berrien, 1968; Bruhn, 1974; Buckley, 1968; Laszlo, 1972).

General ecology has become quite sophisticated in its use of formal quantitative representation and systems theory, but behavioral ecology's use of such concepts is still in its infancy. Systems concepts in behavioral ecology are often common-sensical, crude, and analogical in form, for example, the frequent use of the phrase "environment–behavior system" in contexts in which the speaker or writer cannot specify precisely what that means. Despite this crudeness in usage, it is still possible to illustrate the importance of systems-oriented points of view on behavior.

Ecosystem principles often can be dramatized best by a demonstration that a given intervention or change leads to complicated and unintended ramifications. Since many social, physical, and biological systems function as integrated wholes, even the most positively motivated intrusions into interdependent systems can lead to all sorts of unanticipated effects, many of which are unpleasant and pernicious. To label these unintended effects as "side effects" only compounds the problem. Anticipated and unanticipated effects are all functions of the system's processes. Side effects do not occur in the real world. They exist in our images of events for which we *expect* some things and not others.

In our growing awareness of ecological phenomena, we may have become reluctant to introduce new biotic elements and new chemicals into our ecological systems, but we display dismal irresponsibility when it comes to intervening in behavioral and behavioral–environmental systems. Almost every day we hear of projects or technologies being changed, slowed down, stopped, or disapproved on ecological grounds because of the known complexity or delicacy of ecosystems. The location of a proposed factory is switched, a bridge is not built, a planned freeway is rerouted, a smokestack is modified, someone is restrained from introducing a new animal into an area, or a pesticide is taken off the market. Those who think that no changes are required in the behavioral sciences or that arguments for a new effort in behavioral ecology are just so much window dressing should ask just one question: How often have I heard of a program or project whose target is human behavior being changed, slowed down, stopped, or disapproved on *behavioral*–ecological grounds, because of the *known* complexity and delicacy of ecobehavioral systems? The answer should sober us and point out the need for sophisticated models of ecobehavioral systems. Unintended effects occurring in the short- or long-range outcome of a purposeful intervention in human behavior are viewed by the behavioral ecologist as important aspects of interdependent phenomena that need to be understood (Alexander, Dreher, and Willems, 1976; Willems, 1973d, 1974).

Partly because of their rigor and partly because of the explicitness with which their intended effects can be spelled out, various programs of applied behavior analysis or behavior modification illustrate these problems very clearly for human behavior. Buell, Stoddard, Harris, and Baer (1968) used teacher attention to reinforce a withdrawn girl's use of play equipment in a preschool setting. The intervention was successful (intended effect), but it also affected the girl's interactions with other children, such as touching, verbalizations, and cooperative play (positive unintended effects). Wahler, Sperling, Thomas, Teeter, and Luper (1970) found that parents' successful efforts to reduce non-speech deviant behaviors by their children also led to a reduction in stuttering and that this positive unintended effect was not a function of differential reinforcement of stuttering and fluent speech. Drabman and Lahey (1974) used teacher feedback to reduce the rate of disruptive behavior by a child in a classroom, but they found that the rate of disruptive behavior by other children was reduced as well.

Unintended effects of a more unpleasant and disruptive sort also occur. Herbert, Pinkston, Hayden, Sajwaj, Pinkston, Cordua, and Jackson (1973) trained parents in the use of differential attention to increase appropriate behaviors and decrease deviant behaviors in six children. One child showed some improvement and one showed no change. In the cases of four children, dramatic, intense, and durable (but unintended) effects showed up, both in the treatment setting and in other settings (e.g., assaulting mother, scratching self until bleeding, enuresis, and throwing tables and chairs). The investigators were able to show that these effects occurred despite tenacious programs of differential reinforcement by parents.

Sajwaj, Twardosz, and Burke (1972) found various "side effects" of manipulating single behaviors in a preschool boy. They arranged for the teacher to ignore the child's initiated speech to her (nagging) in one setting of the preschool. This tactic was successful in reducing the nagging but produced systematic changes in other behavior by the child in the same setting and in another setting as well. Some of the unintended effects were desirable (increasing speech initiated to children, increasing cooperative play), while some were undesirable (decreasing task-appropriate behavior, increasing disruptive behavior), and some were neutral (use of girls' toys). The investigators were able to show that the covarying effects were not due to differential attention by the teacher applied directly to those behaviors but were somehow (as yet, mysteriously) a function of modifying another single dimension of behavior.

It seems clear that the simplistic models and technologies of change used by the applied-behavior analyst are not comprehensive enough to lead to the understanding of complex human behavior or to predictable interventions. Extensive research should be conducted to ascertain which *kinds* of unintended effects occur most frequently in various settings and *why* they occur, so that practitioners can begin to predict such effects and plan interventions with these effects in mind.

There are other examples that fall higher in a hierarchy of setting size and complexity. In a mental hospital ward, Proshansky, Ittelson, and Rivlin (Chapters 3 and 43 in 1970a) used some amenities of interior design to increase the rate of sociable occupancy and use of a solarium, and they found that the rate of detached, withdrawn, standing behavior went down. However, they had only succeeded in changing the *location* of the troubling behavior—a great deal of it now occurred at the other end of the corridor, by the nurses' station. At a southwestern rehabilitation hospital (Willems, 1976), a change in staff assignments was accompanied by some anticipated (positive) changes in patient behavior (e.g., greater patient independence) but unanticipated (negative) changes as well (e.g., less environmental diversity in patient performance).

At the level of residential systems, the work of such investigators as Newman (1972) and Galle, Gove, and McPherson (1972) and the accumulation of experiences with arrangements such as Pruitt-Igoe in St. Louis all suggest that a torrent of troubling effects can follow from the concatenation of people in large groupings, high population density, and physical design whose behavioral principles are very poorly understood. The new town of Skarholmen, near Stockholm in Sweden, was built to incorporate the most advanced architectural technology (Dubos, 1971). Among its 20,000 inhabitants, particularly among its children and teen-agers, there followed an alarming rate of restlessness, aggressiveness, and withdrawal that was correlated with nearness to the center of town and the density of living arrangement. Behavioral scientists studying and evaluating the new town suggested that the antisocial behaviors were related to population density and the austere form of architecture. Whether this specific explanation is correct or not, it would appear that the unanticipated behavioral problems are symptomatic not of personal problems but of problems in the relationship of habitat and behavior.

While such examples offer strong reinforcement to the behavioral ecologist and some of his favorite arguments and beliefs about ecobehavioral systems, they are also troubling, partly because they raise serious questions about some of the most promising, most explicit, and most powerful techniques of behavior change available today and partly because we are confronted with the monumental tasks of learning how to monitor and understand the network of influences in such systems and of developing anticipatory and prescriptive models and guidelines for intervention.

Long Time Periods

In keeping with the characteristics of behavior–environment systems and the kinds of behavioral dimensions with which he often works (e.g., adaptation, accommodation, functional achievement, long-range behavior, and sometimes even survival), the ecologist not only allows but sometimes demands unusually long time periods and time dependencies in his research. Over and above the more traditional search for early antecedents (as in developmental psychology), such long-range research often takes the form of monitoring interdependencies continuously, or nearly continuously, for extended periods of time. At least three concerns lead to this emphasis. First, sequential, temporal-emergent phenomena are among the most important properties of behavior (Barker, 1963b; Nesselroade and Reese, 1973; Raush, 1969). Second, ecosystems in general (and therefore probably behavioral–ecological systems) follow rules of succession and internal distribution in which the longitudinal perspective becomes critical. Third, we know by now from other areas (e.g., crop diseases, pollution, public-health problems, and insecticides) that empirical monitoring of very long sequences can be both scientifically illuminating and pragmatically critical. Psychologists must become willing to participate in such long-range concerns.

> Whatever is done to the environment is likely to have repercussions in other places and at other times. Because of the characteristic problems of ecology some of the effects are bound to be unpredictable in practice, if not in principle. Furthermore, because of the characteristic time-dependence problem, the effects may not be measureable for years—possibly not for decades. (Murdoch and Connell, 1970, p. 61)

Two examples illustrate these issues. First, noting that a person's adaptation to the noxious stimulation of high-intensity noise can produce negative aftereffects in behavior (Glass and Singer, 1972), Cohen, Glass, and Singer (1973) studied the long-term effects of noise on children living in a high-rise apartment building. The apartment building was situated directly over a busy interstate highway that produced high noise levels and an echo-chamber effect in the building. Measurements of decibel levels showed that noise levels were much more intense on the lower floors than on the upper floors. Testing of the children showed that the lower the floor of residence (noisier), the more impairment of auditory discrimination and reading ability the children displayed. Most importantly, these relationships increased in strength as length of residence increased (0–4 years, 4–6 years, 6 or more years). If a long time perspective had not been adopted in the research, this cumulative effect of noise on the behavioral performances of hearing and reading would have been missed.

Second, Lee (1972) showed how misleading a data-gathering period of even a whole year can be in understanding the behavior and social life of a tribe of hunter–gatherers. The typical field worker observes at most one or two annual cycles in the life of a tribe. He may well observe the hunting-and-gathering population in a state of mobility that puzzles him, and he is likely to conclude that they are moving more than necessary because of social deterioration or breakdown of the groups. However, from a very long time frame, Lee has shown in the case of the !Kung Bushmen that such a hypothesis, based on a 1-year observation, misrepresents what is happening because it underestimates the amount of movement of such tribes. With data from the !Kung, Lee showed that a group of hunter–gatherers often is able to satisfy subsistence requirements within an area of 100 square kilometers (already a large area) for 4 out of 5 years. However, the group must have access to a much larger area every fifth year, on the average, in order to survive. To survive cycles of environmental fluctuations over the course of 50 years, or up to 200 years, the group must maintain access to areas of up to 1,000 square kilometers. This pattern of extreme environmental mobility and its relation to environmental resources can be understood only within a very long time perspective. Adaptation by the !Kung is a long-term, cyclical process—a very small part of which can be captured by 1 year of observation.

The arguments by Toffler (1970) and the empirical research of Holmes and Masuda (1972) and their associates indicate that the rate and magnitude of change in a person's life affect his health, behavior, and well-being in profound ways, perhaps because of limits on persons' capacities to cope with environmental input and stress. And yet, we know almost nothing about the cumulative, longitudinal aspects of such phenomena or about reversible and irreversible effects. When we consider the possibility of very subtle, subthreshold correlates of change that may aggregate over time into serious problems (Dubos, 1965), the need for longitudinal research becomes evident.

Of course, not all of the important phenomena of human functioning and behavior require very long periods of study. The *ecological* problem is that behavioral scientists often are distressingly unwilling to differentiate those behavioral issues that require the emergent time frame from those that do not, and they are often even less willing to knuckle down and tackle those that do. Many psychologists would much rather do several discrete studies with many subjects each year than work on a phenomenon whose important properties unravel and cycle over a period of months or years. Research with very long time frames is absolutely necessary for the development of an ecological perspective on behavior.

Taxonomy

Behavioral ecology concerns itself with one of the great voids in American psychology—the problem of taxonomy. Together with naturalistic description of the distribution of behavioral phenomena, basic taxonomic research has been grossly neglected by psychologists. What are the units of environment, of behavior, and of environment–behavior linkages? Into what types of classifications do situations, behaviors, and environments fall? It is sometimes argued that behavior is too ephemeral, too spontaneous, too malleable to be fitted into taxonomies. However, that is an evasion because the fleeting and malleable quality of many chemical and biological phenomena have not prevented the creation of useful taxonomies. Furthermore the fact that the behavioral sciences "are in a historical position analogous to 100 to 200 years prior to Mendeleev and Linnaeus" (Altman, 1968, p. 57) is no excuse to avoid the necessary work. It is tempting to view the great advances now occurring in biology and physiology and assert that those scientists are not going through the drudgery of basic taxonomic research. The error here lies in forgetting that all the current work *presupposes* and rests upon the work of taxonomists going all the way back to Linnaeus, Fritsch, Hitzig, and others.

Taxonomies are important for several reasons. First, there is the aesthetic pleasure that accompanies scientific orderliness. Second, systems of classification represent the only comprehensive way to avoid being smothered by a great host of splintered, separate facts (Altman, 1968; Studer, 1972). The development of comprehensive theory depends, in part, upon a coherent classification of the empirical domain. Third, a good taxonomy "can provide a standard metalanguage to describe all concepts and variables in a field" (Altman and Lett, 1970, p. 182). Such translation into a common system permits the comparison of various findings and concepts with each other. Fourth, as Altman and Lett point out (1970), an effective taxonomy can help scientists pinpoint well-established results, confused or contradictory results, and areas of research that have been neglected (i.e., missing data). Fifth, Altman and Lett also argue that a taxonomy can lead to predictions of new relationships that have not become obvious from separate studies. Sixth, a generally useful taxonomy allows any particular investigator to classify what he is working on with sufficient precision so that he is fully aware of how his phenomenon relates to what other investigators are working on, and it will allow him to communicate his phenomenon with enough precision so that other investigators know what he is working on. Consider how far we are from that state of affairs in the behavioral sciences. The behavioral ecologist would argue that the infinite splintering and disparate quality of the behavioral sciences is due, in large part, to the lack of coherent, consensual systems of classification.

Finally, it is not difficult to see from all this that good taxonomies become particularly important to persons engaged in the applied, mission-oriented efforts of environmental design. It is when environmental agents set out to apply the substance of behavioral research to arrangements for living that the lack of orderly classification of knowledge becomes most painful (Barker, 1963a, 1969; Sells, 1966, 1968, 1969; Studer, 1972). When one seeks orderly, cross-classified information and principles and does not find them, it is easy to conclude that psychology and the other behavioral sciences do not know much. We do know much, but without classification systems it is almost impossible to ascertain what we do and do not know.

Molar Phenomena and Nonreductionism

The ecological perspective tends, generally, to place more emphasis upon *molar* phenomena than upon *molecular* ones. Closely related is a relative emphasis upon environmental, behavioral, and organismic holism and simultaneous, complex relationships. This is so in part because all the way from the survival of a species, through adaptive functioning, and down to day-to-day and moment-by-moment adaptive processes, the emphasis is upon the organism's and the population's behavioral commerce with the environmental packages they inhabit. Adaptation to everyday settings and long-range, functional performance in them places focus on coming to terms with the environment, on what Powers (1973) called *results* rather than more molecular movements. Even though it might be possible, in principle, to study the ecology of eye blinks (a relatively molecular phenomenon), the behavioral ecologist usually focuses on larger, setting-sized, functional behavior episodes, for example, cooperation, conflict, solving problems, social interactions, and transporting (Barker, 1963a, 1965, 1969; Sells, 1969; Wicker, 1972; Wright, 1967).

Thus, the ecologist in much more willing than many of his peers in psychology to favor working from the complex to the simple as his strategy of choice and to accept complicated, intact phenomena as his arena. Space does not permit the extensive development of this point, but the ecologist, with some support from other scientists, operates on the assumption that the functioning of his relatively large units of phenomena cannot always be reduced to or understood in terms of more molecular events and that the exhaustive understanding of systemlike phenomena often requires the formulation of models and principles at the level of the system.

Transdisciplinary Emphasis

The behavioral ecologist assumes and *acts* on the assumption that the phenomena of behavior participate in a much larger network of phenomena, descriptions, and disciplines. In fact, as Smith (1966) pointed out, "The ecologist is something of a chartered libertine. He roams at will over the legitimate preserves" of other scientists and "poaches" from other disciplines (p. 5). Ecology tends to be highly eclectic, and the ecologist tends to borrow and lend concepts, methods, and hypotheses freely, with little sense of preciousness about boundaries between disciplines, because he believes that the sciences of behavior thrive on polygamy. The need for eclecticism and professional symbiosis arises because of the nature of the phenomena and partly because of the nature of professional specialization.

Behavior, the principal means by which organisms carry on commerce with the environment, is embedded in and relates to phenomena at many levels, which themselves form hierarchies of embedded systems, for example, molecules, cells, tissues, organs, organ systems, organisms, settings, facilities, institutions, political systems, economic systems. Behavior is a mid-range phenomenon; what organisms *do* is the principal means by which they relate to the various levels of context. Thus, the full contextual understanding of behavior requires models and approaches developed by persons who study the various levels of embeddedness (Barker, 1969; Boulding, 1968; Chase, 1971; Sells, 1969; Shepard and McKinley, 1969).

As scientists and practitioners, psychologists seem to accept the doctrine of the organization of the world in terms of levels. Having picked the level of analysis that clusters around the organism and his behavior, they tend to work *within* that level and not *with* it; that is, they do little to display its relations to the environment as it extends away from the person. Two forms of crossing boundaries must occur. First, we must use the ideas, concepts, measures, and procedures of various disciplines (and levels of analysis) freely. Second, we must develop new forms of intensive, problem-oriented collaboration and cooperation with professionals from various disciplines. In a word, behavioral ecology is too important to be left to psychologists (Craik, 1972).

Habitability

More than many of his peers in psychology, the behavioral ecologist devotes a great deal of effort to the question of *habitability;* that is, to the issue of what kinds of environments are fit for human beings to inhabit. The ecologist does this not only because it sets the stage for human design and social engineering, but because he believes that when he leaves his preoccupation with phenomena that are convenient from the investigative point of view—for example, measures of time, latency, errors, number of trials, thresholds, bar-pressing, and molecular physiology—and concerns himself with such messy and molar problems as safety, convenience, comfort, satisfaction, adjustment, long-term functional achievement, adaptation, and cost, he may well be on the most direct path to basic theoretical understanding as well (see Benarde, 1970; Chase, 1971; Chapanis, 1967; Insel and Moos, 1974).

Small Rates

In drawing conclusions, the behavioral ecologist is more willing than many of his peers to depend upon rate measures across whole populations. Americans and American behavioral scientists look for *whopper* effects; we tend to respond most readily to large increases and decreases in things. We are used to viewing things as effective or ineffective, important or unimportant, good or bad only if they lead to big changes in rate. Another way of saying this is that we do not view things from an ecological perspective. The ecologist lets himself view certain matters in terms of whole populations and in terms of small changes in rates in those populations. A change in a few parts per million in the density of a chemical in the environment can mean the difference between a rate that preserves life and a rate that destroys it. Small changes in percentages or even fractions of percentages in such phenomena as tuberculosis, metallic poisoning, bubonic plague, cholera, or schistosomiasis can bear unambiguous information that something is wrong in the environment and in the relations between persons and the environment.

If this is so, then why should it be different with social and behavioral phenomena? Does nearly everyone in a population have to be involved in rape, murder, suicide, drug addiction, alcoholism, assault, irritability, depression, malaise, uncooperativeness, or lack of social amenity before we conclude that there is something fundamentally wrong in the environment or in the interaction of that population with it? Probably not. However, we are not prepared to take rate measures seriously enough, partly because we know so little about the general adaptive and maladaptive value of behavioral phenomena (we know so little about its symptomatic value in various contexts) and partly because we do not yet have the models and theories that lead us to depend upon such rate measures. These are ecological problems and they are ecological problems for psychology.

Porter's (1972) illustration of the concept of parts per million (ppm) offers us an idea of how far behavioral scientists are from using very small rates. Porter points out that many important measures of toxic metals in the environment are expressed in ppm and dramatizes the concept by describing "The world's driest martini: one ppm of vermouth would be the equivalent of one ounce of vermouth in 7,800 gallons of gin" (p. 477). In the behavioral sciences, we are still very far from attaching significance to such small rates.

Evaluation of Natural Experiments

The final aspect of behavioral ecology is one that, to date, has done most to bring general ecology to the attention of the public. Many events—for example, the introduction of insecticides, the building of dams, the introduction of contraceptive techniques, increases in pollutants, uses of new seed crops, lumbering, and the introduction of organisms into new areas—are out of the direct control of ecologists and, therefore, represent natural experiments whose various effects they are able to study. Such natural experiments, when evaluated by ecologists, have provided data and generalizations that have made ecology a faddish and controversial enterprise; they are phenomena on which ecologists have been able to test models and strategies of investigation.

Behavioral ecology has begun to recognize the potential scientific value of natural experiments and should realize that the possibilities are almost infinite, for example, institutional reforms, refurbishing programs, social-change programs, changes in trafficways and transportation systems, disruption of neighborhoods, increases in population and crowding, shifts from single-family to multifamily dwellings, and programs of behavior modification. Campbell (1969) advocates such research and discusses some of the problems and pitfalls involved. A recent compendium (Struening and Guttentag, 1975) summarizes the major methodological issues of evaluation research.

Concluding Comments

By means of a series of principles, issues, and illustrations, I have tried to communicate some of the essential flavor of behavioral ecology as a vision of how the world of human behavior functions. Included in this vision are key ideas such as complexity, interdependencies across many levels of phenomena, behavior–organism–environment systems, principles of reciprocity and exchange, cycles and emergent phenomena over long periods of time, widespread ramifications of interventions and changes, and many important implications for research methodology.

Research commensurate with that vision will provide comprehensive, progressive, and cumulative information on ecobehavioral systems— homes, schools, and many other institutions and settings. This sort of work will be expensive, complex, demanding, and sometimes of low yield in direct, pragmatic outcomes. In the long run, however, this work will lead to more effective means of dealing with human problems, to more effective prediction and management of unintended effects, and, perhaps, even to new paradigms and theories. If this happens, then the behavioral sciences themselves will also become more ecologically adaptive and more relevant to the solution of human problems. Thus, I would argue that behavioral ecology is central both to psychological perspectives on the environment and to environmental perspectives on psychology.

References

Alexander, J. L., Dreher, G. F., and Willems, E. P. Behavioral ecology and humanistic and behavioristic approaches to change. In A. Wandersman, P. Poppen, and D. Ricks (Eds.), *Human behavior and change*. Elmsford, N.Y.: Pergamon, 1976.

Altman, I. Choicepoints in the classification of scientific knowledge. In B. P. Indik and F. K. Berrien (Eds.), *People, groups, and organizations*. New York: Teachers College Press, 1968, pp. 47–69.

Altman, I. *The environment and social behavior*. Monterey, Calif.: Brooks/Cole, 1975.

Altman, I., and Lett, E. E. The ecology of interpersonal relationships: A classification system and conceptual model. In J. E. McGrath (Ed.), *Social and psychological factors in stress*. New York: Holt, Rinehart and Winston, 1970, pp. 177–201.

Bakeman, R., and Helmreich, R. Cohesiveness and performance: Covariation and causality in an undersea environment. *Journal of Experimental Social Psychology*, 1975, *11*, 478–489.

Barker, R. G. Ecology and motivation. In M. R. Jones (Ed.), *Nebraska Symposium on Motivation*. Lincoln: University of Nebraska Press, 1960, pp. 1–49.

Barker, R. G. On the nature of the environment. *Journal of Social Issues*, 1963, *19*, 17–38. (a)

Barker, R. G. (Ed.). *The stream of behavior*. New York: Appleton-Century-Crofts, 1963. (b)

Barker, R. G. Observation of behavior: Ecological approaches. *Journal of Mt. Sinai Hospital*, 1964, *31*, 268–284.

Barker, R. G. Explorations in ecological psychology. *American Psychologist*, 1965, *20*, 1–14.

Barker, R. G. *Ecological psychology*. Stanford, Calif.: Stanford University Press, 1968.

Barker, R. G. Wanted: An eco-behavioral science. In E. P. Willems and H. L. Raush (Eds.), *Naturalistic viewpoints in psychological research*. New York: Holt, Rinehart and Winston, 1969, pp. 31–43.

Barker, R. G., and Barker, L. S. Behavior units for the comparative study of culture. In B. Kaplan (Ed.), *Studying personality cross-culturally*. New York: Harper and Row, 1961, pp. 457–476.

Barker, R. G., and Schoggen, P. *Qualities of community life*. San Francisco: Jossey-Bass, 1973.

Barker, R. G., and Wright, H. F. *Midwest and its children*. New York: Harper & Row, 1955.

Benarde, M. A. *Our precarious habitat.* New York: W. W. Norton, 1970.

Berrien, F. K. *General and social systems.* New Brunswick, N.J.: Rutgers University Press, 1968.

Boulding, K. E. General systems theory: The skeleton of science. In W. Buckley (Ed.), *Modern systems research for the behavioral scientist.* Chicago: Aldine, 1968, pp. 3–10.

Brandt, R. M. *Studying behavior in natural settings.* New York: Holt, Rinehart and Winston, 1972.

Breland, K., and Breland, M. *Animal behavior.* New York: Macmillan, 1966.

Bruhn, J. G. Human ecology: A unifying science? *Human Ecology,* 1974, *2,* 105–125.

Bruner, J. S. The growth of mind. *American Psychologist,* 1965, *20,* 1007–1017.

Buckley, W. (Ed.). *Modern systems research for the behavioral scientist.* Chicago: Aldine, 1968.

Buell, J., Stoddard, P., Harris, F. R., and Baer, D. M. Collateral social development accompanying reinforcement of outdoor play in a preschool child. *Journal of Applied Behavior Analysis,* 1968, *1,* 167–173.

Calhoun, J. B. Ecological factors in the development of behavioral anomalies. In J. Zubin and H. F. Hunt (Eds.), *Comparative psychopathology.* New York: Grune and Stratton, 1967, pp. 1–51.

Campbell, D. T. Reforms as experiments. *American Psychologist,* 1969, *24,* 409–429.

Caplan, N., and Nelson, S. D. On being useful: The nature and consequences of psychological research on social problems. *American Psychologist,* 1973, *28,* 199–211.

Chapanis, A. The relevance of laboratory studies to practical situations. *Ergonomics,* 1967, *10,* 557–577.

Chase, A. *The biological imperatives.* New York: Holt, Rinehart and Winston, 1971.

Cohen, S., Glass, D. C., and Singer, J. E. Apartment noise, auditory discrimination, and reading ability in children. *Journal of Experimental Social Psychology,* 1973, *9,* 407–422.

Colinvaux, P. A. *Introduction to ecology.* New York: Wiley, 1973.

Cowen, E. L. Social and community interventions. *Annual Review of Psychology,* 1973, *24,* 423–472.

Craik, K. H. Environmental psychology. In *New Directions in psychology—IV.* New York: Holt, Rinehart and Winston, 1970, pp. 1–121.

Craik, K. H. An ecological perspective on environmental decision-making. *Human Ecology,* 1972, *1,* 69–80.

Danford, G. S., and Willems, E. P. Subjective responses to architectual displays: A question of validity. *Environment and Behavior,* 1975, *7,* 486–516.

Desor, J. Toward a psychological theory of crowding. *Journal of Personality and Social Psychology,* 1972, *21,* 79–83.

Downs, R. M., and Stea, D. (Eds.). *Image and environment: Cognitive mapping and spatial behavior.* Chicago: Aldine, 1973.

Drabman, R. S., and Lahey, B. B. Feedback in classroom behavior modification: Effects on the target and her classmates. *Journal of Applied Behavior Analysis,* 1974, *7,* 591–598.

Dubos, R. *Man adapting.* New Haven, Conn.: Yale University Press, 1965.

Dubos, R. *So human an animal.* New York: Charles Scribner's Sons, 1968.

Dubos, R. The despairing optimist. *American Scholar,* 1970–1971, *40,* 16–20.

Dubos, R. The despairing optimist. *American Scholar,* 1971, *40,* 565–572.

Ebbesen, E. B., and Haney, M. Flirting with death: Variables affecting risk taking at intersections. *Journal of Applied Social Psychology,* 1973, *3,* 303–324.

Eisenberg, L. The *human* nature of human nature. *Science,* 1972, *176,* 123–128.

Elms, A. C. The crisis of confidence in social psychology. *American Psychologist,* 1975, *30,* 967–976.

Fawl, C. L. Disturbances experienced by children in their natural habitats. In R. G. Barker (Ed.), *The stream of behavior.* New York: Appleton-Century-Crofts, 1973, pp. 99–126.

Galle, O. R., Gove, W. R., and McPherson, J. M. Population density and pathology: What are the relations for man? *Science,* 1972, *176,* 23–30.

Glass, D. C., and Singer, J. E. *Urban stress.* New York: Academic Press, 1972.

Gump, P. V. Intra-setting analysis: The third grade classroom as a special but illustrative case.

In E. P. Willems and H. L. Raush (Eds.), *Naturalistic viewpoints in psychological research.* New York: Holt, Rinehart and Winston, 1969, pp. 200–220.

Gump, P. V., and Kounin, J. S. Issues raised by ecological and "classical" research efforts. *Merrill-Palmer Quarterly,* 1959–1960, *6,* 145–152.

Herbert, E. W., Pinkston, E. M., Hayden, M. L., Sajwaj, T. E., Pinkston, S., Cordua, G., and Jackson, C. Adverse effects of differential parental attention. *Journal of Applied Behavior Analysis,* 1973, *6,* 15–30.

Holmes, T. H., and Masuda, M. Psychosomatic syndrome. *Psychology Today,* 1972, *5,* 71–72, 106.

Insel, P. M., and Moos, R. H. (Eds.). *Health and the social environment.* Lexington, Mass.: Lexington Books, 1974.

Ittelson, W. H., Proshansky, H. M., Rivlin, L. G., and Winkel, G. H. *An introduction to environmental psychology.* New York: Holt, Rinehart and Winston, 1974.

Ittelson, W. H., Rivlin, L. G., and Proshansky, H. M. The use of behavioral maps in environmental psychology. In H. M. Proshansky, W. H. Ittelson, and L. G. Rivlin (Eds.), *Environmental psychology.* New York: Holt, Rinehart and Winston, 1970, pp. 658–668.

King, J. A. Ecological psychology: An approach to motivation. In W. J. Arnold and M. M. Page (Eds.), *Nebraska Symposium on Motivation.* Lincoln: University of Nebraska Press, 1970, pp. 1–33.

Laszlo, E. *The systems view of the world.* New York: Braziller, 1972.

LeCompte, W. F., and Willems, E. P. Ecological analysis of a hospital: Location dependencies in the behavior of staff and patients. In J. Archea and C. Eastman (Eds.), *EDRA-2: Proceedings of the 2nd annual environmental design research association conference.* Pittsburgh: Carnegie-Mellon University, 1970, pp. 236–245.

Lee, R. B. !Kung spatial organization: An ecological and historical perspective. *Human Ecology,* 1972, *1,* 125–147.

Lewin, K. *Field theory in social science.* New York: Harper, 1951.

Margalef, R. *Perspectives in ecological theory.* Chicago: University of Chicago Press, 1968.

McGuire, W. J. Theory-oriented research in natural settings: The best of both worlds for social psychology. In M. Sherif and C. W. Sherif (Eds.), *Interdisciplinary relationships in the social sciences.* Chicago: Aldine, 1969, pp. 21–51.

McHale, J. *The eoclogical context.* New York: Braziller, 1970.

Menzel, E. W., Jr. Naturalistic and experimental approaches to primate behavior. In E. P. Willems and H. L. Raush (Eds.), *Naturalistic viewpoints in psychological research.* New York: Holt, Rinehart and Winston, 1969, pp. 78–121.

Mischel, W. *Personality and assessment.* New York: Wiley, 1968.

Moos, R. H. Conceptualizations of human environments. *American Psychologist,* 1973, *28,* 652–665.

Moos, R. H. Systems for the classification of human environments: An overview. In R. H. Moos and P. M. Insel (Eds.), *Issues in human ecology.* Palo Alto, Calif.: National Press Books, 1974, pp. 5–28.

Moss, G. E. *Illness, immunity, and social interaction.* New York: Wiley, 1973.

Murdoch, W., and Connell, J. All about ecology. *The Center Magazine,* 1970, *3,* 56–63.

Nesselroade, J. R., and Reese, H. W. (Eds.). *Life-span developmental psychology: Methodological issues.* New York: Academic Press, 1973.

Newman, O. *Defensible space.* New York: Macmillan, 1972.

Porter, W. W., II. One part per million (letter). *Science,* 1972, *177,* 476–477.

Powers, W. T. Feedback: Beyond behaviorism. *Science,* 1973, *179,* 351–356.

Proshansky, H. M., Ittelson, W. H., and Rivlin, L. G. (Eds.). *Environmental psychology.* New York: Holt, Rinehart and Winston, 1970. (a)

Proshansky, H. M., Ittelson, W. H., and Rivlin, L. G. The influence of the physical environment on behavior: Some basic assumptions. In H. M. Proshansky, W. H. Ittelson, and L. G. Rivlin (Eds.), *Environmental psychology.* New York: Holt, Rinehart and Winston, 1970, pp. 27–37 (b)

Raush, H. L. Naturalistic method and the clinical approach. In E. P. Willems and H. L. Raush (Eds.), *Naturalistic viewpoints in psychological research*. New York: Holt, Rinehart and Winston, 1969, pp. 122–146.

Raush, H. L., Dittmann, A. T., and Taylor, T. J. The interpersonal behavior of children in residential treatment. *Journal of Abnormal and Social Psychology*, 1959, *58*, 9–26. (a).

Raush, H. L., Dittmann, A. T., and Taylor, T. J. Person, setting and change in social interaction. *Human Relations*, 1959, *12*, 361–379. (b)

Raush, H. L., Farbman, I., and Llewellyn, L. G. Person, setting and change in social interaction: II. A normal-control study. *Human Relations*, 1960, *13*, 305–333.

Rhodes, W. C. An overview: Toward synthesis of models of disturbance. In W. C. Rhodes and M. L. Tracy (Eds.), *A study of child variance*. Ann Arbor: University of Michigan Press, 1972, pp. 541–600.

Ronnebeck, R. W. A naturalistic investigation of community adjustment of facially disfigured burned teenagers. Unpublished doctoral dissertation, University of Houston, 1972.

Rosenhan, D. L. On being sane in insane places. *Science*, 1973, *179*, 250–258.

Ryan, W. *Blaming the victim*. New York: Pantheon, 1971.

Sajwaj, T., Twardosz, S., and Burke, M. Side effects of extinction procedures in a remedial preschool. *Journal of Applied Behavior Analysis*, 1972, *5*, 163–175.

Schmitt, R. C. Some ecological variables of community adjustment in a group of facially disfigured burned children. Unpublished doctoral dissertation, University of Houston, 1971.

Sells, S. B. A model for the social system of the multiman, extended duration space ship. *Aerospace Medicine*, 1966, *37*, 1130–1135.

Sells, S. B. General theoretical problems related to organizational taxonomy: A model solution. In B. P. Indik and F. K. Berrien (Eds.), *People, groups, and organizations*. New York: Teachers College Press, 1968, pp. 27–46.

Sells, S. B. Ecology and the science of psychology. In E. P. Willems and H. L. Raush (Eds.), *Naturalistic viewpoints in psychological research*. New York: Holt, Rinehart and Winston, 1969, pp. 15–30.

Shepard, P., and McKinley, D. (Eds.). *The subversive science: Essays toward an ecology of man*. Boston: Houghton Mifflin, 1969.

Smith, R. L. *Ecology and field biology*. New York: Harper and Row, 1966.

Stokols, D., Smith, T. E., and Prostor, J. J. Partitioning and perceived crowding in a public space. *American Behavioral Scientist*, 1975, *18*, 792–814.

Struening, E. L., and Guttentag, M. (Eds.). *Handbook of evaluation research*. Beverly Hills, Calif.: Sage, 1975.

Stuart, D. G. A naturalistic study of the daily activities of disabled and nondisabled college students. Unpublished master's thesis, University of Houston, 1973.

Studer, R. G. The organization of spatial stimuli. In J. F. Wohlwill and D. H. Carson (Eds.), *Environment and the social sciences: Perspectives and applications*. Washington, D.C.: American Psychological Association, 1972, pp. 279–292.

Toffler, A. *Future shock*. New York: Random House, 1970.

Wahler, R. G. Some structural aspects of deviant child behavior. *Journal of Applied Behavior Analysis*, 1975, *8*, 27–42.

Wahler, R. G., Sperling, K. A., Thomas, M. R., Teeter, N. C., and Luper, H. L. The modification of childhood stuttering: Some response–response relationships. *Journal of Experimental Child Psychology*, 1970, *9*, 411–428.

Wallace, B. *Essays in social biology* (3 vols.). Englewood Cliffs, N.J.: Prentice-Hall, 1972.

Watt, K. E. F. (Ed.). *Systems analysis in ecology*. New York: Academic Press, 1966.

Watt, K. E. F. *Ecology and resource management*. New York: McGraw-Hill, 1968.

Wicker, A. W. Attitudes versus actions: The relationship of verbal and overt behavioral responses to attitude objects. *Journal of Social Issues*, 1969, *25*, 41–78.

Wicker, A. W. An examination of the "other variables" explanation of attitude–behavior inconsistency. *Journal of Personality and Social Psychology*, 1971, *19*, 18–30.

Wicker, A. W. Processes which mediate behavior–environment congruence. *Behavioral Science*, 1972, *17*, 265–277.

Willems, E. P. An ecological orientation in psychology. *Merrill-Palmer Quarterly*, 1965, *11*, 317–343.

Willems, E. P. Behavioral validity of a test for measuring social anxiety. *Psychological Reports*, 1967, *21*, 433–442.

Willems, E. P. Planning a rationale for naturalistic research. In E. P. Willems and H. L. Raush (Eds.), *Naturalistic viewpoints in psychological research*. New York: Holt, Rinehart and Winston, 1969, pp. 44–71.

Willems, E. P. The interface of the hospital environment and patient behavior. *Archives of Physical Medicine and Rehabilitation*, 1972, *53*, 115–122. (a)

Willems, E. P. Place and motivation: Complexity and independence in patient behavior. In W. J. Mitchell (Ed.), *Environmental design: Research and practice*. Los Angeles: University of California at Los Angeles, 1972, pp. 4-3-1–4-3-8. (b)

Willems, E. P. Behavior–environment systems: An ecological approach. *Man–Environment Systems*, 1973, *3*, 79–110. (a)

Willems, E. P. Behavioral ecology and experimental analysis: Courtship is not enough. In J. R. Nesselroade and H. W. Reese (Eds.), *Life-span developmental psychology: Methodological issues*. New York: Academic Press, 1973, pp. 195–217. (b)

Willems, E. P. Behavioral ecology as a perspective for man–environment research. In W. F. E. Preiser (Ed.), *Environmental design research (vol. 2)*. Stroudsburg, Pa.: Dowden, Hutchinson and Ross, 1973, pp. 152–165. (c)

Willems, E. P. Go ye into all the world and modify behavior: An ecologist's view. *Representative Research in Social Psychology*, 1973, *4*, 93–105. (d)

Willems, E. P. Behavioral technology and behavioral ecology. *Journal of Applied Behavior Analysis*, 1974, *7*, 151–165.

Willems, E. P. Behavioral ecology as a perspective for research in psychology. In C. W. Deckner (Ed.), *Methodological perspectives for behavioral research*. Springfield, Ill.: Charles C. Thomas, in press. (a)

Willems, E. P. Behavioral ecology, health status, and health care: Applications to the rehabilitation setting. In I. Altman and J. F. Wohlwill (Eds.), *Environment and behavior: Advances in research* (vol. 1). New York: Plenum Press, 1976.

Willems, E. P. Relations of models to methods in behavioral ecology. In H. McGurk (Ed.), *Ecological factors in human development*. New York: Academic Press, in press. (b)

Willems, E. P., and Campbell, D. E. Behavioral ecology: A new approach to health status and health care. In B. Honikman (Ed.), *Responding to social change*. Stroudsburg, Pa.: Dowden, Hutchinson and Ross, 1975, pp. 200–210.

Willems, E. P., and Raush, H. L. (Eds.). *Naturalistic viewpoints in psychological research*. New York: Holt, Rinehart and Winston, 1969.

Wright, H. F. *Recording and analyzing child behavior*. New York: Harper & Row, 1967.

Wright, H. F. *Children's behavior in communities differing in size* (5 vols.). Lawrence, Kans,: University of Kansas, 1969–1970.

From Church to Laboratory to National Park: A Program of Research on Excess and Insufficient Populations in Behavior Settings

3

ALLAN W. WICKER AND SANDRA KIRMEYER

In the national office of a liberal protestant church, a researcher looks up and down a row of yearbooks of the 112 dioceses of the church. He selects one, looks for the listing of a particular local church, and copies down the church's average worship-service attendance, average church-school attendance, number of pastors, and number of church-school teachers.

In a social psychology laboratory on a college campus, another researcher listens to the conversation of four students as they race a slot car around an obstacle-laden track in an attempt to improve their team's performance. She codes each statement into one of nine categories.

In a heavily visited national park, a third researcher greets a park-service ranger who has just finished a busy and difficult work shift. She asks the ranger to complete a questionnaire regarding his day's work.

In the same national park, a fourth researcher supervises a work crew installing a network of posts and chains for channeling people (a queuing device) at a heavily used bus stop where he and another researcher have been observing loading procedures for the previous three weeks.

3

ALLAN W. WICKER AND SANDRA KIRMEYER • Claremont Graduate School, Claremont, California. This paper originally appeared in Wapner, Cohen, and Kaplan (1976).

Behavior Settings

We have used the above research activities to study some of the ways human behavior and experience interact with the immediate social–physical environment, or *behavior setting*. As conceived and studied by Barker and his associates (Barker, 1960, 1963, 1965, 1968; Barker and Gump, 1964; Barker and Schoggen, 1973; Barker and Wright, 1955), behavior settings are places and activities, such as banks, piano lessons, church worship services, Lions Club meetings, bus routes, and baseball games. More precisely, a behavior setting has the following characteristics:

1. One or more standing patterns of behavior, that is, regularly occurring human activities. For example, at a church worship service, these activities would include ushering, preaching, and singing.

2. Coordination between behavior patterns and the inanimate objects nearby. Behaviors at a worship service are coordinated with the location and physical characteristics of the pews, altar, hymnals, and offering plates, for example.

3. Definite time–place boundaries, such that the behaviors outside the boundaries are readily discriminable from those within. The boundaries of the worship service, say, would be between 10 and 11 a.m. on Sundays and within the walls forming the church sanctuary.

4. Lack of dependence on specific individuals; the people inhabiting a behavior setting are largely interchangeable and replaceable. Members attending a worship service, or even the church pastor, could change and the setting would function much as before.

5. A hierarchy of positions that influence the behavior setting or have responsibility for its functions. An usher at a church service has more influence and is more essential than a single member who merely attends; the pastor has more authority and responsibility than the usher.

6. The capacity to generate the "forces" necessary for its own maintenance; that is, pressures develop to assure that the program of the behavior setting is adhered to, that necessary components (people or materials) are brought into the setting, shaped, and, if necessary, expelled when they become disruptive. Thus a crying child at a worship service may produce forces leading to such actions as glances from people trying to listen to the sermon or a parent carrying the child out of the room.

(In this chapter, the terms *behavior setting, setting*, and *environment* will be used interchangeably to denote the above concept.)

Much of Barker's work has been devoted to cataloguing and extensively describing all of the public behavior settings in several small towns (see Barker and Schoggen, 1973). The present concern, however, is with a more dynamic aspect of settings: how they influence, and are influenced by, their inhabitants. The interdependence between people and behavior settings could be studied in an almost unlimited number of ways; indeed much research in environmental psychology can be conceived of as being addressed to this general question. Similarly, numerous theoretical approaches can also be applied to the question of how person–environment influences operate (see Wicker, 1972).

Manning Theory

Barker's discussion of the dynamics of behavior settings has focused on the interplay between people and their environments under different conditions of *manning*[1] (Barker, 1960, 1968). Undermanning, the condition of having insufficient or barely sufficient personnel in a setting to carry out the essential tasks or functions, represents a threat to the setting and to the satisfactions that occupants receive from it. In order to maintain the setting under these adverse conditions, the occupants both receive and produce more frequent, stronger, and more varied messages regarding the carrying out of the setting's essential activities than would be the case if the number of persons available were at or above the optimal level.

This greater *claim* of undermanned behavior settings is said to produce the following consequences for setting occupants:

1. Greater effort to support the setting and its functions, either by "harder" work or by longer hours.

2. Participation in a great diversity of tasks and roles.

3. Involvement in more difficult and more important tasks.

4. More responsibility in the sense that the setting and what others gain from it depend on each individual occupant.

5. Viewing oneself and others in terms of task-related characteristics rather than in terms of social–emotional characteristics.

6. Greater functional importance of individuals within the setting.

7. Less sensitivity to and less evaluation of differences between people.

8. Setting of lower standards and fewer tests for admission into the setting.

9. A lower level of best performance.

10. Greater insecurity about the eventual maintenance of the setting.

11. More frequent occurrences of success and failure, depending upon the outcome of the setting's functions.

This set of propositions has stimulated a number of investigations, ship. The research has been recently reviewed elsewhere (Wicker, 1973) and will not be summarized here. We will, rather, continue from about the point where that review ended and present the latest 3- or 4-year slice of our research program, beginning with the conclusions from the archival

---

[1]The choice of the term *manning* is perhaps unfortunate because of the sexist connotations it may have for some people. As will be seen, we have replaced it with more neutral terms in our recent conceptual work.

study of churches, which led to a reformulation of the manning notions (Wicker, McGrath, and Armstrong, 1972). We will then report in some detail two laboratory studies based on the reformulation and using the slot-car task. Finally we will discuss our latest thinking on the theory of manning and show how it guided our recent research in Yosemite National Park.[2]

From the archival study of churches, and for reasons that will not be repeated here, Wicker *et al.* (1972) concluded that future research on manning should be conducted at the level of specific behavior settings rather than at the organizational level. They also suggested that the definition of manning conditions be refined and made more precise in a number of ways: by the introduction of the concept of behavior setting capacity, by clarification of the distinction between optimal manning and overmanning, and by allowance for different levels of manning to be specified for different types of occupants in the same behavior setting.

A Reformulation of the Manning Notions

In an attempt to deal with these needs, Wicker *et al.* (1972) proposed the following reformulation: Degree of manning should be determined separately for two kinds of setting occupants identified previously by Barker: *performers,* who have assigned responsibilities in the setting (for example, the managers, players, umpires, and concessionaires at a baseball game), and *nonperformers* (consumers, clients), who do not have such responsibilities (for example, the baseball fans in the stands). Thus there can be differential degrees of manning of the same setting. For example, a one-man barber shop having insufficient customers would be adequately manned or overmanned at the level of performers but undermanned at the level of nonperformers. And a crowded physician's office would be undermanned at the level of performers yet overmanned at the level of nonperformers.

According to this reformulation, the following basic concepts are applied to each class of potential setting occupants (i.e., to performers and to nonperformers) to determine the degree of manning of a setting: the smallest number of persons required in order for the setting to be maintained (the *maintenance minimum*); the largest number of persons that the setting can accommodate (*capacity*);[3] and the total number of persons who both seek to participate and meet the eligibility requirements (*applicants*).

The maintenance minimum of performers in a behavior setting is the smallest number of functionaries required to carry out its *program*, that is, the time-ordered sequence of events that must occur in the setting. A baseball game requires 18 players (9 per team), for example.

In the case of nonperformers, the maintenance minimum is the smallest number of persons who must be present as consumers (audience, members, customers) in order for the setting to continue. A quorum is the maintenance minimum for a business meeting, for example.

A behavior setting's capacity for performers may be constrained by both physical and social structural factors. The backstage area of a theater may limit the number of persons who can serve on the stage crew, and the size of the choir loft in a church may effectively limit the size of the choir. But the program of the setting may also limit capacity. Examples would include rules specifying the size of the roster of athletic teams, scripts specifying the number of actors in a play, by-laws of organizations, and the like.

The capacity for nonperformers in a setting is largely constrained by physical factors, such as number of seats and available floor space, but social structural factors may operate as well. For example, safety regulations may limit the number of persons who can be admitted to an auditorium to a figure below the absolute physical capacity.

The applicants for performer roles in a behavior setting are those persons who are eligible to participate at the performer level and who wish to do so. A person is eligible for a setting if he can attend at its specified time and place and if he meets all admission standards.

Applicants for nonperformer roles are simply those people who meet the admission requirements and who can and wish to enter.

These concepts can perhaps be more clearly understood if they are related to a particular kind of behavior setting. For example, in a high-school play, the maintenance minimum for performers would include the director; the members of the cast; the persons who handle lighting, props, and costumes; a ticket seller; and possibly a few others. The maintenance minimum for nonperformers would be the smallest audience size that would be tolerated before the setting would be altered or eliminated. Capacity of performers would be the total number of persons who could be accommodated in all functional roles, including, in addition to those listed above, ushers, a house manager, an assistant director, understudies, concessions sellers, and others. Capacity of nonperformers would be the number of persons who could be seated in the auditorium. Applicants at the performer level would be the number of people who sought to or at

---

might be able to get along with 1 exceptionally fast and accurate typist or with 2 persons who type with average speed and accuracy; a church sanctuary might seat 350 thin people in its pews but only 325 people of average build.

least were willing to serve as functionaries in the settings, that is, to direct, act, usher, serve on the stage crew, and so on. Applicants at the nonperformer level would be the number of persons who had the admission fee and sought to enter the play performance.

According to Wicker *et al.* (1972), the condition of manning of a setting depends upon where the number of applicants falls relative to the maintenance minimum and capacity. If the number of applicants is below the maintenance minimum, the setting is *undermanned.* If the number of applicants falls between the maintenance minimum and capacity, *adequate manning*[4] exists. When there are more applicants than capacity, *overmanning* is present. More recently, two subdivisions of adequate manning were also specified: *poorly manned,* when the number of applicants barely exceeds the maintenance minimum; and *richly manned,* when the number of applicants approaches capacity (Wicker, 1973).[5]

Adequate manning is a quasi-stationary state and produces no strong internal pressures toward change. However, in the poorly manned and richly manned regions, the pressures described below would begin to increase as the number of applicants approaches the maintenance minimum and capacity, respectively.

Both undermanning and overmanning are unstable and generate forces toward adequate manning. Undermanning, whether at the performer level or at the nonperformer level, results in pressures to increase the number of applicants—perhaps by recruitment from among the eligibles or by the lowering of eligibility standards—and/or to reduce the maintenance minimum, perhaps by reduction of the scope of the setting or by its reorganization. Overmanning at either level results in pressures to reduce the number of applicants—perhaps by the reduction of recruiting efforts or by the raising of eligibility standards—and/or to increase the setting capacity.

In the example of a high-school play, overmanning at the performer level would exist if more students sought to be in the cast than there were acting parts available. In this case, the eligibility standards might be raised so that only the best actors would be selected. Or an additional cast might be set up ("double casting") to perform on a different night so that twice as many people could serve as actors. At the nonperformer level, the capacity of the play behavior setting might be increased either physically (by the addition of more chairs, the allowing for standing room at the back of the theater, the use of a larger theater) or by repetition of the performance.

In many instances, however, adjustments to overmanning or undermanning cannot be made immediately. Thus these conditions, although unstable, may persist over sufficient amounts of time to be studied.

[4]The term *adequate manning* was deliberately chosen over Barker's term, *optimal manning,* to avoid the connotation of a specific, ideal level of manning in a behavior setting.
[5]The terms *poorly manned* and *richly manned* were suggested by a colleague, Stuart Oskamp.

Questions for Research

The clearer distinction between optimal or adequate manning and over-manning, which the above reformulation provides, led Wicker (1973) to propose that the ecological psychology literature be applied to the study of excess human populations. He suggested that three basic questions be examined empirically over the range of manning conditions:

1. Are different degrees of manning sufficient causes for differential experiences and behaviors of group members?

Previous research had shown that members of small organizations, whose voluntary activities were presumably undermanned, were more often performers and had more experiences of feeling important, being needed, having worked hard, and so on than members of large organizations, whose activities were presumably adequately manned or over-manned. While the findings were consistent with Barker's theory, these studies were limited in that they (a) used correlational designs, (b) compared organizations and not behavior settings known to differ in degree of manning, and (c) provided no information on differences between adequate manning and overmanning.

2. Are there differences in group verbal interaction patterns as a function of different manning conditions?

Barker's theory suggests that with increasing degrees of manning (i.e., from undermanning to adequate manning to overmanning) there are decreases in (a) task-related comments, (b) evaluative comments about the setting and its occupants, and (c) comments that are directed toward modifying the behavior of others, as opposed to comments that seek to eliminate the others from participation. No previous studies had observed group processes in settings varying in degree of manning.

3. Does the degree of manning in a setting have carry-over effects on experiences and behaviors in subsequent situations?

There were no direct data on this question. However, studies at the organizational level suggested that members' subjective experiences in organization behavior settings were related to the size of the organization with which the members had previously been affiliated.

A Laboratory Study of Manning

Two studies dealing with the above questions have been completed. The first investigation (Hanson, 1973; Hanson and Wicker, 1973) examined (1) the differential effects of performer overmanning and adequate manning on group subjective experiences, admissions standards, and group performance; (2) possible carry-over effects on experiences due to the immediately prior manning condition; and (3) possible carry-over effects on experiences due to the manning conditions of settings in the subject's everyday environment. We had reasoned, following Helson's (1964) adaptation-level theory, that both immediately preceding manning conditions (*contextual* stimuli) and earlier manning conditions of activities in everyday environments (*residual* stimuli) might displace ratings of experiences in the current situation.

We studied carry-over effects of the immediately prior environment by exposing subjects to two successive conditions or stages of manning, while we studied carry-over effects of settings in the subject's everyday environment by means of a questionnaire that asked about the manning conditions of several different kinds of settings (work, voluntary organizations) he entered regularly. We found no evidence for carry-over effects due to the everyday environment and only one carry-over effect due to the immediately preceding manning level. With that one exception, the experimental design and findings to be reported thus pertain only to the first of the two stages of manning to which subjects were exposed.

Groups of two or three male college students worked on a task designed for either two or three persons. There were three experimental conditions: (1) groups of three when only two could be accommodated (three-person, overmanned groups, of which there were 24); (2) groups of two when two were required (two-person, adequately manned groups, of which there were 12); and (3) groups of three when three were required (three-person, adequately manned groups, of which there were 12). As can be seen, this design experimentally isolates the variables of group size and degree of manning.

The task for this study was adapted from Petty and Wicker (1974). Each group ran a miniature car, a slot car, 55 laps around a track as quickly as possible in competition for a prize to be awarded to the fastest group in the experiment. The roles of the participants were *driver*, who was blindfolded, who controlled the speed of the car by means of a hand trigger mechanism, and *crew member*, who was not blindfolded and whose job it was to lift obstacles (snap-back hinges mounted across the track) in order to allow the car to pass unhindered each time it completed a lap of the track. Crew members also replaced the car on the track when it went off, informed the blindfolded driver of the location and running speed of the car, and directed him when to change the car's speed.

We varied the minimum number of persons required in order to complete the task by having either one or two track obstacles in operation during the run. For example, in overmanned groups, there were three group members with only one obstacle operating. Thus only two people were required, the driver and one crew member to lift the obstacle, replace the car, and provide feedback to the driver. Prior to the 55-lap run, there was a practice session in which each group member drove the car 10 laps around the track without a blindfold, after which his running time was announced to the group. The groups then decided on role assignments for the 55 competition laps; that is the number of laps each member would drive and the number of laps during which each would be a crew member and/or (in overmanned groups) a watcher.

On the basis of Barker's theory, it was expected that members of overmanned groups, relative to members of adequately manned groups, would (1) have lesser experiences of being needed, having an important role, being involved with the task, being concerned about the group's success, being depended upon, having contributed to the group, having worked closely with others, and having worked hard; (2) set higher standards of admission into the group; and (3) show higher levels of performance on the group task. Since it was believed that manning level, and not group size, is the primary determinant of the dependent variables studied, the two sizes of adequately manned groups were not expected to differ in experiences, admissions standards, or performance.

Group members' perceptions of personnel requirements, subjective experiences, and admissions standards were measured by a semantic differential-type questionnaire administered after the 55-lap run. There were two performance measures recorded for each stage: running time taken to complete the 55 laps and number of penalties. Penalties were assessed each time the car went off the track, which was usually because of the car's going too fast to make a curve. For each penalty, 1 second was added to the running time.

For all analyses to be reported, the unit of analysis was the mean of each experimental group rather than individual scores of group members. Three comparisons were made on variables of interest: (1) overmanned versus two-person adequately manned; (2) overmanned versus three-person adequately manned; and (3) two-person adequately manned versus three-person adequately manned.

Responses to two rated validator items (more men were needed, an additional member would be desirable) and to an item asking judgments about the appropriate number of persons for the task revealed that the manning manipulation was rather weak. There were four comparisons of the rated items on which differences were expected: for each of the two items, overmanned versus two-person adequate and overmanned versus three-person adequate. Although for each comparison the means were in the expected direction, only one was significant beyond the .05 level: overmanned versus two-person adequate on the item "more men were needed." The two adequately manned condition means did not differ on these items. As expected, adequately manned groups with three members gave a larger mean judgment of number of people appropriate for the task (3.0) than did adequately manned groups with two members (2.2, $p < .001$) or overmanned groups (2.7, $p < .005$). However, the average of 2.7 people considered appropriate by overmanned groups was significantly greater ($p < .001$) than the judgment of two-member adequately manned groups (2.2), in spite of the fact that the task setup was identical. Apparently, the number of people present influenced subjects' judgments about personnel requirements.

There were eight subjective experience items dealing with manning theory (see above). Seven of the eight were found to intercorrelate highly; a composite index was derived by the summing of the standard scores for each of the seven items. The composite revealed the expected outcome: the pattern of feeling needed, involved, and so on, was less prevalent for over-manned groups than for two-person adequately manned groups ($p < .01$) or three-person adequately manned groups ($p < .05$). The means for the latter two conditions did not differ.

No support was obtained for the hypothesis that higher standards of admission are set by members of overmanned groups. Average ratings of minimal qualifications required of new group members (based on seven items, such as patience and quickness) did not differ for any comparison.

Adequately manned groups tended to spin the car off the track more and therefore were assessed more penalties than overmanned groups ($p < .10$, $< .05$), but there were no differences among conditions on the running-time measure of performance.

Other analyses revealed that scores on the subjective experience composite tended to be higher for subjects who drove for the entire 55 laps than for those who were crew members or who merely watched for the entire period. Half of the groups in each condition chose to have one driver for all 55 laps; the remainder shared the driving responsibilities.

The carry-over effect due to prior manning conditions was found on the three validator items listed above. In a comparison of adequately manned groups, half of which had previously been overmanned and half of which had been adequately manned, it was found that the groups with a history of overmanning indicated that more people were needed ($p < .01$) or that an additional member would be more desirable ($p < .001$), and they gave larger mean judgments of the number of people appropriate for the task (2.6 vs. 2.0, $p < .001$). And although the differences are not statistically significant, means for all three validator items also suggest that over-manned groups with a history of adequate manning felt that fewer people were needed than did overmanned groups with a history of overmanning. These results thus show that estimates of present personnel requirements in a behavior setting can be considerably influenced by the prior manning conditions that occupants have experienced in the same setting.

The pattern of data for the validator items may be at least partially due to the fact that in spite of our attempts to structure the task roles somewhat rigidly, some overmanned groups increased the setting capacity in effect by fractionating the crewman role. We observed in some cases that the person designated as the crewman would merely remove the obstacle and replace the car on the track, while the other person (nominally a watcher) would give feedback to the driver regarding the car's location and speed.

Even with this weakening of the manipulation, the study showed that the present manipulations for conditions of adequate manning and over-manning did produce differences in subjective experiences that cannot be attributed to group size. The study produced inconsistent evidence regarding the effects of manning on quality of group performance and no evidence to support the assertion that admissions standards vary in groups differing in degree of manning. Carry-over effects of manning conditions were limited to perceptions of personnel requirements. We felt these results were sufficiently promising for us to conduct a second laboratory study of manning to examine several other questions of interest.

A Follow-up Laboratory Study of Manning

In planning and developing the next investigation, we sought to follow an "ecological, social systems" orientation (Altman, 1973) more closely than in the previous study. That is, while we set up the basic experimental conditions, we also sought to avoid excessive experimental control. Groups were allowed more flexibility in dealing with the experimental task (e.g., more opportunities to change roles and equipment), and accurate, periodic feedback on task performance was provided. Moreover we sought to employ measures of several different levels of behavioral functioning that could be monitored over time and whose interrelationships could be determined. Some of our considerations in setting up the study are given below.

Design, Equipment, and Procedure

The slot-car task was retained, as was the two-stage experimental procedure exposing subjects to successive conditions of manning. An attempt was made to strengthen the manning manipulation, and the range of manning was extended to include undermanning. Group size was set at four members for all experimental conditions. We manipulated the degree of manning by varying the number of necessary jobs: undermanned, six jobs; adequately manned, four jobs; and overmanned, two jobs. In the second stage, all groups were exposed to the overmanned condition. As before, we varied the number of jobs by changing the number of track obstacles in operation. In the undermanned condition, crew members had to run from one end of the table to another to remove the obstacles so that the car could pass freely.

Two major equipment changes were made: the track was made longer and more difficult by the addition of more curves, and table-mounted dials were installed to control the car speed, replacing the less reliable hand-held trigger devices.

The number of laps run in each stage was reduced to 23; these were broken down into four "segments" of 6, 6, 7, and 4 laps by "pit stops." At the pit stops, group members were told their running time and penalties for the laps run since the previous stop. Teams were then given a fixed amount of time to discuss strategy for the next set of laps. During these pit stops, members could decide to reassign roles (driver, crew, and watcher), change from one to the other lane of the race track, and/or change from the slot car they had been using to one of three others provided. Each segment thus contained two distinct types of tasks: planning strategy for the next set of laps and actually running the laps. This arrangement permitted an analysis of the influence of type of task on group interaction, in addition to manning influences.

Dependent Variables

The questionnaire measuring subjective experiences and validation of the manipulation was revised and expanded. It included questions on the manning experiences and, in addition, questions about experiences that have been reported in the literature (e.g., Steiner, 1972) to be a function of group size (e.g., perceptions of how well organized the group was and how much influence the member felt he had on the group's decisions and performance). We were interested in learning if responses to these items would vary with degree of manning when group size was constant. A more explicit validator item asked subjects to consider the number of obstacles that had been operating in the experiment and then to estimate the most appropriate number of people for the setup in order to get the car around the track as fast as possible. Finally several questions were asked about experiences suggested in the literature (e.g., Stokols, 1972) as consequences of crowding (e.g., feelings of frustration, pressure, and being restless).

A second questionnaire administered to all subjects after the second stage of the experiment sought to measure individual differences in reactions to situations requiring waiting and/or inaction. It was reasoned that people with different generalized reactions to waiting might report different subjective experiences and show different behaviors in overmanned situations. The format (adapted from Wicker, 1971) was a series of described hypothetical situations to which subjects responded in terms of the likelihood that they would remain in the setting to wait or would leave the setting. Some of the 18 situations described were being told there will be a 45-minute wait at one's favorite restaurant before being seated; being the 12th man on a basketball team and thus having little opportunity to play; being repeatedly asked by a dormitory telephone operator to hold the line when trying to reach a girl to ask for a date.

The group performance measures were the same as in the previous study: the running time to complete the assigned number of laps and the number of penalties assessed.

An observational measure of the distance that subjects positioned themselves from the board on which the group running times and penalties were posted was employed as a possible index of members' involvement in the group and its task. An observer looking through a one-way mirror took this measure at the beginning of each pit stop, just as the performance data were being announced by the experimenter. Bits of tape were placed on the floor of the experimental room at predetermined distances from the board to make the measurement more reliable.

Observation Scheme

In an attempt to study group-interaction patterns in settings differing in degree of manning, we devised the following set of nine interaction categories,[6] some of which were adapted from Bales (1951) and from Carter, Haythorn, Meirowitz, and Lanzetta (1951):

1. Proposes game strategy or role for self or other.
2. Shows agreement concurrence, compliance, acknowledgment.
3. Shows disagreement, skepticism.
4. Questions, asks for information, opinion, or evaluation.
5. Gives information, opinion, evaluation, explanation.
6. Gives directions.
7. Satisfaction or supportive evaluation of setting.
8. Dissatisfaction or negative evaluation of setting.
9. Incidental comments, joking.

Categories 1 through 8 were considered task-related comments, and Categories 7 and 8, evaluative comments. Complete descriptions of each category, with examples, are presented in Kirmeyer (1974).

The unit of analysis of this scheme was the smallest portion of a verbal utterance that had meaning independent of the rest of the statement; it could be a complete sentence, a phrase, or a single word (cf. Bales, 1951). The verbal interaction of each group was tape-recorded for later analysis. All tapes were coded by two raters, and interrater agreement was periodically monitored by a third researcher. When a decline in agreement was detected part way through the experiment, the two raters worked on pilot tapes until their former high level of agreement was achieved. Mean interrater reliability for the entire experiment was .80 for content classification and .86 for unit classification. (Mean r's are based on z-transformations.) See Wicker, 1975, for a more complete report on reliability of the observations.

Subjects

Since it was felt that there would be more group interaction if members were acquainted with one another prior to the experiment, we recruited subjects by asking volunteer male college students to bring three male

---

[6]It had been planned also to include in the coding scheme categories corresponding to Barker's "deviation countering mechanism" (i.e., comments aimed at correcting the inappropriate behavior of others) and his "vetoing mechanism" (i.e., comments directed toward eliminating others from continued participation). Pilot testing revealed, however, that for the present task, there were insufficient numbers of comments in the categories to retain them.

college friends to the experiment. This differs from the earlier study, in which groups were composed of strangers. A total of 180 persons participated; there were 15 four-man groups in each of three manning conditions.

Results

The results to be reported are of two basic kinds: (1) comparisons of manning conditions on the various dependent variables and (2) interrelationships between the dependent variables across manning conditions.

Effects of Manning Conditions

In contrast to the previous study, the validator items for Stage 1 showed highly significant differences across manning conditions ($p < .01$): mean judged appropriate group size was 4.7 for undermanned groups, 4.0 for adequately manned groups, and 3.3 for overmanned groups. It should be noted, however, that participants in the undermanned and overmanned groups did not perceive the task as requiring the exact number of participants intended by the experimenters (six and two, respectively). As in the previous study, judgments were displaced toward the number of people present. In Stage 2, when all groups were overmanned, a residual effect of prior manning conditions on perceived personnel requirements was again noted: mean judged appropriate group size was 2.4 for previously undermanned groups, 2.6 for previously adequately manned groups, and 3.1 for previously overmanned groups ($p < .01$).

Correlational analysis[7] revealed reasonably high intercorrelations among the eight subjective experience items derived from Barker (1968) (median $r = .52$) and among four of six items designed to measure subjective experiences presumably associated with group size (median $r = .45$). The eight Barker items were combined into a single manning-experience composite by the summing of their standard scores, and a group-size experience composite based on the four items was calculated in the same way. As expected, in Stage 1 the pattern of feeling needed, expending effort, feeling one's role was important, and so on was most characteristic of undermanned groups, followed by adequately manned groups, and then by overmanned groups ($p < .01$). It was also found that in Stage 1 the pattern of feeling one's group was well organized, that one had an influence on group decisions and on group performance, and that the group experience was a pleasant one (i.e., the group-size experience composite), was most characteristic of undermanned groups, followed by adequately manned

---

[7]Matrices were calculated for individual and group data for both Stage 1 and Stage 2. Only group data for Stage 1 are summarized here, since the patterns were essentially the same across levels of analysis and across stages.

groups, and then by overmanned groups ($p < .05$). Neither composite showed significant effects of manning-condition history in Stage 2. No differences were found among manning conditions in the frequencies with which subjects reported feelings based on the crowding literature, with one exception: feeling crowded. Although one might expect that feeling crowding would be more prevalent in overmanned groups, we found that members of undermanned groups more often indicated they felt crowded than did members of adequately manned or overmanned groups. Stokols (1974) has suggested a plausible explanation: the greater physical movement and coordination required of the three crewmen to operate five obstacles successfully in undermanned groups might have led to feelings of crowding.

Neither measure of group performance (running time, penalties) was affected by manning condition, either in Stage 1 or in Stage 2. However, as might be expected, there was a strong ($p < .01$) practice effect in Stage 1, with both time and penalties declining with each successive segment. The Stage 2 running-time data showed similar patterns, but the penalties data did not.

It was expected that when running times were posted at each pit stop, members of undermanned groups, who presumably were more involved in the task, would position themselves closer to the board than would members of adequately manned groups, who would be closer than members of overmanned groups. The Stage I mean distances differed significantly ($p < .01$) across manning conditions: undermanned, 81 inches, adequately manned, 105 inches; and overmanned, 87 inches. The contrast between the former two conditions is the largest and is consistent with expectations. It is also less ambiguous than other comparisons because in both undermanned and adequately manned groups, all members had a station at the table (either an obstacle or the speed control) that they had been manning. In contrast, two members of overmanned groups did not have such stations, and in the small experimental room one of the two members nearly always watched from an open area just in front of the board. Thus his proximity to the board was generally not due to his moving forward to learn how well the group performed. This explanation, however, cannot readily account for the pattern of the distance data in Stage 2, when all groups were overmanned. Distances for the groups by prior manning conditions were undermanned, 77 inches; adequately manned, 97 inches; and overmanned, 83 inches ($p < .05$). Correlational data reported below, however, lend credibility to the view that the distance measure may be an indicator of involvement.

Turning now to the group interaction data,[8] contrary to expectation,

[8]The present discussion of results of analyses of the group interaction data does not reflect the actual complexity of the statistical treatment of the data. For example, since the strategy sessions had the same duration (8 minutes) for each group, but the run sessions varied in length, all frequency data for the run sessions were statistically adjusted to 8 minutes. A square-root transformation was then applied to the strategy frequencies and the time-adjusted run frequencies to meet the assumptions of the analyses of variance that were

manning levels did not affect the frequencies of task-related or evaluative comments. And while the group interaction profiles for the three manning conditions were not significantly different at either stage, the profiles for strategy and run sessions were markedly different, as shown in Table 1. At each stage, the strategy-run X coding category statistical-interaction was highly significant ($p < .001$) and accounted for more than 50% of the variance in the frequency data. As might be expected, in strategy sessions there were more proposals of how to improve group performance, and in runs there were more directions given. Perhaps less obvious are the findings that strategy sessions showed more frequent expressions of agreement and disagreement, more requests for information, and more comments unrelated to the task, while run sessions had more expressions of satisfaction and dissatisfaction.

There was a tendency in Stage 1 for overmanned groups to share the driver role more than groups in the other conditions ($p < .10$). The numbers of groups (out of 15 in each condition) that used more than one driver for the four segments were: undermanned, 4; adequately manned, 2; and overmanned, 8. This pattern was even more pronounced in Stage 2, when all groups were shifted to overmanning: previously undermanned, 3; previously adequately manned, 0; and previously overmanned, 8 ($p < .05$). There was thus a pronounced carry-over effect of manning conditions on choice of role assignments.

Interrelationships Between Dependent Variables

We will limit our discussion of correlational results to a summary of significant relationships of the manning-experience composite with other variables.[9] As shown in Table 2, subjective experiences associated with undermanning (higher composite scores) were more prevalent for *persons* who (1) stood closer to the board when running times were announced, (2) had more central roles in the experimental task, (3) estimated greater personnel requirements for the experimental task, and (4) reported that they were more inclined to wait in the hypothetical situations described (especially subjects in the overmanned condition). *Groups* scoring higher on the manning composite also tended to show: in strategy sessions, more expressions of agreement and task-related comments; in run sessions, more expressions of satisfaction, comments providing information, and task-related comments.

---

computed. Two five-way anovas (one for each stage) were applied to the time-adjusted, transformed data. The factors were manning condition (3 levels), coding category (9 levels), rater (2 levels), strategy-run partition (2 levels), and partition for before–after remedial coder training (2 levels).

[9]At this writing we are still digesting results of other correlational analyses, for example, relationships between group performance and types of verbal interaction.

Table 1. Interaction Profiles for Strategy and Run Sessions,
Stages 1 and 2[a]

Coding category	Stage 1		Stage 2	
	Strategy	Run	Strategy	Run
1. Proposes strategy	30.4	3.2	16.7	2.5
2. Shows agreement	22.3	3.4	12.5	3.6
3. Shows disagreement	3.4	1.1	2.0	.9
4. Asks for information	23.7	10.4	15.2	9.4
5. Gives information	59.5	59.0	40.7	63.5
6. Gives directions	3.2	85.6	2.1	88.1
7. Expresses satisfaction	5.9	22.5	6.1	26.1
8. Expresses dissatisfaction	3.0	10.2	2.6	11.1
9. Incidental comments	22.8	5.5	27.0	7.3

[a]Mean frequencies are reported. Frequencies for run sessions were adjusted to equate observation time with strategy sessions (8 minutes). See footnote 8.

Conclusions from the Completed Research

Our experience in conducting the two laboratory studies of manning has convinced us of the value of the ecological, social-systems approach, with its emphases on mutual influences of persons and environments, multiple modes of response, and adaptive behaviors over time (Altman, 1973). There are a number of benefits that may follow from loosening tight experimental controls and allowing a wide latitude of response in laboratory experiments: one may find effects that are understandable after the fact, and indeed consistent with existing theory, but that were not anticipated at the outset of the experiment. Examples are our findings that overmanned groups tended to fractionate the crewman role and to share the driver role

Table 2. Correlation Coefficients Relating Manning Experience Composite with Other Variables[a]

Variable	Stage 1	Stage 2
Distance from board	−.19[b]	−.15
Role index[d]	−.36[c]	−.50[c]
Judged appropriate group size	.18[b]	.16[b]
Hypothetical waiting situations: all conditions	.14	.18[b]
Hypothetical waiting situations: overmanned condition in Stage 1	.19	.33[b]

[a]$n = 180$, except for last row of coefficients, for which $n = 60$.
[b]$p < .05$.
[c]$p < .01$.
[d]An index of the subject's roles for one stage was formed by the summing of the numerical values assigned to the roles (1 = driver, 2 = crew, 3 = watcher) each subject had during the four segments of the stage.

to a greater extent than other groups. One may also find reliable and comprehensible results that were not anticipated. Our finding that perceived personnel requirements are a function of the number of people present to work on a task and of the prior manning conditions in the same setting is an example. One may also be able to examine the same relationships among variables in different ways. We found, for example, that subjective experiences related to manning theory varied not only with different manning conditions but also within manning conditions, depending upon subjects' task roles.

A broad, multiple-variable approach may also provide results that suggest promising strategies for future study. An example would be our finding that type of task greatly influenced group-interaction profiles, but manning did not. Conceivably, manning effects might be found if the observation scheme we used were applied to groups working in a setting in which the nature of the jobs to be done changed with shifts in degree of manning. In any case, the relationships between manning conditions and task roles should be further explored. Finally we would also like to note that researchers who begin to use the ecological, social-systems approach in the laboratory may have to develop a greater tolerance for complexity and ambiguity and to learn to focus on patterns of results rather than to rely on the significance of statistical tests on one or a few variables.

While we were concluding our analyses of the laboratory studies, we were also considering the questions: What would be the most profitable next steps in developing the theory of manning: In what kinds of settings should future research be conducted? Consistent with the ecological orientation, we decided that we should return to real-life situations while attempting to expand the theory. Our long-range goal is to develop a more comprehensive and more "balanced" theory of excess and insufficient populations in behavior settings by focusing upon inner psychological states, such as cognitions and feelings, and related behaviors, and by elaborating upon the consequences of overmanning.

Focus on Service Behavior Settings

In working toward the above goals, we have narrowed our conceptual focus from behavior settings in general to *service behavior settings*, that is, those in which the performers are employees or entrepreneurs whose primary function is to provide a service to consumers, users, visitors, or other nonperformers. In the following discussion, we call performers in service behavior settings *staff* and nonperformers in these settings *clients*. Examples of service behavior settings would be grocery stores, post-office lobbies, attorneys' offices, privately owned campgrounds, police patrols, massage parlors, and hospital emergency-rooms. While the focus on service settings eliminates from present consideration a number of other kinds of settings, such as most voluntary-organization activities and work environments in which nonperformers are not present, it nevertheless clearly includes a sufficient number and diversity of settings to be of general interest.

One advantage of focusing on service behavior settings is the fact that in such settings there is an inverse relationship between manning levels for staff and clients. Increases in number of clients result in greater job demands for staff; decreases in number of clients lessen job demands on staff.[10] In the following discussion, we use the terms *understaffed, adequately staffed,* and *overstaffed* to refer to manning conditions among staff, and the terms *underpopulated, adequately populated,* and *overpopulated* to refer to manning conditions among clients. Three different setting conditions are possible: (1) understaffed–overpopulated, for example, a crowded dentist's office; (2) adequately staffed–adequately populated; and (3) overstaffed–underpopulated, for example a beauty shop with more operators than customers. Obviously staffing and population conditions in service behavior settings can fluctuate widely over periods as brief as a few minutes because of changes in numbers of clients and/or staff. Variations also occur over hours, days, weeks, months, and years. While the selection of a time period for research purposes is somewhat arbitrary, such decisions should take into account the program of the setting, the range of staffing and population conditions that exist in the setting, and whether the investigator is interested in reactions of staff, clients or both.

In our thinking about service settings, we have considered two related yet somewhat distinct problem areas. One focuses more directly on people and examines in greater detail than has been done previously the effects of staffing and population conditions (i.e., manning conditions) on the cognitions, feelings, experiences, and behaviors of setting occupants. The other focuses more directly on selected features of settings and deals with the adaptive mechanisms that have been developed to avoid or reduce setting overpopulation. Our work on both problem areas is in a formulative stage, as will be seen.

Effects of Staffing and Population Levels on Occupants of Service Behavior Settings

Conceptual Considerations

In an attempt to elaborate upon the cognitions and feelings of occupants of service behavior settings, we have drawn upon the psychological-stress lit-

---

[10]Barker's (1968) implicit assumption that the boundary between performer and nonperformer roles is permeable—that is, that when more performers are needed, nonperformers present take over those duties—seems inappropriate for service behavior settings.

erature, particularly the concept of overload. Several writers have linked departures from adequate manning with stress (Barker, 1968; McGrath, 1976; Weick, 1970). Barker and McGrath have proposed very similar models, which deal with the steps by which individuals deal with environmental threats. For Barker (1968), the threats are conditions or events in a behavior setting that jeopardize the functions of the setting and hence the satisfactions of setting occupants. He suggests that when such events are perceived (by a "sensory mechanism"), they are evaluated, and a course of action is chosen (by an "executive mechanism") and then enacted (by an "action mechanism").

McGrath (1976) considers sources of stress to be environmental situations that are "perceived as presenting a demand which threatens to exceed the person's capabilities and resources for meeting it" (p. 1352). He proposes a four-stage, closed-loop cycle for stress situations, which we will relate to staffing and population conditions in service behavior settings. The stages are the following:

1. The objective situation, as it might be recorded by an observer.
2. The perceived situation, as it is experienced by the focal person.
3. Response selection, the strategy chosen by the focal person for dealing with the threat.
4. Behavior, the actual responses emitted to affect the objective situation.

The objective situations of interest are two of the three conditions specified earlier, namely, service behavior settings that are either (1) understaffed and overpopulated or (2) overstaffed and underpopulated. In the first condition, task *overload* is a potential stressor for the staff, who must deal with large numbers of clients over whom they may have little control. For clients in this condition, waiting with nothing to do could be a stressor, particularly if they are not aware of the procedures and policies that constrain the staff's activities (see Kahn and French, 1970, pp. 255–256). In the second condition, both staff and clients might also experience stress: staff because of a task *underload*, that is, few people to be served (see McGrath, 1970, p. 19), and clients because of an uncertainty about the quality of the service, for example, wondering if lack of restaurant patrons means that the food is not good.

The next two stages in the stress cycle, perceived situation and response selection, occur within the focal person. McGrath (1976) and other writers have emphasized the importance of the individual's perceiving the objective situation as stressful. Thus one aspect of the perceived situation is essentially validational. In the understaffed–overpopulated situation, the following feelings might be expected: among staff, feelings of having too much to do, being under pressure, feeling rushed, and needing help; and among clients, feelings of impatience, boredom, and wasting their time. In the overstaffed–underpopulated condition, we should find among the staff, feelings of boredom, not having enough to do, and having too many co-workers; and among clients (in some cases, at least), feelings of insecurity and uneasiness. Since previous research (see Glass and Singer, 1972) has suggested that unpredictable, uncontrollable stressors may have greater effects than predictable, controllable stressors, it might further be expected that these feelings would be more prevalent for unexpected shifts in staffing and population conditions.

Another important aspect of the perceived situation is causal attribution for the stress, that is, who or what is believed to be the source of the offending condition (see Heider, 1958; Weick, 1970). Attributions can be made to the self or to persons or conditions outside the self. For staff in the situations of interest, not only the self but also persons who interact with the focal person in the job situation and who are dependent upon him may be considered to be responsible for the stress. These would include the people being served, one's co-workers, and one's immediate supervisor. Staff could also attribute the stress and its effects to components of the broader organization, such as an employer or the physical features of the behavior setting, such as equipment, the arrangement of physical objects, or the amount of available space. For example, a bank teller in an understaffed setting might consider the long queue of people at his window to be due to his own inefficiency, to the unreasonableness of the customers, to the inefficiency of his fellow tellers, to the failure of his supervisor to assign enough people to windows, to the failure of the organization to hire enough tellers, to an insufficient number of windows, or to the absence of a queuing device. For clients, attributions could be made to the self, to the staff offering the service, to others being served, to the organization as an employer, or to physical features of the setting. For example, a person waiting for service at the bank teller's window might consider his condition to be due to his own failure to arrive at a less busy time; to the inefficiency of the teller, to the unreasonableness of the other customers, to the failure of the bank to employ enough tellers, or to the failure of the bank to provide enough windows.

The third stage in McGrath's stress cycle is response selection, the process by which the focal person selects a strategy from among possible alternatives to deal with the perceived threat. An important factor in response selection is undoubtedly the source to which the stress is attributed: a staff member who sees his own inefficiency as being responsible for a long queue might try to work faster. The attribution–response-selection linkage often may not be direct or one-to-one, however. A staff member might also attribute a long queue to his co-worker's inefficiency, yet try to relieve stress by working faster himself.

Among the response alternatives a staff member might consider in dealing with different staffing conditions are the following: spending less or more time per client served; purposefully reducing or increasing the quality of the service he renders; ignoring or attending to low-priority tasks; inducing his co-workers to change their rate or quality of work; asking his supervisor for additional help or for permission to leave his post;

communicating his feelings to persons higher up in the organization; or activating or deactivating a queuing mechanism (e.g., a "take-a-number" device). A client's response alternatives to various setting-population conditions might include the following: leaving the behavior setting; switching from one waiting line to another; complaining to the other clients or the staff in the setting; questioning other setting occupants about the reasons for the small number of people present; attempting to advance in a queue by cutting in or using other unauthorized methods to obtain service more quickly; releasing emotion, for example, honking one's horn or stamping one's feet; making resolutions for the future, for example, never or always to return at that hour, to make reservations or not to bother with them, or to communicate his feelings to others by letter or in conversation (see Saaty, 1961, p. 10).

Some of the alternative responses described above were derived from Milgram's (1970) discussion of the reactions to sensory overload shown by residents of large cities and from Meier's (1962) list of responses to communications stress. Milgram also suggests two other responses, which probably are gradual adaptations to overload rather than consciously considered strategies; these would most directly apply to persons who repeatedly and/or continuously experience understaffing. They are (1) interacting with clients only in terms of job-role prescriptions, that is, only on an impersonal and relatively superficial level and (2) lacking empathy with or sensitivity to the problems or concerns of the persons served. Another possible adaptation is the development of stereotyped perceptions of clients by the staff, that is, classifying clients into a small number of broad and often derogatory categories.[11]

The notions derived from Milgram may seem somewhat contradictory to Barker's theory, which would predict increasing feelings of job involvement, importance, and concern as staffing levels decrease. Conceivably this relationship may be stronger in voluntary activities (e.g., settings in schools and churches, laboratory experiments) than in work situations. Also the temporal factor may be crucial: first experiences of understaffing may well lead to greater involvement, with later chronic understaffing producing cynicism and dissociation from the task.

The fourth stage in the stress cycle is the actual behaviors by the focal person to deal with the threat. The behaviors will presumably be a subset of the response alternatives considered in the third stage. The outcome of these behaviors in the objective situation is then perceived, considered, and further acted upon if necessary, according to the McGrath (1976) model.

---

[11]For example, Washington, D.C., supermarket checkout clerks have developed the following categories for the people they serve: "hawks," who closely watch the cash register as items are rung up; "scavengers," who attempt to get reductions on prices for dented cans, damaged produce, and the like; "aristocrats," who ask clerks for services no longer provided, such as leaving their station to collect items that the shopper could not locate; and "self-servers," who shoplift in a variety of ways (McCarthy, 1973). See Menmerick (1974) for a further discussion of the use of client typologies by service workers.

Empirical Research

We attempted to examine some of the above notions in Yosemite National Park in the summer of 1974.[12] With the cooperation of the local park administration, we obtained questionnaire responses from National Park Service employees in several different kinds of jobs that involved extensive contact with park visitors. Our sample included some people whose work allowed them to move about and others who had to stay in a single, rather confining location: patrolling rangers, ranger naturalists, entrance-station attendants, and campground-kiosk attendants. The employees answered questions about specific workdays that we had judged from external criteria to be heavy, average, or light in terms of job demands. Questions dealt with such topics as the extent to which the employee felt involved in his work, the extent to which he felt under pressure, the extent to which he saw himself or others as being responsible for the pressure, the alternatives he considered for dealing with the pressure, and the courses he actually took. Other questions asked about general working conditions (e.g., how often the amount of work the employee had to do interfered with how well he was able to do the work and how much freedom he had in deciding the amount of time to spend with any given park visitor) and with perceived characteristics of park visitors (e.g., the percentage of visitors who understand the problems that park employees have to deal with and the percentage of visitors who try to minimize the environmental impact of their visit). Unfortunately we were not able to obtain comparable data from park visitors because of regulations that severely restrict the administration of questionnaires and interviews to visitors on Federal recreational lands. Results of the Yosemite research are not available at this time, as we are just beginning the data analysis. Among other things, we hope to determine the effects of both level of job demands and type of job on the subjective experiences, attributions, and perceptions described above.

Adaptive Mechanisms for Avoiding or Reducing Overpopulation of Service Behavior Settings

Conceptual Considerations

We are also struggling with ways to conceptualize and study adaptive mechanisms that have developed spontaneously or that have been introduced into service settings to lessen problems of overpopulation, that is, having more clients present than can readily be served. There appear to be

---

[12]While there are both conceptual and methodological similarities and differences between our Yosemite research and the laboratory studies reported earlier, it should be understood that we view the Yosemite work as an examination of our most recent elaboration of the manning notions and not simply as a field replication of the earlier laboratory investigations.

at least three basic ways these mechanisms function, by regulating (1) the entrance of clients into the setting, (2) the capacity of the setting, and (3) the length of time clients spend in the setting. Each basic type of regulation may be achieved in a number of different ways, as illustrated below[13]:

A. Regulation of the entrance of clients into the setting

   1. Scheduling entrances
      Example: A dentist might require his patients to make an appointment before being allowed to see him.

   2. Varying recruiting activities
      Example: A restaurant whose business is good every night might stop advertising.

   3. Adjusting standards of admission
      Example: A national park whose wilderness areas are heavily visited might begin to require all backpackers to demonstrate a knowledge of how to minimize the environmental impact of their visit before issuing them wilderness permits.

   4. Channeling clients into holding areas
      Example: Patrons of a busy restaurant might be directed to the cocktail lounge to wait until a table is free.

   5. Preventing unauthorized entrances
      Example: A bus driver might eject a would-be passenger who entered the bus in a discharging zone to avoid waiting in line at the loading area.

B. Regulation of the capacity of the setting

   1. Altering physical facilities and spaces
      Examples: Ushers at an Easter worship service might place folding chairs at the back of a church to accommodate a large crowd of worshipers. On holiday weekends, additional queuing-device stanchions might be placed in the waiting area for a popular amusement-park attraction.

   2. Adjusting duration or occurrences of the setting
      Example: A popular tavern might extend the hours and/or the days of the week it is open.

   3. Adjusting size of staff
      Example: A bank manager might assign an additional employee to teller duty on Fridays.

   4. Varying assignments of nonservice tasks to staff
      Example: Lifeguards at a beach might be asked to suspend all equipment-maintenance tasks during heavy visitation periods.

---

[13]This list is tentative and undoubtedly incomplete. The list and examples have been drawn from our casual observation of service behavior settings, introductions to queuing theory (Cox and Smith, 1961; Goode and Machol, 1957; Panico, 1969; Saaty, 1961) and the literature on sensory overload (Milgram, 1970; Meier, 1962), manning theory (Barker, 1968; Wicker *et al.*, 1972), and general systems theory (Miller, 1971, 1972).

C. Regulation of the amount of time clients spend in the setting
  1. Varying rate of processing clients
     Example: A barber with a number of customers waiting might spend less time on each haircut.
  2. Varying limitations on length of stay
     Example: A public campground might allow campers to stay only 7 days during the summer but 21 days during the rest of the year.
  3. Activating a graduated fee-structure based on time spent in the setting
     Examples: Campers in a public campground might be charged a higher fee each successive night they spend there.
  4. Establishing priorities among clients in the setting on such bases as time of arrival, waiting costs, and service time required
     Example: A hospital emergency ward might have a policy of attending to the most seriously injured first. A computer consultant might first serve those clients having brief questions before helping those with more involved problems.
  5. Altering the standing patterns of behavior by means of procedures, rules, and/or physical facilities that affect the rate of flow of clients into and out of the setting
     Examples: A hamburger stand might be rearranged so that customers place their orders at one counter and pick them up at another. A busy bus system might begin to accept only the exact fare. A restroom in a large sports arena might be redesigned with separate entrance and exit doors. A savings-and-loan bank might post signs asking customers to complete their own deposit slips before approaching a teller.

In addition to the above mechanisms that are aimed at physically processing clients in ways that avoid or reduce overpopulation, there are other mechanisms that seem to be oriented toward reducing clients' *perceptions* and *experiences* of overpopulation and its consequences without really affecting the objective situation. One such mechanism is a distracting or entertaining stimulus located where it can be viewed by people waiting in line. An example would be a closed-circuit television that shows ski movies placed near a queue of skiers waiting for a lift. Another such mechanism is a queuing arrangement that leads people waiting in line to believe that the number of people ahead of them is smaller than it actually is. For example, inside the building that houses an amusement-park attraction, there may be a 100-foot queue that is not visible to those waiting in line outside. A somewhat related mechanism is leading clients to believe that they are making progress by introducing a number of discrete steps in the obtainment of service. For example, a patient in a physician's office may first check in with a receptionist; then wait in a waiting room until his name is called; then be escorted to an examination room, where he waits until a nurse comes to take his temperature and pulse; then be escorted into still another room, where he waits until the physician arrives. Another of these mechanisms involves concealing the setting capacity from clients. A dentist may have several patients in chairs and rotate from one to another without their knowing how many others he is seeing at the same time.

Empirical Research

In Yosemite National Park, we have studied an adaptive mechanism designed to reduce problems of overmanning at a bus stop. The mechanism was a queuing device made of posts and chains arranged in such a way as to get passengers to line up in an orderly fashion in preparation for boarding. In the study, we first systematically observed and recorded a number of measures of the orderliness and rate of loading at two of the busiest bus stops on the free Yosemite Valley shuttle-bus system. During these observations there were many instances of people's being stranded at the stop because the bus filled before they were able to board. There was also much pushing and shoving. After three weeks of observations, with the help of the park-service work crews, we installed the queuing device at one of the two stops. Over the next 3 weeks, we again took the same measures at both stops and also observed the frequency of violations of the queuing procedures. At the end of this period, we gave questionnaires to the bus drivers to get their reactions to the device. It is our impression that the queuing device was successful, but we will be better able to make an evaluation and recommendations regarding its use after the data are analyzed.

We believe that further knowledge of the ways service settings avoid or reduce overpopulation would be valuable for both theoretical and practical reasons. Such knowledge might come from attempts to elaborate and refine the above list of mechanisms and/or from other intensive studies of specific mechanisms in selected settings. The potential conceptual payoffs include a greater convergence between the study of adaptive mechanisms and the study of subjective reactions to staffing and population conditions, and increased understanding of the *processes* by which these mechanisms operate (see Wicker, 1972) and of the ways various mechanisms are related to one another. The potential practical payoffs include detailed information on how, and how well, certain mechanisms operate and availability of a comprehensive list of adaptive mechanisms that could be consulted by persons in charge of settings that are threatened with overpopulation.

Postscript

In this chapter we have tried to *illustrate* the recent activities in our program of research rather than to make formal or general statements about our orientation to the study of how people experience their environments.

Given the nature of programmatic research, it also seems appropriate that the chapter should end by alluding to data still being analyzed and by posing questions for future study.

Acknowledgments

The first author was primarily responsible for the theoretical sections of this paper; the second author had a major role in the empirical work reported. The following persons also participated in the empirical research: in the slot-car studies, Lois Hanson and Dean Alexander; in the Yosemite National Park projects, Lois Hanson, Richard LeBlanc, and Scott Buehler. We are indebted to Joseph E. McGrath for helpful comments on an earlier version of this paper. The research reported here was supported by Grant No. GS 34998 from the National Science Foundation.

References

Altman, I. Some perspectives on the study of man–environment phenomena. *Representative Research in Social Psychology*, 1973, *4*, 109–126.

Bales, R. F. *Interaction process analysis*. Cambridge, Mass.: Addison-Wesley, 1951.

Barker, R. G. Ecology and motivation. *Nebraska Symposium on Motivation*, 1960, *8*, 1–50.

Barker, R. G. On the nature of the environment. *Journal of Social Issues*, 1963, *19*(4), 17–38.

Barker, R. G. Explorations in ecological psychology. *American Psychologist*, 1965, *20*, 1–14.

Barker, R. G. *Ecological psychology: Concepts and methods for studying the environment of human behavior*. Stanford, Calif.: Stanford University Press, 1968.

Barker, R. G., and Gump, P. V. *Big school, small school: High school size and student behavior*. Stanford, Calif.: Stanford University Press, 1964.

Barker, R. G., and Schoggen, P. *Qualities of community life*. San Francisco: Jossey-Bass, 1973.

Barker, R. G., and Wright, H. F. *Midwest and its children*. New York: Harper & Row, 1955.

Carter, L., Haythorn, W., Meirowitz, B., and Lanzetta, J. The relation of categorizations and ratings in the observation of group behavior. *Human Relations*, 1951, *4*, 239–254.

Cox, D. R., and Smith, W. L. *Queues*. New York: Wiley, 1961.

Glass, D. C., and Singer, J. E. *Urban stress: Experiments on noise and social stressors*. New York: Academic Press, 1972.

Goode, H. H., and Machol, R. E. *System engineering*. New York: McGraw-Hill, 1957.

Hanson, L. Effects of overmanning on group experience and task performance. Unpublished master's thesis, Claremont Graduate School, 1973.

Hanson, L., and Wicker, A. W. Effects of overmanning on group experience and task performance. Paper presented at the meeting of the Western Psychological Association, Anaheim, Calif., April, 1973.

Heider, F. *The psychology of interpersonal relations*. New York: Wiley, 1958.

Helson, H. *Adaptation-level theory*. New York: Harper & Row, 1964.

Kahn, R. L., and French, J. R. P., Jr. Status and conflict: Two themes in the study of stress. In J. E. McGrath (Ed.), *Social and psychological factors in stress*. New York: Holt, Rinehart and Winston, 1970.

Kirmeyer, S. The effects of manning condition on group interaction. Unpublished master's thesis, Claremont Graduate School, 1974.

McCarthy, C. Checking out the faces on the supermarket assembly line. *San Francisco Examiner & Chronicle,* December 30, 1973, Sunday Punch, p. 7.

McGrath, J. E. A conceptual formulation for research on stress. In J. E. McGrath (Ed.), *Social and psychological factors in stress.* New York: Holt, Rinehart and Winston, 1970.

McGrath, J. E. Stress and behavior in organizations. In M. D. Dunnette (Ed.), *Handbook of industrial and organizational psychology.* Chicago: Rand-McNally, 1976.

Meier, R. L. *A communications theory of urban growth.* Cambridge, Mass.: M.I.T. Press, 1962.

Mennerick, L. A. Client typologies. *Sociology of Work and Occupations,* 1974, *1,* 396–418.

Milgram, S. The experience of living in cities. *Science,* 1970, *167,* 1461–1468.

Miller, J. G. The nature of living systems. *Behavioral Science,* 1971, *16,* 277–301.

Miller, J. G. Living systems: The organization. *Behavioral Science,* 1972, *17,* 1–182.

Panico, J. A. *Queuing theory: A study of waiting lines for business, economics, and science.* Englewood Cliffs, N.J.: Prentice-Hall, 1969.

Petty, R. M., and Wicker, A. W. Degree of manning and degree of success of a group as determinants of members' subjective experiences and their acceptance of a new group member. *JSAS Catalog of Selected Documents in Psychology,* 1974, *4,* 43. (Ms. No. 616)

Saaty, T. L. *Elements of queueing theory.* New York: McGraw-Hill, 1961.

Steiner, I. D. *Group process and productivity.* New York: Academic Press, 1972.

Stokols, D. A social–psychological model of human crowding phenomena. *Journal of the American Institute of Planners,* 1972, *38,* 72–83.

Stokols, D. The experience of crowding in primary and secondary environments. Paper presented at the meeting of the American Psychological Association, New Orleans, August, 1974.

Wapner, S., Cohen, S. B., and Kaplan, B. (Eds.), *Experiencing the environment.* New York: Plenum, 1976.

Weick, K. E. The "Ess" in stress: Some conceptual and methodological problems. In J. E. McGrath (Ed.), *Social and psychological factors in stress.* New York: Holt, Rinehart and Winston, 1970.

Wicker, A. W. An examination of the "other variables" explanation of attitude–behavior inconsistency. *Journal of Personality and Social Psychology,* 1971, *19,* 18–30.

Wicker, A. W. Processes which mediate behavior–environment congruence. *Behavioral Science,* 1972, *17,* 265–277.

Wicker, A. W. Undermanning theory and research: Implications for the study of psychological and behavioral effects of excess populations. *Representative Research in Social Psychology,* 1973, *4,* 185–206.

Wicker, A. W. An application of the multitrait-multimethod logic to the reliability of observational records. *Personality and Social Psychology Bulletin,* 1975, *4,* 575–579.

Wicker, A. W., McGrath, J. E., and Armstrong, G. E. Organization size and behavior setting capacity as determinants of member participation. *Behavioral Science,* 1972, *17,* 499–513.

SECTION III
Environmental Psychology ☐

This section examines the second major line of research within the environment and behavior field: environmental psychology. Although the areas of ecological and environmental psychology presently share certain substantive and procedural assumptions, they emerged from distinctly different theoretical orientations (see Stokols, Chapter 1). The former area developed from an extension of bioecological principles to the analysis of human groups, whereas the latter emerged largely from developments within psychology that placed increasing emphasis on the interaction between personal and environmental determinants of individual behavior (see Craik, 1970; Ittelson, Proshansky, Rivlin, and Winkel, 1974; Wohlwill, 1970).

The initial chapter by Harold Proshansky and Timothy O'Hanlon offers a detailed analysis of the intellectual and societal forces which contributed to the emergence of environmental psychology. The authors link these forces to a set of "value-methodological properties" which characterize contemporary research in environmental psychology. Among the distinguishing features of this research discussed by the authors are its emphases on (1) the psychological and social processes that mediate the effects of the molar physical environment on behavior, and (2) the development of solutions to community problems based on behavioral science theory and interdisciplinary research. Several other aspects of environmental psychology are mentioned, including its emphasis on naturalistic, longitudinal, and descriptive research, and the prospects for future development and conceptualization of the field are assessed.

The remaining chapters reflect many of the substantive and procedural emphases discussed by Proshansky and O'Hanlon. The program of research described by David Glass, Jerome Singer, and James Pennebaker clearly emphasizes the interaction of personal and environmental determinants of behavior. A substantial amount of evidence is presented, indicating that the impact of the physical environment (e.g., noise) on people is mediated largely by situational and intrapersonal factors (e.g., perceived controllability of noise; the "coronary-prone behavior pattern"; see Jenkins, Rosenman, and Zyzanski, 1974). Moreover, the concern of this research with the measurement of delayed (or "post-stressor") aftereffects of noise reflects the importance of temporal factors in regulating human-environment transactions, an issue also emphasized by Proshansky and O'Hanlon.

Chalsa Loo's chapter on human crowding further illustrates certain key features of environmental psychology. First, it traces the rapid expansion of crowding research to a growing concern among scientists and policy-makers over community problems such as overpopulation, pollution, and resource depletion. The linkage between crowding research and societal concern over these issues reflects the social-problems orientation of environmental psychology, mentioned earlier. Furthermore, the model of social and spatial crowding stress, presented by Loo, exemplifies the interactionist perspective (see Bowers, 1973; Lewin, 1935) of research in environmental psychology. Specifically, crowding is viewed as an experiential state whose occurrence cannot be predicted on the basis of spatial factors alone but, rather, depends on an interplay of psychological, social, and physical variables.

The chapter by George McKechnie also reflects the community-problems orientation of environmental psychology. Mckechnie presents a typology of environmental simulations and a description of ongoing investigations in which the responses of individuals to simulated environments are being analyzed. Future refinements of the assessment procedures discussed in this chapter may facilitate the design of physical settings that are maximally congruent with the needs and preferences of specific user groups.

The chapters included in this section reflect varying levels of emphasis on the three modes of human-environment transaction, discussed in Section I of this volume. Orientation processes, or the ways in which people perceive and interpret the environment, are emphasized in the analyses of cognitive and personality determinants of individuals' reactions to environmental stressors, presented by Glass, Singer, and Pennebaker and by Loo. At the same time, operation processes, or the ways in which people are affected by, and act upon, their surroundings, are emphasized in the noise and crowding research described by these authors. And evaluation processes, which involve assessments of the environment in terms of its suitability as a context for future goal attainment, are given greater emphasis in the environmental simulation research discussed by McKechnie.

In summary, the chapters included in this section provide an overview of empirical developments within some of the major problem areas of environmental psychology. Although the programs of research described in these chapters diverge in many ways (e.g., in terms of their relative emphasis on laboratory vs. naturalistic methodologies, and on physical vs. social dimensions of the environment), they collectively reflect the key substantive and procedural emphases of environmental psychology.

References

Bowers, K. S. Situationism in psychology: An analysis and a critique. *Psychological Review*, 1973, *80*, 307–336.

Craik, K. Environmental psychology. In K. Craik, B. Kleinmuntz, R. Rosnow, R. Rosenthal, J. A. Cheyne, and R. H. Walters (Eds.), *New directions in psychology* (vol. 4). New York: Holt, Rinehart and Winston, 1970.

Ittelson, W., Proshansky, H., Rivlin, L., and Winkel, G. *An introduction to environmental psychology*. New York: Holt, Rinehart and Winston, 1974.

Jenkins, C. D., Rosenmann, R. H., and Zyzanski, S. J. Prediction of clinical coronary heart disease by a test for the coronary prone behavior pattern. *New England Journal of Medicine*, 1974, *290*, 1271–1275.

Lewin, K. *A dynamic theory of personality*. New York: McGraw-Hill, 1935.

Wohlwill, J. The emerging discipline of environmental psychology. *American Psychologist*, 1970, *25*, 303–312.

Environmental Psychology: Origins and Development

4

HAROLD M. PROSHANSKY
AND TIMOTHY O'HANLON

Historical analysis is never a simple matter. This is true whether it involves tracing the origin and development of an individual, a group, or, as in this instance, a new field of scientific inquiry. The intention to be "historical" in the premeditated sense of keeping an ongoing record of people, events, and activities seldom, if ever, occurs. And even if it did, the problems of how much should be recorded, what is relevant and what is not, and how to organize and interpret what is recorded are no less formidable problems. In this chapter, we shall be, of course, looking back at the origins and development of the recently developed field of environmental psychology, and in undertaking this task we were beset with all of these problems and even more. More in a number of ways: the field is interdisciplinary and so the sources of its origins and development range through not just the more established behavioral sciences but the design professions as well; modern communication and media technology have accelerated the accumulation and dissemination of information such that even in a short period of time, "new fields" show a remarkable accumulation of people, scientific papers, conferences, research programs, educational curricula, and other signs of scholarship and scientific inquiry; and finally we ourselves—as the "historians" in this case—have been part of and involved in the development of this fledgling field.

Whatever the limitations in our historical analysis, our chronicle of the ideas, the research, the people, and the events that led to the emergence of environmental psychology is quite accurate. The usefulness of this chronicle and the various interpretations that can be made of it are twofold: for

HAROLD M. PROSHANSKY AND TIMOTHY O'HANLON ● City University of New York.

relevant theorists, empirical researchers, and "interested bystanders" alike, it provides, first, some understanding of the major underlying assumptions that structure and direct the thinking and research in the field at the present time; and second, it provides a basis for thinking about where the field may be going in the future—or indeed whether or not it has a future—and what kind of priorities it must establish to ensure its continued growth and development as a scientific field of inquiry.

Perhaps it is best to begin with the operational but obviously tautological statement that environmental psychology in its most inclusive sense is concerned with the study of the environment. The fact is that even now, some 15 years after it first could be distinguished as a problem area with some distinctive, relatively "untouched" conceptual and empirical questions, it remains a "big buzzing confusion." Although the field is now most frequently identified by behavioral scientists and design professionals as environmental psychology, there are still other designations that remain— for example, "ecological psychology" and "architectural psychology"—and whose particular orientations, despite the less frequent use of the designations, continue to have influence on the field.

What we have, then, at the present time is a broad interdisciplinary problem area that in no sense whatsoever represents a well-defined field of scientific inquiry. It lacks the conceptual and theoretical structure that would identify its boundaries for analysis and research and the kind of knowledge or understanding it would accumulate. Not only are meaningful theoretical definitions of the field virtually impossible at the present time, but the usual operational definitions of a behavioral science, in which one simply "points to" the kinds of problems and research it engages in, are not a simple matter either. Theorists and researchers who identify themselves as environmental psychologists vary so greatly in what, how, where, and for what purposes they formulate and do research, that at this point the term *environmental psychology* serves as a huge umbrella with room enough for anyone concerned with problems of human behavior and experience in relation to some recognizable dimension, description, or property of the person's environment.

It is true, of course, that not all researchers or practitioners who are involved in environmental research care to have themselves identified by means of this umbrella. Many *human factor* researchers, for example, concerned with the individual's responses and performances in relation to the functional requirements of given tasks and activities in a variety of environmental settings, would argue that they do not need this umbrella because they have been involved in environmental research for at least five decades, if not longer. It is also true that experimental psychologists concerned with psychophysical relationships in the study of illumination, auditory stimulation, and other sensory systems would undoubtedly take this same view. And not to be outdone, there are social psychologists, sociologists, and certainly anthropologists who view the very long concern of their respective fields with the behavior and experience of individuals or groups in relation to sociocultural systems as clear evidence that "environmental psychology" or the field by any other name is neither a new idea nor a very young one.

How then can we identify this "new" field that began to show itself at the very end of the 1950's and the beginning of the 1960's? What distinguished it operationally or substantively, if not conceptually, in its concern with the environment so that it eventually developed a place of its own in that scheme of activity we call behavioral science research?

First, and perhaps most important, was its primary concern with the physical environment in particular rather than with the human environment in general. The use of the term *environment* by social psychologists and all other behavioral scientists almost invariably refers to the psychological, social, organizational, or cultural systems that characterize human environments. For the environmental psychologist, the lens of analysis is focused on the physical systems that by definition also characterize these environments: physical systems that are expressed as spaces, places, and the objects in them that provide the locus and not a small part of the meaning of these other kinds of systems or environments and the people and activities they encompass and in turn define. For the environmental psychologist, there was a shift in the figure–ground relationships in considerations of the various systems, empirical and abstract, that comprise a person's environment. Now it was the physical setting that was moved to the foreground to be studied and conceptualized against the background of the far-more-frequently-investigated psychological, social, and cultural environments of individuals and groups.

Their concern with the physical environment was not enough to provide a place in the sun for environmental psychologists. Stimuli, in the form of light, sound, temperature, shape, and height, and more complex patterns of environmental stimuli in the form of equipment and machine systems are also means of studying the physical environment of the person. For the environmental psychologist, however, the physical environment of interest goes well beyond the stimuli and patterns of stimuli of interest to experimental and human-factor psychologists. Indeed he rejects these conceptions of the physical environment because they represent analytical abstractions of this environment rather than a realistic description of it as it relates to the actual behavior and experience of the individual. The physical environments to be observed and studied are all those places and spaces that provide the locus and definition of the varied multiple of human activities that characterize day-to-day existence. And these spaces and places are in turn defined by the social realities we identify as community settings, playgrounds, housing developments, hospitals, transportation systems, and courthouses and, on a smaller scale, as bedrooms, hospital wards, classrooms, bathrooms, diners, hotel suites, operating rooms, secretarial work spaces, bus stops, and many others.

This means, of course, that the physical setting to be investigated, whatever its scope and complexity as defined by a particular problem needing analysis, is the intact environment, or said differently, a physical environment whose phenomenal integrity as a real-life experience for the individual is to be maintained. This in turn requires not only a necessary collaboration with architects, designers, landscape specialists, space managers, and other environmental specialists but a commitment to research in the real-life settings with directed attempts to maintain the integrity of the setting and the activities and events that take place in them. Applied or field researchers in social, industrial, and still other fields of psychology had left the laboratory many decades ago, but not in the "environmental sense" we have just described. And it is in just that environmental sense that environmental psychology is operationally defined, either explicitly or implicitly, by many of those who were initially involved in its beginning development: the study of the behavior and experience of the person or groups of persons in relation to their physical setting, and in particular that real-life setting now most commonly referred to as the "built environment."

Although this definition reduces the size of the very wide umbrella involved in our initial definition of environmental psychology, those still covered by it hardly agree on more precise definitions of the field, that is, on what problems should be studied, for what purposes, and by what means. These differences are to be expected in any fledgling field of inquiry, particularly when its interdisciplinary nature ranges well beyond the usual behavioral sciences. Some of these differences will be revealed in the discussion that follows, particularly in the section on the value-methodological orientations of the new field. Having given the reader at least a working definition of the field, we turn our attention now to our first task of providing a brief history of the field: when, how, and who was involved in its birth and growth.

Environmental Psychology: Some History

When did it all begin? This is always a difficult question to answer, particularly about the origin of a field of scientific inquiry. Many particular writings and research activities of one or another behavioral scientist, going back as far as the early 1920's, might in fact be characterized as "environmental psychology." However, in terms of the origins of the field as we know it today, these sporadic papers are not relevant since in most instances the physical setting was a secondary consideration in relation to other environmental influences or conceptual concerns. For instance, Festinger, Schacter, and Back studied in 1950 the development of informal social groups in university housing as a function of spatial proximity. However, this research was far more concerned with group process and social communication than with the properties of the physical setting. Evidence of "a beginning" of the environmental psychology presented in this volume occurred in the late 1950's.

In 1958–1959, Ittelson, Proshansky, and Rosenblatt took the first steps toward initiating a research program on the influence of ward design on patient behavior in mental hospitals (Ittelson, 1960). These steps involved a review of the relevant literature and a set of working papers to guide the specific formulation of problems. By 1962, Leanne Rivlin had joined the research team, and this was the year that the first systematic studies of psychiatric wards were undertaken. They continued over the next 8 years. At the same time Ittelson, Proshansky, and Rosenblatt began their effort. Humphrey Osmond, a research-oriented psychiatrist, published a scientific paper on "Function as the Basis of Psychiatric Ward Design" (1957). Equally important was the work of Robert Sommer, a social psychologist, who collaborated with Osmond on the problems of the behavioral symptoms of institutional care, especially as they reflected the physical setup of psychiatric wards (Sommer and Osmond, 1961). In addition, Sommer, working with Ross, had published one of the earliest papers on social interaction on a geriatric ward in which the concept of territoriality was clearly demonstrated (Sommer and Ross, 1958).

Not to be overlooked, and also taking place at more or less the same time, was the research performed by Paul Sivadon, a French psychiatrist, on the role of the design of mental hospitals in facilitating patient recovery. He and his architectural associates published a monograph on this problem for the World Health Organization in 1960 (Baker, Davies, and Sivadon, 1960). At the University of Utah and the University of Kansas, including the Topeka State Hospital, there was psychiatric-ward research being formulated and carried out. Thus both universities became additional sites for research in the design of space in mental hospitals in relation to the behavior and experience of patients and staff. In 1961 the first Architectural Psychology and Psychiatry Conference was held (Bailey, Branch, and Taylor, 1961). It was supported by the community services branch of the National Institute of Mental Health. Included in the conference were psychologists, architects, psychiatrists, and medical planners.

It is interesting that during the same period, other environmental psychology stirrings of a very different sort were going on. Kevin Lynch, a city planner at M.I.T., and his students became involved in the individual's perception of urban settings. Lynch was concerned with how urban dwellers used the space of the city and the images they formed of it as a consequence of its design and their day-to-day experience in moving about it. He published his now classic *Image of the City* in 1960, and it was only a few years later that he, Donald Appleyard, and John Meyer got involved in their research in the aesthetics of urban design. Here they attempted to determine how urban highways looked to automobile drivers and their passengers for the purpose of determining how such highways should be designed (Appleyard, Lynch, and Meyer, 1966).

Immediately following the 3-year period of the "glimmerings" of an environmental psychology, the development of the field during the 1960's was sharply accelerated. And it was during this decade that the term *environmental psychology* as the designation for the field began to be more commonly used than such terms as *architectural psychology* and *man–environment relations,* among others. The term *architectural psychology* was first used to describe cooperative research activity between architects and psychologists in the very late 1950's and the early 1960's at the University of Utah. Even to this day, British psychologists and sociologists, like David Canter, Terrence Lee, and others, still use this term to describe their cooperative activity with architects. *Man–environment relations* was a term used to name an interdisciplinary environmental program established at Pennsylvania State University in the late 1960's by Raymond Studer. The designation *environmental psychology* was first used in 1964 at a conference (Ittelson, 1964) and, as we noted above, has been readily adopted by other psychologists and other behavioral scientists. Still other terms were used for brief periods of time, such as *psychogeography,* but are rarely seen now.

Let us examine now what happened in the 1960's by looking at the major writings and research conferences held and the creation of newsletters, journals, professional associations, and training programs. By 1965, some significant writings and research had appeared that attracted other behavioral scientists and design professionals to the field. Clearly a classic work was Alexander's volume *Notes on the Synthesis of Form,* published in 1964. Alexander, an architect with computer and behavioral-science training, conceived of the design of environmental settings as derived from the functions or goals of the various institutional structures in that setting. At about the same time, the architect James Fitch (1965) took the position that architectural design and aesthetic decisions had to rest on the biological needs and cultural experiences of the user. Also responding to the work of Alexander was Raymond Studer, who agreed with him in some respects but differed in others. Studer (1966) saw needs or goals expressed in terms of patterns of behavior as the correct unit of analysis for designing and programming human physical settings.

Meanwhile the growth of an environmental psychology was being mobilized by behavioral scientists and architects concerned with more specific environmental problems. The work of John Calhoun on crowding and territoriality in rats and other animal groups played a critical role in this respect. Although the basis for his environmental emphasis in this research began as early as 1956, it was in the early 1960's, that his concept of "behavioral sink" became widely known (Calhoun, 1962, 1964). Probably as influential was the anthropologist Edward Hall (1959, 1966), whose focus was on the anthropology of space or *proxemics,* the term used to define the interrelated observations and theories of how people use space. For Hall there are fixed features of space representing the underlying normative means for organizing the activities of individuals and groups, for example, the rooms inside a house or the public spaces of buildings. Cultures vary in this respect as they do in their use of the semifixed features of space or in their use and arrangement of furniture. Perhaps what deserves the greatest attention in Hall's formulation is his emphasis on how individuals establish distances from each other during social interaction as a function of their cultural setting, the nature of the interaction, and their social-status relationships.

By the second half of the decade, the growing interest of geographers in the behavioral aspects of broad geographical settings became apparent. Thus in 1967, the geographer David Lowenthal edited the monograph *Environmental Perception and Behavior,* which included environmental research by geographers as well as architects. Clearly we cannot cite all of the significant work that developed during the 1960's, but it is important to identify at least by name the other important researchers during this period: Altman and Haythorn (1967), Esser, Chamberlain, Chapple, and Kline (1965), Kira (1966), Gans (1959, 1961, 1962), Gutman (1965–1966), Winkel and Sasonoff (1965), and Izumi (1965). Of course, deserving of special mention is the work on ecological psychology developed and carried on by Barker and his associates (1963, 1968). While not concerned directly with the physical setting and far more with its social and cultural definition as a basis for organizing human activities, ecological psychology directed attention to the properties of the physical environment and its continuing study in natural, ongoing settings.

By 1967, the architectural psychology group at the University of Utah was publishing the *Architectural Psychology Newsletter,* which later combined with a newsletter published by Esser and his associates to become *Man–Environment Systems.* Esser now also serves as the editor of this newer endeavor, which reviews research, meetings, and other activities relevant to problems in environmental psychology. It also serves as an organ of the Association for the Study of Man–Environment Relations. Still another newletter publication with more or less the same purposes is the *Architectural Psychology Newsletter,* which was started in 1969 by Honikman, Bridge, and Lee in England and which is still periodically published. And as late as 1974, the first issue of *Environmental Sociology Newsletter* was published by Charles Wolfe in Washington, D.C. In terms of general publications during the 1960's, theoretical and empirical papers in environmental psychology were published in various established journals of the design professions and the behavioral sciences. Viewed against the variety of other kinds of research published in these journals, the environmental papers published were clearly only a tiny fraction of the total. However, at various times particular journals devoted entire issues of their journals to such papers. This was true of the *Journal of Social Issues* (1966) and *Representative Research in Social Psychology* (1973). Thus the environmental sociologist Robert Gutman published a paper on "Site Planning and Social Behavior" in this *J.S.I.* issue. This issue also included significant papers by Calhoun, Wohlwill, and others. It is important to note that the single paper that probably served to introduce environmental psychology to the widest audience of psychologists was the Wohlwill paper on "The Emerging Discipline of Environmental Psychology" that appeared in the *American Psychologist* in 1970. And similarly there can be no question that Milgram's paper on "The Experience of Living Cities," appearing in *Science* in 1970, also served to bring considerable attention to the field.

By the end of the 1960s', however, environmental psychology had truly come into its own with the creation of the journal *Environment and Behavior* edited by Gary Winkel. The variety of papers published truly reflect the interdisciplinary nature of the field, and its readership has grown considerably since the publication of its first issue in 1969. Also important in this respect, but giving far more attention to the thinking and research of architects and designers, is the *Journal of Architectural Research* published in Washington, D.C., by the Royal Institute of British Architects and the American Institute of Architects. The first issue appeared in 1971. Still a third journal is *Design and Environment,* which began publication in 1969 and, like the *Journal of Architectural Research,* gives emphasis primarily to the needs of practitioners in these fields.

During the 1960's various conferences in environmental research were initiated, with some now occurring on a regular basis. Taylor, Bailey, and Branch at the University of Utah held a second conference on architectural psychology in 1966. In England, David Canter organized and later edited the proceedings of the Dalandhui Conference in Architectural Psychology (1970). This conference is now held on a biannual basis, with subsequent conferences held in Kingston (Honikman, 1971) and Surrey (Canter and Lee, 1974). What began as a loosely organized group of architects, planners, designers, and behavioral scientists, holding their first conference in 1969 and designating themselves as the Environmental Design Research Associates (EDRA), has emerged as the first truly organized effort of researchers and practitioners in the United States interested in human–environmental problems. The organization continues to hold annual conferences with each succeeding year, giving evidence of an increasing membership involved in the exchange of information and the formation of new research-and-design networks at these conferences.

In terms of training programs at the graduate and undergraduate levels, there were important developments in the 1960's and 1970's. However, growth of the field in this respect has been far less than expected. Clearly environmental psychology courses given in departments of psychology, sociology, architecture, and design grew in number during this period. Although Altman who is at Utah and continues to be highly productive as an environmental psychologist, the jointly sponsored master's level program in architectural psychology that began with Bailey, Branch, and Taylor has apparently been phased out. On the other hand, there are specializations at the graduate or undergraduate levels in environmental psychology at the City University of New York, the University of British Columbia in Vancouver, the University of California at Irvine, and Arizona State University, and the Department of Psychology at the University of Arizona at Tucson is just initiating such a program at the graduate and undergraduate levels. Courses on environmental research are also being taught at M.I.T., Harvard, the University of California at Berkeley and Los Angeles, the University of North Carolina, the University of Michigan, the University of Surrey (England), and the University of Kansas at Lawrence. This training is taking place in architecture, sociology, urban planning, and psychology departments. The joint program efforts of the departments of geography and psychology at Clark University seem to have slowed down, although work in environmental research continues there.

Worthy of special mention is the Ph.D. specialization in environmental psychology established at the Graduate School and University Center of the City University of New York in 1968. Also important in this respect are the broader and still more interdisciplinary undergraduate and Ph.D. programs in man–environment relations established at Penn State by Raymond Studer in the late 1960's. Whether these and other efforts will continue to develop remains to be seen, given the funding problems facing most universities and the fierce competition among specializations, disciplines, and schools for available resources.

At this point, we are ready to conclude our brief history by looking at some major publications and events of the last 4 or 5 years. Of considerable significance in this respect is the first major reading volume, *Environmental Psychology: Man and His Physical Settings,* edited by Proshansky, Ittelson, and Rivlin and published in 1970. A revision of the volume was published in 1976. Since that time other readers have appeared, including one sponsored by the American Psychological Association entitled *Environment and the Social Sciences: Perspectives and Applications,* edited by Wohlwill and Carson and published in 1972 (see also Moos and Insel 1974; Gutman, 1972; and others).

Not to be overlooked is the volume on *Personal Space* written by Robert Sommer and published in 1969. Here Sommer reviews a good deal of his own research and touches on many relevant problem areas, such as privacy, territoriality, and space-related behaviors in specific physical settings. And in 1974 a set of readings on theory and empirical research relevant to the problems of *Crowding and Behavior* was edited by Loo. In this same year the first textbook on environmental psychology was published by Ittelson, Proshansky, Rivlin, and Winkel. And finally it is important to note that the American Psychological Association has established a Task Force on Environment and Behavior, which has organized an information-exchange effort in the field facilitated by symposia, special meetings, and selected publications in relation to the APA's annual meeting.

Undoubtedly we have omitted some significant events, people, and research efforts in this brief history. Quite early in the 1960's, Leon Pastalan at the University of Michigan was involved in important research on physical settings of geriatric patients, and on this same problem, some of the earliest work and sustained effort was and is being carried out by Powell Lawton (1974). Finally special reference must be given to Oscar Newman, whose research on *Defensible Space* focuses on the design of housing projects in relation to crime and security in urban settings (1973).

It should be evident that with all that we have presented in this history of the development of environmental psychology, its boundaries and basic approaches remain blurred. In part, this may be the fault of the rapid-fire account we have presented. However, even if we had slowed down and had given the reader more discussion and detail, it is very likely that he or she would still find the picture unclear. There are two reasons for this: first, the complex interdisciplinary nature of the field; and second, its relative infancy as a scientific field of inquiry despite its meteoric growth in little more than a decade. To some extent, the picture will clear with respect to the nature of the field when we consider the factors that gave rise to it and the value-methodological orientations in its approach that express the influence of some of these factors.

Factors Underlying the Emergence of Environmental Psychology

Now that we have considered the people, places, and events out of which the field of environmental psychology arose, it is important to look back again, this time to ask, "Why?" What factors accounted for the emergence and the development of the field? Of course, in no sense can we expect to answer this question in any complete sense, nor even with the certainty that we have identified the essential determinants. On the other hand, some of these determinants can only be described as "self-evident," and in these instances "certainty" is more or less assured. The value of an analysis of the determinants or causes that gave rise to environmental psychology is twofold: first, it provides a basis for understanding the nature and direction the field took during its first 15 years, and indeed what directions it *might* continue to take for the next decade or two; and second, it is only in the broader context of considering its underlying determinants that the kaleidoscopic nature, the multitude of approaches, and the very intense and rapid development of the field can be understood.

There was a series of events in the decade following World War II that combined in a way to exert very strong pressures on architects, designers, and others in the design professions to produce a great many structures for many purposes. The primary sources of these pressures were the high-level government and private administrators responsible for the unprecedented need for new physical facilities in the form of schools, hospitals, private homes, office buildings, mental institutions, transportation systems, high-rise housing projects, theaters, factories, and other structures. As a result the environmental ethos of American life came very sharply into view: an ever increasing urbanism rooted in an expanding suburban setting engulfing a more densely contrived inner-city life, all of which was being fostered by and having consequences for a growing modern technology. The demands for—and the actually accelerated pace of—changes in living, working, and leisure-time activities in American life reached the point where those who were putting up the money, or at least were responsible for spending it, began to seek assurance and evidence that a "better life" would result. For the school superintendent, a more "educational" school was needed; for the hospital director, the facilities providing the best medical care; for the housing-development director, everything the resident would need to be comfortable and happy; and so on.

A common concern underlying all of these demands was the desire to ensure that, in a complex and bureaucratic society in which electronic devices, rapid speed, and growing uniformity portended a highly ritualized and impersonal life, somehow or other a humanistic existence would be preserved for those who lived in the society. In effect such concepts as "bureaucracy," "organizational man," "prefabricated," "data bank," and "high rise" seemed to echo louder and louder the cry of a new "mass society" in which speed, impersonality, and uniformity increasingly made difficult the development of strong friendships, interpersonal relationships with meaning, and cohesive group-life. Somehow architects and other design professionals had to provide a better balance between technological advances and achievements on the one hand and social and personal needs on the other.

The push for people-oriented spaces and places in modern life came from within as well as from without. A careful review of the value orientations of the design professions would undoubtedly reveal that probably from the very beginning there were always those architects, designers, and landscape specialists who saw human needs and individual experiences as the value nexus of their design efforts rather than simply aesthetic satisfactions and symbolic meanings. As is often the case, the views of dissidents, mavericks, and value deviants are not heard unless they are joined by many, many other voices outside the profession that demand they be heard. Thus the fact that architect-designers such as Izumi (1970), Fitch (1965), Alexander (1964), and Lynch (1960) were poised and ready to act out new professional values in response to growing external pressures consistent with their own views was not enough. And no one knew it better than these dissidents, because it was they who challenged the traditional underlying assumptions being made about the needs, values, feelings, and conceptions of people in relation to the places and settings that defined their day-to-day existence; and it was they who recognized and faced the need for input from psychologists, sociologists, anthropologists, and other behavioral-science specialists. However, by the late 1950's and the early 1960's, the stage was set. Following World War II—with the hue and cry for growth and change we have already noted—the behavioral sciences extended the scope of their theoretical conceptions and methodological approaches to the point that they were indeed willing and able to come to grips with major social problems such as poverty, learning disabilities, ethnic prejudice, international conflicts, and urban stress. If there was to be a "new society," then indeed the paths to be taken in the search for human dignity and individual fulfillment were to be shaped and realized in part by the analysis and findings of the behavioral sciences.

It is probably true that a poised and eager group of behavioral scientists and design professionals, aided and abetted by the demands of those decision makers who controlled the funding resources, provided the right mix for the emergence of an "environmental psychology." What is not so clear is whether that mix could have jelled so quickly and decisively without the advent of the environmental crisis of the late 1960's. Earth Day in 1970 was merely the culmination of the environmental crisis that had been edging into public consciousness beginning in the mid 1960's. Suddenly the sporadic and relatively ineffective protests of some environmental groups concerned with urban blight, the desecration of wilderness areas, and the increasing tinsel-like, neon-lighted culture of the American city gave way to a wave of public protest and public concern. A threat to human sensibilities is one thing. A threat to human life is still another. Air pollution and food and water contamination, along with the hasty and therefore reckless introduction of new chemical compounds, electronic devices, and other technological innovations, all carried with them the stark reality of a great loss of human life.

Far less threatening but far more difficult to come to grips with were matters of human dignity. There was a growing awareness that the quality of urban life went well beyond the question of human survival. A physical setting in which the individual's day-to-day existence robbed him of his right to realize his full capacity as a human being because of crowding, intense noise, physical inconveniences, and still other stresses clearly cast doubt on the value of technological and scientific progress. But the question of human dignity went well beyond the matter of living in urban settings that were clean, efficient, and safe. There was the matter, for example, of increasing numbers of individuals' being forced into smaller and smaller physical settings in which efficiency, speed, and uniformity assumed greater importance than individual variation, freedom of choice, and aesthetic expression. What the "environmental crisis" in human dignity did, then, was to focus, extend, and intensify the interest of a small but increasing number of design professionals and behavioral scientists in the problems of the relationships between human behavior and experience and the nature of physical settings, whether at the level of a school classroom, a city street, an apartment house, or an entire cosmopolitan area. And of course it also directed the attention of many more administrators and environmental managers to the need to consider these kinds of environmental problems as well as those that threatened human life.

Without detracting from the singular importance of the environmental crisis for the development of the field of environmental psychology, it is important to stress the significance of two other determinants in this development. One, indeed, gave impetus to the environmental movement itself. We are referring to the college-campus student uprisings during the late 1960's and early 1970's. While undergraduates—and in some instances graduate students—expressed their dismay over the war in Vietnam, the violation of the civil rights of minorities, and the inexorable and unyielding social ills of our society, no less a key issue was the precedence of research over teaching, made even more profound by the lack of *relevance* in both. What they campaigned for were courses, experiences, and even research endeavors (nonmilitary) that would give them a better understanding of the day-to-day political, social, and economic worlds in which they lived; and this understanding, they believed, would increase the probability of their bringing about, through active participation and intervention as citizens, a better existence for all groups in society.

It is easy enough to look back now and be amused by, if not critical of, the open-ended influence that the concept of "relevance" had on the training given graduate and undergraduate students in the various behavioral-science fields. On the other hand, one should not ignore the very important positive aspects of this influence, including the long-needed review of these training programs. Furthermore the emphasis on "relevance" tended to legitimize, for many hesitant and overly cautious behavioral scientists trained in the laboratory tradition of "pure research," the possibility of studying major social problems in the real-life context in which they occurred and indeed to follow Lewin's (1948) dictum of doing research that was "theoretically meaningful and socially useful." The physical settings of modern urban communities—with all the problems that living in these communities entailed—were a conspicious part of this context. If crowding, urban decay, loss of privacy, and water and air pollution were not relevant, then no other problems could be.

Whatever the lure of the "relevance" of the real world for some behavioral scientists—particularly in the fields of social psychology and sociology—it did not represent the sole influence that caused them to venture out into that world. The writers can speak with some authority only about what was happening in their own field, social psychology, but there is evidence that other behavioral-science areas were deriving similar results. By the late 1970's, there were more than a few indications that social psychologists had failed to deliver the many promised solutions required to bring about the "great society." Furthermore the research process itself was being subjected to serious scrutiny because of ethical issues being raised about research done on individuals and social groups. To make matters worse, some behavioral scientists began to question whether the research findings produced in a spate of experimental laboratory studies following World War II had any real value for the analysis and understanding of the complex social problems that they were now being asked "to solve" (Katz, 1972). The consequence of all this was a malaise among social psychologists and other behavioral scientists: a sense of futility about the research being done largely because of the growing belief that the field was not going to "arrive" as a science achieving a cumulative, and therefore useful, body of knowledge (Berkowitz, 1970; Smith, 1972; Elms, 1975; Proshansky, 1976). And at the core of this scientific anomie was the apparent failure of the laboratory-experimental paradigm for the study of human problems. Where to turn and what to do? We can only answer for a small but increasing number of social, personality, and experimental psychologists. There was not only the lure of relevance and the real world embodied in the environmental crisis, but there was also the dissatisfaction with their own fields of interest and what they had produced in the context of a scientific model that failed to realize its promise. In effect, not only were they pulled by the possibility of a new approach, they were pushed into it.

Value-Methodological Properties of the Field

Early in the discussion we made it clear that the field of environmental psychology cannot be defined by means of a particular theoretical structure. Although increasing, theory and empirical research in this field have yet to come even close to the productive level of the other behavioral-science fields. And systematic theory in the field has moved at a snail's pace. Theoretical developments have been sparse and fragmentary in substance (Proshansky, 1973). Environmental psychology is and probably will remain for some time an amorphous field of scientific inquiry in which highly diverse patterns of empirical research are tied together by very loose and unconnected strands of theoretical conceptualization.

What this means is that at best it is possible to define the field only in substantive or operational terms, that is, to distinguish the activities of various groups of researchers in terms of the kinds of problems they study and the types of empirical strategies they employ in attacking these problems. Given the variation and diversity of efforts in this respect, little would be gained from a close look at the scientific fabric we call environmental psychology. If we stand back, however, and view this fabric at a distance, there are to be seen woven into it some fundamental strands in approach that add greater definition if not clearer boundaries to the field. We refer to these strands as *value-methodological properties,* and while not all of them will pertain to the empirical approaches of every environmental psychologist, one or more of them in various combinations do pertain.

Given the pattern of influences underlying the emergence of environmental psychology, it should come as no surprise that a basic orientation of many researchers in this field is a direct and clearly stated concern with solving environmental problems in order to achieve a better society. Such solutions should enable the members of this society to create environmental settings most congruent with their values and social aspirations.

It is important not to confuse this value commitment with the rather trite conception of science as theory-oriented, basic research concerned first with the accumulation of knowledge, which is then applied to the solving of complex human problems. For the environmental psychologist, the traditional distinction between "pure" and "applied" research is not a fruitful or valuable distinction. Nor is the related assumption that the behavioral sciences must *first* establish general principles of human behavior and experiences and that it is only after such principles have been established that complex human problems and issues can be solved.

The value commitment of the environmental psychologist to a "better world" through systematic investigation is expressed in the problem-centered focus of the new field. Theory and research begin and end with particular human–environment problems that characterize a society—at any level of social organization—at a given period of time. It is by means of such problem-centered research that appropriate theoretical principles will be established and the solutions to these problems made evident or at least approximated. In this sense it can be said from the point of view of the environmental psychologist that all applied research is basic research and all basic research is applied research.

In its basic emphasis on problem-centered research that will lead to better human–environment relations, environmental psychology has to assume a number of other major methodological properties as a field of scientific inquiry. Since the problems involved in these relations are rooted in the interplay of factors at the psychological, group, and societal levels of human organization, and since at each of these levels situational, historical, and cultural events condition this interplay, environmental psychology almost by definition had to be interdisciplinary in its research orientation. Whatever the conceptual, heuristic, and practical values in distinguishing among various kinds of analysis as different fields of scientific inquiry, a problem-centered research program cannot afford the luxury of this type of research approach. What must be emphasized is that as an interdisciplinary research activity concerned with environmental problems, the field must necessarily include the conceptions and basic assumptions of those in the design professions. Since the environmental psychologist seeks to establish the relationships between people and their physical world, particularly in the form of their built environment, then the assumptions and methods of those who define, implement, and change this environment over time are critical inputs in the attempt to determine these relationships through systematic research.

It should be evident that the problem-centered, interdisciplinary orientation of environmental psychology makes its primary if not exclusive arena of research the real-life settings in which individuals eat, sleep, work, play, learn, recuperate from illness, express their grief, listen to music, and do other things. And it is these basic methodological orientations expressed in their emphasis on the real-life setting of person–environment interactions that give rise to still other, more specific, value-methodological properties of the field.

Thus a move into real-world settings in order to study individuals' reactions to and relationships with their physical settings has carried with it a fundamental constraint insofar as research and analysis are concerned: the integrity of the person–environment events have to be maintained at any cost. These events must be defined, analysed, and observed in the natural, ongoing context in which they occur. What is to be scrupulously avoided, regardless of circumstances, are distortions of these events engendered by the research process itself, extending from such matters as the role of the researcher in the natural setting to attempts to manipulate environmental settings in order to meet the standards of "scientifically controlled" investigations. To some extent environmental psychologists have received fair warning about the need to maintain the integrity of events that are of interest to them. The problem of the demand characteristics of social psychological experiments in the laboratory was clearly in evidence in the early 1960's (Rosenthal, 1966), and by the late 1960's, the failure of an experimental social-psychology concerned with social perception, social interaction, and small-group processes to establish even a few valid principles based on highly controlled and contrived investigations was fully revealed (Katz, 1972). When confronted with challenges from practitioners, community leaders, and government officials to render insights into, if not solve, major social issues in the late 1960's, behavioral scientists representing more than a few of the fields of psychology found their generalizations and indeed even their research techniques far less than useful, if not almost useless. Although the "names were the same" the problems and issues they had studied in the laboratory and outside of it under highly controlled conditions held little relationship to the problems and issues that were of concern in the real-life settings. The original real-life issues had been so "peeled," "cleaned up," and rendered researchable that in the final analysis these problems were no longer recognizable, so that the findings, concepts, and methods of this type of research had no generalizability to nonlaboratory settings.

The emphasis on the integrity of events or phenomena in environmental psychology involved more than the fear of failure. It took this direction because its problem-centered focus confronted its initial enthusiasts with a number of givens that made it quite evident where the path to success was to be found. First, it was patently evident that psychologists and sociologists had virtually ignored the physical environment in their research and analysis of social interactions and social processes, other than making programmatic statements that it was there and that it was a condition necessary and essential for such interactions and processes to take place. Since there were no available data of any kind, the environmental psychologist had to begin with person–environment events in pure state, so to speak. The first and indeed critical task is to observe and define the dimensions of these events and the problems related to them as they occur and are experienced by the individuals and the groups involved. To take but one example, there literally existed no systematic behavioral-science data on the problem of human privacy until roughly 5–8 years ago.

A research orientation that requires maintaining the integrity of real-life person–environment relationships implies still another methodological property of the field. Part of that requirement is a recognition of the human characteristics of the setting occupant: a goal-directed and purposive organism continually monitored by cognitive and affective processes, these processes, in turn, influencing and being influenced by a physical setting that itself reveals enduring properties and continual change. What this means is that attempts to establish general principles of human behavior and experience based on abstractions that transcend the evident properties of people and places in given situations was next to useless. A model in which physical settings constituted stimuli or stimulus patterns and individuals making responses or having response patterns, or any other variation of the S–R paradigm, was completely inconsistent with a problem-focused environmental psychology. What was needed was a model or approach in which the integrity of the evident properties of people and places was maintained during the examination and interpretation of the stable and changing transactions between them.

This brings us to a fifth value-methodological orientation of the environmental psychologist. The integrity of person–environment relationships involves maintaining not only the reality of the processes involved but the *content* or substance of these processes as well. To understand people–place interrelationships and interactions, the researcher must be concerned with questions of what people, carrying out what activities, for what purposes, in what physical setting with what properties of its own. As a consequence of the goal of psychology to establish universal principles of human behavior, social, personality, general or experimental, and other fields of psychology have emphasized motivational, cognitive, and affective processes rather than the specific content of those psychological-response systems. In social psychology, for example, far more attention has been given to the structure, organization, and functional nature of social attitudes than to the substantive nature of the social attitudes that indeed influence our responses to other people. In small-group research, it was the dynamics of group structure and process and not what groups carrying out what activities and functions in what kinds of social and physical contexts that determined the nature and definition of the research undertaken.

It should be evident from the previous discussion that environmental psychologists see little value in the laboratory–experimental paradigm. There is more involved here, however, than the need to maintain the integrity of the phenomena being studied. The underlying assumption of the paradigm that one can establish causal relationships by varying one variable (or even a number of variables) while holding all others constant and then determining the particular effects of this variable runs directly counter to the view taken by environmental researchers. Person–environment interactions are viewed as rooted in a patterning of enduring and changing relationships between the properties of the physical setting and characteristic behaviors and experiences of the individuals. The objective, then, is to establish the nature of these patterned relationships through an appropriate methodology that seeks to maintain the integrity of environmental events.

What are required, then, are neither methods of experimental control nor sophisticated techniques of quantification. Perhaps with the increasing development of the field and the accumulation of knowledge, precise quantitative relationships established through systematic experiments may have a special role to play in detailing our understanding of particular problems. What is required now, however, is to establish the descriptive properties and relationships of person–environmental transactions by means of systematic observations and other forms of unobtrusive recordings of these events and their changes over time. For the environmental psychologist, qualitative accounts of people and places and their relationships to each other in the form of case histories, longitudinal observations, open-ended descriptions by participants, and visual and auditory records of what has and will go on are basic methodological tools.

There are two rather intriguing aspects of the task of examining and determining the relationships between the individual's behavior and experience and his physical setting. First, a great deal of this behavior and, indeed, even what is being experienced takes place without the person's being consciously aware of its occurrence and influence. Not walking into a wall of a room or walking around a chair usually takes place because an "awareness" or "knowing" that they are there has been established and is effective without requiring the individual's conscious awareness of his seeing, judging, and avoiding them. Thus, as has been pointed out many times, interviewing people about what they think, feel, or usually do in a given physical setting can be a hazardous procedure. As in the case of attitudes, values, and beliefs that individuals either do not hold or are not consciously aware that they hold, interviews of such individuals often lead to responses that are "creatively produced," usually because the respondent thinks he should make them since this is what he thinks the interviewer wants or what most other people would probably say.

Of course changes in a physical setting increase the individual's awareness of where he is and what is happening, whether the lights suddenly go out, the temperature drops sharply, or someone plays a radio very loudly. Furthermore as he or she carries out particular activities that require and indeed depend on physical-setting supports, even for the most routine of activities, the substantive features of one or more aspects of this setting drift in and out of conscious awareness. Sitting down to read, we do often consciously select the place, the position of the chair, and the lighting; the same is true of cooking a meal, having a private conversation, taking a shower, and so on. The essential consideration here is that at varying levels of momentary awareness the individual always knows where he or she is. The significance of this fact becomes clear if we think once again of contrived laboratory or even field situations. Except for extraordinary and unthinkable measures of deception, there is no way in the laboratory setting or in contrived field situations of substituting for the individual's immediate awareness of the reality of the particular physical setting that he or she happens to be in. It may be possible to get individuals to believe they are actually part of some "real" work group or that they are taking a test that measures their intellectual ability, but it is impossible to get them to believe through systematic instructions and descriptions that they are at home, or in a crowded subway train, or in their doctor's waiting room, when in reality they are in a research laboratory or a field setting. Just the process of *getting them not to believe* what they know better than anyone else—that is, where they are and what they are doing there—immediately invalidates the attempts to create "their reality" for research purposes.

All behavioral sciences are predicated on the assumption that regularities are expressed both in the interplay of significant variables in given settings at a given time and in the changing character of these variables and their relationships over extended periods of time. Yet to a large extent time as a significant dimension of human behavior and experience has been ignored in the theory and research of psychologists, sociologists, and cultural anthropologists. Ostensibly, given the costs involved, the nature of scientific research work, and still other reasons, it is easier to study human behavior and experience at given points in time than to attempt studies over lengthy periods of time. Yet this is an escape the environmental psychologist cannot afford, that is, not if he desires to study person–environment events in their natural settings, while exerting every attempt to maintain the integrity of these events. Included in this integrity is the time structure of person–environment interactions. This means that systematic research must be designed so that the course of interactions between persons and their physical environment over time is part of the research strategy. This, then, is still another essential methodological orientation of the environmental psychologist.

It is important to reiterate at this point what we said earlier about the various value-methodological properties that characterize the approach of the environmental psychologist. While all of them would be embraced by some environmental psychologists, including the authors, only one or more of them would be acceptable to still others involved in the study of physical settings. While the variations in approach among all environmental psychologists are undoubtedly many, there is a key issue or factor that divides them into at least two major groups. It can be said with relative certainty that almost all, if not all of them, subscribe to a problem-centered, interdisciplinary orientation in which particular problems in, or relevant to, real-life settings are to be studied. The need to resolve these problems and thereby provide a better physical world or built environment for members of our society is a commonly held value among, as we said, almost all, if not all, environmental psychologists.

The difference occurs over the more specific value-methodological properties we discussed earlier. For some environmental psychologists, the designation of these properties has far more to do with a shift from sociocultural problems—for example, small-group process and family conflict—to those focused on physical settings. In making the shift, these psychologists see no need to forsake the established methodologies, including the laboratory–experimental model they have always employed when carrying out research on basic problems that identified them as a "social psychologists," "urban sociologists," "clinical research psychologists," or "personality researchers." The shift for them is far more a matter of the particular kind of problems studied than of the nature of the methodology to be employed.

Other environmental psychologists, including the authors, see more involved in the new field than a shift of an interdisciplinary, problem-centered approach from one set of problems (e.g., changing community attitudes) to another (e.g., privacy and territoriality in apartment dwelling). The other value-methodological properties described earlier—including the emphasis on content, the integrity of person–environment settings in research and analysis, the goal-directed and cognitively organized person as the unit of analysis, and the importance of the time dimension, as well as the need to describe and search out patterned relationships between individuals and their physical settings—clearly suggest the need for a new scientific approach to knowledge other than the paradigm underlying the advances in the natural and physical sciences.

The Future of Environmental Psychology: Some Analysis and Speculation

The forecasting of the future of environmental psychology as a field of scientific inquiry is like the forecasting of most complex institutional systems, a hazardous undertaking to say the least. As we have already indicated, it emerged from an array of determinants that have far less to do with behavioral-science priorities dictated by systematic theoretical and empirical developments than with institutional demands generated by a

changing and troubled society. We can expect that its future will undoubtedly be subject to similar types of influences. Given the present state of the
behavioral sciences—that is, their achieved level of accumulated
knowledge—and the general methodological orientation we have described
above as characterizing environmental psychology, one thing is certain:
there is little if any chance that some startling breakthrough by environmental psychologists will establish its theoretical and empirical structure
and, therefore, its significance for the understanding of human behavior
and experience. On the other hand, the field may grow and indeed establish itself not because of any "breakthrough" but as a result of a still more
accelerated technology, an intensified urban life, and other problems of
modern society that require continued investigation of the planning and
the consequences of the built environment.

In the various chapters that follow in this book, the trends in thinking
and research in environmental psychology will undoubtedly be revealed.
Furthermore there now exist a number of texts that provide extensive
reviews of theory and findings for the diversity of problem areas that
characterize the field (Moos and Insel, 1974; Gutman, 1972; Wohlwill and
Carson, 1972; Proshansky, Ittelson, and Rivlin, 1970, 1976). Given all this,
little would be gained by a look at the field in terms of such a review,
however brief it might be. What would be useful—particularly before we
examine the future of environmental psychology—would be to ask what
relationships its research endeavors must necessarily have to the design
professions. Said differently, we must ask what practical functions environmental research can serve with respect to these professions. After all,
if there are critical environmental problems on the one hand and the purpose of environmental psychologists to help resolve them by providing
knowledge on the other, then the data requirements of the design professions regarding the relationships between people and physical settings
must be met to activate research purposes with existing problems. Meeting
these requirements should improve the capabilities of architects, designers,
and individuals and groups generally to plan and to execute their plans by
a more effective technology.

To speak of a society's technological processes is to refer to its means of
transforming *knowledge* about the physical environment into *instruments of
control* over this environment in order to achieve its *goals*. It is evident,
therefore, that the first task of an environmental psychology is to provide a
knowledge base from which may be derived guidelines for implementing
the purposes of these processes. Knowledge of the dynamic interrelationships among components of environmental settings should provide the
guidelines for implementing these goals by means of the patterns of action
necessary to achieve them. If we look at the present array of research
findings, we are hard-pressed to find any that fulfill this function. On the
other hand, there is evidence of at least a rudimentary beginning in the
form of research that explores the meaning and implications of concepts

such as social impact assessment (Wolf, 1975), personal space (Leibman, 1970), crowding (Saegert, 1975), social space (Buttimer, 1972), spatial cognition (Downs and Stea, 1973), and life styles (Michelson, 1970).

If research on such concepts is needed to provide the understanding that will transform our technological goals into the patterns of action necessary to meet these goals, then this kind of research necessarily serves another function in the design process. It helps to delimit the range of practical action fruitful in the meeting of our technological goals. Through an understanding of the dynamics of environmental settings, it should be possible to discriminate between those actions that will or will not be instrumental in achieving these goals. As an example, one can point to research that has been performed on the traditional design elements of public housing (layout of public spaces) and their relationship to personal security (Yancy, 1971; Newman, 1972). Similar research has been performed on playgrounds (Haywood, Rothenberg, and Beasley, 1974), subways (Bronzaft, Dubrow, and O'Hanlon, in press), and psychiatric hospitals (Ittelson, Proshansky, and Rivlin, 1970).

A third important function of environmental research for the design professions is its potential for explaining why particular technological strategies or approaches fail to meet their anticipated goals. Having methods and concepts for exploring the relationships between components of settings should help to explain why certain space-related activities and functions have been successful or unsuccessful. At the moment, the only way to investigate the consequences of a large-scale environmental project is to examine the project after it has already been built, and this function represents one of the most significant contributions of environmental psychology to the design profession and those responsible for these projects. This function includes explicitly examining the behavioral and social goals of the project, evaluating the project in terms of its ability to meet these goals of the project, evaluating the project in terms of its ability to meet these goals, and investigating the underlying processes that account for these goals' being met or not met. Some notable examples of this type of research concern the evaluation of housing projects (Cooper, 1975; Zeisel and Griffin, 1975; and Zehner, Burby, and Weiss, 1974) and psychiatric hospitals (Rivlin and Wolfe, 1972).

Still another function of environmental research is to expand our ability to anticipate the full range of the impact of any technological changes we undertake. Traditionally the objectives of environmental changes have been formulated only in terms of the immediate goals of the project. It is now commonly recognized that this is a very narrow conception of the requirements of socially acceptable planning. Technological innovations can no longer be evaluated in isolation from the larger environmental setting in which they are introduced. The full range of the impact of modern technology on the environment must be considered. This area of research is generally termed *environmental–impact assessment,* and it is undoubtedly one of the most difficult and challenging fields of inquiry. Theoretical and empirical investigations in this area are rather recent (Wolf, 1974, 1975), but its social importance has already been institutionalized in Federal legislation (National Environmental Protection Act of 1969, P.L. 91-190) and in similar state legislation. The roots of this type of research can be found in investigations of the impact of urban renewal and highway construction on residential communities (e.g., Fellman and Brandt, 1973; Fried, 1972; Hartman, 1974).

The four functions of environmental research we have described up to this point lead to the need for the development of a fifth and perhaps an even more basic function, namely, establishing methods and concepts that will provide a more rational basis for the definition and selection of our technological goals. In this regard, two sets of problems come immediately to mind. It has been pointed out that scientists, planners, and technological experts do more than merely put the goals of the public into operation. They also interpret the goals of the public, define the instruments for obtaining these goals, and describe the implications of these plans. It is evident that these interpretations are rooted in their specialized views of the world as determined by their professional training and their institutional positions (Ackerman, Ackerman, Sawyer, and Henderson, 1974; Barker, 1972; Sewell, 1971). It would be surprising if it was otherwise. A second set of problems is no less evident: the various groups in society are rarely unanimous in their definition of problems or their statement of priorities, nor is the impact of technological processes without differential effects on various groups (Althoff and Greig, 1974; Wolf, 1975). The fifth function, then, of environmental research looms as a critical one, for if, in fact, technological or environmental goals are not rationally based, what follows in terms of actions or means loses its rational significance regardless of the validity of the criterion employed.

What does the future look like for environmental psychology? Clearly no one can really predict with any sense of certainty. At best, we can indicate some favorable signs for its continued growth and development and, as one might expect, just as many unfavorable signs. Such an analysis, however, must be put into proper perspective. A fundamental question that must be answered before any analysis is made concerns the meaning of "the growth of a scientific field of inquiry." Clearly a field can grow because it does more research, is found in many more universities, increases its number of researchers, gets increasing amounts of funding, and in general produces more papers, books, research reports, and so on. Such growth may be necessary for scientific growth, but by itself it is not sufficient. Clearly this has been the case in many of the behavioral sciences over the last 50 years. By *scientific growth* we mean that advancement in theory and information that expresses itself in the cumulation of scientific knowledge about a particular problem or a set of problems. Such knowledge becomes a basis not only for the understanding of events but for their alteration in directions consistent with the expressed personal and social values of a society.

The forecasting we will engage in below will represent the analysis of influence that will have consequences for environmental psychology as an organized institutional endeavor rather than as a particular system of scientific knowledge. In effect, at this stage in its development it is important to ask whether it can survive as a new, interdisciplinary field. Its validity—theoretically and empirically—can be judged only if it survives and has that time and those conditions necessary to "test" its value as a science. And yet even if that time is adequate and the resources for research ample, the eventual significance of the field is not rooted simply in the validity of its own underlying assumptions. Because in its problem-centered focus it depends on the advances made in the other behavioral sciences—particularly psychology, sociology, and anthropology—however bright its future appears at this point, it is necessarily tied to the scientific future of these fields of inquiry.

In many ways, the future of environmental psychology looks good. First, the problems of the physical environment do not seem to be disappearing. While immediate threats to human life have been mitigated, other problems related to the dignity of the individual, an ever-accelerating technological existence, and urbanism as *the* rather than *a* way of life loom ever larger than before. It is becoming a common practice at least to ask not only whether the building is safe, whether the equipment functions properly, whether there is enough room, whether we can make it a cleaner and prettier place, and so on, but also to ask what those who use it think about it, what they feel about it, and what it is doing to them and for them.

Perhaps more important for the growth of environmental psychology than the increasing number and persistent presence of physical-setting problems is a new way of looking at problems—a new way engendered by experiences in medicine and spatial technology. Involved is the now-common but only recently established approach in medical and technical innovation that asks what are the *unintended consequences* of the new drug, the new device, or the more modern equipment. Furthermore experience has shown that such consequences must be measured not just today but tomorrow and perhaps many, many tomorrows after that. This new way of viewing technological change and innovation in a modern society, coupled with even more accelerated changes in modern urban life, has certainly made the *evaluation* and the *understanding* of physical settings, and therefore of the role of environmental psychology, that much more important. Perhaps it can be said even more trenchantly that our society—notwithstanding its problems, conflicts, and catastrophes—is becoming increasingly humanistic and democratic in the sense that each individual has a greater opportunity to know more about what is going on and to make himself or herself learn if she or he doesn't like it. Under such circumstances, it becomes increasingly difficult for those who plan, design, create, establish, and administer our existences to do so on the basis of a series of false or untenable assumptions about what people are like, what they want, and what are their goals in life. Evaluations of the products of the architect, the designer, and the physical planner will become commonplace; the criteria they will employ will include far more than the usual economic, technological, and aesthetic criteria or standards that have been used.

Still another factor that suggests a future for environmental psychology is the self-evident validity of the phenomena it seeks to identify and study as a basis for increasing our understanding of human behavior and experience. The fact is that the failure of the behavioral sciences to pay even the slightest attention to the role of the physical setting in relation to complex forms of individual experience, social interaction, and institutional process is a failure they can no longer afford to endure. There is already evidence that, regardless of the future of a "field of environmental psychology," the concern with physical-setting variables will grow in the fields of sociology, psychology, and anthropology and the various specializations within these disciplines.

Looking at environmental psychology as still another institutional system within the structure of the behavioral sciences, we find, then, a final influence that will operate in favor of its continued growth. The fact that it already has a number of professional organizations associated with those who identify themselves as environmental psychologists (e.g., EDRA) and that at least one journal has emerged to provide a publishing outlet for environmental psychologists, all contribute to the field's institutionalization and therefore to its continuity. Furthermore within the government funding agencies EPA, HEW, and NSF, it has been given recognition by the establishment of sections that either specifically or generally fund research and training in various environmental problem areas.

It would seem that the future looks good for the field of environmental psychology. There are, however, other factors that cast doubt on this future despite the rosy picture suggested by the favorable influences we have noted above. By now one would have expected many more graduate and undergraduate psychology programs to have established the field as an area of specialization—if not a major or specialization in these departments, then at least as part of interdisciplinary programs for those with these interests. Of course, it may well be a problem of whether the chicken or the egg comes first. The number of faculty members with this interest who are available is quite small, and until they are available to become members of relevant behavioral science departments, faculty who specialize in other problem areas are far less likely to move to establish a program in environmental psychology.

Courses in environmental psychology both at the undergraduate and the graduate levels have been given at more departments in the last 5 years than were given between 1965 and 1970. In many instances they have been given by faculty members who have other areas of research interest and expertise. While the field may continue in that these individuals and many others can no longer ignore the role of physical-environment variables in many complex problem areas, the particular value-methodological orientation of the new field may well disappear in short order. In time, "environmental psychology" studied through the traditional approaches of the behavioral sciences may be relegated to the role of another problem area to be studied if any faculty member and student became interested in it.

Still other threats to the continued existence and development of the field are far more difficult to contend with. Fields with interdisciplinary requirements have yet to fare well in the behavioral sciences. Even now, great lip service is given to this property of the field, with very little evidence either in research or in the organization of university departments that this is being taken into account in any systematic way. The established behavioral-science fields and their areas of specialization have their own identities and research agendas, and since they are far older and more established institutional structures, they control the existing resources. In this respect, these fields can exert great influence on the future insofar as the growth of environmental psychology is concerned. What makes matters worse is the critical financial problems being faced by universities, research-funding agencies, and private corporations that support research enterprises. To put it simply the "pot" has grown smaller, and established disciplines or specializations are less likely to be willing to share at this point. At best, a university chairperson or administrator might be willing to support a new specialization in environmental psychology if some other specialization or program were phased out.

As we indicated from the beginning, no one can really tell how all of these factors will ultimately influence the future of the field of environmental psychology. At a time when the behavioral sciences have become self-consciously aware of the need to study critical social problems in their ongoing social context, when behavioral science is becoming a powerful influence on public policy, when it is now apparent that existing approaches to several behavioral sciences are being questioned, and finally when there is a growing emphasis on the need for institutional change, environmental psychology has a critical role to play both inside the arena of behavioral-science disciplines and outside of it in the real world of environmental complexities and problems. Whether or not the field will emerge to fulfill these roles remains to be seen.

Conferences

1961
Bailey, R., Branch, C., and Taylor, C. W. (Eds.). *Architectural Psychology and Psychiatry: An exploratory national research conference.* Salt Lake City: University of Utah, 1961.

1966
Taylor, C. W., Bailey, R., and Branch, C. H. *Second National Conference on Architectural Psychology.* Salt Lake City: University of Utah, 1967.

1969
Canter, D. (Ed.). *Architectural Psychology: Proceedings of the Dalandhui Conference.* London: RIBA Publications, 1970.

Sanoff, H., and Cohn, S. (Eds.) *Proceedings of EDRA I.* Raleigh, N.C.: University of North Carolina, 1970.

1970
Honikman, B. (Ed.). *Proceedings of the Architectural Psychology Conference at Kingston Polytechnic.* London: RIBA Publications, 1971.

Archea, J., and Eastman, C. (Eds.). *Proceedings of the Second Annual Environmental Design Association Conference.* Pittsburgh: Carnegie-Mellon University, 1970.

1972
Mitchell, W. J. (Ed.). *Environmental design: Research and practice.* Proceedings of the EDRA 3/AR 8 Conference. Los Angeles: University of California, 1972.

1973
Preiser, W. F. (Ed.). *Environmental design research:* Proceedings of the 4th international EDRA conference at Blacksburg, Virginia. Stroudsburg, Pa.: Dowden, Hutchinson and Ross, Inc., 1973.

Canter, D., and Lee, T. (Eds.). *Psychology and the built environment.* Proceedings of the Architectural Psychology Conference at Surrey, England. New York: John Wiley and Sons, 1974.

1974
Carson, A. D. *Man environment interactions: Evaluation and Application.* Proceedings of the 5th Annual EDRA Conference at Milwaukee. Stroudsburg, Pa.: Dowden, Hutchinson and Ross, Inc., 1974.

1975
Honikman, B. (Ed.). *Responding to social change: Companion to Sixth International EDRA Conference.* Stroudsburg, Pa.: Dowden, 1975. Hutchinson and Ross, Inc.

References

Ackerman, B., Ackerman, S., Sawyer, J., and Henderson, D. *The uncertain search for environmental quality.* New York: The Free Press, 1974.

Alexander, C. *Notes on the synthesis of form.* Cambridge, Mass.: Harvard University Press, 1964.

Althoff, P., and Greig, W. Environmental pollution control policy-makers: an analysis of elite perceptions and preferences. *Environment and Behavior,* 1974, *6*(3), 259–288.

Altman, I., and Haythorn, W. Ecology of isolated groups. *Behavioral Science,* 1967, *12*, 169–182.

Appleyard, D., Lynch, K., and Meyer, J. *The view from the road.* Cambridge, Mass.: M.I.T. Press, 1966.

Baker, A., Davies, R., and Sivadon, P. *Psychiatric services and architecture.* Geneva, Switzerland: World Health Organization, 1960.

Barker, M. Information and complexity: The conceptualization of air pollution by specialist groups. *Environment and Behavior,* 1974, *6*(3), 346–377.

Barker, R. (Ed.). *The stream of behavior.* New York: Appelton-Century-Crofts, 1963.

Barker, R. *Ecological psychology.* Stanford, Calif.: Stanford University Press, 1968.

Berkowitz, L. Theoretical and research approaches in experimental psychology. In A. R. Gelgen (Ed.). *Contemporary scientific psychology.* New York: Academic Press, 1970.

Bronzaft, A., Dubrow, S., and O'Hanlon, T. Spatial orientation in a subway system. *Environment and Behavior,* in press.

Buttimer, A. Social space and the planning of residential areas. *Environment and Behavior,* 1972, *4*(3), 279–318.

Calhoun, J. B. Population density and social pathology. *Scientific America,* 1962, *206,* 139–148.

Calhoun, J. B. The social use of space. In W. Mayer and R. Van Gelder (Eds.), *Physiological mammalogy.* New York: Academic Press, 1964.

Cooper, C. *Easter Hill Village.* New York: The Free Press, 1975.

Downs, R., and Stea, D. *Image and environment.* Chicago: Adline Press, 1973.

Elms, A. The crisis of confidence in social psychology. *American Psychologist,* 1975, *30*(10), 967–976.

Esser, A., Chamberlain, A., Chapple, E., and Kline, N. Territoriality of patients on a research ward. *Recent Advances in Biological Psychiatry,* 1965, *7,* 36–44.

Fellman, G., and Brandt, B. *The deceived majority.* Rutgers, N.J.: Transaction Books, 1973.

Festinger, L., Schachter, S., and Back, K. *Social pressures in informal groups.* Stanford, Calif.: Stanford University Press, 1950.

Fitch, J. Aesthetics of function. *Annals of the New York Academy of Sciences,* 1965, *128,* 706–714.

Fried, M. Grieving for a lost home. In R. Gutman (Ed.), *People and buildings.* New York: Basic Books, 1972.

Gans, H. The human implications of current redevelopment and relocation planning. *Journal of the American Institute of Planners,* 1959, *25*(1), 15–25.

Gans, H. Planning and social life: friendship and neighborhood relations in suburban communities. *Journal of the American Institute of Planners,* 1961, *27,* 176–184.

Gans, H. *The urban villagers.* New York: The Free Press, 1962.

Gutman, R. The questions architects ask. In R. Gutman (Ed.), *People and buildings.* New York: Basic Books, 1965–1966.

Gutman, R. Site planning and social behavior. *Journal of Social Issues,* 1966, *22*(4), 103–115.

Gutman, R. *People and buildings.* New York: Basic Books, 1972.

Hall, E. T. *The silent language.* New York: Doubleday, 1959.

Hall, E. T. *The hidden dimension.* Garden City, N.Y.: Doubleday, 1966.

Hartman, C. *Yerba Buena: Land Grab and Community Resistence in San Francisco.* San Francisco: Glide Publications, 1974.

Haywood, D. G., Rothenberg, M., and Beasley, R. Children's play and urban playground environment. *Environment and Behavior,* 1974, *6,* 131–168.

Ittelson, W. *Some factors influencing the design and function of psychiatric facilities.* Progress Report, Brooklyn College, 1960.

Ittelson, W. Environmental psychology and architectural planning. Paper presented at the American Hospital Association Conference on Hospital Planning in New York, 1964.

Ittelson, W., Proshansky, H., and Rivlin, L. Bedroom size and social interaction of the psychiatric ward, *Environment and Behavior,* 1970, *2*(3), 255–270.

Ittelson, W., Proshansky, H., Rivlin, L., and Winkel, G. *Introduction to environmental psychology.* New York: Holt, Rinehart and Winston, 1974.

Izumi, K. Psychosocial phenomena and building design. In H. Proshansky, Ittelson, W., and Rivlin, L. (Eds.). *Environmental psychology.* New York: Holt, Rinehart and Winston, 1970.

Katz, D. Some final considerations about experimentation in social psychology. In C. McClintock (Ed.), *Experimental social psychology.* New York: Holt, Rinehart and Winston, 1972.

Kira, A. *Bathroom criteria for design.* Ithaca, N. Y.: Cornell University Center for Housing and Environmental Studies, 1966.

Lawton, P. The human being and the institutional building. In J. T. Lang, Moleski, W., and Vachon, D. (Eds.), *Designing for human behavior.* Stroudsburg, Pa.: Dowden, Hutchinson & Ross, Inc., 1974.

Leibman, M. The effects of sex and race norms on personal space. *Environment and behavior,* 1970, *2,* 208–246.

Lewin, K. *Resolving social conflicts.* New York: Harper & Brothers, 1948.

Loo, C. *Crowding and behavior.* New York: MSS Information Service, 1974.

Lowenthal, D. (Ed.). *Environmental perception and behavior.* Research Paper No. 109, Department of Geography, University of Chicago, 1967.

Lynch, K. *Image of the city.* Cambridge, Mass.: M.I.T. Press, 1960.

Michelson, W. *Man and his urban environment: A sociological approach.* Reading, Mass.: Addison-Wesley, 1970.

Milgram, S. The experience of living in cities. *Science,* 1970, *167,* 1461–1468.

Moos, R., and Insel, P. *Issues in social ecology: Human milieus.* Palo Alto, Calif.: National Press Books, 1974.

Newman, O. *Defensible space: Crime prevention through urban design.* New York: Collier Books, 1973.

Osmond, H. Function as the basis of psychiatric ward design. *Mental Hospitals,* 1957, *8,* 23–30.

Proshansky, H. Theoretical issues in environmental psychology. *Representative Research in Social Psychology,* 1973, *4,* 93–107.

Proshansky, H. Environmental psychology in the real world. *American Psychologist,* 1976, *31* (14), 303–310.

Proshansky, H., Ittelson, W., and Rivlin, L. *Environmental psychology: Man and his physical setting.* New York: Holt, Rinehart and Winston, 1970, 1976.

Representative Research in Social Sociology, 1973, *4* (1).

Rivlin, L., Proshansky, H., and Ittelson, W. Changes in psychiatric ward design and patient behavior. *Transactions of the Bartlett Society,* 1969–1970, *8,* 7–32.

Rivlin, L., and Wolfe, M. The early history of a psychiatric hospital for children: Expectations and reality. *Environment and Behavior,* 1971, *3* (1), 23–60.

Rosenthal, R. *Experimental effects in experimental research.* New York: Appleton-Century-Crofts, 1966.

Saegert, S. (Ed.) *Environment and Behavior,* 1975, *7* (2).

Sewell, W. Environmental perceptions and attitudes of engineers and public health officials. *Environment and Behavior,* 1971, *3* (1), 23–60.

Smith, M. B. Is experimental socieal psychology advancing? *Journal of Experimental Social Psychology,* 1972, *8,* 86–96.

Sommer, R. *Personal space: The behavioral basis of design.* Englewood Cliffs, N.J.: Prentice-Hall, 1969.

Sommer, R., and Osmond, H. Symptoms of institutional care. *Social Problems,* 1961, *8,* 254.

Sommer, R., and Ross, H. Social interaction on a geriatrics ward. *International Journal of Social Psychiatry,* 1958, *4,* 128–133.

Studer, R. On environmental programming. *Architectural Associates Journal,* 1966, *81,* 290–296.

Winkel, G., and Sasonoff, R. *Approaches to an objective analysis of behavior in architectural space.* Seattle, University Park: College of Architecture and Urban Planning, 1965.

Wohlwill, J. The emerging discipline of environmental psychology. *American Psychologist,* 1970, *25* (4), 303–312.

Wohlwill, J., and Carson, D. (Eds.). *Environment and the social sciences: Perspectives and application.* Washington, D.C.: American Psychological Association, 1972.

Wolf, C. Social impact assessment: the state of the art. In C. Wolf (Ed.), *Social impact assessment.* Milwaukee, Wis.: Environmental Design Research Association, 1974.

Wolf, C. (Ed.). *Environment and Behavior,* 1975, *7* (3).

Yancy, W. Architecture, interaction and social control: The case of a large-scale public housing project. *Environment and Behavior,* 1971, *3* (1), 3–22.

Zehner, R., Burby, R., III, and Weiss, S. Evaluations of new communities in the United States. Paper presented at the 69th annual meeting of the American Sociological Association, Montreal, August 26–29, 1974.

Zeisel, J., and Griffin, M. *Charlesview housing: A diagnostic evaluation.* Architectural Research Office, Graduate School of Design, Harvard University, 1975.

Behavioral and Physiological Effects of Uncontrollable Environmental Events

5

DAVID C. GLASS, JEROME E. SINGER, AND JAMES W. PENNEBAKER

Introduction

This chapter examines the influence of noise and related environmental stressors on human behavior. It is concerned with the cognitive context in which stressful stimulation occurs and with the behavioral aftereffects that such stimulation produces. The presentation deals, in large part, with relatively immediate aftereffects of exposure to uncontrollable and unpredictable aversive events. The demonstration of these aftereffects is primarily confined to performance deficits and only minimal attention is given to physiological processes. However, a final section presents more recent findings that have direct implications for the understanding of long-term effects of uncontrollable stressors on physiology, specifically cardiovascular functioning. This research, though also behavioral, has as its principal focus psychological antecedents of coronary heart disease (CHD). We shall

DAVID C. GLASS • The University of Texas, Austin. JEROME E. SINGER • State University of New York at Stony Brook. JAMES W. PENNEBAKER • The University of Texas, Austin. Dr. Singer was involved in the stress-aftereffect research discussed in the first part of the chapter. Mr. Pennebaker was involved in the research on uncontrollability and the coronary-prone variable described in the last section of this chapter. The research was made possible by grants from the National Science Foundation (GS-2405, GS-2412 and GS-34329), Russell Sage Foundation, and The Hogg Foundation for Mental Health. A modified version of this chapter appeared in *Representative Research in Social Psychology*, 1973, *4*, 165–183.

begin with the line of thought leading to the noise aftereffect studies and later introduce the rationale for the CHD research.

Though seemingly obvious, the direct effects of noise on behavior are difficult to demonstrate. For, in time, people learn to ignore noise. However, the proposition that man is adaptable has an important corollary, namely, that man pays a price for adaptation that is observable in behavior (Selye, 1956; Dubos, 1965; Wohlwill, 1970). Our program of noise research was undertaken as a test of this hypothesis. But, as we shall see later, the results suggested a somewhat different interpretation.

The idea for our initial study was to allow subjects to adapt to repeatedly presented high-intensity sound and then determine whether the process of adaptation or habituation[1] left subjects less able to cope with subsequent environmental demands. The basic notion was that the mental effort entailed in the adaptive process affects subsequent behavior adversely. Following Lazarus and his colleagues (e.g., 1968), we assumed that adaptation is a cognitive process involving reevaluation of the noise stressor as benign or the use of more direct action strategies for coping with noise, for example, "filtering" noise out of awareness by becoming engrossed in some task. We did not attempt to measure the various adaptive strategies. Instead we simply assumed that subjects used one or another strategy and that this would be reflected in a decrement in autonomic response to noise. This decrement was, in effect, our principal index of adaptation.

Noise and Task Performance

Before describing some of the behavioral aftereffects of noise adaptation, we will first consider noise effects occurring during the process of acoustic stimulation. Noise may be defined as any sound that is physiologically arousing and stressful, subjectively annoying, or disruptive of performance (Anastasi, 1964). But do we really have any evidence that noise is a stressor with measurable consequences resulting from its repeated application? There are dozens of newspaper accounts and magazine stories that suggest an affirmative answer. However, psychoacousticians are not at all convinced that noise has deleterious effects on man. Comprehensive reviews of systematic research on noise (Broadbent, 1957; Kryter, 1970; Ward, 1974) conclude that there is no compelling evidence of adverse effects of high-intensity noise *per se* on human performance. Laboratory-produced noise does not affect the subject's ability to do mental and psychomotor tasks ranging from the boringly simple to the oftentimes interesting and challenging. Other than as a damaging agent to the ear, or as a source of

[1]We use the terms *habituation* and *adaptation* interchangeably throughout this chapter. The convention is adopted with full knowledge that not all forms of adaptation necessarily involve the same basic processes (cf. Thompson and Spencer, 1966; Lazarus, 1968).

interference with tasks requiring communication, noise does not seem to impair human task-performance.

Data from our own research provide support for this conclusion (Glass and Singer, 1972). On relatively simple mental tasks—arithmetic addition, number comparison, verbal skills—there appears to be little evidence of task impairment during noise stimulation. Over 200 subjects have been tested to date. Typically there are no differences in task errors between loud and soft noise-conditions during the first part of the noise session, but whatever errors do occur tend to decline during the second part of the session. We interpret these error decrements as evidence of noise adaptation.

Our research has customarily used broad-band noise consisting of a specially prepared tape recording of the following sounds superimposed upon one another: (1) two people speaking Spanish (2) one person speaking Armenian; (3) a mimeograph machine; (4) a desk calculator; and (5) a typewriter. We selected this particular concatenation of sounds as an analogue of the spectrum of complex noises often present in the urban environment. A sound-spectrographic analysis of the noise recording showed that energy did indeed occur over a broad range from 500 Hz to 7000 Hz, with the mode at about 700 Hz. Free-field stimulation was used throughout most of the research, with the noise delivered over a speaker mounted on a wall directly behind the subject.

We have asserted that noise *per se* has minimal effects on task performance. There are several exceptions to this conclusion, however. In particular, task performance is impaired when (1) long-term vigilance demands are placed on the subject; (2) the task is otherwise complex; (3) noise is intermittent. Evidence for vigilance-task impairments have been extensively documented elsewhere (e.g., Broadbent, 1971) and need not be repeated at this time. Evidence of intermittency effects have also been reported by other investigators (Broadbent, 1957), but a word or two are needed here. Briefly, this research has shown that intermittent noise is experienced as more aversive than continuous noise, and if the intermittency is aperiodic (i.e., unpredictable), felt aversiveness is still greater. Other studies have reported corresponding effects for task performance; for example, aperiodic noise degrades performance more than does continuous or periodic noise (e.g., Sanders, 1961). The tasks used in most of this research were relatively simple verbal and numerical tasks.

We have not been able to replicate the aperiodicity effect in our own laboratories. Our results have shown that aperiodic noise does not produce more task deficits than periodic noise (Glass and Singer, 1972). It should also be noted that unsignaled noise does not result in greater performance errors than signaled noise. Signaling and periodicity are each a form of predictability, and we have studied the influence of both variables in our research.

Though unpredictable noise does not degrade *simple* task performance, it does exert a greater impact on *complex* task performance than does predictable noise. In two of our experiments, deterioration of performance was observed if excessive demands were placed on the subject's information-processing capacities, as when he worked on two tasks simultaneously or maintained continual vigilance on a tracking task (Finkelman and Glass, 1970; Glass and Singer, 1972). It would appear that unpredictable noise directly affects performance only when the subject is working at maximum capacity.

There is one general consistency in these exceptions to the earlier conclusion that noise *per se* does not have adverse effects on performance. All three appear to reflect the operation not of noise alone but of noise mediated by cognitive processes. Two are presumably situations in which the organism becomes overloaded; that is, task inputs are so numerous as to inhibit adequate information-processing, and noise becomes still another input for the organism to monitor. The noise continually overloads the subject and in such a situation produces performance deficits that do not wane with repeated exposure. The deleterious effects of aperiodic noise probably reflect the fact that unpredictable stressors have a more aversive impact on behavior than predictable stressors (e.g., Berlyne, 1960). These conclusions underscore the importance of cognitive factors in mediating the effects of noise on behavior. For unpredictability is an extrastimulus variable, and task complexity and vigilance may be viewed as instances of cognitive overload.

Aftereffects of Unpredictable Noise

The implicit assumption in all of our research has been that individuals expend "psychic energy" in the course of the adaptive process and that this leaves them less able to cope with subsequent environmental demands and frustrations. Since there is some evidence to suggest that unpredictable noise is more aversive than predictable noise, we anticipated that adaptation to the former type of stimulation would be more costly to the individual. Specifically we hypothesized that unpredictable noise, in contrast to predictable noise, would lead to greater reductions in tolerance for post-noise frustration and greater impairment of performance on a task requiring care and attention.

The prototypic procedure used to test this general hypothesis is as follows. Upon entering the laboratory, the subject was told that the purpose of the study was to investigate "the effects of noise levels on task performance and physiological processes." The use of skin electrodes was then explained and leads were attached to the subject. After a brief resting period, the experimenter explained the tasks the subject would be working on during noise exposure—usually verbal and numerical tests. The noise session began immediately following the task instructions. Noise was delivered intermittently—at either random or fixed intervals—throughout a

23-, 24-, or 25-minute period, depending on the particular experiment. In fixed conditions, noise was presented at the end of every minute for about 9 seconds. In random conditions, delivery of noise was randomized with respect to the length of the bursts and the intervals between them. The intensity of each type of noise was also varied, such that half the subjects in the random and fixed conditions heard 108-dbA sound, whereas the other half heard 56-dbA sound. The total time to which subjects were exposed to noise was identical in all conditions—about 3.5–5 minutes, again depending on the particular study. Following termination of noise, the experimenter reentered the laboratory chamber and administered the tasks designed to measure aftereffects of adaptation. Subjects assigned to no-noise control conditions were treated identically to experimental subjects, with the obvious exception that noise stimuli were not presented during the performance of the verbal and numerical tasks.

Let us now consider illustrative results from the first of these noise experiments (Glass, Singer, and Friedman, 1969, Experiment I). We begin with evidence pertaining to noise adaptation. Phasic skin conductance (GSR) was monitored throughout the noise session, and as noted earlier, the decrement in reactivity on this measure was taken as an index of adaptation. Figure 1 shows these adaptation data as average log conductance-change scores within each of four successive blocks of noise trials. There is a significant decline in GSR on successive blocks in each noise condition. Since initial reactions to loud noise (108 dbA) were greater than to soft noise (56 dbA), the magnitude of GSR decline is understandably greater in the former condition. However, the magnitude and rate of adaptation are

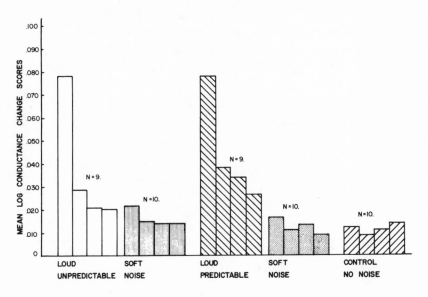

Figure 1. Mean log conductance-change scores for four successive blocks of noise bursts.

virtually identical in predictable and unpredictable conditions within each noise-intensity treatment; that is, subjects were equally reactive at the beginning of the noise session and equally unreactive at the end.

To sum up, phasic skin-conductance responses to noise appear during initial exposure, but they wane with repeated stimulation. Assuming that physiological stress-reactions interfere with performance efficiency, we may expect initial task errors, which decline over the course of noise exposure. Recall that the task results presented earlier conformed to such expectations. This phenomenon of adaptation is indeed pervasive. It occurred in almost every subject in each of our experiments, and it appeared on several different autonomic channels—GSR, vasoconstriction of the peripheral blood vessels, and muscle-action potentials. We may thus conclude that there is a generalized stress response to noise that habituates with repeated stimulation.

We began our research with the hypothesis that adaptation to noise is correlated with deleterious behavioral aftereffects. This expectation was in fact confirmed. Exposure to unpredictable noise, in contrast to predictable noise, was followed by impaired task-performance and lowered tolerance for postnoise frustrations. Despite noise adaptation in both predictable and unpredictable conditions, the magnitude of adverse aftereffects was greater following unpredictable noise. Before presenting results in support of this general conclusion, we must first explain how frustration tolerance was measured.

Following noise termination, subjects were given a task consisting of four line-diagrams (Figure 2) printed on 5″ × 7″ cards arranged in four

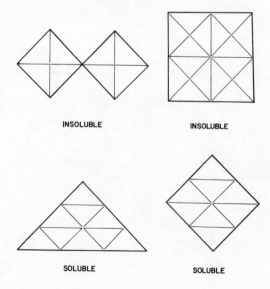

Figure 2. Insoluble and soluble puzzles.

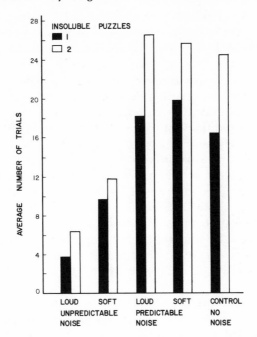

Figure 3. Average number of trials on the first and second insoluble puzzles.

piles in front of each subject (Feather, 1961; Glass and Singer, 1972). The subject's task was to trace over all of the lines of a given diagram without tracing any line twice and without lifting his pencil from the figure. The subject was told that he could take as many trials at a given item as he wished. However, he was also told that there was a time limit on how long he could work on a particular trial and that the experimenter would inform him when his time was up. At the end of that time, he had to decide whether to take another card from the same pile or to move on to the next pile. If he decided to move on, he could not go back to the previous pile.

Two of the line diagrams were in fact insoluble, but very few subjects were able to see this. These insoluble puzzles were presumed to lead to failure and frustration. Indeed we repeatedly observed outward signs of exasperation as subjects attempted over and over again to solve the insoluble. While this was going on in the experimental chamber, the experimenter was in the control room observing and recording the number of trials taken by a subject on each puzzle. These data provided us with a measure of his persistence on the insoluble puzzles; namely, the fewer the number of trials, the less the persistence, and by interpretation, the lower the subject's tolerance for an inherently frustrating task.

Typical results on this task are shown in Figure 3. As can be seen, subjects took significantly fewer trials following exposure to loud unpredictable noise than following the loud and soft predictable noise. This effect was true for both of the insoluble puzzles. It would appear, then, that lowered tolerance for frustration is a consequence of exposure to the presumably more aversive unpredictable noise. There is also an unexpected tendency for this effect to appear even when the unpredictable noise is not particularly loud. Soft unpreditable noise was associated with lower frustration tolerance than loud predictable noise. Unpredictability is indeed a potent factor in the production of noise aftereffects.

It should be noted that our measure of frustration tolerance could be regarded alternatively as an index of adaptive lack of persistence on an insoluble task. Put somewhat differently, it may be that taking fewer trials on an insoluble puzzle is an adaptive rather than a maladaptive response. Such an interpretation is theoretically possible, but we find it difficult to understand why unpredictable noise would lead to more adaptive responses to insoluble problems than predictable noise. Unpredictable stressors have been shown by others to exert a more aversive impact on behavior than predictable stressors (e.g., Berlyne, 1960), and thus we might expect maladaptive consequences after exposure to the former type of stimulation.

The alternative interpretation of our frustration-tolerance measure is also difficult to maintain in the face of results obtained on another postnoise task. It was expected that unpredictable noise, in contrast to predictable noise, would impair quality of performance on a task requiring care and attention. Subjects were given a proofreading test immediately following completion of the insoluble puzzles. They were asked to correct errors, such as transpositions and misspellings, that had been deliberately introduced into a seven-page passage. Each subject was given 15 minutes on this task, and quality of performance was measured as the percentage of "errors not found" of the total number of errors that could have been detected at the point the subject was told to stop work.

There were no significant differences between noise conditions in the total amount read by subjects. However, Figure 4 shows the predicted differences in average percentage of errors missed in the completed part of the proofreading task. Loud unpredictable noise was associated with a greater percentage of proofreading errors than either loud or soft predictable noise. Though soft unpredictable noise resulted in greater impairment of proofreading accuracy than loud predictable noise, the difference was not statistically significant, as was the case with frustration tolerance.

Taken together, the findings suggest that people adapt to noise but behavioral deficits appear after noise termination. We cannot say that these deficits are the result of noise adaptation; it is just as likely that they occur in spite of adaptation. Later we refer to data that in fact support the second interpretation. For the moment, however, we have simply shown that exposure to unpredictable noise leads to more adverse aftereffects than exposure to predictable noise. Though noise intensity affects the magnitude of these aftereffects, a psychological factor, unpredictability, appears

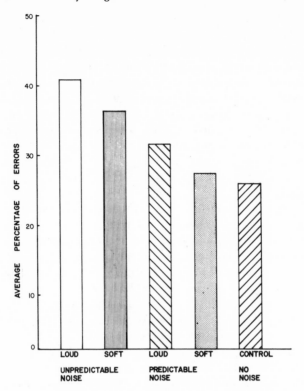

Figure 4. Average percentage of errors missed in the proofreading task.

to be more important than physical parameters in producing post-noise deficits. The case for the existence of this phenomenon is strengthened by the range of conditions over which it has been obtained in various replications. These include (1) different ways of manipulating unpredictability; (2) different levels of physical noise intensity; (3) different subject populations; and (4) different laboratory settings. A very recent study provides additional support for the generalizability of noise-aftereffect phenomena: adverse aftereffects occurred regardless of whether subjects worked on a task during noise exposure (Wohlwill, Nasar, DeJoy, and Foruzani, 1975).

Perceived Control over Noise

The preceding studies do not, however, provide precise theoretical understanding of the relationship between unpredictable noise and adverse aftereffects. It is not enough to assume that unpredictable noise is more aversive than predictable noise, for we still need to specify why it is more aversive and why the negative effects appear *after* noise termination. A possible answer to the first question is based on the notion that exposure to an unpredictable stressor induces feelings in the individual that he cannot control his environment—or at least certain stressful aspects of it. Under these conditions, we might well expect lowered frustration-tolerance and impaired proofreading-accuracy. The individual has experienced not only the aversiveness of noise but also the "anxiety" of being incapable of doing anything about it. On the other hand, providing him with information about when to expect the noise affords a measure of cognitive control over the situation that reduces the adverse effects of unpredictability. The validity of this line of reasoning was tested in a series of eight experiments. We present only one illustrative study here (Glass, Singer, and Friedman, 1969, Experiment II).

Two groups of subjects listened to the unpredictable-noise tape played at 108 dbA. One group (hereafter referred to as Perceived Control) was given control over the noise, whereas the other group (No Perceived Control) did not receive this option. At the beginning of the experiemnt, each subject in the Perceived Control condition was shown a microswitch attached to the side of his chair and told he could at any time terminate the noise for the remainder of the session by pressing the switch. He was further informed that the experimenter preferred that he did not press the switch but that the choice was entirely up to him. The latter half of the instruction was given particular emphasis in order to induce forces against pressing the switch, while at the same time allowing the subject to feel that he could press it if he desired. In fact, few subjects used the switch throughout noise exposure. All other details of procedure and measurement were virtually identical to those used in the previous noise experiments.

In order to determine whether or not the experiment was successful in inducing perceptions of control, all subjects were asked to respond to the following rating scale in a postexperimental questionnaire: "To what extent do you feel that you really could have had the noise stopped during today's session?" where 1 = "No control at all" and 9 = "Complete control." The mean for the Perceived Control condition was 7.4 and for No Perceived Control 3.0. The difference was statistically significant at less than the .05 level.

Subjects in both conditions adapted to the noise as measured by GSR decrements and decline in task errors. The aftereffect results present a somewhat different picture, however. Figures 5 and 6 show these data. It is immediately obvious that the perception of control over noise termination had a dramatic impact on the aftereffect measures. Tolerance for postnoise frustration was appreciably increased and proofreading errors substantially reduced.

These ameliorative effects have been obtained with a number of experimental variations of perceived control, including the induction of a

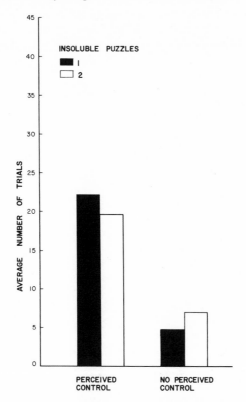

Figure 5. Average number of trials on the first and second insoluble puzzles.

perceived contingency between instrumental responding and avoidance of noise (Glass and Singer, 1972). The results of our research, then, suggest that perceptions of control reduce the aversive impact of unpredictable noise, hence the deleterious aftereffects of exposure to such stimulation. To reiterate our earlier conclusion, psychological factors, not simply physical parameters of noise, are important elements in the production of noise afereffects.

Perceived Control and Helplessness

But what specific stress-reducing mechanisms are aroused by the manipulation of perceived control? In answering this question, we reasoned that inescapable and unpredictable noise confronts the individual with a situation in which he is powerless to anticipate and influence the occurrence of the stressor. We may describe his psychological state under these circumstances as one of helplessness (Lazarus, 1966; Seligman, Maier, and Solomon,

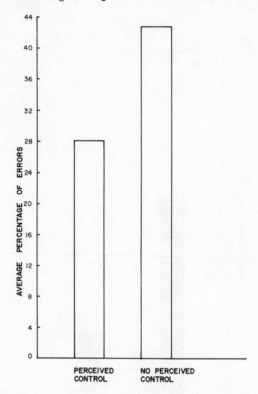

Figure 6. Average percentage of errors missed in the proofreading task.

1971; Seligman, 1975). Such a mechanism provides a nice explanation of the relationship between uncontrollable noise and deleterious aftereffects. If the impact of a repeatedly presented aversive event is greatest where feelings of helplessness are maximal, it follows that adverse aftereffects will also be maximal. Our working thesis is that exposure to uncontrollable noise produces feelings of helplessness that interfere with later functioning. Perceived Control subjects label their situation as one in which they have control over their environment and, therefore, are not helpless. By contrast, No Perceived Control subjects do not develop these expectations.

Subsequent performance after noise stimulation is affected in a way that is consistent with prior experience, when control was or was not available. Presumably the helpless group not only experiences the aversiveness of unpredictable noise *per se* but also the "anxiety" connected with their felt inability to do anything about it. Perceived Control subjects, on the other hand, are exposed only to the stress of the noise itself; they do not experience additional anxiety produced by feelings of helplessness. We tentatively conclude, therefore, that unpredictable noise produces more adverse aftereffects than predictable noise because unpredictability leads to a sense of helplessness in individuals who are unable to control and/or predict the onset of noise.

Other Stressors

Noise was the principal stressor used in our research. However, we do not believe our findings or interpretations hinge upon characteristics unique to noise. The pattern of results obtained with noise—almost universal adaptation followed by adverse aftereffects as a function of the unpredictability and uncontrollability surrounding noise exposure—has been obtained with other stressors. For example, data from two laboratory experiments using electric shock demonstrated that adverse behavioral consequences were reduced if this form of stimulation was both predictable and controllable (Glass and Singer, 1972; Glass, Singer, Leonard, Krantz, Cohen, and Cummings, 1973). Still other research (Glass and Singer, 1972; Sherrod, 1974) indicates that these two variables (predictability and controllability) produce similar effects with social stressors, such as bureaucratic frustration, arbitrary discrimination, and crowding, thereby permitting the general conclusion that deleterious aftereffects of stress are probably a function of the unpredictability of aversive stimulation and the belief that one has little control over stimulus occurrence.

Psychic Costs of Stress

Physical and social stressors have few direct effects on performance. People adapt to stress. But stressors do have disruptive aftereffects, and these tend to be a function of the cognitive circumstances in which stimulation occurs rather than of the sheer magnitude of intensity of stimulation. These conclusions do not mean that aftereffect phenomena are the "psychic price" paid by the individual for his adaptation to aversive events. This hypothesis was indeed the original basis of our research, but the results presented thus far do not provide the necessary confirmation. It is entirely possible that aftereffects are as much poststressor phenomena as postadaptation phenomena. The designs and findings of our research do not indicate whether aftereffects occurred in spite of adaptation or because of the effort entailed in the adaptive process. Further analysis and experimentation with noise enabled us to reach a partial adjudication of this rather nice theoretical issue.

As we noted earlier, adaptation is assumed to be a cognitive process involving one or another mechanism designed to filter out of awareness certain aspects of the aversive event or in some other way reappraise it as benign. It is also assumed that physiological adaptation is one index of this process and that the effort entailed in achieving adaptation is reflected in the magnitude of decline of physiological response to the stressor. Given these assumptions, we were able to conclude that greater amounts of adaptation are not systematically related to greater postnoise deficits. We inferred this lack of association from two analyses (see Glass and Singer, 1972).

First, there was a low correlation ($-.20$) between aftereffect scores (i.e., proofreading) and indices of GSR-adaptation magnitude for subjects in various unpredictable and uncontrollable noise conditions. Second, we conducted still another noise experiment in which we failed to find differences in adverse aftereffects in two unpredictable conditions—one in which the usual autonomic adaptation occurred, and one in which GSR decrements were inhibited by the use of long interstimulus intervals between noise bursts. On the basis of these and related data, we suggest that aftereffect phenomena represent behavioral residues of cumulative exposure to uncontrollable noxious stimulation. It is not the adaptive process itself that causes deleterious aftereffects but the fact of continued exposure to a stressful event in spite of adaptation (Glass and Singer, 1972).

Uncontrollable Events and Coronary Heart Disease

Adverse aftereffects have been attributed to the stressful impact of uncontrollable aversive events. We have argued that (1) helplessness develops in individuals who are unable to control the onset and/or offset of a stressor and (b) this cognitive-affective state interferes with efforts to cope with subsequent task demands. The effects of uncontrollability and helplessness are not limited to immediate poststress performance deficits, however. Recent work in psychosomatic medicine indicates that helplessness is a general precursor of various types of physical and psychic disease that often take years to develop (e.g., Engel, 1968). A patient experiencing a sense of helplessness is described as attributing this state to failures emanating from the environment to which he looks for a solution. Of particular relevance here is the finding that sudden death due to CHD occurs in men who have been depressed for several months prior to the attack (Greene, Goldstein, and Moss, 1972). Since there are major parallels between behaviors that define helplessness and symptoms of depression (Seligman, 1975), it is not unreasonable to assume that helplessness may be an antecedent of CHD. However, helplessness is alleged to figure in the etiology of disease generally, in which case we may ask what set of factors interact with helplessness to predispose an individual toward CHD rather than some other disorder.

Pattern A and CHD

A partial answer to this question comes from the work of Friedman and Rosenman on the "coronary-prone behavior pattern" (e.g., Rosenman and

Friedman, 1974; Friedman and Rosenman, 1974). This overt behavior pattern reflects a style of life characterized by a sense of time urgency, competitive achievement-striving, and hostility. Persons manifesting the behavior pattern are designated Type A; those who exhibit the pattern to a lesser degree are called Type B.[2] The Type A pattern is a set of characterological predispositions that are elicited under appropriately challenging situations. Recent behavioral studies provide empirical support for this hypothesis. Glass, Snyder, and Hollis (1974), for example, report that Type A's react with irritation when experiencing interference with the customary rapid pacing of their activities. The study also showed that Type A's performed more poorly than B's on a task requiring a low rate of response. Other research has indicated that A's display an excessive drive to achieve that leads them to work with maximum effort, irrespective of the requirements of the task confronting them (Burnam, Pennebaker, and Glass, 1975). Still another experiment indicates that A's react with greater hostility and aggression than B's to threats directed at their sense of mastery over a situation (Glass, 1977).

Retrospective and prospective epidemiological research shows that the Type A designation is associated with about two times the prevalence of clinical CHD than the Type B classification, even when the influence of traditional risk factors (e.g., serum cholesterol) is removed (Rosenman, Brand, Jenkins, Friedman, Straus, and Wurm, 1975). Other studies indicate that Type A is not only associated with the actual occurrence of CHD, but is also related to the disease process that culminates in myocardial infarction or angina. Thus one postmortem study found that coronary atherosclerosis in Type A men is approximately twice that of Type B men (Friedman, Rosenman, Straus, Wurm and Kositchek, 1968), and two recent experiments found even more striking differences in the degree of atherosclerosis shown by coronary angiography (Jenkins, Zyzanski, Lefkowitz, Everist, and Ryan, 1974; Blumenthal, Kong, Rosenman, Thompson, and Williams, 1975).

Classification of subjects as Type A or Type B is customarily based on a standardized interview (Rosenman, Friedman, Straus, Wurm, Kositchek, Hahn, and Werthessen, 1964) or a self-administered questionnaire called the Jenkins Activity Survey for Health Prediction (JAS) (Jenkins, Zyzanski, and Rosenman, 1971). The JAS has shown approximately 72% agreement with the diagnostic interview, the procedure used to predict clinical CHD in the Friedman–Rosenman research. Retrospective and prospective studies with the JAS itself indicate that it can distinguish between noncoronary and coronary groups almost as well as the interview (e.g., Kenigsberg, Zyzanski,

---

[2]It should be noted that there are minimal correlations between Pattern A and seemingly related psychological variables, such as need for achievement, fear of failure, and internal–external control. The relevant product–moment coefficients from one study of approximately 300 cases are .15, .02, and .17, respectively.

Jenkins, Wardwell, and Licciardello, 1974; Jenkins, Rosenman, and Zyzanski, 1974).[3]

Pattern A, Uncontrollable Events, and CHD

The Type A behavior pattern may well mediate a helplessness–coronary disease relationship. The descriptive elements of the pattern suggest someone who is continually striving to avoid loss of control over his environment. In contrast to B's, A's work hard, show little tolerance for interruption, are unable or unwilling to reduce the pace of their activities, and react with hostility to threats to their sense of mastery. Failure and frustration resulting from their efforts at environmental control should result in initial attempts to reassert control. However, when direct coping-responses are found to be ineffective with uncontrollable stressors, the Type A individual eventually experiences helplessness and gives up efforts to exert direct control over his environment.

Systematic support for this line of thought comes from several recent experiments conducted in our laboratory (Glass, 1977). The results indicate that the initial reaction of Type A's to uncontrollable events is to exert greater efforts than Type B's to reestablish control. Thus one study showed greater performance enhancement on a psychomotor task among A's following exposure to noncontingent as opposed to contingent reinforcement. Noncontingency may be considered an instance of loss of control (Seligman, 1975; Wortman and Brehm, 1975). A second experiment demonstrated that uncontrollability potentiated time-urgent behavior in Type A subjects. When speed was defined as the criterion of task mastery, A's accelerated the pace with which they worked following exposure to inescapable noise. A third study indicated that the initial response of Type A's to inescapable high-intensity noise (105 dBA, 3000 Hz) was to increase their efforts to escape relative to their Type B counterparts. More recent research indicates that variable ratio schedules, perceived as more uncontrollable by subjects than fixed ratio schedules, led to enhanced efforts to obtain monetary rewards among Type A's compared to type B's.

The results of this research are based on relatively brief exposure to the uncontrollable stimuli. Extended experience with uncontrollable stress has been found to result in more passive behavior among A's than B's. For example, one study shows that the efforts of A's to escape from intense inescapable noise by pressing a button extinguished over the course of the noise session, whereas as a comparable pattern did not emerge for Type B subjects (Glass, 1977). A more direct test of this "learned helplessness" hypothesis (Seligman, 1975) is contained in an experiment by Krantz, Glass,

---

[3]The A–B classification used in the studies reported in this chapter is based on the original JAS or its modification for college students (Krantz, Glass, and Snyder, 1974).

and Snyder (1974). The results showed that repeatedly exposing subjects to an uncontrollable noise stressor (pre-treatment phase of the study) interfered with escape learning in a subsequent experimental situation in which the stressor was in fact controllable (test phase). Interference with learning occurred under both moderate and high levels of noise, but the Type A classification placed an important qualification on the results. Type A's experienced helplessness (i.e., gave up efforts to escape) only after pretreatment with an uncontrollable stressor of high intensity. There was minimal evidence of this effect among A's following moderate-stress pretreatment. These results were consistent with data from a study using 9- to 11-year-old children classified in terms of the A–B variable, and additional confirmation was found in an experiment with college students that manipulated uncontrollability in a nonnoise context (Glass, 1977). Taken together with the findings on initial reactions to uncontrollable events, we may thus characterize the Type A individual as one who exerts greater efforts than the Type B individual to reassert mastery over events that clearly threaten his sense of control. However, initial controlling behavior is followed by helplessness as it becomes apparent that stressful events are actually uncontrollable.

We have suggested that the interaction of the Type A behavior pattern and a state of helplessness may be the psychological condition needed to produce myocardial infarction. A direct test of this hypothesis obviously requires a study of CHD patients. We have just completed such a project using 45 male patients in the coronary-care unit of the VA Hospital in Houston, Texas. Two principal control groups were included in the design: 77 patients in the psychiatric and general-medical-service wards (excepting patients with organic disorders, psychotics, and drug addicts), and a group of 50 "healthy" maintenance employees from the Austin campus. *Healthy* was defined as being free of CHD, psyciatric problems, and physical disease requiring hospitalization within the preceding year. The groups were frequency-matched on the following variables: age in decades; social class, as measured by the Hollingshead index; race; and religion. The age range was 35 to 55.

Two principal measures administered to the subjects were the JAS and a modified form of the Schedule of Recent Experience (e.g., Hawkins, Davies, and Holmes, 1957). This self-administered questionnaire asks the respondent to document the number of occurrences of each of 47 life events over a 10-year period. Five specific time segments are used: 0 to 3 weeks prior to the time the subject is completing the questionnaire; 3 weeks to 3 months; 3 months to 1 year; 1 year to 3 years; and 3 years to 10 years. Previous research (e.g., Greene, Goldstein, and Moss, 1972) suggests that stressful life events cluster in the 1-year period preceding CHD and other ailments. Since many of these life events constitute a loss that may be categorized as inducing helplessness (e.g., death of a spouse; son leaving home; financial decline), we combined these data to form a "helplessness index" for the 1-year period preceding the time the questionnaire was completed.

The specific hypothesis at test was that CHD patients would show a higher A–B score and a greater helplessness-index score than matched noncoronary patients and the "healthy" control group. The results provided confirmation of the hypothesis. We may tentatively conclude, therefore, that CHD is more likely to occur among individuals who exhibit Pattern A and also report an excess of recent events that may be described as arousing feelings of helplessness. This conclusion must be viewed with some caution, for the results are based on a retrospective study that requires replication in some type of prospective design. The evidence is, nevertheless, consistent with laboratory data suggesting that Pattern A is a specific response style for coping with uncontrollable environmental events.

Directions for Future Research

There are probably a set of physiological processes that mediate the association between cardiovascular disease, Pattern A, and differential responsivity to uncontrollable stimuli. We know that the probability of CHD is greater for Type A men than for Type B men, but there is precious little data indicating the precise nature of the mediating mechanisms. What is known, however, suggests that these mechanisms may involve traditional risk factors for CHD. For example, one experiment has shown that the stress of deadline pressures can produce substantial elevations of the serum-cholesterol level (Friedman, Rosenman, and Carroll, 1958). Other studies indicate that norepinephrine levels remain elevated when subjects are engaged in active efforts to escape or avoid stressors (Frankenhaeuser and Rissler, 1970; Weiss, Stone, and Harrell, 1970). Since A's seem to have higher serum cholesterol and norepinephrine levels than Type B's (Friedman, 1969), it may be that persistent concern with environmental control—and ensuing controlling behavior—contributes to cholesterol and norepinephrine elevations. Serum cholesterol is, of course, an important risk factor in CHD, and catecholamines are believed to potentiate coronary artery disease (Friedman, 1969). It may be, therefore, that the specific reactions of A's to uncontrollability increase the risk of CHD by directly and indirectly affecting their cardiovascular system. Systematic research is currently underway aimed at exploring the possible interaction between physiological and psychological factors in the development of CHD.

Still another line of inquiry being pursued in our laboratory concerns the emergence of the Type A behavior pattern. The precise antecedents remain obscure at this time, although genetic factors may play a part in the genesis of Pattern A (Rosenman, Rahe, Borhani, and Feinleib, 1975). The possibility that components of the behavior pattern are inherited does not reduce the importance of environmental influences, however. Type A behavior ensues only when the milieu presents suitable challenges, such as a threat of loss of control. The pattern is defined by the interaction of characterological predispositions and appropriate eliciting situations. Undoubtedly Pattern A is partially shaped by contemporary sociocultural values that emphasize competitive-achievement striving and time urgency. Western society may encourage the development of Pattern A by rewarding those who can think, perform, communicate, and, in general, master their environment more rapidly and effectively than their peers. Karen Matthews is currently exploring the possibility that this reward system appears in exaggerated form in the child-rearing practices of parents whose children subsequently show Pattern A behavior.

Concluding Remarks

We have considered a broad range of issues from postnoise performance deficits to the impact of uncontrollable events on the genesis of cardiovascular disease. The findings on which our discussion was based emerged from a continuing research program on the effects of perceived lack of control on human behavior and physiology. Because this chapter represents a progress report on the project, it would be premature to offer a theoretical integration of data at this time. Suffice it to say that a common theme underlying the research is the notion that uncontrollability has profound effects on human behavior. The stress-aftereffect studies (particularly those dealing with noise) provide adequate documentation for this hypothesis. We also believe that a hyperreactive style of coping with the experience of uncontrollability, such as the Type A behavior pattern, is related to long-term impairments of cardiovascular functioning. While we presented evidence consistent with this hypothesis, more systematic support must await future experimentation and analysis that combines both behavioral and physiological measurement.

References

Anastasi, A. *Fields of applied psychology.* New York: McGraw-Hill, 1964.

Berlyne, D. E. *Conflict, arousal, and curiosity,.* New York: McGraw-Hill, 1960.

Blumenthal, J. A., Kong, Y., Rosenman, R. H., Thompson, L. W., and Williams, R. B. Type A behavior pattern and angiography documented coronary disease. Submitted for publication, 1975. Abstract, American Psychosomatic Society, March, 1975.

Broadbent, D. E. Effects of noise on behavior. In C. M. Harris (Ed.), *Handbook of noise control.* New York: McGraw-Hill, 1957.

Broadbent, D. E. *Decision and stress.* New York: Academic, 1971.

Burnam, M. A., Pennebaker, J. W., and Glass, D. C. Time consciousness, achievement striving, and the type A coronary-prone behavior pattern. *Journal of Abnormal Psychology,* 1975, *84,* 76–79.

Dubos, R. *Man adapting.* New Haven, Conn: Yale University Press, 1965.

Engel, G. L. A life setting conducive to illness: The giving-up–given-up complex. *Annals of Internal Medicine,* 1968, *69,* 293–300.

Feather, N. T. The relationship of persistence at a task to expectation of success and achievement related motives. *Journal of Abnormal and Social Psychology,* 1961, *63,* 552–561.

Finkelman, J. M. and Glass, D. C. Reappraisal of the relationship between noise and human performance by means of a subsidiary task measure. *Journal of Applied Psychology,* 1970, *54,* 211–213.

Frankenhaeuser, M., and Rissler, A. Effects of punishment on catecholamine release and efficiency of performance. *Psychopharmacologica,* 1970, *17,* 378–390.

Friedman, M. *Pathogenesis of coronary artery disease.* New York: McGraw-Hill, 1969.

Friedman, M., and Rosenman, R. H. *Type A behavior and your heart.* New York: Knopf, 1974.

Friedman, M., Rosenman, R. H., and Carroll, V. Changes in the serum cholesterol and blood clotting time in men subjected to cyclic variation of occupational stress. *Circulation,* 1958, *17,* 852–861.

Friedman, M., Rosenman, R. H., Straus, R., Wurm, M., and Kositchek, R. The relationship of behavior pattern A to the state of the coronary vasculature: A study of 51 autopsy subjects. *American Journal of Medicine,* 1968, *44,* 525–537.

Glass, D. C. *Stress and coronary prone behavior.* Hillsdale, New Jersey: Lawrence Erlbaum Associates, 1977.

Glass, D. C., and Singer, J. E. *Urban stress: Experiments in noise and social stressors.* New York: Academic, 1972.

Glass, D. C., Singer, J. E., and Friedman, L. N. Psychic cost of adaptation to an environmental stressor. *Journal of Personality and Social Psychology,* 1969, *12,* 200–210.

Glass, D. C., Singer, J. E., Leonard, H. S., Krantz, D. S., Cohen, S., and Cummings, H. X. Perceived control of aversive stimulation and the reduction of stress responses. *Journal of Personality,* 1973, *41,* 577–595.

Glass, D. C., Snyder, M. L., and Hollis, J. F. Time urgency and the type A coronary-prone behavior pattern. *Journal of Applied Social Psychology,* 1974, *4,* 125–140.

Greene, W. A., Goldstein, S., and Moss, A. J. Psychosocial aspects of sudden death: A preliminary report. *Archives of Internal Medicine,* 1972, *129,* 725–731.

Grinker, R. R., and Spiegel, J. P. *Men under stress.* New York: McGraw-Hill, 1945.

Hawkins, N. G., Davies, R., and Holmes, T. H. Evidence of psychosocial factors in the development of pulmonary tuberculosis. *American Review of Tubercular and Pulmonary Diseases,* 1957, *75,* 768–780.

Jenkins, C. D., Rosenman, R. H., and Zyzanski, S. J. Prediction of clinical coronary heart disease by a test for the coronary-prone behavior pattern. *New England Journal of Medicine,* 1974, *290,* 1271–1275.

Jenkins, C. D., Zyzanski, S. J., Lefkowitz, S., Everist, M., and Ryan, T. Psychological correlates of coronary angiographic findings. Presented at the American Heart Association meetings, November 1974. Abs. Circ. 50: *69,* 1974.

Jenkins, C. D., Zyzanski, S. J., and Rosenman, R. H. Progress toward validation of a computer-scored test of the type A coronary-prone behavior pattern. *Psychosomatic Medicine,* 1971, *33,* 192–202.

Kenigsberg, D., Zyzanski, S. J., Jenkins, C. D., Wardwell, W. I., and Licciardello, A. T. The coronary-prone behavior pattern in hospitalized patients with and without coronary heart disease. *Psychosomatic Medicine,* 1974, *36,* 344–351.

Krantz, D. S., Glass, D. C., and Snyder, M. L. Helplessness, stress level, and the coronary-prone behavior pattern. *Journal of Experimental Social Psychology,* 1974, *10,* 284–300.

Kryter, K. D. *The effects of noise on man.* New York: Academic, 1970.

Lazarus, R. S. *Psychological stress and the coping process.* New York: McGraw-Hill, 1966.

Lazarus, R. S. Emotions and adaptation: Conceptual and empirical relations. In W. J. Arnold

(Ed.), *Nebraska Symposium on Motivation*. Lincoln, Neb.: University of Nebraska Press, 1968.

Rosenmann, R. H., Brand, R., J., Jenkins, C. D., Friedman, M., Straus, R., and Wurm, M. Coronary heart disease in the western collaborative group study: Final follow-up experience of 8½ years. *Journal of the American Medical Association*, 1975, *233*, 872–877.

Rosenman, R. H., and Friedman, M. Neurogenic factors in pathogenesis of cornary heart disease. *Medical Clinics of North America*, 1974, *58*, 269–279.

Rosenman, R. H., Friedman, M., Straus, R., Wurm, M., Kositchek, R., Hahn, W., and Werthessen, N. T. Predictive study of coronary heart disease: The western collaborative group study. *Journal of the American Medical Association*, 1964, *189*, 15–26.

Rosenman, R. H., Rahe, R. H., Borhani, N. O., and Feinlieb, M. Heritability of personality and behavior pattern. Unpublished manuscript, Harold Bruun Institute, Mount Zion Hospital and Medical Center, San Francisco, Calif., 1975.

Sanders, A. F. The influence of noise on two discrimination tasks. *Ergonomics*, 1961, *4*, 253–258.

Seligman, M. E. P. *Helplessness: On depression, development, and death*. San Francisco, Calif.: Freeman, 1975.

Seligman, M. E. P., Maier, S. F., and Solomon, R. L. Unpredictable and uncontrollable aversive events. In F. R. Brush (Ed.), *Aversive conditioning and learning*. New York: Academic, 1971.

Selye, H. *The stress of life*. New York: McGraw-Hill, 1956.

Sherrod, D. R. Crowding, perceived control, and behavioral aftereffects. *Journal of Applied Social Psychology*, 1974, *4*, 171–186.

Thompson, R. S., and Spencer, W. A. Habituation: A model phenomenon for the study of neuronal substrates of behavior. *Psychological Review*, 1966, *73*, 16–43.

Ward, W. D. (Ed.). *Proceedings of the International Congress on Noise as a Public Health Problem*. Washington, D.C.: U. S. Government Printing Office, 1974.

Weiss, J. M., Stone, E. A., and Harrell, N. Coping behavior and brain norepinephrine levels in rats. *Journal of Comparative and Physiological Psychology*, 1970, *72*, 153–160.

Wohlwill, F. F., Nasar, J. L., DeJoy, D. M., and Foruzani, H. H. Behavioral effects of a noisy environment: Task involvement versus passive exposure. Unpublished manuscript, Pennsylvania State University, 1975.

Wohlwill, J. F. The emerging discipline of environmental psychology. *American Psychologist*, 1970, *25*, 303–312.

Wortman, C. F., and Brehm, J. W. Responses to uncontrollable outcomes: An integration of reactance theory and the learned helplessness model. In L. Berkowitz (Ed.), *Advances in experimental social psychology* (vol. 8). New York: Academic, 1975.

Beyond the Effects of Crowding: Situational and Individual Differences

6

CHALSA LOO

Research on crowding represents one of many attempts on the part of the field of psychology to address issues born of a rapidly changing world. The issues most relevant to the study of crowding include overpopulation, rapid urbanization, and environmental deterioration. With the environmentalist movement of the late 1960's as a forerunner, the field of psychology formally responded to the issue of overpopulation in 1970 (Bartz, 1970; Craik, 1970; Fawcett, 1970; Wohlwill, 1970). More comprehensive demographic data on population and urbanization growth-trends were available. With such data as an existential backdrop, psychologists contributed some useful research to further the understanding of crowding and population issues.

Demographic Data

Several demographic statistics provided fuel for the ecological fire. The world-population growth-rate was calculated to be approximately 2% per year, equivalent to adding two people per second to this planet (net growth, births minus deaths) or 70 million people per year. Speaking more concretely, this growth is equivalent to adding a city the size of San Francisco to this world every 6 days. Our world doubling-time is 35 years.

CHALSA LOO ● Merrill College, University of California at Santa Cruz. A portion of this research was presented under the title "Deriving Hypotheses for Researching the Effects of Crowding in Experimental Settings" at a symposium at the American Psychological Association, Montreal, August, 1973, and another portion was presented under the title "A Social–Spatial Model of Crowding Stress" at a symposium at the Western Psychological Association, San Francisco, April, 1974.

Although the United States rate of population growth has dropped to .8%, increasing urbanization has created (and continues to create) crowded conditions. Mobility to the cities and affluence have been considered to be the primary factors leading to environmental deterioration and problems of crowding in the United States (Kirk, 1973). Increasing density is a problem in the United States primarily because of the large numbers of our population who migrate to urban areas. Our problem is not that we have a small land area; our problem derives from the very uneven distribution of our population across a large land area. According to Kirk (1973), 70% of the American population lives in less than 2% of the total land area. The rapid move to urban centers is represented in the comparison between the percentage of the population living in urban areas in 1790 and today. In 1790, only 5% of the United States population lived in urban areas, whereas today 75% of the population lives in urban areas (*Population Bulletin*, 1974, Vol. 19, No. 2).

Moreover most people are not aware that consumption and world-resource depletion are connected to the relationship between overpopulation, resource depletion, and unemployment in other countries. America cannot fool herself into believing that because her population is growing at a much slower rate than that of other countries she does not contribute to a worldwide problem. Note that America consumes much more than her "share" of world resources on the basis of population. The United States accounts for about 30% of the world's consumption of raw materials (*United Nations Statistical Yearbook*, 1971). Based on calculations of power and steel consumption, one American produces roughly 50 times the stress on the environment as one Indian. Based on calculations of per capita steel consumption, one American puts 342 times the demand on nonrenewable materials as does one Indonesian (Ehrlich and Holdren, 1973). For the United States to maintain (or increase) her technological state and affluent life-style (relative to other countries), she must depend on obtaining natural resources from other countries whose populations are growing at far greater rates than her own. Since many of these natural resources are finite and since these countries have and will come to realize the value of their possessed resources coupled with their own aspirations for a more affluent life, conflicts between nations are likely. Otherwise the United States must face new and hard solutions as other alternatives.

Research on Crowding

With an understanding of the growth trends of population and urbanization, many psychologists sought to research the behavioral effects of crowding through controlled experimental studies. The empirical studies of Freedman, Klevansky, and Ehrlich, published in 1971, received widespread attention both outside of and within the discipline of psychology.

What was most startling about the notoriety given to these experiments was the fact that Freedman and his colleagues found no significant effects of crowding on the task performance of adults. One might expect notoriety to result from the finding of significant effects, but it is unusual that "the acceptance of the null hypothesis wins the Nobel prize." It is my belief that attention was drawn to the Freedman *et al.* studies for one basic reason: the purposes of the research filled a felt need, a need for research pertaining to a critical issue of both social and environmental relevance, a need that prior psychological research had not directly addressed. The research addressed the need to understand the effects of crowding on human behavior. It might be argued that the unexpectedness of Freedman *et al.*'s findings contributed to its notoriety. I suspect however that this factor may have had less import than the fact that it filled a research need.

Since 1971 psychological research on crowding has grown considerably, not just in number but also in kind. Initial research on crowding focused on the effects of crowding. Of late, research on the effects of crowding has investigated a fuller sample of effects; besides the more obvious task effects, research has been pursued on the more subtle aftereffects, the less detectable physiological and emotional effects, and the interpersonal effects. While research on crowding effects is essential to our understanding of crowding, a comprehensive study of crowding must also include research on the *determinants* of crowding effects, the *process* of crowding, and the *perception* of crowding. These issues are now being addressed in more detail and with greater interest. The interplay between individual needs and spatial conditions needs to be more fully understood, for it cannot be assumed that what holds for one holds for all. There is also the need for psychological research to examine the effects of crowding on the individual (i.e., particular individuals) as well as on the group. Moreover, as noted by Moos and Insel (1974), environments have personalities. Thus just as it is naïve to assume that everyone reacts similarly to an individual who has a particular personality, it is naïve to assume that all persons respond to their physical environment in a similar way.

Lastly there is a need for replication of research, given the neophyte nature of this research area and the complexities of crowding determinants.

Some research on crowding effects pursue either/or purposes; that is, they seek to answer the question of whether or not crowding adversely affects people. Such research might well be supplemented with empirical inquiry into the determinants of crowding effects. Such an approach is in keeping with the complexities of understanding the phenomenon of crowding. Two researchable questions, answers to which could potentially contribute substantial knowledge, include: *Under what conditions* does crowding affect or not affect people? and *For whom* does crowding have or not have effects? This chapter discusses these two issues: (1) the determinants of crowding effects and (2) the interaction between individual needs and spatial conditions. A conceptual model of crowding stress is presented as an illustration of the role of individual differences in human response to environmental-space factors.

Determinants of the Effects of Crowding

Thus far no research on crowding offers conclusive evidence that crowding does or does not significantly affect human behavior. This is because the factors affecting the findings are multiple and complex. Any environment or situation contains more than just a manipulated density factor; there are *environmental factors* (physical and social), *situational factors,* and *intrapersonal factors* that contribute to the objective definition and the subjective experience of a condition.

Environmental factors include inside and outside factors, both of which have physical (or nonsocial) and social components. *Inside physical factors* includes the two-dimensional area (length × width of floor) as well as the three-dimensional area (length × width × ceiling height), since ceiling height may alter the experience of crowdedness. Inside physical factors also include room shape, since research findings indicate that room shape affects the perception of degree of crowdedness. Given identical areas, it was found that a square-shaped room was perceived to be more crowded than a rectangular-shaped room (Desor, 1972). Other inside physical factors include (1) the absence or provision of personal territories through the use or inclusion of certain furniture or furniture arrangements; (2) the quality of the territorial boundaries (permeable or impermeable); and (3) architectural designs that affect the experience or perception of crowding. The absence or presence of windows or mirrors, or of locked or unlocked doors and the number of doors are examples of inside structural factors that may determine the degree of experienced crowdedness.

Outside physical factors of the environment include census-tract data or geographical factors. Census-tract data include: number of apartments in a hallway; number of apartments in a dwelling; height of the apartment in terms of floor; number of dwellings in a unit; number of units in an acre; population size and density of the neighborhood, town, city, and country; length of residence; degree of mobility; and quality of territorial space (public, semiprivate, or private). Geographical factors include terrain and weather conditions.

Inside social factors of the environment include number of occupants and number of people per square foot. *Outside social factors of the environment* include cultural and societal variables such as values, norms, and expectations.

Social situational factors include characteristics of the individual's interactions with others (type of interaction and degree of interaction), his or her relationship to the other occupants (friends, acquaintances, or strangers), or his or her interpersonal attraction to the other occupants. *Nonso-*

cial situational factors include the type of ongoing activity, the duration of the condition, and the purposes of the activity.

Intrapersonal factors consist of idiosyncratic characteristics of the person, including age; sex; personal space needs; degree of perceived control over the environment; temperament; state of arousal; personality traits; need for privacy, enclosure, stability, safety, and affiliation; and personal expectations.

Having reviewed some of the factors involved in any density condition, let us now consider a few of these factors in regard to the understanding of research findings. Research findings of the either–or variety that appear to be discrepant may actually point to factors that determine the experience of crowdedness regardless of the density factor or in interaction with the density factor. When Freedman, Klevansky, and Ehrlich (1971b) failed to find significant effects of density on adults' task performance, Freedman (1971a) concluded that crowding is not particularly detrimental to human beings. Additionally the research of Stokols, Rall, Pinner, and Schopler (1973) found no significant effects of density on adults' task performance. Yet research on the effects of density on children have shown significant findings. Significant effects of density have been found for amount of social interaction and aggression (Hutt and Vaizey, 1966; Loo, 1972) and for amount of motor activity (Smith, 1973).

It is not sufficient to take an either–or position with regard to discrepant findings in terms of density effects. One must ask how the conditions differed in terms of factors other than density, such as environmental, situational, and intrapersonal factors.

Environmental factors other than density that need to be considered include the degree to which architectural arrangement provides personal territories for the occupants. Situational factors such as the activity of the occupants must be considered. Intrapersonal factors such as the age, the relationship, the coping skill, and the test sophistocation of the occupants must be considered. Finally, any interaction between the aforementioned factors must be examined.

Crowding Effects as a Function of Architecture and Personal Territory

The effects of architectural design (especially partitioning) on the occupants perception of crowdedness has been investigated (Baum, Riess, and O'Hara, 1974; Desor, 1972; Stokols, Smith, and Prostor, 1975). These findings support the notion that feelings of crowdedness can be altered by certain kinds of changes in architectural design while density is held constant. In addition to the effects of partitioning, the provision of personal territories by the allotment of furniture is likely to influence the perception of crowdedness.

Nearly all of the research on the effects of crowding on adult behavior have been performed in rooms with furniture such as chairs or chairs with desk-type arms, and each subject has been given a chair. It should be noted that structuring the environment with desk-chairs or chairs is one way of providing a personal territory for each individual that has clearly defined boundaries. Since these territories were equal among all persons and determined beforehand by the experimenter, several factors were eliminated that may often be present in crowded conditions in the real world. These factors include ambiguity of personal territory, competition for the more valued or larger territories, and anxiety over anticipated or actual intrusions of others into one's personal territory. Architectural structures that create territorial havens for individuals are likely to reduce greatly the probability that a state of crowdedness will be experienced or that negative effects of crowding will be demonstrated.

Studies of crowding using children (Hutt and Vaizey, 1966; Loo, 1972) were performed with highly unstructured architecture. No furniture was provided, and the only contents (toys) were portable. Personal territories were undefined; the experimenters did not provide nor assign them. The resources of toys and space were undetermined and ambiguous. No attempt was made to eliminate physical discomfort that might result, unless it proved physically dangerous to a child. There was no architectural structure behind or within which a child could retreat for safety or solitude. No architectural arrangement existed to eliminate uninvited stimuli from others, such as noise, physical intrusions, or social overtures. In such a situation, it is expected that the level of anxiety will be higher because of greater competition for resources, greater possibility of anticipated and actual intrusions, greater fear of loss of resources, greater uncertainty about establishing a personal territory, and greater insecurity born of a lack of an area in which to retreat. Thus it is assumed that the availability of architectural structures to provide territories, boundaries, spatial screens, and solitude will affect the degree to which crowding is experienced.

Degree of architectural structuredness alone, however, may not be a necessary or sufficient condition to determine whether or not crowdedness will have measureable effects. Research on the effects of spatial density on adults in architecturally *unstructured* experimental settings (Sherrod, 1974; Dooley, 1974) has shown that even in settings where no furniture to define personal territories was provided, there were no effects on task performance. However, while Sherrod failed to find a relationship between task performance and crowding, he did find a relationship between behavioral aftereffects and crowding. Subjects who had been placed in the crowded condition were less persistent in solving unsolvable puzzles than were subjects who were placed in noncrowded conditions. Dooley found that although spatial density did not significantly affect computational accuracy on a marketing task, it did affect emotional tone. Subjects in the high spatial-density condition felt more negative, uncomfortable, crowded, and irritated and perceived others as more unfriendly and aggressive than did those in the low spatial-density condition. Moreover crowded conditions adversely affected subjects' enjoyment of the task.

In summary, then, it is hypothesized that the effects of crowding are more likely to be found where the architecture fails to allow for the structuring of individual territories, privacy, and a sense of control over one's environment. If structure does provide territories or resources but they are of unequal value or the supply fails to meet the need, negative effects of crowding are more likely to be found. Negative effects of crowding are also more likely to occur if the personal territories and/or resources are insufficient for the completion or mastery of the activity by any one or more individuals. Yet the degree to which architectural arrangement can ameliorate or alleviate the harmful effects of crowding most likely depends on other factors as well, such as the activity of the occupants or the characteristics of the occupants.

Crowding Effects as a Function of Type of Activity

While crowding is more than just a matter of space, it is also more than just a matter of architectural design. Research (Cozby, 1973; Desor, 1972) has demonstrated that the type of ongoing activity significantly affects the degree to which occupants perceive crowdedness. Comparing four activities, Desor found that given the same area, the number of people that constituted a state just under "overcrowded" was largest for (1) a cocktail party, followed in order by (2) waiting in an airport, (3) sitting and talking, and (4) sitting and reading. Generalizing from Desor's findings, it appears as though standing activities should require less space per person before overcrowdedness is felt than should sitting activities. Within each position, standing or sitting, social activities were perceived to necessitate less space per person before overcrowdedness was felt than solitary activities. Thus activities that are more solitary in nature and require a greater horizontal body position can be hypothesized to require greater personal space for the individuals.

Studies on the effects of crowding on adults have examined crowded conditions in which the activity of the participants has been highly structured and have often involved tasks that must be performed individually. In Freedman's study (1971), the adult subjects who worked alone at their desks were assigned specific pencil-and-paper tasks such as doing anagrams, crossing out numbers, and forming words. In Sherrod's study (1974), subjects who worked alone sitting on the floor were asked to complete pencil-and-paper tests of mental abilities. In Dooley's study (1974), subjects who worked alone while standing calculated mathematical problems on paper. Solitary activities simultaneously performed by all persons reduce or eliminate the probability of interference from others. Like architectural designs that provide individual boundaries, solitary activities,

which draw attention to a nonsocial task, function to "cocoon" the individual from the stimuli bombardment of others. Take as an example the common actvity of riders on crowded subways, planes, or buses; restricting
one's vision to one's immediate field by reading or writing serves to help
"tune out" outside stimuli. Furthermore, since solitary tasks frequently do
not involve mobility, there is little threat of being intruded upon.

Comparing the effects of individual and group tasks is an important
researchable issue. The study by Stokols, Rall, Pinner, and Schopler (1973)
did not assign individual tasks. While their study does not truly compare
tasks done individually with tasks done cooperatively, it approaches this
question. No significant effect for perceived crowdedness between group
tasks that were competitive or cooperative was found. This finding was
contrary to their hypothesis that subjects would experience more crowding
under a competitive task set than under a cooperative one. However, the
authors noted that the enjoyment of the game was high for all conditions,
which may have minimized task differences, and that both the cooperative
and the competitive conditions were located toward the cooperative end of
the rating scale.

In contrast to the activities of adults in studies of crowding, the activities in all studies of crowding using children have been highly *unstructured.*
Children have been studied under free-play conditions in which activities
are solely the choice of each child, for example, which and how many toys
are played with and who and how many other children are interacted with.
Interactions among participants are much more likely and participant activities vary with each individual. Consider, for instance, a situation in
which Child A wishes to play alone, while Child B, who carries a doctor's
bag, eagerly seeks out a "patient" to cure. If all the other children are
involved in "cops and robbers," Child A may be coerced to play the role of
"patient," particularly if Child B exceeds A in dominance and strength. Or
consider the situation in which Child D decides to sleep and needs quiet to
accomplish this solitary activity, yet Child E decides to play "Frankenstein
wakes up the dead!"

In summary, it is hypothesized that negative effects of crowding are
more likely to be found where people's activities involve social interaction
or where the accomplishment of one person's task necessitates certain behavior from another that is incompatible with the needs of the other. It is
also hypothesized that negative effects of crowding are more likely to be
found where the activity of some occupants involves mobility in directions
that intersect the direction of others, for then the probability of congestion,
interference, and territorial intrusions is most likely.

The factors considered to affect human response to crowded conditions that have been addressed so far have included: (1) the capacity of the
environment to provide personal territories for the occupants; (2) the degree of social interaction characteristic of the activities of the occupants or
the degree to which the activities of the occupants are structured individual

tasks; (3) the degree of physical intrusiveness and congestion characteristic of occupant activities; and (4) the degree of similarity of the activity needs of the occupants.

Crowding Effects as a Function of Individual Differences

Now that we have discussed two determinants of crowdedness—architectural structure and occupant activities—it is appropriate to ask: For whom does crowding have an effect? The study of individual differences in response to crowding has barely been explored, which is surprising since the few studies that have analyzed for individual differences have reported significant findings. In a study that compared autistic, brain-damaged, and normal children in terms of social-density effects (Hutt and Vaizey, 1966), more aggressive–destructive behavior was found in the high social-density condition than in the low-density condition for the normal and for the brain-damaged subjects, while the autistic subjects showed no main effect for density. Further differences were found for territoriality behavior. As social density increased, autistic subjects spent more time on the boundaries of the room, while normal subjects spent more time in the central areas of the room. In a study that compared spatial-density effects on men with different personal space needs, Dooley (1974) found that subjects with large personal-space needs experienced more adverse aftereffects and affective reactions in the spatially crowded condition than did subjects with small personal-space needs. Individual differences seemed to be a stronger determinant in response to crowding than were the crowding conditions themselves to all subjects as a whole.

In general, the study of sex differences has received considerably more attention than the study of individual differences. In some senses, however, sex differences can be subsumed under the heading of individual differences and, as such, are mentioned here. Significant effects of density on sex have been found (Freedman, Levy, Buchanan, and Price, 1972; Ross, Layton, Erickson, and Schopler, 1973; Stokols, Rall, Pinner, and Schopler, 1973). In general, males find crowded conditions to be more emotionally unpleasant than do females, although this pattern of results appears to be mediated by group size, composition, and task set (cf. Aiello, Epstein, and Karlin, 1975; Marshall and Heslin, 1975).

Returning to our comparison between findings from density studies on adults with those on children, the question of how crowding differentially affects persons of different ages should be asked. Obviously crowding may affect children differently than adults, although it is difficult to know to what one should attribute these differences. Are differences attributable to coping skill? Are adults more adaptable? Are they able to cope with a greater range and severity of conditions than children? Are differences attributable to test consciousness? Are adults who participate in

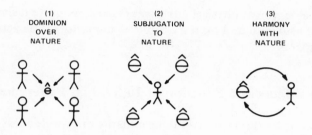

Figure 1. Three person–environment relationships.

laboratory psychology experiments more wary than children and thus less likely to respond spontaneously and naturally in experimental settings than children? Are differences attributable to the nature of the activities in which persons of various ages engage or to age-related capabilities? Children generally have a shorter attention span, have a lower capacity for concentration, and indulge in more mobile than stationary activity than do adults. These questions are at present empirically unanswered.

Psychological Effects as a Function of Relationship to the Environment

Individual differences in response to environmental conditions can be conceptualized in terms of the relationship (or interaction) between individual predispositions or traits and environmental factors. In the most general terms, Kluckholn and Strodtbeck (1961) distinguished among three basic relationships that persons can have with nature: (1) dominion over nature, (2) subjugation to nature, and (3) harmony with nature (see Figure 1). Applying this model to the degree of psychological stress experienced, I contend that stress is usually not experienced when persons are either in harmony with the environment or when they have dominion over the environment. Where there is harmony, the environment accommodates the social and spatial needs of the individual. Where there is dominion over the environment, individuals have freedom of choice and control to alter the environment to fit their spatial and social needs. But where individuals are subjugated to their environment, they have little or no control over their surroundings: the environment places constraints on the individual.

Many writers have generalized about the adaptive responses of the human species, that capacity of human beings to change or modify themselves according to new environmental conditions, the ability to accommodate without difficulty. Wohlwill (1970), for example, states that while all behavior occurs in some environmental context and the environment imposes constraints on the range of behaviors permissible in it, people develop forms of adaptation to environmental conditions. Dubos (1965) also comments on the incredibly adaptive capacities of the human species.

Sommer (1969) comments that people will "not only . . . adapt to crowding, noise, and traffic in the city, they will find it difficult to live in any other environment" (p. 169) and that "man will be reshaped to fit whatever environment he creates" (p. 172).

Statements of people's adaptive responses do not address the issue of individual differences. A study of individual differences must also include nonadaptation, the process whereby an individual does not cope with or accommodate his needs to the demands of the environment. Whether the relationship between the individual and the environment is harmonious or stressful will be partly determined by the individual's spatial and social needs, which are individually and situationally variable and which are partly related to cultural norms and values. Personal space or body-buffer zones, defined as the area surrounding a person within which the presence of another person creates feelings of anxiety, are measures of social–spatial needs. Research evidence exists to demonstrate that measures of personal space and body-buffer zones are distinct among people, although they can vary somewhat as a function of time, situation, and level of emotional anxiety or arousal. Every environmental context contains spatial and social features that can either accommodate or frustrate the satisfaction of the individual's social–spatial needs. Where such needs are frustrated, stress and anxiety are experienced, sometimes resulting in clinically dysfunctional behavior.

A Model of Social and Spatial Crowding Stresses

A model for the relationship between environmental constraints and individual differences integrates social–spatial needs of the individual, a continuum of states of crowdedness, and pathological classifications that serve as descriptive examples of a disharmonious relationship between the environment and the self. The model combines clinical and social–psychological phenomena (see Figure 2).

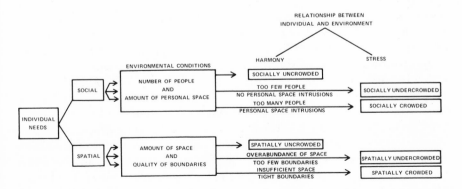

Figure 2. A social–spatial model of crowding stresses.

Although social and spatial needs are often intertwined, the distinction between them has been discussed (McGrew, 1970; Loo, 1973). The *social need* of the individual can vary in terms of the number of people that are desired and the amount of personal space needed (or size of body-buffer zone). The number of people desired can range from a desire to be alone (high need for social privacy) to a desire to be among crowds (low need for social privacy). The size of the body-buffer zone will be a function of the individual and the situation. *Spatial needs* can vary from closed to vast space (boundaries relevant) and from a small to large area (boundaries irrelevant).

Uncrowded, crowded, and *undercrowded* represent points on a continuum of states of crowdedness (Stokols, 1972). Integrating these points with the social and spatial dimensions results in states characterized as: socially uncrowded, socially crowded, socially undercrowded, spatially uncrowded, spatially crowded, and spatially undercrowded. Harmony between the individual and the environment exists in the socially uncrowded and spatially uncrowded state. In the socially uncrowded state, the number of people and the amount of personal space achieved all meet the individual's social needs. In the spatially uncrowded state, the amount of space and the boundary characteristics meet the individual's spatial needs for psychological and performance functioning. Crowding stress exists when individual needs and characteristics are not synchronous with the constraints of the environment; stress can be measured by affective responses and/or physiological changes or by behavioral indices of anxiety.

Normally there is a balanced interaction between the individual and the environment. The environment affects the individual but the individual still maintains some degree of control over the environment. However, in clinical cases of environmental phobias, the influence of the environment upon the individual vastly outweighs the effect that the individual has on the environment. Environmental phobias represent a persistent and irrational fear of certain environmental conditions, in which the individual is psychologically overwhelmed by his or her surroundings to the point that severe anxiety is felt and demonstrated.

Social-crowding stress (defined as a response) results from situations in which the number of people present or the amount of personal space allowed are contrary to individual needs, causing anxiety or frustration. Social-crowding stress is experienced in the socially crowded and socially undercrowded condition. In the socially crowded condition, stress is due to the presence of either too many people or to intrusions on one's personal space by others. *Ochlophobia* an outdated term referring to a fear of crowds, is a clinical description of *social-crowding stress* and exemplifies a dysfunctional relationship between the individual and the social environment. Intrusions on personal space may also be present in ochlophobia but are not dependent upon a crowd to precipitate anxiety or discomfort. Intrusions into one's personal space require only one other person.

In the *socially undercrowded condition,* stress is due to the absence of people or to a need for closer interactional distance between oneself and another. There is a need for affiliation with others, intimacy, and social contact either because of an insecurity in being alone or a strong need for physical closeness. *Monophobia,* the fear of being alone, is a clinical diagnosis representing one type of *social-undercrowding stress.*

Spatial-crowding stress refers to a situation in which the amount of physical space surrounding the individual is contrary to the individual's level of comfort. How this space is bounded can also create feelings of discomfort to certain individuals. On the spatial dimension, stress is experienced in the spatially crowded and spatially undercrowded conditions. In the *spatially crowded condition,* stress is due to having insufficient space available for individual comfort and normal functioning. There is a feeling of spatial restrictiveness and a need for more space. *Claustrophobia* represents an exaggeration of such a stress, in which persons suffering from this condition are fearful of closed places. Claustrophobics may fear being in closets or may go to great lengths to avoid entering a small room or passageway even when it is essential for them to do so.

In a *spatially undercrowded condition,* there is an individual need for spatial crowding or spatial enclosure. Stress is due to an individual's experience of an excessive abundance of space. *Agoraphobia,* narrowly defined as a fear of open spaces, represents such a stress. Apparently, environmental boundaries provide a sense of security, and minor visual features of the environment affect the intensity of the anxiety of agoraphobia. Anxiety is greatest when there are no perceivable boundaries to a large, open visual field. Where boundaries to the space exist, the fear is greatest where the space walked into is wide and high. The phobia diminishes as soon as a visual boundary is imposed, be this a hedge, a fence, trees, undulation of the ground, or simply an umbrella held above the head of the agoraphobic (Clevenger, 1890; Weiss, 1964). One of the common fears expressed by agoraphobics is that they will go mad and lose control; they fear an inability to control unacceptable urges in an environment which is so vast and open as to not provide external constraints or controls for them (Marks, 1969).

Environmental phobias are not commonly diagnosed or treated, but for the purposes of this paper, they are used as examples of extreme conditions in which certain characteristics of the environment elicit anxiety and feelings of discomfort in certain individuals. Differential responses to environmental conditions are a function of many factors, including an individual's personal-space needs, interpersonal-space needs, needs for solitude and privacy, needs for affiliation, needs for physical space and the arrangement of such space, past experiences, cultural values, and idiosyncratic symbolism of or association with certain environmental situations. Crowding is dependent upon the individual's perception and experience of the environment; thus definitions of crowdedness, uncrowdedness, and undercrowdedness are individually defined. And since all individual per-

ceptions are made within a particular cultural context, definitions of crowdedness, uncrowdedness, and undercrowdedness are culturally as well as
individually defined.

Summary

The effects of crowding are individually and situationally variable. Thus
research and theory on crowding must address the question of "for whom"
and "under what conditions" crowding has and fails to have an effect.
Another important question, that of how or which behaviors crowding
affects has not been addressed in this chapter, although it is of no less value.
It is assumed that answers of "how" are dependent on "for whom" and
"under what conditions." More importantly, conclusions as to how crowding affects human beings are incomplete without an analysis of situational
and individual differences. Research on crowding must proceed "beyond
the effects of crowding."

More research is needed on individual differences with respect to social and spatial environmental conditions. In addition, closer examination
is needed to understand the complex and interacting variables in the setting that affect human behavior and emotion. Provision of personal territories by architecture and by the characteristics of the activity are only two
such variables. Generally persons function most securely and effectively
when they have a sense of control over and involvement with their environment, where their environment accommodates their needs and preferences, and where their environment provides the greatest flexibility of
behaviors and conditions to suit the individual's changing and variable
functions and emotional needs. Control over the environment also involves
a sense of predictability and permanence in the environment. Interest in an
environment involves the appropriate combination of stimulation and
familiarity in a perceptual and cognitive sense.

Without predictability and interest, environments can cause anxiety
and stress for the individual, and the severity of the stress and discomfort is
largely determined by individual needs and vulnerabilities as they conflict
with the constraints of the environment. Certain environmental conditions
can induce stress, either through change that comes about so quickly as to
create cognitive confusion and insecurity in relation to the environment or
through conditions of stimulus overload such as traffic congestion and
noise pollution that test the limits of our capacity to cope (cf. Glass and
Singer, 1972; Milgram, 1970). Crowding in the cities has led to a new style
of living, that of the condominium and the high-rise. We need to know how
such changes affect human behavior. Our advancing technology, born of a
society seeking to dominate nature, frequently advances to a point beyond
our control. The ability to cope is a healthy one for it means our survival.
Yet consciousness of one's environment and its effects are of primary im-

portance. If human beings continue always to cope, without being conscious of what we are creating and what it is in turn creating in us, we may never initiate the actions or alter the attitudes necessary to modify these conditions.

Going beyond naïve and simple thinking to sophistication in research and theory in environmental psychology would do justice to the complexity of the relationship between the individual and his or her environment. Psychology has a long way to go before achieving a sophisticated understanding of the phenomena of crowding, but some headway is being made and important directions for future research are clear.

Acknowledgments

I wish to thank Adam Geballe, M. Brewster Smith, Dan Schag, Dan Stokols, and Pavel Machotka for their helpful comments on the manuscript. I also wish to dedicate this chapter to those whose support of my early work on crowding was so valuable—Charles Wenar, Dean Coddington, Malcolm Helper, Herbert Rie, and Paul Ehrlich.

References

Aiello, J., Epstein, Y., and Karlin, R. Methodological conceptual issues in crowding. Paper presented at the Western Psychological Convention, San Francisco, April, 1974.

Bartz, W. While psychologists doze on. *American Psychologist,* 1970, *25*(6), 500–503.

Baum, A., Riess, M., and O'Hara, J. Architectural variance of reaction to spatial invasion. *Environment and Behavior,* 1974, *6*(1), 91–100.

Clevenger, S. Heart disease in insanity and a case of panphobia. *Alienist and neurologist,* 1890, *7,* 535–543.

Cozby, P. Effects of density, activity, and personality on environmental preferences. *Journal of Research on Personality,* 1973, *7,* 45–60.

Craik, K. Environmental psychology. In *New directions in psychology* (vol. 4). New York: Holt, Rinehart and Winston, 1970.

Desor, J. Toward a psychological theory of crowding. *Journal of Personality and Social Psychology,* 1972, *21*(1), 79–83.

Dooley, B. Crowding stress: The effects of social density on men with "close" or "far" personal space. U.C.L.A.: Unpublished dissertation, 1974, also presented at the Western Psychological Association Convention, Sacramento, California, May, 1975.

Dubos, R. *Man adapting.* New Haven, Conn.: Yale University Press, 1965.

Ehrlich, P., Ehrlich, A., and Holdren, J. *Human ecology.* San Francisco: W. H. Freeman and Co., 1973.

Fawcett, J. *Psychology and population.* New Haven, Conn.: The Population Council, 1970.

Freedman, J. The crowd—Maybe not so maddening after all. *Psychology Today,* 1971a, *5*(4).

Freedman, J., Klevansky, S., and Ehrlich, P. The effect of crowding on human task performance. *Journal of Applied Social Psychology,* 1971b, *1,* 7–25.

Freedman, J. L., Levy, A. S., Buchanan, R. W., and Price, J. Crowding and human aggressiveness. *Journal of Experimental Social Psychology,* 1972, *8,* 502–517.

Glass, D., and Singer, J. *Urban stress: Experiments in noise and social stressors.* New York: Academic Press, 1972.

Hutt, C., and Vaizey, M. Differential effects of group density on social behavior. *Nature*, 1966, *209*, 1371–1372.

Kirk, D. The misunderstood challenge of population change. The Population Reference Bureau report, selection No. 44, November 1973, Washington, D.C.

Kluckholn, R. R., and Strodtbeck, F. L. *Variations in value orientations.* Evanston, Ill.: Row, Peterson, 1961.

Loo, C. The effects of spatial density on the social behavior or children. *Journal of Applied Social Psychology*, 1972, *2*, 372–381.

Loo, C. Important issues in researching the effects of crowding on humans. *Representative Research in Social Psychology*, 1973, *4*, 219–226.

Marks, I. *Fears and phobias.* New York: Academic Press, 1969.

Marshall, J., and Heslin, R. Boys and girls together: Sexual composition and the effects of density and group size on children. *Journal of Personality and Social Psychology*, in press.

McGrew, P. Social and spatial density effects on spacing behavior in preschool children. *Journal of Child Psychology and Psychiatry*, 1970, *11*, 197–205.

Milgram, S. The experience of living in cities. *Science*, 1970, *167*, 1461–1468.

Moos, R. and Insel, P. (Eds.). *Issues in social ecology: Human milieus.* Palo Alto, Calif.: National Press, 1974.

Population Bulletin, 1974, *19*(2).

Ross, M., Layton, B., Erickson, B., and Schopler, J. Affect, facial regard, and reactions to crowding. *Journal of Personality and Social Psychology*, 1973, *28*(1), 69–76.

Sherrod, D. Crowding, perceived control, and behavioral aftereffects. *Journal of Applied Social Psychology*, 1974, *4*(2), 171–186.

Smith, P. Aggression in a preschool playground: Effects of varying physical resources. Presentation at the International Conference on Origins and Determinants of Aggressive Behavior. Monte Carlo, Monaco, July, 1973.

Sommer, R. *Personal space.* Englewood Cliffs, N.J.: Prentice-Hall, 1969.

Stokols, D. A social–psychological model of human crowding phenomena. *Journal of the American Institute of Planners*, 1972, *38*, 72–83.

Stokols, D., Rall, M., Pinner, B., and Schopler, J. Physical, social, and personal determinants of the perception of crowding. *Environment and Behavior*, 1973, *5*, 87–116.

Stokols, D., Smith, T., and Prostor, J. Partitioning and perceived crowding in a public space. *American Behavioral Scientist*, July–August, 1975, *18*(6), 792–814.

United Nations Statistical Yearbook, 1970. New York: United Nations, 1971.

Weiss, E. *Agoraphobia in the light of ego psychology.* London: Grune and Stratton, 1964.

Wohlwill, J. The emerging discipline of environmental psychology. *American Psychologist*, 1970, *25*, 303–312.

Simulation Techniques in Environmental Psychology

7

GEORGE E. McKECHNIE

Introduction

This chapter is concerned with the problem of anticipating human response to future environments—environments that are now being planned but are not yet a reality. Specifically, it focuses on the development of techniques for "presenting" future environments to potential users and other observers via physical and symbolic replicas and other such laboratory analogues of real environments. In addition, the chapter presents a discussion of the psychological issues involved in the attempt to present these simulations of reality to the observer in such a way that his responses will accurately predict the responses of observers of the real environment, should it actually be constructed as planned.

The family of techniques utilized for replicating—or, more precisely, previewing or otherwise anticipating—in the laboratory everyday environments that have not yet been built, modified, or otherwise actualized are known collectively as *environmental simulations.* The empirical question of whether a specific technique (or medley of techniques) fulfills the intent of "standing in" for the target environment—so that observers' responses to the simulation are predictive of subsequent observers' responses to the real environment—raises the issue of *ecological validity,* the applicability of the results of laboratory analogues to nonlaboratory, real-life settings.

In this chapter, various types of environmental simulations will be surveyed, and the uses of simulation most relevant to environmental psychology will be explored. One specific application of simulation techniques—to the decision-making processes of environmental designers—will serve as a focal point for subsequent discussions in the

GEORGE E. McKECHNIE ● University of California at Berkeley.

chapter. The development of the Environmental Simulation Laboratory at the University of California at Berkeley[1] will be described, followed by a description of the physical operating characteristics of the laboratory. The problem of ecological validity in environmental-simulation research will be discussed, and a program of field research designed to evaluate the psychological-response capability of the Berkeley simulator outlined. Finally, a discussion of the generalizability of this evaluation research will be presented, together with suggestions for further validational research and technical development and for application to problems in environmental psychology.

Varieties of Environmental Simulation

The idea of simulation as a simplified laboratory rendition of a naturally occurring environment or event is new neither to the behavioral sciences nor to the design professions, having been an integral part of the decision-making apparatus of both disciplines for many years. Numerous distinct research methods in both fields—some older than environmental psychology itself—may legitimately be included under the rubric of simulation techniques. For the purposes of this chapter, it is not possible or desirable to review all of these. Rather, a brief survey of notable representatives from psychology and the design professions is given in order to suggest the scope of the simulation approach.

Experimental research in such areas of psychology as social, personality, clinical, and developmental psychology have for many years utilized laboratory analogues of real-life settings. To the extent that this research strategy involved attempts on the part of the experimenter to set up laboratory replicas that extracted functionally essential features of the presumed "real" environment, it partook of the notion of simulation.[2] With the ad-

[1]Development of the Berkeley Environmental Simulation Laboratory was funded through National Science Foundation Grant #GS-30984-X, "Environmental Dispositions and the Simulation of Environments," to Donald Appleyard and Kenneth H. Craik, Co-Principal Investigators. The author wishes to thank Professors Craik and Appleyard for permission to present here details on the development and validation of the simulation laboratory. Many of the ideas presented in this chapter evolved through discussions of the author with Professors Craik and Appleyard, and with other members of the Environmental Simulation Project staff. The influence of their contributions to the content of this chapter is gratefully acknowledged. The opinions expressed herein are those of the author, and not necessarily those of the principal investigators or of the National Science Foundation.
[2]A formal analysis of this argument yields an analogy, as follows: the responses of observers of the simulation are to the responses of observers of the actual environment represented in the simulation as the characteristics of the environment selected are represented in the simulation are to the actual environment being represented (after Dennett, 1968). Although the sufficiency of this analogy is of theoretical interest, and—to a limited extent—may be evaluated empirically, its adequacy does not, in itself, guarantee (nor its insufficiency rule out) the utilization of a simulation technique as a system for predicting behavioral response to future environments.

vent of electronic computers in the 1950's came a more self-conscious concern with simulations *per se,* especially in the field of cognition. Investigators began to use the computer as a formal means of testing psychological theory. By submitting his theory to the formal rigors of programming language and to the empirical rigors of comparing the articulation of the program in the computer (the machine trace) with the behavior of real subjects, the psychologist could test both the logical consistency and the sufficiency of his formulations. Thus did investigators study, among other things, cognitive processes (Feigenbaum and Feldman, 1963) and personality (Tomkins and Messick, 1963).

Because these uses of simulation in psychology are all so closely aligned with the experimental method, it is necessary to turn to the environmental professions for examples that more fully delineate the broad scope of simulative techniques. Within these disciplines, the term *environmental simulation* refers to a number of distinct research and applied techniques currently employed for representing and exploring various aspects of man–environment interaction. Although all of these methods are of at least tangential interest to the environmental psychologist, only one is of specific concern in this essay.

The simulation techniques perhaps most widely known and discussed over the past several years are those that use computers to elaborate conceptual models of the environment, much like the psychologists' use of computers to explore cognitive or personality processes within the person. These *conceptual simulations* program in the computer equations and parameters interrelating such ecological processes as population growth, resource utilization, and pollution levels in an attempt to anticipate future ecological events and trends, for example, the collapse of the ecosystem. The famous Club of Rome *Limits to Growth* study (Meadows, 1972; Cole, Freeman, Jahoda, and Pavitt, 1973) is a good example of this type of study.

Closely allied to these conceptual models of the environment are the gaming techniques used in urban planning (Kibel, 1972) as well as in operations research, business, industry, and sundry other fields of endeavor.[3] As employed in urban-planning studies, these simulations resemble the familiar game of Monopoly. The game materials and rules embody development pressures, regulatory principles, and other facets of a situation currently at play in a given region or anticipated for the future. Participants "play" the simulation game according to the rules, sometimes in conjunction with a computer that remembers all the rules and keeps track of everyone's play. Researchers monitor the behavior of the players, hoping that it will provide insight into the likely real-life behavior of per-

[3]Simulation/gaming techniques have been used in such disciplines as operations research (Chorafas, 1965), management decision-making (Dardin and Lucas, 1969), international relations (Giffin, 1965), and marketing (Greenlaw and Kniffin, 1964). A journal, *Simulation and Games,* is devoted to the reporting of research in this general area.

sons involved in the planning and development of the environment and that the outcome of the game can be taken as an indicator of the probable outcome of the situation modeled in the game, should the process be allowed to come to fruition.

Both the computer-modeling and the simulation/gaming techniques are *abstract* in that they emphasize the functional, operational properties of the man–environment interaction under investigation. Each is concerned with the formal analysis of complex and interacting processes, rather than with the representation of concrete physical detail.

In contrast with these abstract approaches are the simulation tools of the architect, the landscape architect, and the urban designer. In these contexts there is a concern with developing simulations that are as *concrete* and perceptually lifelike as possible. The purpose of simulation in design work is to communicate tangibly what a given environment will look, feel, sound, and even smell like, after it is built or otherwise modified according to a proposed plan.[4] Of course, the simulation tools traditionally available to the environmental designer—scale models viewed from above, artists' renderings, construction floor-plans, etc.—vary among themselves in the degree to which they emphasize *concrete perceptual* information versus *abstract conceptual* information. Building plans, for example, provide much conceptual information—dimensions, angles, abstract shapes; when perceptual information is given, it usually involves construction details that subsequently will be hidden from view in the finished building. Little is provided in a set of blueprints to show the observer how the building will look. In contrast, the scale model at its best provides abundant perceptual information: colors and actual three-dimensional shapes of building, textures of vegetation, variations in terrain and ground cover, etc.

Thus the perceptual–conceptual dimension is very useful for distinguishing among environmental simulations. Simulations can be classified also in terms of the extent to which the information they provide is *static* and unchanging versus *dynamic* and variable. For conceptual simulators, the dynamic capability usually consists of an iterative change in the structure or

---

[4]Concrete simulations almost invariably utilize visual perception to the exclusion of the other sense modalities. This emphasis reflects the fact that much of the information man gleans about the everyday physical environment is acquired visually. In principle, one might easily extend the notion of environmental simulation to encompass auditory, kinesthetic, tactile, olfactory, and gustatory stimuli. For the Berkeley simulator, it is at present feasible to add only auditory stimuli. Motion simulators, like those used by NASA and commercial airlines to train pilots, are very costly and are likely to be of little specific value in much environmental research. Although olfactory and tactile simulations may be of value in research on proxemics and crowding, their practical feasibility is at present unknown.

The issue of importance here is that of incremental validity (Sechrest, 1963); that is, to what extent adding an additional sensory channel to the simulator will increase the amount of information communicated and enhance the predictive validity of the technique. The incremental-validity issue is similarly relevant to evaluation of the relative advantage of complex and expensive simulation techniques over more primitive ones.

parameters of at least one component of the system as a function of the interaction of the environment represented in the simulation with humans or with other machines. The result is an open system, yielding a variety of possible outcomes, some of which might not have been anticipated on the basis of static examination of the input materials (i.e., formal specifications of initial parameters and of functional relationships). In the case of the *Limits to Growth* study, for example, the actual behavioral outcome of the system was not known in advance. Even though the researchers knew and understood specific details of the input parameters, it was not until the model was elaborated or played out in the computer that the now-famous implications became apparent.[5]

For perceptual simulations, the dynamic capability consists ideally in the provision of an infinite variety of continuously variable concrete "views" of a place. The Berkeley simulation lab, discussed below, possesses this dynamic capability to a substantial degree. It consists of a remote-controlled miniature optical system, capable of movement in all directions, suspended above a high-detail, precision physical-model of a planning region. The lab provides highly realistic eye-level views (on color film, videotape, or live closed-circuit TV) of a potentially infinite number of different lifelike "tours" through the model. Although the resulting views are entirely a function of—and are limited by—the extent and veridicality of the physical model, great flexibility is achieved in the exploration of a given model.

Static simulation-techniques exist for both conceptual and perceptual modes. Still photographs, scale drawings, and artists' renderings are examples of static perceptual devices. They permit but a single, unchanging view of the represented environment. The perceptual interrelationships among the various elements of the environment (e.g., buildings, doors, and streets) are fixed and cannot be transformed, except in the imagination of the skilled user of such materials.

Land-use maps, printed flow charts, and other schematics are examples of static abstract simulations. They systematize environmental information but do not in themselves lead to the generation of consequences not already contained in the schematic. They merely abstract known or specified aspects of the man–environment interaction.

Figure 1 schematizes these two dimensions of simulation—conceptual–perceptual and dynamic–static—and provides examples of each type. These aspects of simulation should not be taken as dichotomies but rather as continua, for analysis of these and other examples will lead the reader to the conclusion that few "pure" simulation types exist. Many combine to some extent features of both ends of the continua.

A simulation technique of particular interest in this regard is known as

---

[5]Meadows *et al.* (1972) discovered in their simulation computer-runs that almost every combination of parameters led eventually to the collapse of the ecosystem, unless population growth was held in check.

	PERCEPTUAL (Concrete)	CONCEPTUAL (Abstract)
STATIC	PHOTOGRAPHS ARTIST'S SKETCHES	MAPS FLOOR PLANS
DYNAMIC	BERKELEY SIMULATOR	LIMITS TO GROWTH SIMULATION

Figure 1. A typology of environmental simulations, with examples.

computer graphics (Greenberg, 1974). Systems of this sort store information on the physical environment in a computer program: locations of buildings, trees, streets, shapes of building, colors, textures, etc. Without having a physical model of the area, the computer can use this program to generate "scenes" on a television screen or even to simulate a "walk" through the environment. Moreover the system can be used to produce detailed plans or other schematics. Computer-graphic simulators, thus, are capable of both perceptual and conceptual simulation. This versatility and freedom from the constraints of a physical model are achieved at considerable cost. At present, computer-graphic systems are very expensive, require heroic amounts of computer programming for a complex everyday environment, and most importantly, may not be sufficiently realistic for use in decision-making contexts where psychological response to the perceptual environment is of crucial concern.

In summary, we can say that conceptual simulation represents the processes underlying man–environment interactions and transformations through formal, abstract analysis. Perceptual simulation attempts to provide tangible, concrete replicas or isomorphs of environments—often future environments—that can be displayed to observers for their evaluation or other response. Dynamic simulations provide a recursive or interactive capability, such that often unanticipated new information is generated from the multiple, complex parts of the system. Static simulations lack this interactive capability and instead merely extract known aspects of the environment.

Development of the Berkeley Environmental Simulation Laboratory

The Berkeley Environmental Simulation Laboratory had its beginnings in 1968, when a prototype simulator was purchased from Yale University. In 1971, a National Science Foundation grant to the Institute of Urban and

Regional Planning and the Institute of Personality Assessment and Research on the Berkeley campus of the University of California permitted the design, construction, and validational appraisal of a new and vastly improved simulator under the direction of Professors Donald Appleyard and Kenneth H. Craik. This collaboration reflected Appleyard's interest in simulation as a research and design tool (Appleyard, Lynch, and Myer, 1965), begun in 1958 at M.I.T. as part of a study of the environmental experiences of the urban traveler, and Craik's (1970, 1973) increasing involvement in research issues surrounding human comprehension of the everyday physical environment and the application of psychological-assessment techniques to problems in environmental psychology.

The simulator lab consists of (1) a gantry system (capable of movement in all three directions, plus pitch, roll, and yaw rotations), which guides (2) an optical probe and an associated (3) video or color-film camera through (4) a physical model of a block, neighborhood, or region and which is controlled by (5) a digital computer with associated software. In addition, (6) special lighting is provided to allow adequate photographic exposures of film and videotape. Figures 2, 3 and 4 show several views of the simulation equipment.

In its present form, the simulator will allow an operator to prepare color movie or black-and-white videotape "tours" through a scale model. For any model down to a scale of approximately 1 inch = 30 feet, the lab can provide a human eye-level "drive" or "walk" through the simulated setting.[6] For models below this scale of miniaturization (e.g., 1 inch = 100 feet), the apparatus provides "helicopter passes" over the model. The total land area that can be simulated in the lab is a function of the model scale. The simulator can span a model 24 feet wide by 3 feet high and approximately 44 feet long. At the present standard scale of 1 inch = 30 feet, this represents a land area of 4.9 square miles (1.64 miles wide by 3.0 miles long), with a maximum elevation of 1,080 feet above the model base.

One simulates tours through the model by first installing the closed-circuit TV camera in the gantry, having the operator "drive" the probe along a selected route using electronic hand-controls, and watching the view through the probe displayed on a TV monitor. As it is driven along, the computer digitizes and stores in memory the various locations traversed, along with the corresponding velocities, accelerations, and turning rates. After an acceptable tour has been made, control is given to the computer, which then executes a stop-frame movie of the tour. Computer-controlled, stop-frame photography was necessitated by a number of problems encountered in the design of the optical probe. The

---

[6]The diameter of the optical probe at its lower end determines the minimal model-scale through which the simulator can be "driven." At 1″ = 30 feet, the probe would have to be of less than a .4-inch diameter in order to center on a 12-foot-wide traffic lane. The actual probe used in the Berkeley simulator is of a .5-inch diameter for its lower-most 6 inches. It has a 60-degree horizontal angle of view and a 45-degree vertical angle of view.

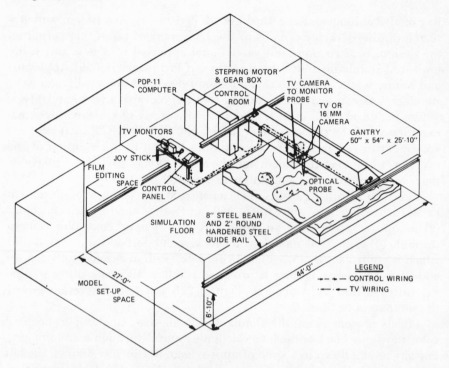

Figure 2. Schematic drawing of the Berkeley Environmental Simulation Laboratory showing simulation floor, control room, and ancillary spaces.

need for a wide-angle optic with high resolution and adequate depth-of-field, small enough to be contained in a probe having a maximum diameter of 0.5 inches, resulted in a lens having a relatively small effective aperture (high f-ratio). Conventional real-time motion-picture photography with slow-speed, high-resolution film would have required that great quantities of light be used to illuminate the model. This illumination would produce enough heat to burn up the model! Therefore it was necessary to turn to the longer exposures of the stop-frame method. This necessitated the use of a computer to position the gantry accurately for each stop-frame exposure. A secondary advantage of this method was that vibration problems (which had plagued the prototype machine) could be eliminated simply by a pause for a second or two after the movement of the gantry to a new "location" and before the exposure was made at that location. Finally the use of the computer allowed the operator to record and subsequently play back on demand a perfect run through the model, thus maximizing the reproducibility of the system and minimizing film waste.

The choice of a standard scale for the lab that permits the modeling of areas several square miles in extent allows users of the lab to address issues at the planning level in addition to those of purely architectural scope. This capability was achieved at a considerable expenditure of funds and of engineering, construction, and model-making effort. Had the lab been built to accommodate only architectural scale-models (i.e., at 1 inch = 8 feet), much less research and development would have been necessary (especially in the design of the optical probe), and the innovations in model making achieved in the project would not have been required. At architectural scales, simulators and models of a quality comparable to that of the Berkeley simulator could be built at a more modest cost. Of course, they would be of relatively little value for simulating large areas.

Uses of Dynamic Perceptual Simulation

The dynamic simulation of perceptual information embodied in the everyday physical environment is of interest to students of man–environment relations for at least three purposes: (1) as a research technique for the laboratory evaluation of environmental theory; (2) as a device for communicating environmental-design solutions to the public; and (3) as a decision-making tool within the environmental-design process (Appleyard and Craik, 1974). As a research technique, dynamic perceptual-simulation

Figure 3. The Berkeley simulation laboratory in action.

Figure 4. Detail of the model and optical probe.

allows the experimental psychologist to encompass, within the controlled conditions of the laboratory, complete replicas of everyday physical environments—streets, neighborhoods, even entire cities. It is thus possible to manipulate these environments systematically to test hypotheses and build environmental theory. Using dynamic simulation-techniques, it is feasible, for example, to study experimentally (using classical experimental designs) such interesting and important topics as the imageability of cities (Lynch, 1960) and the effect of imageability on human behavior, the consequences of architectural aesthetics (Craik, 1971) for mood, or the effect of visual pollution on spatial orientation.

As a communications tool, simulation allows the environmentalist to provide to the public information representing the ways they experience everyday environments and is thus directly relevant to valid evaluations of proposed environmental alterations. All too often the meetings of architect and client or planning hearings employ abstract simulation-techniques such as land-use maps that provide the layman with information he is unprepared to assimilate, yet they fail to provide the kind of visual data on which he can form impressions and base decisions (see S. Kaplan, Chapter 11).

Environmental-design solutions, such as those involving public housing or urban redevelopment, embody hundreds—sometimes thousands— of small-scale decisions that sequentially focus the solution and narrow down subsequent options. Unfortunately the simulation media traditionally available to the designer tend to emphasize irrelevant detail, such as the roofs of buildings on models viewed conventionally from a bird's-eye view or construction detail in the case of scale drawings. As a design aid, dynamic perceptual simulation provides the architect or urban designer with highly realistic visual feedback *during* the design process, rather than after all of the interlocking, lower-order decisions have been made. In the same way that the piano provides the music composer with a tool for evaluating the auditory implications of a phrase or passage, simulation allows the designer to scrutinize the various visual implications of a particular design decision.

The potential uses of simulation in man–environment relations are thus both theoretical and applied. Because of the urgency with which environmental decision-makers must confront everyday design decisions, because of the increasing tendency within the design professions to turn to social scientists for solutions to these problems, and because many readers of this chapter are undoubtedly more conversant with the details of laboratory psychological research than with the press of everyday environmental decision-making, the applied uses of simulation will be emphasized throughout the remainder of this chapter. This emphasis should not dissuade the researcher interested in using simulation techniques for validating man–environment theory or for modeling psychological response to environments.

The Environmental Decision-Maker as Applied Psychologist

How can the psychologist help professionals concerned with the design, alteration, and maintenance of physical environments to anticipate successfully the psychological responses of users of the environments they create? Although a concern with the human consequences of environmental modifications is implicit in the environmental decision-making process (Lipman, 1969; Craik, 1972a), until recently little progress had been made in providing the decision-maker with either relevant psychological theory or research methodology to aid him in his attempts to meet more adequately the social, psychological, and aesthetic needs of the people who must live with the products of his imagination.

This author has often challenged architecture students with the assertion: "Every time you draw a line (on a plan, a sketch, or other rendering), you are making a hypothesis about human psychological response." Although in some ways an obvious overstatement, this assertion does suggest the appropriateness of viewing the architect or other environmental manager as an applied psychologist—or at least potentially a regular consumer of the products of psychology. Given this role as a necessary part of the profession, the question then arises: What can psychology provide of value to the environmental designer in his difficult task of creating environments that are well suited to specific and diverse human purposes? Three qualitatively distinct "products" are available to the psychologically minded environmental professional: theories, research techniques, and philosophical views on the nature of man:

1. Theories, models, or laws that involve a simplification or reduction of reality into a more-or-less formal statement relating behavior (or, less often, experience) to sociophysical parameters of the environment. Much of the research on territoriality, proxemics, and density/crowding is of interest in this regard to environmentalists.
2. Research techniques and methods that permit the environmentalist to assess systematically the effects of a given environment on a specified subject population. The ecological (e.g., Barker, 1968) and assessment[7] (e.g., Craik, 1972b) approaches in psychology are of this type.
3. A theory or philosophy of man, either explicitly (e.g., Skinner's operant psychology) or implicitly (e.g., experimental-social research on territoriality) embodied in a theory or a methodology.

Depending upon the circumstances under which the designer is working, he may feel the need for one or another of the "products," perhaps even all three.

The current discussion of simulation techniques in environmental psychology emphasizes the second type of product: the development of a simulative research-technique for predicting human response to future environments before they are built, or before existing environments are modified, plus the empirical evaluation of the predictive capability of the technique. The latter would be achieved through systematic field-experiments to appraise the ecological validity of the simulation system.

[7]Applications of this approach to environmental psychology have been sketched out in recent articles by Craik (1972b, 1976). Conceptual origins of the assessment approach in psychology may be traced back to the work of Murray et al. (1938). For useful summary treatments of the contemporary psychological-assessment paradigm, the reader is referred to Wiggins (1973), Insel and Moos (1974), and Craik (1971).

For the question of importance to the applied psychologist is not whether a given formulation is consistent with the results of a series of laboratory experiments, but rather whether a given methodological tool will allow him to make decisions that are subsequently justified in terms of their human consequences.

Theoretically the simulation technique is relatively neutral, save that it emphasizes visual perception to the exclusion of other sense modalities. No single view of man is embodied in the simulation apparatus *per se,* although the research design for its validation does embody assumptions about both the nature of man and the nature of the environment (as perceived and understood by man). We turn now to a presentation of these assumptions.

The Everyday Environment as a Complex, Multidimensional Entity

No science is ever really free of a *priori* bedrock assumptions about the nature of its universe, assumptions that are never amenable to direct empirical evaluation. Psychology is no exception to this rule. In fact, it outdoes most sciences in encompassing within its boundaries multiple competing sets of assumptions, such as those of phenomenology and behaviorism (Wann, 1964).

The assumptions underlying this essay, and offered as appropriate for the evaluation of simulation as an applied technique in environmental decision-making, are those associated with *assessment psychology.* Briefly, this approach asserts that the psychological world can, for convenience, be divided into three components: the personality system, the social system, and the environmental system (Craik, 1972a). Human behavior is thought to be attributable to both personality and environmental components, as well as their interactions. Environments, like people, are assumed to be complex, multidimensional entities, capable of being represented psychologically as well as physically; we can assess environments by employing methods analogous to those used in personality assessment (Insel and Moos, 1974). Furthermore this approach asserts that individuals may vary in the ways they comprehend a given environment and that multiple procedures are often necessary to tap the full array of human response to the environment.

Craik (1971) has systematized these assumptions in his Process Model for the Assessment of Environmental Displays. The model identifies four sets of variables pertinent to the analysis of human response to environments:

1. Observers: *Whose* impressions are being studied?
2. Media of presentation: *How* is the environment presented to the observer?

3. Response formats: *What* measures of response are of interest?
4. Environmental dimension: What *physical* characteristics of the environment shall the psychological responses be related to?

Category 1, the observer, takes into account individual differences in the observer, defined in terms of demographics (e.g., professional membership), environmental dispositions (McKechnie, 1974), or relevant environmental behaviors, such as recreation activities (McKechnie, 1975). The question of interest here is whether some observers "see" a given environment differently or more accurately (given some suitable criterion) than do others. For example, do architects notice different features of the environment than highway engineers or real-estate appraisers? Are environmental specialists, because of their visual skills, better able than nonspecialists to compensate for inadequate simulations?

Category 2, the media, addresses the question of the adequacy of simulation *per se.* Which techniques are subjectively the most realistic? Which yield the human responses that are most similar to responses of observers of the real environment? Which medium yields the psychological judgments that are most highly correlated with the physical parameters of the environment?

Category 3, the response format, explores some of the many possible ways and levels of recording the observer's response to the environmental display. Is the concern with aesthetic responses, memory for environmental detail, spatial orientation, judgments of environmental quality, or other such topics? Shall we employ an open-ended interview, map-drawing techniques, checklists, or other formats? Two points are important here. First is the notion that a given observer may respond to a molar environment at a number of different levels. Also important is the idea that a given psychological measurement contains both content and method components of variance. Often it is desirable to evaluate to what extent data collected by the use of a particular response format (e.g., a map-drawing task) are contaminated by method variance (e.g., ability and willingness to draw), and thus fail to converge with a different measure of the same construct. Multitrait–multimethod analysis (Campbell and Fiske, 1959) may be used to evaluate such components of measurement.

Category 4, environmental dimensions, refers to the standardized description or measurement of the environment being displayed. Such standards, to which the responses of a given observer may be related, usually take the form of physical dimensions (e.g., morphology, climate, size, color, and temperature) measured with instruments of known validity and reliability, or they take the form of psychological descriptions made by experts and based upon long-term exposure to the displayed environment.

The outcome of a given simulation study is thus a function of the choices made for each of the four sets of variables. Because of its interest in individual differences among persons, as well as between physical and social environments, assessment psychology is open to the possibility that unforseen and divergent findings may result from various combinations of these variable sets and that a full account of the man–environment interaction must ultimately encompass all combinations.

Validation of the Berkeley Simulator

Given the above perspective on human response to the environment, the question of the validity of the Berkeley simulator is not a simple yes–no question. Rather it involves a methodological charting-out of a new research area. Validity research must specify not only the extent to which the simulation is psychologically equivalent to the corresponding real environment but also under what conditions it is valid: for what kinds of observers, under what sorts of instructions, using what types of response measures, for models representing what kinds of environments.[8] It may turn out, for example, that dynamic perceptual simulation shows high validity for observers who work at professions requiring good visual memory, when subjects are instructed to focus on aesthetic factors in the display, and when the environment being observed includes suburban single-unit dwellings, but it may be that the technique does not work well for laymen, for responses involving spatial orientation (i.e., mental mapping), or for environments that are heavily urban in character.

Because of the great potential of the use of simulation in applied psychological contexts, the validity question of greatest moment is that of *ecological validity* (Brunswik, 1956): the extent to which findings utilizing the simulation laboratory are generalizable to the real environment represented in the model. The logic of simulation as a communications and design tool requires that the responses of target observers (i.e., the user–public or the designer) to the simulation material be sufficiently predictive of subsequent observer responses to the corresponding real environment (given that the environmental transformation under evaluation actually takes place).

In the case of the Berkeley simulator, the question of ecological validity has been approached by a reversal of the usual sequence of application. Instead of the modeling of an environment planned for the future, a model is constructed and simulation films are made for an environment already in existence. Responses of subjects who see the simulated tour of the area are compared with those who are driven through the real environment along the same tour. A comparison of the results for these two conditions provides a direct answer to the question of the generalizability of simulation data to real-world environments.

[8]Validation research for various types of perceptual simulation has been conducted by a small number of researchers, including Winkel and Sasanoff (1970) and Wood (1972).

The details of the actual validation study are more complex than the above description suggests. First, it was necessary to select a site that was sufficiently "difficult" to provide a fair evaluation of the simulation technique.[9] Then it was necessary to set up a field station at which to conduct the research. Several distinct samples of subjects were recruited: a large, representative sample of residents of the entire county, a smaller sample of persons who lived on or adjacent to the site, and a group of environmental professions (architects, landscape architects, planners, real-estate appraisers, and highway engineers). Four separate experimental conditions were run: some subjects took a ride along the tour in American sedans driven by project staff. Others saw a color film made from an automobile driven through the real environment. Still others saw a color film of the model made on the simulator. A final group saw a videotape of the model made on the simulator.

Although color film was anticipated to be the *best* medium for presenting simulation information, black-and-white videotape was also included because of its low cost and great flexibility. The color film of the real-world condition was included so that if substantial differences were found between the real-life auto tour and color-film simulation conditions, it would be possible to estimate what portion of the difference was due to the use of a simulation medium (i.e., color film) and what portion was due to inadequacies in the simulation model and mechanical apparatus.

After the completion of the various "tour" conditions, subjects spent several hours recording their impressions of the environment they had just experienced in the form of map sketches, Q-sort and adjective checklist descriptions, information quizzes, and judgments of environmental quality. Then, after a break for lunch, subjects described themselves on a number of personality, demographic, and environmental-experience measures.[10]

All in all, 1,043 subjects participated in the field experiment over a period of 2 years. The long duration of the experiment necessitated that a number of additional control conditions be run and analyzed to evaluate possible confounding of the experimental results because of history, maturational, and experimental mortality effects (Campbell and Stanley, 1963).

Although many of these data are still being analyzed 1 year after the

[9]The site ultimately chosen is the Terra Linda section of San Rafael, Marin County, California. This site encompasses state highway 101 and surrounding areas, just north of the Marin County Civic Center. The route "traveled" by the experimental subjects begins at the Northgate Shopping Center, passes north along the freeway, turns left through the undeveloped open space of Lucas Valley Road, then heads south into the suburban residential neighborhoods of Las Gallinas Road, back past the shopping center, then along the old highway commercial strip adjacent to route 101, through an industrial park, and then southbound on the freeway back to the regional shopping center.

[10]Details of the validational appraisal study are provided in a technical report to the National Science Foundation and will appear in a forthcoming book on the development and validation of the simulator.

completion of the field research, preliminary findings suggest that it is possible to predict real-world responses of observers from responses of observers who see Berkeley simulation-laboratory material with very high accuracy. For example, correlations between mean descriptions on the Q-sort task for the auto tour versus the model-film or model-video conditions are rather high, typically above .90. It is, of course, premature to jump to conclusions regarding the validity of simulation on the basis of these early returns from the computer. Current analyses must be fully interpreted and perhaps a second generation of analyses performed before a thorough and balanced appraisal of the Berkeley simulator's validity emerges. Nonetheless early results are encouraging.

According to conventional canons of science, validation of the Berkeley environmental simulator as a laboratory technique may well be regarded as nearly complete, assuming that the preliminary findings hold up under closer scrutiny. Indeed the present writer can think of no other instance in the history of psychology as an experimental science in which such considerable amounts of time, energy, and research funds have been invested to evaluate systematically the validity of a laboratory technique. Given the potential for direct applications of the environmental-simulation technique to the decision-making contexts of architecture and planning, however, the present writer regards this intensive evaluation as not only desirable but prudent.

During the period when plans for the validation research were first being formulated, the Federal truth-in-lending legislation had just been signed into law. Staff members on the project often joked about the need for a *truth-in-simulation* law aimed at ensuring the veridicality of environmental simulations upon which design decisions are based. From the beginning of the project, it had been clear that various environmental special interest groups would be interested in using environmental simulation to show how *good* or *bad* a given environmental transaction might be. For example, both the U.S. Army Corps of Engineers and a conservation group opposed to a project proposed by the engineers might want the simulator to show their point of view to best advantage, thus reducing a scientific technique to a propaganda device. The principal investigators for the project even envisioned themselves appearing, at some future date, as expert witnesses in court cases involving litigation among environmental interest groups, when simulation techniques had been used and were in dispute as evidence in the case.

In a formal sense, however, the validation study currently being completed pertains to a specific environment—or, perhaps more liberally, to the type of mixed land-use suburban environment embodied in the Terra Linda site model—and thus represents but a first step in the full validation process. The present study leaves unevaluated the adequacy of the simulation technique in representing downtown urban areas or exclusively rural areas or—for that matter—in representing features of landscape morphology and vegetation types other than those that were salient in the Terra Linda site. Even though the site was chosen in part because of the heterogeneity of land use and its complement of both indigenous and nonnative flora, the possibility exists that various interactive and/or threshold effects operate in the site to limit the generalizability of the validation findings to other environments.

In one sense, then, the validity of the simulator for urban areas or New England villages, for example, has not yet been established, and the technique should not be employed in a decision-making context until such validational-research findings become available to justify this use. In a more practical sense, however, the issue of generalizability of the simulation technique is more complex and less straightforward than it might at first appear. Although for convenience in this essay the process of validation has been described in global terms, from the model maker's perspective, each object on the model represents a validity challenge. During the process of fabricating trees, fences, houses, and autos, and later in dressing the model, the model maker is constantly confronted with the question: Will it look right through the optical probe of the simulator? In one sense, then, the model maker may be an important arbiter of validity at the molecular scale. Indeed it may be upon his or her judgments and decisions that the entire enterprise stands.

From this perspective, it is the model maker's critical eye and model-making technique (rather than a type of environment) on which the simulator is being evaluated. To some extent, it may be possible to record the fabrication specifics of successful techniques (e.g., for a live oak tree or a particular type of fence) and to document the process of discriminating adequate from inadequate solutions. In fact, many of the data analyses currently under way for the Terra Linda site will, to some extent, permit this sort of fine-grain analysis of the model-making technique. However, given the great number of such objects and such decisions in the typical model, and their often highly specific nature, it ultimately may be most cost-effective to regard model making as an art rather than a science and to seek out and employ qualified practitioners.

At present, no additional studies are planned having as their sole purpose the validation of the simulator for different environments. It is likely, rather, that further validation of the technique will occur as a consequence of applying the technique to actual environmental decision-making contexts. One possible application is the use of the Berkeley simulator to provide demonstration movies allowing subjects to evaluate alternative types of clear-cut fire breaks in fire-hazard regions adjacent to residential areas. Although such validations must be regarded as less than optimal from a scientific perspective because of the limited control such applied contexts provide, from the point of view of the environmental decision-maker, they are indispensable because they take into account the numerous methodological and practical obstacles inherent in naturalistic settings.

Further Development and Application

Refinement of the model-making technique and further development of the simulation apparatus *per se* will occur as current data analyses are digested and a second generation of analyses are performed. Hopefully subsequent adjustments will firmly establish the Berkeley simulator as a state-of-the-art international facility for environmental simulation at the city and regional planning level.

Although the cost of fabricating additional simulators similar to the Berkeley machine would be a fraction of the cost entailed in the development of the original, it is unlikely that additional facilities of this scope will be either necessary or supportable through public research-funding in the near future, given that the original facility can be made available to qualified investigators who require the technical sophistication available in the Berkeley simulator. It is probable that (as a spinoff of basic research and development of the Berkeley project) smaller simulators of more modest scale (i.e., the architectural scale of 1 inch = 8 feet) and cost will become available to city and regional planning agencies, university architecture and planning departments, and larger private environmental-design firms. This trend would make simulation available both as an educational tool and as an aid in the everyday context of environmental decision-making.

The utilization of environmental simulation in environmental psychology will permit experimentally oriented psychologists to manipulate in a systematic manner perceptually accurate and ecologically valid molar environments. To some extent, the development and validation of the simulation technique allow the psychologist to surmount both the limitations of external validity associated with laboratory-based experimental techniques and the internal validity-threats inherent in field research. To the extent that it achieves these ends, it represents a rapprochement between the experimental and ecological sciences of psychology (Cronbach, 1957).

Specific researches planned for the simulator include a study of cognitive representation of the spatial environment utilizing yoked-subjects design. Subjects in the active condition will be allowed to "explore" the site via the simulator. The computer will record the exploration route, then "play it back" to a yoked control subject in the passive condition. This design will allow an unrestricted evaluation of the effect of choice making on spatial memory and evaluation.

Another study proposed for the laboratory involves research on adaptation to new environments. One can make a microgenetic evaluation of adaptation (à la Beck, Cohen, Craik, Dwyer, McCleary, and Wapner, 1973) by having subjects play the role of a person recently moved to a new neighborhood and by scheduling daily commuting trips from home to office or routine shopping trips through the surrounding areas.

Finally, the capability of the simulator for altering the location of socially important or otherwise visible buildings and landscape features in an area—and indeed for systematically manipulating entire areas—makes the experimental study of imageability (Lynch, 1960) very attractive.

The Berkeley environmental simulator provides the environmental psychologist with a convenient, efficient, and precise means of systematically testing research hypotheses at a level of molarity that heretofore has not been amenable to direct laboratory manipulation and control. In so doing, the simulator offers environmental psychology an empirical technique that may help bridge the gap between research and application, a problem that for too long has characterized the field.

References

Appleyard, D., and Craik, K. H. The Berkeley Environmental Simulation Project: Its use in environmental impact assessment. In T. G. Dickert and K. R. Domeny (Eds.), *Environmental impact assessment: Guidelines and commentary.* Berkeley: University Extension, University of California, 1974.

Appleyard, D., Lynch, K., and Myer, J. R. *The view from the road.* Cambridge, Mass.: M.I.T. Press, 1965.

Barker, R. G. *Ecological psychology: Concepts and methods for studying the environment of human behavior.* Stanford, Calif.: Stanford University Press, 1968.

Beck, R. J., Cohen, S. B., Craik, K. H., Dwyer, M., McCleary, G., and Wapner, S. Studying environmental moves and relocations: A research note. *Environment and Behavior,* 1973, 5, 335–349.

Brunswik, E. *Perception and the representative design of psychological experiments.* Berkeley: University of California Press, 1956.

Campbell, D. T., and Fiske, D. W. Convergent and discriminant validation by the multitrait–multimethod matrix. *Psychological Bulletin,* 1959, 56, 81–105.

Campbell, D. T., and Stanley, J. C. *Experimental and quasi-experimental designs for research.* Chicago: Rand McNally, 1963.

Chorafas, D. N. *Systems and simulation.* New York: Academic Press, 1965.

Cole, N. S. D., Freeman, C., Jahoda, M., and Pavitt, K. L. R. (Eds.). *Thinking about the future: A critique of the limits to growth.* London: Chatto and Windus, 1973.

Craik, K. H. Environmental psychology. In K. H. Craik, B. Kleinmuntz, R. Rosnow, R. Rosenthal, J. A. Cheyne, and R. H. Walters (Eds.), *New Directions in psychology IV.* New York: Holt, Rinehart and Winston, 1970.

Craik, K. H. The assessment of places. In P. McReynolds (Ed.), *Advances in psychological assessment (vol. 2).* Palo Alto, Calif.: Science and Behavior Books, 1971.

Craik, K. H. An ecological perspective on environmental decision-making. *Human Ecology,* 1972, 1, 69.-80. (a)

Craik, K. H. The individual and the physical environment: Assessment strategies in environmental psychology. In W. M. Smith (Ed.), *Behavior, design, and policy: Aspects of human habitats.* Green Bay: University of Wisconsin, 1972 (b)

Craik, K. H. Environmental psychology. In P. H. Mussen and M. R. Rosenzweig (Eds.), *Annual review of psychology (vol. 24).* Palo Alto, Calif.: Annual Reviews, Inc., 1973.

Craik, K. H. The personality research paradigm in environmental psychology. In S. Wapner, S. Cohen, and B. Kaplan (Eds.), *Experiencing environments.* New York: Plenum Press, 1976.

Cronbach, L. J. The two disciplines of scientific psychology. *American Psychologist,* 1957, 12, 671–684.

Dardin, W. R., and Lucas, W. H. *The decision-making game: An integrated operations management simulation.* New York: Appleton-Century-Crofts, 1969.

Dennett, D. C. Machine traces and protocol statements. *Behavioral Science,* 1968, *13*, 155–161.

Feigenbaum, E. A., and Feldman, J. *Computers and thought.* New York: McGraw-Hill, 1963.

Giffin, S. F. *The crisis game: Simulating international conflict.* Garden City, N.Y.: Doubleday, 1965.

Greenberg, D. P. Computer graphics in architecture. *Scientific American,* 1974, *230*, 98–106.

Greenlaw, P. S., and Kniffin, F. W. *Marksim: A marketing decision simulation.* Scranton, Pa.: International Textbook, 1964.

Insel, P. M., and Moos, R. Psychological environments: Expanding the scope of human ecology. *American Psychologist,* 1974, *29*, 179–188.

Kaplan, S. Participation in the design process: A cognitive approach. In D. Stokols (Ed.), *Psychological perspectives on environment and behavior.* New York: Plenum Press, 1976.

Kibel, B. M. *Simulation of the urban environment.* Commission on College Geography Technical Paper No. 5. Washington, D.C.: Association of American Geographers, 1972.

Lipman, A. The architectural belief system and social behavior. *The British Journal of Sociology,* 1969, *20*, 190–204.

Lynch, K. *The image of the city.* Cambridge, Mass.: M.I.T. Press, 1960.

McKechnie, G. E. *Manual for the Environmental Response Inventory.* Palo Alto, Calif.: Consulting Psychologists Press, 1974.

McKechnie, G. E. *Manual for the Leisure Activities Blank.* Palo Alto, Calif.: Consulting Psychologists Press, 1975.

Meadows, D. L., and Meadows, D. H. *The limits to growth.* New York: Universe Books, 1972.

Murray, H. A. *Explorations in personality.* New York: Oxford University Press, 1938.

Sechrist, L. Incremetal validity: A recommendation. *Educational and Psychological Measurement,* 1963, *23*, 153–158.

Tomkins, S. S., and Messick, S. (Eds.), *Computer simulation of personality: Frontier of psychological theory.* New York: Wiley, 1963.

Wann, T. W. (Ed.), *Behaviorism and phenomenology: Contrasting bases for modern psychology.* Chicago: University of Chicago Press, 1964.

Wiggins, J. S. *Personality and prediction: Principles of personality assessment.* Reading, Mass.: Addison-Wesley, 1973.

Winkel, G. H., and Sasanoff, R. An approach to an objective analysis of behavior in architectural space. In H. Proshansky, W. A. Ittelson, and L. G. Rivlin (Eds.), *Environmental psychology: Man and his physical setting.* New York: Holt, Rinehart and Winston, 1970.

Wood, W. *An analysis of simulation media.* University of British Columbia, School of Architecture, 1972 (unpublished B. Arch. thesis).

SECTION IV
Applications of Behavioral   □
Research to Environmental
Design

The environment-and-behavior field, as noted in the first section of this volume, is uniquely concerned with the processes of human–environment optimization, or the ways in which individuals and groups rationally guide their transactions with the environment in accord with specified goals and plans (Stokols, Chapter 1). The theme of environmental optimization is clearly evident in the chapters of this section, all of which explicitly emphasize the utility of behavioral-science theories and interdisciplinary research as a basis for developing solutions to community problems.

Robert Sommer begins with a discussion of the relationship between theoretical and applied research in the environment-and-behavior field. The necessity of maintaining a creative tension between these reciprocal orientations is emphasized, for design interventions implemented in the absence of environmental assessment and evaluation are doomed to failure, while untested theories become irrelevant and useless. Lewin's (1948) conception of action research provides the basis for Sommer's recommendations concerning the design of graduate programs in environmental psychology, as well as his discussion of the criteria for effective collaboration among behavioral scientists and design professionals. In each of these instances, the sustained involvement of the student or the consultant in the sequential processes of assessment (orientation), intervention (operation), and evaluation is viewed as a prerequisite for developing effective strategies of environmental optimization.

The chapter by William Michelson elaborates on an important criterion of environmental optimization, namely, behavior–environment congruence (or "intersystem congruence"; cf. Michelson, 1970). Congruence is measured in terms of the degree to which the physical environment facilitates or impairs the desired activities of its users. Several criteria of congruence are discussed, including behavioral, cognitive, and cultural factors.

191

A major point raised by Michelson is that attempts to enhance behavior–environment congruence through design interventions should be preceded by an analysis of the societal and cultural factors (e.g., economic trends and historical developments) that might explain current conditions of incongruence. Thus the optimization of micro environments is linked directly to an understanding of macrosocial forces as well as those circumstances operating within the immediate situation.

The chapter by Stephen Kaplan addresses the issue of client participation in the design process. An important assumption of this chapter is that the assessment of user preferences by design professionals can enhance the process of environmental optimization. Communication among designers and clients, however, is often hampered by the fact that these groups perceive and describe physical environments in very different ways. In an effort to confront this problem, Kaplan develops an analysis of the perceptual and cognitive differences between designers and clients based on information theory and a method for assessing user preferences that transcends earlier communication gaps through the use of scale-model buildings.

A different form of citizen participation in the community planning process is considered by Rachel Kaplan. In her chapter, procedures for the assessment of users' preferences concerning the natural environment are described. Pictorial representations of natural scenes are administered to a sample of community residents, and their evaluations of these scenes are recorded. In this instance, client participation in the design process is accomplished through the provision of environmental-assessment data by community members. From analyses of such data, basic dimensions of environmental preference have been identified, including spaciousness, coherence, and familiarity.

The optimization of learning environments is the focus of Martin Krovetz's chapter. The importance of designing "pluralistic" educational settings, which incorporate a variety of physical and social structures to meet the diverse needs of different students, is emphasized. As a basis for creating learning environments that are maximally congruent with students' needs, Krovetz proposes an integration of social, psychological, and architectural strategies of design. These strategies essentially are intended to enhance students' perceptions of competence and personal control. To illustrate how social–structural and physical interventions might be combined, a series of diagrammatic plans for prospective learning environments is presented.

Finally, the chapter by Mark Baldassare and Claude Fischer examines the potential relevance of crowding research for the amelioration of urban problems. The authors conclude that crowding studies, to date, have not been relevant to an analysis of urban problems because researchers have made few efforts to specify the logical connections between experimental situations and urban conditions of high density. In relation to this problem, the authors suggest a number of strategies for increasing the relevance of future crowding-research to an analysis and enhancement of urban settings. These include a more extensive utilization of field-experimental methods and a systematic assessment of density-related hypotheses derived from sociological theories of urbanism (e.g., Durkheim, 1893/1933; Simmel, 1905/1950).

References

Durkheim. E. *The division of labor in society.* (Trans. by G. Simpson.) New York: Free Press, 1964. (First published, 1933.)

Lewin, K. *Resolving social conflicts.* New York: Harper and Brothers, 1948.

Michelson, W. *Man and his urban environment.* Reading, Mass.: Addison-Wesley, 1970.

Simmel, G. *The metropolis and mental life.* In K. Wolff (trans. and Ed.), *The sociology of Georg Simmel.* New York: Free Press, 1950. (First published, 1905.) Pp. 409–424.

Action Research   8

ROBERT SOMMER

There is a split in the ranks of environmental psychologists between those in universities who view the most critical need to be the development of a sound theoretical framework, and those in the applied fields whose main concern is the application of theory and method to practical problems. This division has characterized many fields and there is no inherent reason why environmental psychology should repeat all the mistakes of other disciplines. Many of the problems connected with the widening schism can be avoided through good design. We are challenged to construct a field that makes optimum use of both theorists and practitioners. Viewing this as a design problem will compel us to take into account structural realities, available materials, and individual differences. We are not designing a prototype for cheap mass production; rather we are in the custom-design business to help a single field make the most of scarce resources.

Because so much of my own career has been bound up with the development of environmental psychology, I tend to view the present situation in personal terms. I find myself being impatient both with theorists for ignoring urgent social problems and with the applied psychologists who don't see beyond the immediate constraints of their jobs. If either theory or practice takes over environmental psychology to the exclusion of the other, the field is doomed. Overspecialization is a sure prescription for extinction. A science that does not move beyond description, analysis, and discussion into implementation will become sterile and irrelevant, and a field involving action without reflection will be blind and stupid.

The difficulties of combining theory and action within a single discipline have produced the sort of schisms that exist between physics and engineering, sociology and social work, art and architecture, and psychology and clinical psychology. The Boulder Conference on Training Clinical Psychologists (Raimy, 1950) designed a prototype that was called a

ROBERT SOMMER • University of California at Davis.

scientist–practitioner. Despite the good intentions of the designers, the model didn't sell and it was extraordinarily difficult to produce. It meant in most programs that clinical students were expected to fulfill all the regular experimental requirements in addition to the clinical courses and internships. Most of the academic courses were not relevant to the students' interests and were barely tolerated. The required dissertation became the first and the last piece of research that the students ever did. Clinical psychologists on the faculty of university departments were treated with disdain by their colleagues. Rather than "a new product's" coming off the academic assembly line, the clinical student was the old model of research psychologist with a few new accessories. This compromise satisfied no one—not the clinical students, who resented taking uninteresting and irrelevent courses, and not the academic faculty, who resented the disinterest of clinical students and clinical faculty in traditional areas of psychology. So often it seemed a student's motivation to do testing and therapy dissipated during the arduous years of a training program that stressed academic subjects. Recognizing the basic hypocrisy of training clinicians in academic departments, many universities drastically curtailed or eliminated their clinical programs. The need for clinical training was then filled by special programs, often outside universities.

The largest of these nonuniversity programs is the California School of Professional Psychology, which has branches in Los Angeles, San Francisco, and Fresno. I have not checked the figures recently, but I suspect that the CSPP is training 10 times the number of clinical Ph.D. students enrolled in all 10 campuses of the University of California. There is no evidence that graduates of the CSPP are any less effective as practitioners, or even scientist–practitioners, than the graduates of university programs. Indeed, given the reluctance of university departments to evaluate their own activities objectively, one is hard put to make any comparison between the two programs at all. Some psychologists would like to see the university confine itself to training clinical theorists and clinical researchers while the professional programs train practioners.

The situation in clinical psychology should give pause to those who proposed that environmental psychology programs produce a hybrid scientist–practitioner. There is very little evidence that the research-oriented American university is willing or able to do this effectively. The scattered programs in environmental psychology, such as those at Arizona State, The City University of New York, Cornell, Penn State, and the University of California at Irvine, are young, and their origins are very different. In some programs environmental psychology is another specialty within an academic department, on a par with social psychology, industrial psychology, comparative psychology, and so on. There is a set of courses and exams that the student takes in order to become a properly certified environmental psychologist. This is a method that has been reasonably successful in producing academic specialists in other subareas of psychology. For producing professionals who will teach in universities and train other psychologists and who will write articles and do research into basic issues, it is probably the most practicable model available. However, it is deficient in training people who can work collaboratively with members of other professions on applied problems to meet tight deadlines. University departments of psychology are isolated both conceptually and spatially from the practical concerns of the design professions.

Other environmental-psychology programs have developed within applied departments such as architecture, home economics, and human factors. To provide a wider purview, academic psychologists have been brought into applied departments, and perhaps the entire department or school is renamed. Such programs have in the past been effective in training practitioners, but there has always been some doubt among psychologists whether the faculty and the students in these programs are sufficiently academic. The ideal solution from many standpoints would be establishing entirely new departments of environmental psychology with a commitment to the scientist–practitioner model. Unfortunately interest in environmental psychology has peaked during a time of economic recession. The era of large government grants to fund new university programs has passed. Whether it will ever return is doubtful. Like it or not, the resources for developing new programs will have to be begged, borrowed, stolen, or diverted from existing programs.

Institutionalization of the field has been developing at a rapid pace. In 1974 the first two introductory textbooks of environmental psychology were published (Heimstra and McFarling, 1974; Ittelson, Proshansky, Rivlin, Winkel, and Dempsey, 1974) and an APA task force was established. It is likely that this will bring some consensus about the terminology, the method, and the scope of the field. Right now the extent and range of topics studied and the methods used are almost beyond comprehension. This has produced great variation in staffing patterns and areas of emphasis in different programs. Environmental psychologists concerned with experimental aesthetics, cognitive mapping, personal space, and environmental decision-making derive their data base and methods from perception, cognition, social psychology, and sociology, respectively. This diversity reflects the initial area of specialization of most of these researchers, all of whom had other interests before moving over into environmental psychology. Prior to 1970, it was possible for a single individual to keep abreast of several lines of research. By 1975 research in areas such as cognitive mapping, crowding, and personal space was being produced at such a pace that it became very difficult for a person to stay current with the experimental literature in more than one area. A frequent complaint about environmental research is that there is no theory, only a seemingly endless collection of observations of and experiments on people in different kinds of situations. This has created a niche for theory builders (who are not necessarily researchers) to move into the field and fit concepts together, develop mathematical models, and relate the research to other areas of psychology. The distinction between research and application cuts across all the boundaries between interest areas. Most psychologists seem to have as much difficulty in spanning both research and application as they do in covering several different research topics. In spite of one's best intentions, often it seems that in any particular project either the research or the application is excess baggage. I find myself working on applied problems such as the design of bicycle paths when there is no existing data-base or theory. My immediate goal is to learn something about the behavior of bicycle riders, motorists, and pedestrians under different conditions of density, visibility, weather, grade separation, etc. I also find myself working with architects designing a student residence hall that provides variety, flexibility, and personalization, as well as a good learning environment and adequate social space. Being required to come up with the recommendations for a Tuesday afternoon meeting requires a tremendous eclecticism.

However, such applied projects can be tremendously exciting. They represent the payoff from all those years spent observing and interviewing people, endless tabulations and compilations, and time spent reading other people's work. When I am finally asked to help design a residence hall, everything I have seen, read, and thought about student behavior, university planning, and architecture comes together. The challenge is to synthesize this information in the context of the immediate problem and to come up with specific recommendations within a tight deadline. At this point I am tempted to describe some of the projects on which I have worked. I am bombarded with images of the Seattle airport, a resort island in Fiji, a data-processing center in San Francisco, FAA offices in Los Angeles, bicycle paths in Oregon, and all those strange places and fine people whom I have interviewed and worked with. I believe it would be a distraction to present the material here. Case studies of collaboration between designers and social scientists are becoming readily available (Deasy, 1974; Sommer, 1972; Zeisel, 1975).

If psychologists are to be helpful members of the environmental movement, we will have to cease talking jargon and stop mystifying our field. We will have to write so that we are understood by the people who make decisions and by those who are affected by those decisions. We will have to apply concepts of practical significance to complement, and often to replace, statistical significance. Most difficult of all will be learning to work to impossible deadlines. We are going to have to develop a sense of research economics even if we never teach any courses on the subject. On most practical projects, computer analysis of 200 interviews with all the cross-tabulations, will be worth less than a quick hand-tabulation of 100 replies in a week's time. Some years ago, I accepted the "essential difference" between doing a graduate thesis on a topic and undertaking a practical study. I have come to realize that if we are teaching graduate students to do thesis research in a particular way, it will be difficult to induce them to switch methods when they are hired to do research professionally. The elitist model of research taught in the United States is somewhat similar to our model for surgery. The expensive selection and training process has meant that only a few people can become surgeons, and their services are available to only a few, usually the wealthy and the powerful. To tell the public and our students that only a few highly selected, highly trained, and highly supervised individuals can do environmental research is to ensure that research will become the tool of the wealthy and the powerful and often will be used to deceive and oppress other segments of society. Too much of social psychology has been built on blatant deception; let us hope that environmental psychology will find more ethical means of obtaining information.

Students should be involved in practical design problems in order to acquire the skills necessary to work in poorly articulated, chaotic, and seemingly irrational field situations. The best sorts of projects are those in the student's immediate environment, such as classroom spaces, dormitories, outdoor campus areas, and various aspects of the local city environment. Working on proximate projects will enable the student not only to observe and interview the users directly but also to talk with the people responsible for the space and find out how it got that way and, finally, to report back to these people afterward and attempt to put the results to some practical use. Whenever possible, I try to direct students to projects in which they can have a direct and tangible impact on a real setting. I want them thinking ahead to the stage at which they will discuss their results with people directly involved in the situation. Surveys should be not ends in themselves but means of gathering information that will help guide policies, renovations, and new construction. I try to avoid at all costs the view that research is inherently good and focus instead on what kind of research, who will benefit from it, and what can be done with the results afterward. Projects that can be justified solely as training efforts should *not* involve significant amounts of time and attention from people who are interviewed and affected, yet receive nothing in return.

Environmental psychologists can utilize their new-found status as standard bearers of a critical research area to become personally involved in significant problems. We are also going to have to establish more formal relationships with practicing designers. Environmental psychologists cannot keep publishing articles and expect that designers will read them and apply the findings. Such hope rests on a very naïve model of behavior change. All of us who have done consulting with architects know the difficulty in transforming behavioral data into design criteria. More often than not, the entire consulation process is somewhat of an embarrassment. Hit-and-run consulting is unsatisfying and in many respects scientifically irresponsible. Yet it is difficult to do more when one is brought in too late with too little authority to have a significant impact on the final outcome and when there is no follow-up invitation after the project is completed.

I spent one afternoon (!) 10 years ago in an architect's office discussing seating arrangements for the proposed Bay Area Rapid Transit. Based on my studies of small-group arrangements, I was considered some kind of expert on seating. I gave them the best advice I could, we had a splendid dinner in San Francisco, and eventually I received payment for one afternoon's consulting. That's the end of the story, except that I have ridden BART a number of times since it was opened and find the seating arrangements very comfortable, although I cannot recall whether or not the final product resembles what I had suggested.

I spent another afternoon 2 years ago with the data-processing department of a large bank discussing a major renovation project. I have never heard from any of the officials since our meeting. They seemed quite receptive to my suggestions, and perhaps they put them into practice, but I don't know. This kind of activity is probably more helpful to me as a teacher than as a researcher since it provides some good stories for my students. Yet if my consultation has not been able to improve these various buildings, I must regard myself as a hypocrite, and a worse one for having regaled my students with these anecdotes.

Another time I spent several weeks working with an interdisciplinary team to design an island resort. We came up with a very good program statement, which we turned over to the owners of the island. Ownership of the island has changed hands five times since then and the project has still not been built. Apparently it is more profitable to take capital gains on a resale of the island than to build a resort, even a resort that has behavioral-science input. While I can continue working like this, I am not sure that I want to. I feel some obligation to follow through on my recommendations, at least on a few projects. I realize that the only way this is going to happen is if I have some direct access to the client or, even better, if I have some role in the client's organization. My most satisfying design collaborations have been of a nonremunerative sort for my own university and my own city. Here I have seen actual projects completed in which my contribution was clearly evident and I could follow the project throughout.

One cannot expect to be an effective consultant operating on a hit-and-run basis. A psychologist cannot simply walk in off the street, tell other people what they are doing wrong, walk away, and expect them to change their behavior. Rather one must work with people who acknowledge their client status and help to facilitate the change process. Behavior change is a very complex and difficult process, and if you don't control any of the reinforcers it may even be hopeless. Most of us who have attempted architectural consultation employ an education model rather than a reinforcement model. We rely upon the goodwill of the designer and the client. This may be why our consultation efforts have born so little fruit. I look forward to the day when environmental psychologists are employed directly by government agencies, architectural firms, and client organizations in positions in which they establish guidelines, write contracts, and participate in all the deliberations involving specific projects. It is not enough merely to do a postoccupancy evaluation and publish the results. We are also going to have to get input into projects during the planning stage and then follow them beyond the construction phase into occupancy in order to ensure that our recommendations are used properly and learn how they worked in practice.

If I had to nominate a single person to serve as a model for training environmental psychologists, it would be Kurt Lewin, whose interests span theory, research, and application. With the field as it is today, I believe we could do no better than design graduate programs to produce Lewin's (1948) brand of action researcher–psychologists who undertake research on important social problems, either in the field or in the laboratory, and then apply their findings to improve social institutions, while monitoring and documenting the entire process.

This can only be done if we begin emphasizing field research and practical collaboration with other disciplines in our graduate programs. We must at all costs avoid a Tower of Babel model of graduate education. An interdisciplinary program is not merely psychologists teaching architects, or architects teaching psychologists, or architects and psychologists being taught by urban planners, but members of different professions working collaboratively, each drawing upon his or her own skills to solve practical problems. When students and faculty are attempting to improve a factory, they will quickly realize that they must become knowledgeable in the area of health-and-safety codes, union regulations, labor legislation, and company policies. Such knowledge is required by the situation and it means checking new sources and areas of expertise. One quickly becomes aware how little solid factual information is available even in such comparatively well-researched areas as color, lighting, and noise. Learning to read the relevant research in the area means sorting out the few decent research studies from the plethora of assumptions, opinions, and myth. Reading available research on almost any practical topic has a demystifying effect on students. For example, the standards on acceptable lighting levels are so variable as to be almost meaningless. When we undertook our research on bicycle-path design, about the only solid information available came from Japanese and German studies, and the applicability of this research to conditions in Davis, California, seemed highly doubtful. Eventually we were able to generate our own data, which then served as a model for bicycle paths in much larger and very different American cities (!).

Environmental psychology still has not come to grips with the implications of the case-study method of research. An investigation of a single mental hospital that involves hundreds of interviews and observations is still basically an $n = 1$ study. While there may be aspects of the results that are applicable to other mental hospitals, it would be hazardous to apply them directly to other institutions in other places. We have not yet evolved the ground rules for extrapolating from one case study to another. For this task, the skills of the clinical psychologist who is sensitive to the individual nuance of a particular client seem at least as appropriate as those of the researcher. Yet the researcher's deliberate attempt to document the entire process will help to refine the case-study method down to a teachable, workable research–consultation approach. Even in as modest a project as interviewing patrons of a laundromat or a supermarket, the student should maintain a journal or a research diary of experiences. As a project progresses it is easy to forget how one perceived things initially. Such field notes are at least as valuable as questionnaire responses or observations in describing and interpreting the results afterwards.

What I have given is a model of an environmental psychologist whose interests span research and practice, who is able to read the research literature and apply it to particular situations, and who can generate new knowledge from his or her research to enlarge the data base available in the field. If we train environmental psychologists to be narrow academic specialists, or applied psychologists in the mold of human-factors researchers, then we cannot expect them to operate as action researchers. Generally speaking, we will get what we design and what we reinforce. Criteria for advancement in academic positions must be enlarged to include provision for applied projects. Most of the colleagues in my own department are uncertain whether or not my studies of bicycle riders are "real psychology." Incidentally I found this same skepticism in visits to other campuses, where they wanted me to talk about something important and relevant like personal space. The fact that 13 million bicycles are sold each year, more bicycles than cars sold in the United States between 1971 and 1974, still didn't make this a valid topic for psychological investigation. In a similar vein, the study of rats in mazes seems more like "real psychology" than a study of students in dormitories, even though the average rat never encounters laboratory mazes; besides, the rats used have been bred in captivity for dozens of generations and behave differently than wild rats. The development of a field that spans both research and application will necessarily involve broadening the criteria of acceptable research areas. Fundamental to field research, as distinct from laboratory research, is that one never changes only one item at a time. Rather one deals with a dynamic field in which a change in one part will affect every other part of the field. It is no accident that Kurt Lewin, who developed the notion of action research, is best known for his field theory of behavior.

In conclusion, I believe it is healthy that some people are complaining that our field is too theoretical while others complain that it is too applied. When people stop making these complaints, it is time to worry. I am content to retain an evolutionary view of environmental psychology as a field characterized by dynamic, irreconcilable tensions among research, theory, and application.

References

Deasy, C. M. *Design for human affairs.* New York: Halstad Press, 1974.

Heimstra, N. W., and McFarling, L. H. *Environmental psychology.* Monterey, Calif.: Brooks/ Cole, 1974.

Ittelson, W. H., Proshansky, H. M., Rivlin, L. G., Winkel, G. H., and Dempsey, D. *An introduction to environmental psychology.* New York: Holt, Rinehart and Winston, 1974.

Lewin, K. *Resolving social conflicts.* New York: Harper and Brothers, 1948.

Raimy, V. C. (Ed.). *Training in clinical psychology.* Englewood Cliffs, N.J.: Prentice-Hall, 1950.

Sommer, R. *Design awareness.* San Francisco: Rinehart Press, 1972.

Zeisel, J. *Sociology and architectural design.* New York: Russell Sage Foundation, 1972.

From Congruence to Antecedent Conditions: A Search for the Basis of Environmental Improvement

9

WILLIAM MICHELSON

Neither long ago nor very recently, I wrote a book that expressed and illustrated a conceptual scheme that I thought captured the essence of how sociological research could help in the creation of more adequate human environments. In retrospect, however, I think that the book in some ways obfuscates the complexity of factors relevant to this context, even though what I said in the fine print might have been suitably oriented.

Therefore in this chapter I should like to trace the development of some of the relevant strands of thought with which I began, indicating at least two interacting sources of complexity affecting fruitful design: (1) the content of various complementary disciplinary perspectives and (2) the consideration of not just the *effects* of environmental practices but also their own *causes* or *conditions*. I shall draw on some recent research to illustrate the latter.

I have been interested for a good percentage of my years in the relationship between people and their built environment. This interest is not a detached, purely scholarly one, but one built on a personal feeling that we are capable of building far better places in which to live than we have in the past.

Making this happen, however, is not just a matter of rhetoric, and therefore I have always felt that there are things that we can learn that will make the job one that is based more on knowledge and less on instinct. I

WILLIAM MICHELSON ● Centre for Urban and Community Studies and Department of Sociology, University of Toronto, Ontario, Canada.

therefore have always taken an empirically positivistic point of view that the results of research on man and his built environment can produce information that, if adopted, will enable the building of better communities.

As part of this system of beliefs, I wrote a book published in 1970 entitled *Man and His Urban Environment,* in which I tried to provide a paradigm for the understanding of man–environment relations that would be useful for organizing discrete findings for both theoretical and practical purposes. I also attempted to assemble the results of many studies conducted previous to that time, so as to indicate what, from a sociological perspective, may have been known and what not known in this context. The paradigm centered on the concept of *congruence.*

Ideas are frequently timebound. Indeed ideas in print are often bound to a time several years before they see daylight. People therefore frequently ask if I still hold to my original formulation on congruence, as well as in what direction my thinking may have pointed since that formulation. Some of this has appeared in obscure bits and pieces (e.g., Michelson, 1971, 1974; 1975a,b,; Michelson and Reed, 1974), while detailed statements are in the process of publication.[1]

Therefore, I shall attempt here to indicate concisely my retrospective view of congruence, as well as where my occasional thoughts, encounters, and research findings appear to have led in the last 8 years. This account is surely egocentric,[2] for which I offer my apologies, but perhaps a personal exercise such as this has at least the potential for illustrating phenomena of more general import.

Congruence

When I wrote of congruence in the book (Michelson, 1970), I meant treating certain relevant aspects of the man-made environment (at various levels of scale, from the most microscopic to the macroscopic) as scientific factors to be viewed in conjunction with nonspatial factors. Environment had previously been conceived of by sociologists and geographers as a location or a container in which things happened, but without any effective force of its own on what happened. While a small number of writers (e.g., Festinger, Schachter, and Back, 1950; Whyte, 1956; and, by implication, Calhoun, 1963) took a very deterministic stance about the effects of man-made environment *on* behavior, their stance was not the predominant one.

My paradigm suggested placing spatial factors in a position of equality *vis-à-vis* the nonspatial factors studied by social scientists and subsequently

[1]A revised edition of *Man and His Urban Environment* was published in the spring of 1976, while a new volume reporting in greater detail the theoretical and empirical substance of my research since 1969 is scheduled for publication by Oxford University Press in 1977.
[2]See, for example, the references for the crowning touch.

assessing how they related, without the shackles of prior notions as to which factors are the "only" important ones.

My position was that spatial factors are mostly permissive. Although some activities may be made difficult or impossible by specific spatial contexts, most others are permitted. When the spatial parameters of the man-made environment prove no hindrance to desired activity, I called this a state of *congruence*. When these parameters made such activity impossibly difficult, I called this *incongruence*. I suggested that incongruence would be accompanied by consequences generally considered negative (e.g., anger, isolation, and mental and physical illness).

I differentiated two types of congruence—mental and experiential. *Mental congruence* referred to whether people *think* a given environment accommodates their desired activity—a critical perception underlying public acceptance or rejection of newly built settings. On the other hand, *experiential congruence* referred to the actual degree of environmental accommodation of activity once people are actually exposed to the setting. Creating a better human environment was thought to require an understanding of both mental and experiential congruence.

Having established this central set of concepts, I proceeded to argue in favor of gathering as complete a collection of known relationships between spatial and aspatial aspects of man-made environment as possible, noting the types and degrees of congruence characteristic of each. This collection would serve as a resource for future design work.

A number of chapters were then devoted to an examination of a major aspatial factor each (e.g., family patterns, life-cycle stage, and socioeconomic status), assessing the relationship of this factor to spatial factors as found in existing social-science and design-research literature. The issues of pathology and environmental determinism were treated in additional chapters.

Although the actual text had, I think, a suitably realistic perspective, I fear now that the organization of the chapters falsely suggests that all the various aspatial factors have the same kind of relationship with the man-made environment and that they should be considered of equal importance. I do not think that this is the case at all.

Such a formulation, if intended, would resemble a simplifying bias long present within the design professions; the conception of clients as *unidimensional,* not *multidimensional.* The unidimensional conception involves planning for people in terms of only one of the various complementary ways in which they should be viewed. Although a particular state of poverty or family structure may be easy to spot and to accommodate, it does not represent the sum total of the simultaneously relevant characteristics of a family or a group of people.

Planners and city officials, for example, focused only on poverty when creating the early, conventional types of public housing. They concentrated on providing adequate shelter for those who could not pay for it themselves, but they were less likely to take into consideration the widely differing needs of their various clients, generated by heterogeneous social characteristics and problems.

A second example of unidimensional planning is the North American suburb of the 1950's and 1960's, which seemed predicated on the presence of a perennial toddler and a housewife without interests other than home and family. The creation of detached homes with private yards and residential streets—*and little else*—was surely suitably oriented to young children. But the kinds of amenities and opportunities required by the same young people within a few years were usually lacking without expensive private means of transportation. Even when the children were small, however, other members of their families were not as well served by the local environment. Mothers generally found it difficult to find adult companionship during the day apart from immediate neighbors, let alone more complex sorts of activities. Fathers often paid the price of longer trips to work for the opportunity to live in a suburb. Indeed even the positive aspects of suburban life appear to be based on the unidimensional assumption of warm (but not hot) weather, clearly only a small part of the reality of most temperate and northern climates.

To be fair to myself, I did state in the last chapter of the book that the considerations of the preceding chapters had to be integrated to be of use for ameliorative efforts in the real world, a task for which the various discrete research findings were not good preparation. But I did not give much of an idea as to the basis for such integrative efforts.

Similar to the foregoing, a typical mode of procedure in the social sciences is to disaggregate people, giving names to each of the factors, such as class or ethnicity, that may influence behavior. Nonetheless when it comes time to predict or to take action predicated upon behavior, we do not know which of the "named" characteristics will be relevant. It is common for two or more characteristics of the same person to lead to greatly differing behavioral outcomes. Two nominally similar people may act quite differently as a consequence of giving different priorities to their component characteristics. Hence even perfect knowledge of the influence of individual human characteristics is not necessarily sufficient for efforts requiring integrated knowledge.

Planning and architectural efforts presumably are intended to satisfy the wants of clients. Hence one has to ask what it is that is to be satisfied. Although all generalizations are inherently false, it is not foolish to say that seldom, if ever, is a nominal characteristic of a person itself a want to be satisfied through design. Rather it is behavior derived from that characteristic that must be accommodated. Since, however, there is a considerable degree of indeterminacy between the presence of any one nominal characteristic and what a person chooses to do in the context of his or her many cross-cutting characteristics, it seems to make much more sense to design for known *patterns of behavior* rather than for nominal characteristics.

I do not intend to demean the relevance of general social-science prac-tice for other purposes. People's nominal characteristics are surely prior to behavior when one is seeking an explanation for what has already hap-pened. Nonetheless they are far more remote from the spatial factors in design than is behavior. *The relationship between the man-made environment and behavior is what I see as the crucial one for the creation of a better environment.*

I called such patterns of behavior *life style* within the confines of a single chapter. With the benefit of hindsight, I would have oriented the book more explicitly around life style, as indeed this concept was implicit in all the substantive chapters, not just the one bearing its name. In terms of the aims of the book (and hopefully of the design disciplines), life style is of greater relevance than the other factors. It represents a different kind of phenomenon, and it has a different structure. One should still assess the potential effects of the other, more nominal factors on life style, but life style acts as a *synoptic* factor integrating the various influences of the other factors at a level appropriate for design activity.

Utilizing a single factor such as life style does not reduce the need to consider populations as internally heterogeneous, as there is usually a di-versity of life styles within any large number of people. In practical terms, however, one can operate under the assumption that the number of rele-vant life styles one should consider is somewhere reasonably between one (monolithy) and infinity (complete idiosyncracy). Utilizing this concept, however, at least tells one what to look for with respect to design purposes when dealing with human complexity.

In short, I give very much more emphasis to patterns of everyday behavior than *Man and His Urban Environment* appears at face value to give. It is the behavioral output of many factors, rather than the factors them-selves, that enters the equation with spatial factors in my current concep-tion of congruence—rather a definite and critical refinement since my formulation of the book.

In this respect, I now conceive of man-made spatial contexts as *oppor-tunity fields* that provide more or less chance for a wide range of behavior (intended, desired, expected, or otherwise) to take place. Many are usually possible; some are constrained. But focusing on the extent to which the measurable parameters of a given environment (e.g., capacity, flow, acous-tics, equipment, and distance) make it impossible to do certain things ena-bles more of a feeling of the process present in a relationship among factors than was the case under the original conceptualization, which used more nominal and hence less process-oriented factors.

The Context of Man–Environment Relations I

At this point, the reader must wonder if I really intend that no social or psychological phenomena other than behavior be treated in the context of design. Are there not other factors still that shed light on man in his built environment? Surely the work of so many psychologists, geographers, sociologists, educators, and others neither focuses exclusively on behavior nor escapes relevance? In the book, I mentioned in passing such perspectives as perception, culture, and the behavior setting, contributed by authors such as Lynch (1960), Hall (1966), Sommer (1969), and Barker (1968). Although acknowledging the validity of such other perspectives at the start, I then went on to develop my own without explicit reference to how it fit with the others in the more general context of man–environment relations. At that period in history, it seemed sufficient to make a fruitful approach to such a neglected subject without integrating the various approaches simultaneously emerging.

In the 8 years that have passed since I actually wrote *Man and His Urban Environment*, I believe that a variety of valid perspectives on man–environment relations has become relatively well established. I believe also that these perspectives are complementary, although any given perspective may have more or less value according to the question being asked. In any case, the total context of man–environment relations has clearly outgrown the inherent constraints of any single perspective.

The kind of complementarity I see was sketched in a fable I wrote a few years ago (Michelson, 1971). It took as its theme the old saying, "You can lead a horse to water but you can't make him drink." The theme by itself suggests my position that man–made environment serves as an opportunity field but not normally as a deterministic factor. However, I attempted to develop the theme further to indicate the place of several of the perspectives *vis-à-vis* each other.

It centered on the hypothetical assignment of a design team to produce an improved trough for five horses. Following each of various trials and errors, the team was always forced to explain why horses did not drink from the design solutions. The team was forced to eliminate social, physiological, and psychological reasons as to why the troughs were not used, such as a preference for playing cowboys-and-Indians or lack of thirst. They had to rule out a coffee cup and a trough built for two because these did not provide adequate opportunity for the five horses to drink. The designers had to eliminate the use of chlorinated water, as this was not perceived as suitable for imbibing by the horses. They found that a building with crosses and a bell tower did not inspire drinking, while swinging doors and a bar stimulated the prospects. Indeed even when the design was maximal in all these ways and the horses were suitably motivated, they still would not drink if compelled to do something else like plow or race. Nonetheless, all these hurdles cleared, the designers finally saw the horses slake their thirst. And this had seemed at one time a simple design problem!

The context is one in which the explanation of behavior with respect to environmental factors requires the examination of many kinds of criteria. The creation of a successful environment requires the satisfaction of these criteria.

From the design standpoint, the very first criterion to be satisfied is whether or not physical opportunity is provided for the specified behavior to occur. If this is not done, no amount of perception, normative appropriateness, or symbolic sensitivity can save the design. Nonetheless the provision of an adequate opportunity field is hardly sufficient to ensure that the behavior will actually occur. Other criteria must be satisfied as well, with the factors involved in them providing a more compelling explanation of why the particular behavior observed is found to occur. By this reasoning, the perceptual perspective is a better explanatory factor for behavior than the opportunity perspective, while the cultural perspective (including both normative and symbolic elements) is better yet. However, in terms of primacy regarding the process of design, one might well reverse the order in which one should consider these perspectives—placing opportunity first, perception second, and culture third, although not failing to consider any.

Hence, my original concentration on one perspective must surely now be placed within a larger man–environment relations context, in which the various perspectives (1) are complementary but (2) vary in salience according to the kind of task facing the researcher or designer.[3]

The Context of Man–Environment Relations II

The preceding discussion suggests that the accumulated efforts of man–environment researchers and theorists are surely such that design practice is enjoying considerable improvement and producing fruitful results. In fact, I think tremendous strides have been made in the past decade. However, I have become increasingly mindful of the fact that simply because you may understand how to make a better design or plan does not mean that you can bring it to fruition. The context in which design issues unfold is certainly larger than the factors internal to the design equation. This context involves many other factors often considered "external," such as more macroscopic considerations in social structure, politics, and economics, to start with just a few.

The more general context of man–environment relations is reached if we take conventional cause-and-effect relationships and "unfold" them backward in time to their genesis. The typical scientific approach that characterizes the perspectives I discussed earlier has to do only with what the consequences are of that environment (or those environmental practices) that we have right now. Yet if we are to make a better environment,

---

[3]A more detailed statement of this paradigm may be found in Michelson, 1974.

we must assess what conditions brought about the status quo and whether or not these so-called antecedent conditions represent barriers to alternative designs or practices in the future.

In many cases, if not in most, an investigation of antecedent conditions shows that the status quo does not reflect the previous intentions of professionals, whether scientific or nonscientific, let alone those of users, but rather reflects more the terms of reference of those concerned with such other non-client-oriented criteria as full employment, political control, and security in mortgage lending.

This is surely not a situation unique to the design sciences. Several years ago, I was appointed to a national committee to help design Canada's Man and the Biosphere Programme, in conjunction with the international program sponsored by UNESCO. This program takes environment in a very much broader way than the design professions normally do. Yet it increasingly struck me that the "two-way" scientific outlook—*back* to antecedent conditions that explain the creation of environmental practices and *forward* to the consequences of these practices—is necessary as a general framework for the amelioration of the environment. Such a paradigm became expressed in its most concrete form during an international working-group's deliberations on "The Impact of Human Activities on Mountain and Tundra Ecosystems" (UNESCO, 1974), a far cry from the man-made environment, yet very similar in its analytic context.

Figure 1 illustrates this paradigm. Although this schema was formulated in the above-mentioned working group, I intended the greater part of it to be of equal relevance to both natural and man-made environments.

According to the paradigm, Steps *C* and *D* refer to the normal scientific approach to research: careful measurement of the effects of an environmental stimulus. The so-called environmental impact study, now required as a prerequisite for many types of projects dealing with both natural and man-made environments, deals with the same steps, but in *hypothetical* fashion: What *would* happen if thus and such a project were built, or practice instituted?

Nonetheless what actually results is not always the same as what people think occurs or notice. If one is to evaluate built space or current practices, it is necessary to include Steps *D* and *E*. These steps acknowledge that (1) evaluation may be made by many persons from various points of view and (2) the evaluation made by any particular group of persons is partly a function of their perception of the situation.

As an example of the first of these points, one might point to the creation of a public housing project, which might have very different consequences for and evaluations by such people as (a) the architect, (b) the contractor, (c) the taxpayer, (d) the politician, (e) the police force, and (f) the resident. One rather infamous project, Pruitt-Igoe in St. Louis, was dynamited after not many years of operation by the local housing authority

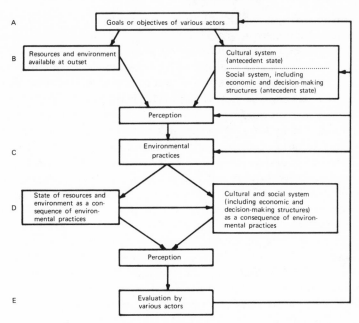

Figure 1. General framework for investigations on man–biosphere interrelations (adapted from UNESCO, 1974, p. 13).

because it was thought so unsuitable for its particular tenants; yet its architect had won acclaim for its design on obviously different grounds.

Regarding the filtering effect of perception on evaluation, studies of noise have shown that persons may be physiologically bothered by noise without necessarily being continually conscious of the cause of the problem. The noise level may become second nature, as is often the case among those living near airports or railroads. In this case, the evaluation of the noise (and its source) may be more positive than the documented effects may justify. In other cases, the situation may be reversed. The point is not to discard either opinion or reality but to be aware of the processes linking them, so that each can be taken for what it is worth.

It is largely a more political, nonscientific matter to determine for any particular issue *whose* evaluation *should* be accorded the most attention. In the public housing example, a classic argument follows from the diverse interests of the tenant, the housing-authority bureaucracy, and the taxpayer. From an outside, impartial view, we would probably side with the actual users or residents, but theirs is not necessarily the only interest critical to the ultimate feasibility of a given project. In any case, the actual process whereby certain interests are given priority over others is seldom explicit or public.

It is also relevant to consider whether those whose interests are not given priority are not, at times, therefore subject to "cruel or unusual punishment" as a consequence.

However, even if the selection of high-priority interests and the reconciliation of perception and evaluation occur relatively unambiguously, this does not mean that environments or practices judged negative can necessarily be rectified very easily. And it is in this connection that Steps A and B become of more than academic interest.

When we look at A and B, we are at first examining who was responsible for bringing about the current setting or practice, what this person or these persons intended, what resources they had available, and under what conditions (social, economic, political, etc.) all this occurred. The "actors" prominent in A and B may not be those judged as most relevant in D and E. It is entirely possible that many environmental practices cannot be changed in such a form as to produce a "satisfactory" D or E for the chosen interest group without the implementation of changes in A or B or both A and B. Hence change in the form of amelioration of environmental problems may not always be solved through the examination of C and D or even C, D, and E but may require knowledge of the whole paradigm.

When an exploration of a problem indicates the need for change, the above paradigm should be "unfolded" laterally, so that alternative variations in environmental practice (e.g., C', C'', etc.) are viewed both with respect to their differential consequences and evaluations (D', D'', E', E'', etc.) and with respect to the differing needs and antecedent conditions thought to underly them (A', A'', B', B'', etc.). Putting such relevant information side by side for alternative environmental practices then enables a choice of the practices seen to be desirable, with a firm understanding of the societal implications of these alternative practices. In some cases, it may be necessary to insist on changes in the way things are done (i.e., more generally than with respect to environmental management) within a given society. In other cases, it may be necessary only to choose an alternative environmental practice that is in fact supported by local conditions and culture and that serves the needs of those groups most involved.

Let me give an example of this situation from my recent research work. For the past 6 years, I have been pursuing a study that focuses on, among other things, the implications of family living in high-rise apartments.[4] It is relatively instructive to examine the various findings of this study with respect to the logic of Figure 1.

Concisely, the results showed that families living in high-rise apartments (C) found grave inadequacies (D) in a wide range of attributes of these buildings, from storage space to soundproofing. The residents also

[4]This research has been carried out under the sponsorship of Central Mortgage and Housing Corporation (Canada), with substantial financial support as well from The Canada Council. It is this study that serves as the empirical base for the volume mentioned earlier to be published by Oxford University Press in 1977.

thought that these shortcomings were important, not just trivial annoyances. The residents thought that they could not themselves provide remedies and that virtually the only thing they could do to bring about improvement was to move.

Nonetheless when questioned about satisfaction (E), the overwhelming majority of high-rise residents professed to be satisfied—mildly so in comparison with those living in houses but surely not dissatisfied. They also said that they would not themselves move on the basis of the specifically named deficiencies in their high-rise units.

This apparent discrepancy between dysfunctions of the units (D) and satisfaction (E) is resolved by an examination of the perceptual basis on which evaluation is made. Perception is not just something that occurs with eyes. What people find salient is the result of a largely subconscious selective process, during which some criteria by which to observe or evaluate an object come to the fore, while others recede, at least temporarily.

In the present case, the families in high-rise apartments had almost all intended these homes to be interim accommodation. They had virtually all said, even before moving in, that they expected to move again within 5 years—mostly to single-family homes. Therefore their evaluation of their high-rise units was conditioned by the fact that they did not view them as permanent. Their main criteria for evaluation of high-rise units were not the same as their most important goals in housing; these criteria largely centered on a small number of pragmatic gains they hoped to achieve during the anticipated short term of residence in their units: proximity to work, on-site recreation facilities, etc. These goals were largely fulfilled, despite the many dysfunctional consequences of living in high-rise apartments, and hence the residents were midly satisfied.

The critical aspect that allows families to focus on those criteria of housing that *are* fulfilled rather than on the many that are not is the assumption of future mobility. Without this assumption, it is clear that the evaluation of the same environment and its consequences would be far more negative. This assumption was in fact shown valid, as we continued to study the same families over a longer period of time, and most of them moved exactly as expected, regardless of their satisfaction with their housing units.

Nonetheless the people studied were chosen because they were relatively affluent and because their actions would reflect their own choices, not simple economic constraints. These actions showed that even though these people were satisfied with the high-rises, they did not prefer them. Furthermore although the outcome can not be regarded as problematic for these people, life in a high-rise had become defined as difficult for many families without this degree of affluence—something which prompted the study in the first place, since most new housing units in recent years in the Toronto area have been in high-rise buildings. What emerges is the notion that evaluation of the same dwelling can be based on quite different criteria and with varying degrees of salience, depending on the plans and prospects for mobility on the part of residents.

If we assume that these findings imply something about the desirability of an alternative environmental context (C'), how do we proceed? One way would be to make specific improvements in the deficiencies noted in conventional high-rise buildings. While these would undoubtedly contribute marginal improvements in satisfaction for all those living there—justification in itself—such improvements are not directly related to the basis for satisfaction of those who assume that they will move elsewhere (who are satisfied despite the presence of these deficiencies), nor do they address the plight of families whose dissatisfaction lies in their inability to make the desired move to another kind of dwelling. The problem for the latter families is that the high-rise cannot become what it is not by definition, while it will be evaluated on this basis unless these families feel they will eventually be able to achieve their aspirations. In short, when the housing market can satisfy dynamically sequenced family wants, a decent measure of satisfaction is possible.

The second alternative way to a more satisfactory situation is therefore to alter the distribution of completed new housing units—away from a heavy concentration on the high-rise and toward a more balanced array of housing types—while keeping the costs of the various alternatives within reason. This alternative way would allow satisfaction in the choice of certain housing types, such as the high-rise for interim periods, under the understanding that it will still be possible to move elsewhere subsequently. Insofar as housing policy is concerned, this is surely a more constructive step than is making more livable that in which families would rather not live on more basic grounds, although the two are not mutually exclusive.

If, however, one wishes to pursue this second alternative, an irony appears. The solution to the problem faces the same set of difficulties as created the problem in the first place! It is at this point that reference to Steps *A* and *B* in the paradigm become helpful.

When we ask under what conditions and under whose responsibility high-rises became predominant in Toronto, we have to rule out consumer demand *for this type of housing* from the start. Although there clearly was and is a market for high-rises among some young people, some elderly people, some families in which both spouses work, and highly mobile people, the results of no study of preferences support the creation of little other than high-rises in Toronto in recent years. Rather most people credit this phenomenon to a marked increase in the value and hence the price of land during this period. When land becomes highly expensive, it is quite rational to divide such a cost among many potential residents rather than to create other forms of housing that are priced outside the borderlines of marketability.

Asking why land became so expensive—something that would have to be altered if alternatives to high-rises are to be considered realistic—then produces a variety of complementary answers, centering around (1)-unbridled speculation both in raw land and in existing residential buildings (the latter also tending to drive up the price of land and of new housing units); (2) a shortage of serviced land meeting government regulations for residential construction; and (3) other governmental practices that tend to delay projects and to make them more expensive. Expense is not just a burden in its own right; it has a decided influence on the qualitative nature of what a builder sees fit to put on the market at any time. The more that expenses *not* associated with labor or materials rise, the more pressure there is to build more units on a given plot of land.

The logical next question is why these practices are allowed to continue. In each case, the structured prerogative of a certain number of people is involved, as embedded in current social, economic, and political structures:

1. In most areas of North America, it is traditional for people to earn money from real-estate speculation, above and beyond both the general rate of inflation and any improvements they might have made to property themselves. Although this practice may have adverse effects that strike almost everyone to a greater or lesser extent, such speculative efforts have not been strongly challenged. They are taxed but not in a way that makes them extinct.[5]

2. The various levels of government affecting the Toronto area are hesitant to relinquish the tight control over the timing and the location of new development they possess through land-servicing regulations and practices, even though the relative inflexibility and slowness of their efforts bring about qualitative effects in what does get built (not to speak of a residue of higher costs as well).

3. The same desire for maintenance of control, together with the laudable desire for the voice of the public to be registered at various stages of the planning and design process, contributes to a lengthy bureaucratic process of preconstruction approvals—often totaling several years, during which time a developer faces expenses such as taxes on the land and interest on money borrowed.

The point is not to praise one alternative and to condemn all others. It is rather to illustrate how what would have to be done to help remedy a problem may fly in the face of those antecedent conditions that helped create the problem in the first place. If someone really wants to face this problem, he or she may have to challenge the fruitfulness of speculative practices and the necessity for the current modes of implementation of governmental controls, for example. The usual governmental procedure of dealing with a problem like this in North America, that of providing a subsidy to lower the costs of certain units by a little, simply does not relate

---

[5] I obviously do not equate speculation with private effort which provides needed new housing units and ought be *encouraged.*

to the nature of the problem. Governments in other parts of the world have taken other types of steps, some of them relatively successful.

What I suggest, then, is that while the scientific isolation of a problem may require only the Steps after C in Figure 1, its *solution* may require the steps backward in time and in causality to A and B.

This discussion has come a long way from the concept of congruence, but hopefully not along random paths. In retrospect, I have come to think that congruence is best understood in terms of behavior patterns and that it stands as one element in a complementary and ordered array of perspectives on man–environment relations. Nonetheless even this integrated view of man and environment may be of little practical value without knowledge of how environments get to be formed and environmental practices instituted or changed. Each concern becomes a constituent element in a subsequently wider context of understanding.

In sum, then, this chapter was intended to indicate that an interest in the ultimate solution of the kinds of issues dealt with by designers has led me to increasingly complex and macroscopic paradigms, which, perhaps, are ultimately necessary even for the solution of microscopic issues. This may make the terms of reference facing design professionals much more difficult, but I would like to think that it might make them more realistic and constructive.

Acknowledgments

This paper was originally presented in the form of a talk to students in urban sociology of the University of Michigan, Flint, on October 25, 1974. I am grateful to Bill Marston for his encouraging me to talk retrospectively and chronologically about my work and to Dan Stokols for the legitimation necessary to formalize such thoughts into writing. Cathy Barth transcribed and typed the first draft of the manuscript. The Institute for Building Functions Analysis, University of Lund, Sweden, provided a stimulating setting for the writing of the last draft.

References

Barker, R. *Ecological psychology*. Stanford, Calif.: Stanford University Press, 1968.
Calhoun, J. B. Population density and social pathology. In L. J. Duhl (Ed.), *The urban condition*, New York: Basic Books, 1963. Pp. 33–43.
Festinger, L., Schachter, S., and Back, K. *Social pressures in informal groups*. New York: Harper, 1950.
Hall, E. T. *The hidden dimension*. Garden City, N.Y.: Doubleday, 1966.
Lynch, K. *The image of the city*. Cambridge, Mass.: M.I.T. Press and Harvard University Press, 1960.
Michelson, W. *Man and his urban environment: A sociological approach*, Reading, Mass.: Addison-Wesley, 1970.

Michelson, W. The case of the equine fountains: Local neighborhood as design opportunity. *Design and Environment,* 1971, *159,* 129–131.

Michelson, W. The reconciliation of subjective and objective information in environmental research: The case of social contact in high rise apartments. *Sociological Inquiry,* 1974, *43*(3–4), 147–173. Also in Marcia P. Effrat (Ed.), *The community.* New York: Free Press, 1974. Pp. 147–173.

Michelson, W. Editor's introduction. In W. Michelson, (Ed.), *Behavioral research methods in environmental design.* Stroudsburg, Pa.: Dowden, Hutchinson and Ross (distributed by Halsted Press of John Wiley), 1975. Pp. 1–8. (a)

Michelson, W. Urbanism as ways of life. *Ekistics,* 1975, *236,* 20–26. (b)

Michelson, W., and Reed, P. B. Life style in environmental research. In C. Beattie and S. Crysdale (Eds.), *Sociology Canada: Readings.* Toronto: Butterworths, 1974. Pp. 406–419.

Sommer, R. *Personal space.* Englewood Cliffs, N.J.: Prentice-Hall, 1969.

UNESCO. *Final Report of Working Group on Project 6: Impact of human activities on mountain and tundra ecosystems.* Paris: MAB Report Series No. 14, 1974.

Whyte, W. H., Jr. *The organization man.* Garden City, N.Y.: Doubleday (Anchor), 1956.

Participation in the Design Process: A Cognitive Approach

10

STEPHEN KAPLAN

A group of us landscape architects were to work with a small community on a playground project. So we went to them and said, "What do you want?" and they said, "Well, what have you got?" So we went back and worked up some drawings of what we thought they should do. When we showed them the drawings, they said, "Oh, no, that's not it at all." So we said, "Well, what do you want?" and they said, "Well, what have you got?"

This dialogue, related to me by a student, constitutes an instance of participation, although not a particularly satisfying one. In the context of design problems, there are in fact many opportunities for participation, ranging from public hearings to meetings with governing boards, both public and private. Sad to say, such participatory sessions are characteristically of limited value and, at times, even counterproductive.

Each failure of designers and ordinary humans to interact effectively is a lost opportunity and in addition a source of stress as well. Environmental design inevitably alters the interface between people and their environment. If people care about their environment, about the setting in which they live and act, then it follows that they wish to be knowledgeable and even influential as far as changes in their environment are concerned.

The pervasiveness of this problem is directly linked to the pervasiveness of environmental design. Designers and planners are involved in tampering with the future, at all levels. They may be concerned with designing a new building, a new town, a new amusement park, bridges, highways, or what have you. In all these cases they deal with nonexistent environments

STEPHEN KAPLAN ● University of Michigan, Ann Arbor. The work reported here was supported, in part, by the Institute for Environmental Quality, University of Michigan.

and with the ramifications such altered environments might bring with them.

Unfortunately designers are not always effective in incorporating input from the public into such considerations. Equally unfortunate, and more surprising, designers often are unable even to communicate the constraints and possibilities of these nonexistent environments. Useful inputs from the public are more unlikely when the public is unable to comprehend the issues involved. (As an informal check on the severity of this problem, we recently sent an assistant to a variety of local public meetings dealing with environmental design issues. The frequency of problems of this kind turned out to be impressive—or appalling, depending on one's perspective. A particularly striking example occurred at a meeting of the planning commission, a relatively experienced and sophisticated citizen group. Their deliberations were hindered by their explicitly stated inability to comprehend maps prepared for them by the professional planning staff.)

There is thus reason to believe that all is not well with participation as it is now practiced. The purpose of this chapter is to attempt to provide a different conception of the nature, the possibilities, and the tools for this process. Hopefully the proposed approach can help the exchanges that are going to occur anyway, as well as encourage participation in settings where environmental design now occurs without such assistance.

The proposal for a new conception inevitably raises the issue of the old conception. What was it like, what was the matter with it? It turns out that the designer and the people have often harbored very different conceptions, and this may be part of the problem. Quite often designers approach sessions with the public as occasions requiring salesmanship. Such an attitude is understandable, given that the public is often brought in rather late in the process, when the designer's commitment to a particular solution is already substantial. Thus the designer's graphics and models tend to be oriented to please, to impress, and to convince. The public, in turn, comes to see sessions with designers as times when one is sold a bill of goods, when one has the wool pulled over one's eyes by an adroit but not particularly receptive professional. Given this expectation, it is hardly surprising that some people have come to see the participatory setting as an opportunity for confrontation.

The positive feedback potential of these views is considerable as public aggressiveness and designer defensiveness come to feed each other. Clearly these attitudes are unlikely to foster a particularly constructive interaction among the parties involved. An alternative approach would be to view the participatory process as an opportunity for problem solving. Humans can be, after all, highly effective problem-solvers under appropriate conditions. If we could identify what these conditions are, it might be possible to make participation considerably more fruitful and satisfying than is now the case.

Problem Solving and the Expert

"Rich people," it is often noted, "are different from the rest of us." So too, and perhaps more importantly, are experts. It is quite obvious, of course, that they know more, at least in their own special area. And it has long been suspected that they think differently. But only relatively recently has it become clear that they *see* differently too, that their actual perception is somehow altered by their acquisition of expertise.

In our quest for ways to make the participatory setting a more likely occasion for problem solving it may be worth a brief digression into the thought and perception of the expert. This is an area that could be particularly engaging for the psychologist interested in aiding the design expert (or any other expert, for that matter). Its fascination lies in the fact that experts tend to be largely unaware of how different they are from ordinary people. Failing to recognize this difference in turn leads to behavior that is often counterproductive and even self-defeating. It is a classic example of a circumstance in which insight could have highly beneficial effects.

Recent developments in cognitive psychology make it clear that the initial representation of a problem—that is, the way it is perceived—has an enormous impact on whether, and how, it is solved (Posner, 1973). With respect to experts, the point is perhaps most clearly made in the research of DeGroot (1965), who studied chess masters. He found that masters differed from ordinary players in the initial conception of the board and not in any subsequent manipulation. Thus the representation of the problem is central to problem solving; much of the expert's expertise may be expressed in the perceptual process itself.

When we speak of a "representation of a problem," we are referring to that aspect of an individual's cognitive map or internal model of the environment that is involved in perceiving *this particular problem*. In other words, the elements involved are assumed to be a portion of the individual's cognitive repertoire, a collection of concepts acquired through previous experience.

Everyone represents problems in terms of previously learned elements—this does not distinguish the expert from anyone else. But the elements corresponding to areas of extensive experience or expertise are different in three important respects:

1. They are both compact and abstract. Through many experiences extraneous material is eliminated, leaving only what is essential or characteristic. Since humans have a limited capacity for what they can think about at any one time, the more compact the elements of thought are, the more of them one can contemplate at any one time. This greatly aids grasping "the larger picture."

(If the idea of cognitive compactness does not bring forth any intuitive imagery, recall your experience in learning some complex task like driving a car. Initially there seemed to be more going on than fit in one's head at one time. But with experience, and increasing compactness, the same content fit into the same head with room to spare, room for listening to the radio, or conversation, or even problem solving.)

With still further experience, another aspect of cognition comes into play, strengthening still further that grasp on the larger picture. This is the development of hierarchy, of *higher-level* cognitive elements that come to stand for a large class of the more basic elements. These higher-level elements, too, become more compact with increasing experience. Abstractions of this kind are easily illustrated in the context of environmental design. When the designer uses the term "space" it might at first sound like the straightforward concept in everyday usage. But after one listens to designers talk for a while about a "good space" and a "sense of space" and the like, it becomes clear that it is a highly abstract and specialized concept. Like the chess master, they have come to see the world in ways that simultaneously make them effective and cut them off from the rest of us. Other examples of abstractions often used by designers are "scale," "density," and "circulation." These are not merely jargon; they are concepts difficult to acquire in the first place and still more difficult to explain once acquired. (For a more extensive discussion of the development of hierarchies in cognitive structure, see Kaplan, 1976.)

2. The cognitive elements in the head of the expert are part of a rich and highly developed network. As such they can be reached in many different ways—there is far less problem of access or retrieval.

Thus the designer might be able to imagine the same structure given a photograph or a plan view or an elevation or a verbal description. The ordinary person, by contrast, might find the photograph the only satisfactory means of eliciting the representation in question. Note that the designer has access to appropriate cognitive elements through the use of inputs that have little in common with the basis upon which they were originally built.

3. This high level of compactness and access makes possible another vital cognitive facility, the capacity to manipulate the critical elements of the problem. Having elements that can be combined in various ways, or that can even be ignored if necessary, is often considered the very essence of the problem-solving process. It should be noted, however, that this could not occur if the elements were not compact and separable in the first place and if they did not have a richness of connections allowing varying access and various patterns of connections.

Differing in these (and undoubtedly other) respects from ordinary mortals is enough of a handicap in itself when communication—that is, the sharing of internal models—is called for. But there is another facet of perceiving differently that makes the difficulty greater still. Perceiving feels natural to the perceiver. In most cases it feels effortless, ordinary, routine. The expert characteristically does not know that he sees differently from anyone else—indeed, he feels that he sees simply what's there, what anyone else not blinded by preconceptions would also see. Psychology long ago discovered that the human capacity for introspecting applies primarily to content; the nature of our own process is largely inaccessible to consciousness. Not perceiving *how* one perceives is thus presumably a rather widespread human limitation and not one that typically causes particular difficulties. In the case of the expert, however, the blindness to his own special way of seeing is far from harmless.

If indeed a major part of expertise is perceptual and if one tends to be oblivious of one's own perception, then experts could readily fall into the trap of doubting that they know anything particularly special that sets them off from other people. From there one readily slips into the uneasy state of wondering if one possesses a generally useful ability and whether others might not ultimately figure this out too. Two strategies for dealing with such self-doubt and self-uncertainty are well known. One is to make clear to one's clients (or the public or whoever is in hearing distance) that one has done one's homework. A second and sometimes not unrelated task is to "snow" the potential listener with a huge quantity of (preferably technical) information. (It should be pointed out that this description of the expert's uncertainties and defensive strategies is in no way limited to the designer. Experts in all fields often find themselves playing the "witch-doctor" role. Physicians are perhaps the best known for adopting this territorial stance, but it is not unknown to engineers, lawyers, and even psychologists.)

These strategies sometimes make the expert feel better. But the public rarely wants to see someone's homework. They almost never like being snowed. And they may well be frustrated in any problem-solving aspirations they secretly harbor.

The picture painted so far may seem a bit discouraging. After all, experts are likely to *continue* to see things differently even if we can convince them that their perception is special rather than universal. But the discussion so far has concerned only the cognitive properties of the expert. The ordinary human, too, is an information-processing system, and a high-powered one at that. If we could find ways of providing information that would link up with the high-powered capacity of this system, problem solving might take place after all.

On Some Intellectual Assets of Ordinary People

The cognitive capacity of the expert is not, of course, unique to the expert. Or, to put it another way, most people have areas of expertise, or at least areas of considerable experience in which they function in essentially similar fashion. But when we consider the area of environmental design, we are dealing with a domain in which people are clearly not expert, although a basic familiarity is widely shared. We must, then, attempt to find ways of achieving compactness (although probably not a high level of abstraction), access, and manipulative capacity that do not rely on extensive training or unusual talent. Three intellectual assets that people can be counted upon to have are particularly salient here:

1. People have great facility in nonverbal cognition. Many of the tasks and circumstances in which humans appear to be incompetent depend heavily upon verbal facility. Differences in school learning are probably particularly important here; cultural factors too may play a central role. But considerable recent evidence points to a separation of visual/spatial capacity from the verbal (Brooks, 1967; Shepard, 1975) and possibly of the visual from the spatial as well (Teuber, 1966; Kinsbourne, 1971). Although much has been made of humans as visual animals, there is reason to believe that they are highly spatial as well (Peters & Mech, 1975) and that they use their spatial processing capacity in dealing with a variety of not obviously spatial concepts and problems (Potts, 1974; cf. Kaplan, 1976).

2. People have highly developed and efficient internal models of the environment (Kaplan, 1973). An individual, in other words, carries around an elaborate cognitive structure that is, under appropriate circumstances, a tremendous asset in problem solving. Although lacking many of the designer's higher-level abstractions, people are thoroughly familiar with the basic elements of the physical environment. They have compact representations for houses and buildings, streets and sidewalks, grass and trees, and the like. This compactness leads to what is technically referred to as "object constancy," the capacity to recognize these things in many versions and guises. As with the expert, this facility rests on the achievement of economy, of simplicity, if you will, of the elements of thought.

3. People have a capacity for involvement, for putting themselves into a hypothetical situation. This "as if" stance is central to the capacity to try something out in the head before trying it out in the world. People have concepts of themselves and the ability to imagine that self in various situations (Hebb, 1960; Kaplan, 1972).

Engaging the Human Capacity

The central problem, then, is how to engage these assets in problem solving about the environment. How can the ordinary human achieve the compactness, the access, the capacity for manipulation that are such an asset to the expert in thinking about environmental design? A possible solution follows rather directly from this abbreviated overview of intellectual assets. What is required must (1) be in a visual/spatial form, (2) be composed of familiar elements, and (3) permit an "as if" stance. And to further enhance compactness, it should entail a minimum of extraneous information. One rather direct approach to this problem would be to use a highly simplified physical model of the environment in question. Alternatively, two-dimensional graphics that achieve the same effect could be comparably useful. (Models and other graphics in this context achieve what is essentially an externalization of the thought process, a bringing of what is or should be inside into full view.)

Although the direction of the solution is straightforward, the contrast with present practice is perhaps less so. After all, do not designers utilize models all the time? Are not graphics the stock in trade of the skilled designer? The answer to these questions is, as one might expect, yes and no. Indeed designers do use models, but traditionally very detailed and very beautiful ones that serve a quite different function from that proposed here. They appear late in the design process and their role is to sell the project.

The proposed role for the model in the present context is to communicate *possibilities*, to give people something to think with and about. They are presumably simple rather than detailed for several reasons: (1) They could hardly be detailed so early in the planning when not even the basic outlines are worked out; (2) they must be simple because detailed models are too expensive to use to present a variety of alternatives, as is appropriate to the beginning of problem solving; and (3) they are appropriately simple because the cognitive elements they call up are themselves highly simplified.

The traditional use of graphics, too, differs from what is proposed here. Traditional graphics are usually "elevations," that is, drawn from an eye-level perspective. While the argument that this mirrors the experience of an individual viewing the scene has some merit, it is the individual with the least experience with the setting who is most likely to experience it that way. With experience, an internal model is developed, and it becomes increasingly likely that the visual stimulus of the setting calls forth the internal model. In other words, the individual comes to see it *as it is known*, as if viewing it from above. Thus the graphics proposed here would be from an oblique perspective—to provide an overview, a compactness comparable to that of a model. Graphics would also be simplified, for similar reasons to those indicated for models. This is in contrast to the more frequently used graphics, which are far from being simple and direct but rather are elaborated, expensive, and obscure.

Sometimes this is the result of a mode of expression that is essentially symbolic—the tree in a plan view *stands for* but does not look much like a tree. Likewise certain textures employed only look like the ground plane to another designer. Another problem is the graphic summary of a design analysis—a map upon which is overlaid a variety of comments, forms, and hues. The mixture of text, arrows, symbols, and regional designations upon a base map that might not have been recognized in the first place provides a classic case of overload. Fortunately the pain involved is brief; the slide bearing this clutter of information is rarely presented for longer than 30 seconds. The point of this discussion is not to complain about the misuse of graphics; rather it is to show that the use of graphics is not in itself synonymous with the approach proposed here.

The proof of the usefulness of the spatial, familiar, simple, and compact model (or related graphics) does not, of course, lie in its difference from traditional procedures, but in hard evidence, in information gleaned from uncompromising reality. There are two sources of such information that seem most likely to be helpful. One of these is research—that is, relatively well controlled experiments. The other involves practice—the use of these guidelines in producing the material the environmental designer requires in the day-to-day process of conceptualizing and presenting alternative futures.

The Interface with Reality: Experimental Evidence[1]

Given a certain reserve (incredulity might be a more accurate term) on the part of some designers we had talked with concerning the utility of simple models, we felt a first and critical step was to determine whether or not people without training in design could make reasonable sense out of material of this kind.

One way to study the effectiveness of simple models is to see whether people's judgments based on them are different from judgments based on the highly detailed models traditionally used. Another strategy would be to show people photographs of reality after they had seen the simple models and ask them to what degree they felt they had been misled. Our study involved both strategies. Since the "comparison-with-reality" procedure required that there be a reality, we decided to select a site (1) where construction and landscaping were completed, (2) that was not known to the participants in the study, and (3) where the plans were available to guide the construction of the models. The apartment complex was decided upon as a useful scale project to consider, and, to avoid any features unique to one particular place, two such complexes were selected.

The process of developing the physical models for use in the study was rather instructive in terms of the attitude among certain designers toward simplicity in model making. The assistant hired to do the work was a graduate student in landscape architecture with a previous degree in architecture and a reputation as a superb model-builder. He had no difficulty constructing the highly detailed models but seemed considerably less comfortable with the task of devising simple ones. The result, at least to the untrained eye, was only a little less detailed than the high-detail models. He was convinced only with great difficulty that what was really desired was something *extremely* simple. (The result, out of blocks of wood, was something of a parody on simplicity. Although cruder than necessary, they were used anyway, since time pressures made it unfeasible to develop still other versions.)

---

[1]For a preliminary summary of this study, see Kaplan, Kaplan, and Deardorff, 1974. A series of papers describing the results in more detail is currently in preparation.

To control the viewing angle and to make the procedures easier to administer to large numbers of people, photographs of the models were used. Groups of seven or eight photographs, providing different views of the same model, were mounted on a single board. A given participant would look at a board, answer a set of questions about it, and go on to the next board, through a series of six boards. A given participant saw only one level of model—either simple or detailed—for both of the apartment complexes. The participant also saw a board depicting how that complex actually looks and was asked to indicate any areas in which the models had been misleading.

The first, and most important, question addressed by the study was whether people could make sense of the simple models. The results make it abundantly clear that they can. Seeing the pictures of simple models produced reactions no different from seeing detailed models. Likewise the feelings about the adequacy of presentation (as compared with photographs of "reality") were no different, except that people who saw the simple models felt (quite correctly) that they could not make judgments of the architecture given the information they had. In general, people did not feel misled by the models, with the single exception of trees. The diversity of trees is an important factor in the appearance of one of the real sites; it was not adequately communicated by the yarrow sprigs on the model.

Among the numerous other facets of this study, one that may be of particular interest involves the way the ground plane was represented in the models. Traditionally the ground plane is built up out of layers cut to correspond to contour lines. The result is a stepwise approximation to the elevation differences on the site. While designers are familiar with this artifice, it creates a horde of extraneous lines that might be a source of confusion to the untrained eye. To determine if this was the case, some participants saw the models with the traditional layered site and others saw them in a much simpler and cleaner version. This involved a flat board with the roads, walkways, and grassy areas depicted by the use of different chalk tones. It is a version of what designers call a rendered site plan. (For those concerned with the technicalities of the experimental arrangement, there were three different combinations of models and sites: detailed models/layered site, detailed models/flat site, and simple models/flat site.)

The layered site did, as expected, cause confusion in interpretation. It was clear that these layers were frequently interpreted as steps, with the results that one site was perceived as being a fun place for children since there were all those steps to play on.

The rendered site plan (two-dimensional site presentation) has an added advantage as far as the model-as-problem-solving tool is concerned. This simplification greatly enhances the flexibility of how the model can be used. Unless the site depicted is totally flat, the layered site must be cut out to accommodate the placement of buildings. This means that each different arrangement acquires a new (laboriously produced) site. Presenting alternatives is made more difficult this way and the manipulation of buildings by participants is precluded. A rendered site plan is not restrictive in this way, and a new one can be quickly developed (or an old one altered) as a phase of the ongoing participation process.

While the use of simpler forms of three-dimensional graphics is an apparently minor or even trivial development, it brings with it some interesting implications for the role of the designer. One of the ways in which participation poses a threat to the designer is that it appears to involve the abandoning of his hard-earned skills in favor of the skills appropriate to the public arena. In fact, the use of simple models early in the design process calls on two of the designer's particular strengths. It requires his considerable skill in graphic communication as well as facility in the generation of alternatives. It is rumored, in fact, that designers are very adroit at this, that they come up with all sorts of alternatives in the back room before "the one right way" is discovered and brought out for public viewing.

The role of the public would undergo a complementary change. At present the public is most often cast in one or both of the following roles: the "what do you want" role and the "isn't it beautiful" role. Recall the frustrating dialogue quoted at the beginning of the chapter. The plaintive "What have you got?" can be viewed as a request for help in envisioning possibilities. Being unable to imagine choices or alternatives, the public is unlikely to provide fruitful answers to the "what do you want" question. On the other hand, the new role for the deisgner as a provider of possibilities thus creates for the public the unfamiliar role as participant in a joint problem-solving activity.

The other traditional role for the public, the acknowledgement that it is beautiful, is of course the consequence of seeing only the final solution. If participation is permitted to begin early in the process, such a unique decision point can be replaced by a more extended and continuous problem-solving process.

Applications

The research described above was carried out by Rachel Kaplan and myself in collaboration with Howard Deardorff, a landscape architect and colleague at the University of Michigan. While appreciative of the benefits of research, Deardorff, like a true designer, is impatient and deeply practical. While this research was being carried out, an incident occurred that led to a practical implementation of these ideas at the same time.

It all began when Deardorff returned from a presentation concerning a plan for a branch campus to a group of vice-presidents of a large midwestern university. Despite the presentation of many handsome slides including photographs, maps, and graphic analyses, there had been little response from the vice-presidents. In fact, they just sat there with what might be interpreted as a rather glazed look in their eyes. When Deardorff expressed his dissatisfaction, we suggested that he might try a very simple model and save the maps and charts for when they were requested. The resulting model, a rendered site plan with the buildings made of glued-up stacks of foam board, is pictured in Figure 1. The buildings that in fact already existed on the site were glued down. The proposed buildings were attached with double-faced tape so they could be moved around readily.

This simple and inexpensive medium resulted in a completely altered atmosphere at a second presentation. There was a high level of participation, a great deal of enthusiasm, and a sense of constructive problem-solving entered into on both sides. This mechanism has since been employed in a variety of other settings with comparable success.

A related procedure involves the creation of two-dimensional graphics that provide the comparable information to looking at a simple model. A bird's-eye or oblique view is employed, and the elements involved are depicted in highly simplified form. Figure 2 illustrates this sort of presentation. Again the procedure met with considerable enthusiasm and is readily comprehended.

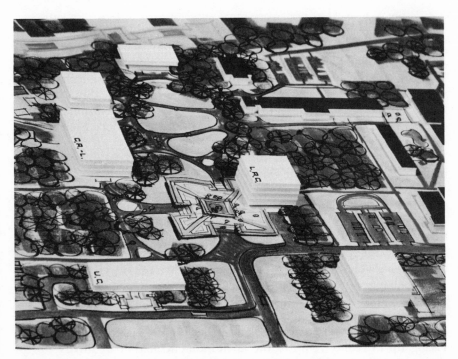

Figure 1. A simple model composed of a rendered site plan with foamboard stacks used to represent buildings (by H. L. Deardorff).

Figure 2. A simplified oblique view (from a larger drawing by H. L. Deardorff).

Thus some implications of a cognitive approach to human nature have, in the hands of a talented designer, proved exceptionally effective in involving people and in helping to provide the comprehension that is requisite for problem solving. The designer, in turn, found these developments satisfying in a number of different respects. He found his tools sharpened and made more flexible. He welcomed the increased level of interest and participation on the part of the consumers of his expertise. And, as he is the first to point out, the resulting freer participation led to a distinct improvement in the final design.

There is a potential gain for the researcher as well. Quite apart from the obvious (but reassuring) fact that theory seems to have made a difference, and apart even from the model of collaboration the work provides, there is the potential boon of a new research tool. It is now apparent that simple and inexpensive means can be effective in simulating an environment. Being able to study environments that are readily constructed and readily changed permits the kind of control dear to the experimentalist. Hopefully this development will help blur still further the distinction between laboratory and field and between basic and applied. Hopefully, too, opportunities of this kind will be able to coax the researcher out of his shell. Facing up to reality requires the abandonment neither of theory nor of rigorous method—although it admittedly might require letting go a few treasured misconceptions.

References

Brooks, L. R. The suppression of visualization by reading. *Quarterly Journal of Experimental Psychology*, 1967, *19* (Part 4), 289–299.

DeGroot, A. D. *Thought and choice in chess.* The Hague: Mouton & Co., 1965.

Hebb, D. O. The American Revolution. *American Psychologist*, 1960, *15*, 735–745.

Kaplan, R., Kaplan, S., and Deardorff, H. L. The perception and evaluation of a simulated environment. *Man–Environment Systems*, 1974, *4*, 191–192.

Kaplan, S. The challenge of environmental psychology: A proposal for a new functionalism. *American Psychologist*, 1972, *27*, 140–143.

Kaplan, S. Cognitive maps in perception and thought. In R. M. Downs and D. Stea (Eds.), *Image and environment.* Chicago: Aldine. 1973. Pp. 63–78.

Kaplan, S. Adaptation, structure and knowledge. In G. T. Moore and R. G. Golledge (Eds.), *Environmental knowing.* Stroudsburg, Pa.: Dowden, Hutchinson & Ross, 1976.

Kinsbourne, M. Cognitive deficit: Experimental analysis. In J. L. McGaugh (Ed.), *Psychobiology.* New York: Academic, 1971. Pp. 285–348.

Peters, R. P., and Mech, L. D. Behavioral and cultural adaptations to the hunting of large animals in selected mammalian predators. In R. Tuttle (Ed.), *Antecedents of man and after.* Chicago: University of Chicago Press, 1975. Pp. 279–300.

Posner, M. I. *Cognition: An introduction.* Glenview, Ill.: Scott, Foresman, 1973.

Potts, G. R. Incorporating quantitative information into a linear ordering. *Memory and Cognition*, 1974, *2*, 533–538.

Shepard, R. N. The form, formation, and transformation of internal representations. In R. C. Solso (Ed.), *Information processing in cognition* (The Loyola Symposium). Hillsdale, N.J.: Lawrence Earlbaum, 1975. Pp. 87–122.

Teuber, H. L. Alterations of perception after brain injury. In J. C. Eccles (Ed.), *Brain and conscious experience.* Cambridge: Cambridge University Press, 1966. Pp. 182–215.

Preference and Everyday Nature: Method and Application

11

RACHEL KAPLAN

In the posters, nature is grand: dramatic waterfalls, craggy mountains, magnificent canyons, lush foliage. Poster places are likely to be remote, spectacular, and extensive. It is reassuring to know that such places exist. Wilderness, in the mind at least, is a Good Place.

Fortunately there exists another realm of nature; it is more immediately accessible to a broader range of the population. It is, literally, the common, backyard variety of nature. The most common version of it, in fact, is the plot of land where people try to grow things. But "everyday nature" is also the tree to sit under and the view of the roadside just outside town. In many places, the open and flowing storm drain provides another example of the nearby and readily available natural environment.

Although these areas are "natural," as opposed to "built," most of them involved human intervention. In the vegetable garden, this is obvious. The bigger shade trees around are more likely to be viewed as "given" and the drainage creek is readily seen as carving its own course. But mostly these natural elements were put there, and each day brings new opportunities for such human assistance with the natural, immediate environment. Sometimes these opportunities go unrecognized and the urbanscape is devoid of everyday nature. Often changes are made with minimal recognition of what would make attractive scenery from the perspective of those whose "backyard" was altered.

The purpose of this chapter is not so much to document that everyday nature is of vital significance to people's well-being. This is a worthwhile (and illusive) topic that is slowly gaining empirical support (R. Kaplan, 1973; Lewis, 1974) to bolster the considerable anecdotal and literary recognition it has long enjoyed. Rather I would like to show some ways in

RACHEL KAPLAN • University of Michigan, Ann Arbor.

which the assessment of preference can provide useful input for those who effect changes in our everyday natural environment. In the context of this volume, I would like to highlight some contributions that are particularly appropriate for psychologists to make—both in terms of a people-oriented perspective and in terms of approaches for generating useful and usable data.

Two case studies will be used to illustrate these points. One of these grew out of a project involving the identification of a scenic route through a region where the scenery is rarely more spectacular than "everyday rural" (Zube, 1973b). Engineers and designers have been working on designating scenic highways for some time, using a variety of procedures. These generally involve schemes for weighting various components of the physical environment to emerge with a quantity to assign each route or route segment. The decision as to what components are important, what their relative values "should" be, what combinatorial rule to follow, and how to score each route segment are generally made by the chief-in-charge and an assistant. From the perspective of one trained in psychology, and in doing research, these procedures are lacking in several respects: (1) there is no check on whether the key ingredients in the formula have any bearing on what people experience in their environment; (2) there is no check on whether the composite value for the route or route segment is in any sense valid; and (3) there is no recognition that even a slight alteration in the metric utilized can lead to vastly different conclusions.

The second case study involved a storm drain that runs through several residential communities and can be described as anything from a delight to a blight, as it winds its 5-mile course. Drains, too, have existed without the help of psychologists. Their routing, repair, and visual quality have been the province of engineers, by and large, with possible input from landscape architects. With the drains, as with the scenic highways, the form of expertise that has been applied cannot be described as sensitive to "the people." (The principal engineer on the drain project offered as an additional item for the questionnarie, "What do you think of impoundments?"—a term intended neither in the context of confining an animal nor of retaining federal funds.) The contribution of an environmental psychologist in this context can be along the more theoretical lines of recognizing the role of the drain in the lives of the people and their community and in its potential as "everyday nature," as well as along the more empirical lines of gathering input from the people who live with it.

Unfortunately it can also happen that the expertise of the psychologist can lead to a noncontribution. His (or hers) is not the magical hand that will set all things straight. Many issues need be raised along these lines to reduce the likelihood that our colleagues or students, despite best intentions, might do more harm than good. In the final section of this chapter I will return to some of these issues, specifically ones pertaining to the research process and how this can go awry.

The Case of the Roadside

There is by now a sizable literature dealing with the identification of scenic landscapes and highways (e.g., Fabos, 1971; Zube, 1973a). Much has been written about the subjectivity of aesthetics, about the idiosyncracy of taste, about the difference between the designer's "standard" and people's opinions (e.g., Craik, 1972; Zube, 1973b). Much effort has also been devoted to the actual designation of some places as scenic and to the development of procedures that are applicable in a variety of circumstances (e.g., Burke, Lewis, and Orr, 1968; Cerny, 1974; Edwards and Kelcey, 1972). These procedures can be viewed as entailing two phases: identification of coherent components and stipulation of their relative "merit." While these activities usually are not presented as distinct, by viewing them as separable phases one can perhaps make clear the difficulties of efforts in this area (cf. R. Kaplan, 1975).

Two approaches have been used with some frequency in the identification of salient components of the (scenic) environment. One of these is based on dividing a particular scene into zones or regions, often corresponding more or less to foreground, midground, and background. The other approach, particularly expedient when one is dealing with large-scale or regional environments, relies upon categories shown on topological maps. This approach identifies as pertinent both the geological or landform and the geographic or land-use categories. The study we undertook involved an attempt to evaluate whether these approaches correspond to "salience" as perceived by the folks for whom the "scenic" designations are to be made. It also permitted evaluation of designer-generated "merit" weightings against people's judgment of preference. In addition, we considered an approach to the identification of salient components that was based on visual-content considerations, cutting across the various other classification systems.

It is characteristic of "applied" research that it falls short of the ideal. This project was not carried out as a general test of the various approaches in a variety of settings. Rather it was an offshoot of a specific project involving a scenic-highway system for the Upper Great Lakes (Polakowski, 1974). It used photographs taken in Michigan's Upper Penninsula and 61 participants approached in public places in the general region depicted in the photographs.[1]

The participants were shown a loose-leaf notebook with 20 cardboard pages. Each page consisted of four photographs, and they were asked to rate each of these 20 pages using a 5-point preference scale. They were told

[1]I want to thank my colleague Kenneth J. Polakowski of the Landscape Architecture Program at the University of Michigan for inviting us to participate in the project and for underwriting the photography. Robert Good took all the pictures and collected the data. A more complete discussion of our part of the project is in Kaplan and Kaplan (1973).

the project involved locating scenic roadways and were asked to imagine "traveling along in an area like the one represented by the four pictures on the page."

The 20 sets of pictures were constructed to permit evaluation of the role of land use, landform, zone distinctions, and visual categories in preference. Each set of four pictures was homogeneous with respect to at least one of the classifications. Thus, for example, three of the sets were classified as "varied farm/forest" in terms of land use and "flat farmland" in terms of the visual classification. Two of these fell in the "outwash plain/old lake-bed" landform designation, while the third was of "ground moraine." To permit adequate sampling of these various categories, the pictures were selected so as to exclude such elements as water and industrial, commercial, or clearly residential settings.

Two distinct questions can be asked with respect to the preference data. One of these involves the actual preference values for different subsets of pictures, corresponding to the various classification categories. The other, and prior question, involves the issue of how meaningful or coherent each category is in terms of the experience of such an environment. Quite apart from whether people like moraines, let us say, there is the problem of whether different instances of moraines are experienced in any similar fashion. If one could determine what the meaningful or coherent groupings of the visual environment are, at least within the context of a specific region, it would make the task of designating particular routes a more enlightened process.

With the aid of the computer there now exists a variety of procedures for determining such groupings. These approaches utilize relationships among the obtained ratings to discover patterns in the responses. Over the course of many years, we have found two such procedures (nonmetric factor analysis and a hierarchical cluster analysis) to be particularly useful both in terms of the "sense" they make of the data and because the combination of the two, based on different mathematical assumptions, underlines the importance of viewing any such grouping as but one realization of a "truth" (R. Kaplan, 1974, 1975).

Using these procedures, three major groupings were found:

Flat, open farmland: These six sets of pictures can be characterized visually as predominantly farmland with woods in the distance and considerable sky above the vast open area. In terms of land use, a majority fell in the "varied farm/forest" category, but "continuous forest" and "farmland" were also included. In terms of landform, all four categories were represented by the pictures.

Open forest and dense forest: The forested scenes, using one of the dimensional procedures, formed one large grouping. Analyzed in terms of the other procedure, they divided into two groupings, one depicting more open and inviting woods and the other showing denser, less penetrable forest. Each of these groupings includes a complete scramble of landform and land-use distinctions. In terms of zonal categories, they do not correspond to whether the forest is in the midground or the foreground. (It is interesting in this context that the ratings show that the participants in the study made the inference that such scenes are equivalent, differing only in the relative distance of particular aspects of the scene. As you keep driving, after all, the midground of a moment ago becomes foreground.)

The coherence of each classification category can be measured by an index of internal consistency (coefficient alpha) that assumes values between 0 and 1.00. Coherence, as defined by this index, does not mean that everyone likes (or dislikes) all the items in a given category or scale. Rather it requires that each individual react in a relatively similar fashion to the items in a given category. The three empirically derived groupings were found to be relatively high in coherence (between .76 and .84). Of the visual categories, four were equally respectable (between .70 and .79), while one was totally irrelevant to the pattern of preference ratings. The land-use and landform categories were found to be of poor to mediocre coherence (alpha between .23 and .63).

There remains the question of whether the designer's notion of the scenic value of the various categories corresponds to people's indication of how much they like the scenes. To the extent that such weighting schemes would lead one to expect a forest category to be preferred to a flat farmland, the results would agree. In terms of more specific land-use patterns, such as the relative preference of "varied farm/forest" and "continuous forest," the results are opposite some of the expectations (cf. Polakowski, 1974). And the expected preference for "bedrock" to "moraine" did not find empirical support.

Conclusions and Implications

The dimensions, based on the participants' preference ratings, provide insight both to a better understanding of the critical variables that distinguish different landscapes and to an improved capacity to predict preference. The flat-farmland category is quite obvious and clearly least preferred. Among the woodland scenes, an important distinction seems to be based on the opaqueness of the setting, with the more open, more spacious forest (Figure 1, lower right) highly preferred to the denser, less penetrable woods (Figure 1, lower left).

The importance of spaciousness showed up in some other scenes as well. A few scenes showing open fields beyond a roadside screen of trees were highly preferred (Figure 1, upper right). Interestingly these scenes differ from the unappreciated flat farmland because of the presence of a few nearby trees, suggesting that a relatively modest manipulation of the environment can have a substantial payoff in scenic quality. The most-preferred set of photographs in the study (mean preference of 4.55 on a 5-point scale) consisted of the four scenes (one of these is shown in Figure

Figure 1. These four photographs from Michigan's Upper Penninsula were included in the scenic roadside study. While participants saw the scenes in sets of four, it should be noted that the four scenes shown here were on four different "pages." If nothing else, the photographs show that the roadside can be scenic without being in any way spectacular!

1, upper left) of relatively open, transparent woodland. (See S. Kaplan, 1975, for a fuller discussion of the role of spaciousness in preference.)

From some points of view it would be comfortable and convenient if the categories already printed on the map were sufficient for the awesome task of designating scenic quality. From other perspectives it is encouraging to find that preference is more accurately predicted by more psychological dimensions, by visual aspects of the environment that people in fact experience. The dimensional approach is a method of discovery; it allows the factors that are particularly salient to scenic value in a particular region to emerge. This has practical benefit both in providing explicit guidelines to experts as to what to look for and in suggesting aspects of the landscape that could be manipulated to enhance scenic potential. (Cf. Forest Service, 1974, for a discussion along these lines.)

The Case of the Drain

Rivers, streams, and lakes of virtually any size are highly appreciated landscape features. Yet the literature on the scenic aspects of storm drains is virtually nonexistent. Many an urban dweller thinks of drains either as part of the underground invisible city or as ditches, or possibly as related to the whole matter of sewers. If the basement is dry and there are no floods to reckon with, storm drains are hardly salient in the perceived environment.

My own ignorance about drains was rapidly corrected when I was asked to do a study of the perception of a particular drain on the part of the residents who live along it. If it were not for the topo map, we would never have been able to follow this 5-mile long creek as it winds its way through residential neighborhoods representing the full range of socioeconomic differences. In many places it was clearly an "amenity," an unspectacular but very welcome touch of nature; in other places it would not have taken much professional training to surmise that the residents had gripes.

It was clearly a foresightful county-drain commissioner who had been willing to inquire about the people's views of the drain. Traditionally drain problems have engineering solutions! In this case, a landscape architect/planner consultant[2] had been hired to analyze possible modifications and improvements. But it seemed that the information that would be even more helpful to this design process than the perception of the drain would be the residents' perceptions of possible alterations to their "backyard" environment. It furthermore appeared to us that these were questions that required visual format; the questionnaire would have to include pictures of various portions of the existing drain and of similar waterways.

The questionnaire was distributed to each household bordering the drain. In the cases of apartment complexes, however, a sampling procedure was used that included about one-third of the units nearest the drain. The questionnaire included a cover letter on the drain commissioner's letterhead and a postage-paid return envelope addressed to him. The letter stated that "We are beginning to consider some alternatives for parts of this drain" and that "We are particularly interested in your feelings about the ways things are now, but the pictures and your reactions to them will also help us consider alternatives for the future."

The return rate was 50%, based on a single distribution. This value varied from about 28% for the areas with relatively transient populations to 81% for the highest-income areas, with the 50% rate characteristic for most of the regions. While the sample size varied for different portions of the questionnaire, a total of 115 citizens are included in the discussion here. The tone of the returned questionnaires was very positive; people commented on finding the task interesting and appreciated the opportunity to provide their reactions.

After some six pages of questions, the questionnaire concluded with four picture pages. Each of these had eight scenes and asked for two ratings: "How similar your view of the waterway is to what is in the picture"

[2]Again thanks to Kenneth J. Polakowski for contacting us for this project, as well as for some of the pictures of "other drains." S. Kaplan was responsible for the photography of all the local places. Janet Frey was a most helpful research assistant.

and "How much you would like the waterway near your home to look like what is pictured."

The same two statistical procedures mentioned in the context of the scenic-highway study were used here to determine meaningful groupings of the drain pictures. Using the preference ratings (5-point scale) for the 32 scenes, we established four major picture groupings. Once again, the content of these clusters is a thought-provoking step in figuring out how people experience the environment.

Covered drain: All the photographs that showed no water formed one grouping; however, three of these, depicting parklike settings with trees (e.g., Figure 2, top left), were considered a separate subgrouping.

Impoundment: These scenes showed larger bodies of water that seemed contained, or pondlike. Two such scenes are presented at the bottom of Figure 2.

Creek in parklike setting: The creek seen in these pictures is in residential areas, but the houses are not as noticeable as is the setting (upper right, Figure 2).

Backyard creek: Here the residential context is much clearer. The name adopted for this grouping suggests both the creek's locus with respect to houses and also the less than idyllic views of the waterway (see Figure 3).

Figure 2. Four alternative views of a storm drain are shown here. All but the lower right picture were taken along the waterway under study here. In the top left instance, the drain is actually piped underground; the bottom two pictures have the water retained, while the upper right scene shows an open, flowing drain.

Figure 3. Three of these scenes (excluding the lower left) were taken along the same waterway as were the Figure 2 photographs. But the open, flowing quality of the drain in these instances leaves something to be desired.

Unlike the "parklike" creek that "belongs," the "backyard" creek is separated from residential property both by fences and by withholding of the care applied to the adjacent lawns.

Verbal and Visual Parallels

The picture-preference groupings provide data on alternative drain treatments, present or potential. The questionnaire also included items dealing with alternatives presented verbally. For example, the verbal analogue to the "covered-drain" pictures was a set of three items regarding piping the water underground, and the verbal version of "impoundment" consisted of two items dealing with a "larger pool of water" (either "planted with some fish" or "left natural, marshy"). People's responses to the verbal and visual renditions led to some rather striking differences.

Residents in one of the regions were generally quite fond of the set of "impoundment" pictures, and their reaction to the verbal items was glowing. For the residents living nearest such an arrangement, however, the pictures were much to their liking, but the bald statement of such an alternative was far less desirable. The latter combination, a high preference for the pictured version and relatively negative response to the verbal, was even more outstanding in the case of the "covered-drain" grouping. One segment of the drain is in fact underground and the residents along this region are extremely fond of the *visual* appearance of their "invisible" drain (top left in Figure 2). On the other hand, for the area with the most problem with respect to the drain, the thought of "piping it underground" is far more attractive than are the visual alternatives provided.

These differences between responses to verbal and visual formats of the same idea are not simply a reflection of the visual pattern nearest to home. While it is the case that only the residents of the "covered-drain" area were particularly fond of that set of pictures, perceived similarity in other contexts did not relate to increased preference. Rather these findings suggest how easily one can be misled by having only one set of responses, either verbal or visual. Each approach can provide only partial insight into the domain being sampled. When the drain is perceived as a mess, having it "go away" is attractive without much imagery for what would be there instead. On the other hand, appreciation of particular pondlike arrangements need not conjure up the "health hazards" a few people mentioned in reaction to the verbal description of a body of water "left natural, marshy."

Preference, Regional and "Universal"

Another important outcome of the study was the realization that the various regions could be characterized by distinctly different preferences and problems. Accordingly the set of solutions proposed by the planner/ designer are strikingly different for the different segments of the drain. While these solutions are in part a function of physical constraints, the questionnaire data played an important part in the process.

Despite the diversity of reactions, a few generalizations can be made with respect to the picture preferences. The "backyard-creek" grouping was consistently among the least preferred alternatives. The "creek in parklike setting" was consistently among the most preferred. In answer to the engineer's question, as it were, "impoundments" (given the pictured version) was relatively favored.

By looking at these general preferences, as well as the pattern for individual pictures, one can appreciate some principles underlying preference for everyday nature. Once again, as was the case with the scenic routes, a sense of spaciousness enhances preference. This is particularly the case in comparisons of the "backyard creek" with the "creek in parklike setting." The former seems to limit or block the passage; the latter tends to show a well-defined, extended space. Indeed, to the degree they promise more as one goes deeper, while at the same time blocking a direct view, they contain a degree of mystery, another factor that is often effective in enhancing preference (R. Kaplan, 1975).

Perhaps the most apparent determinant of preference here is related to a sense of orderliness. The four scenes in Figure 3 are among the consistently and strongly disliked. In all these, the water is not well defined, there is an unkempt look, and there is little sense of order. By contrast, in the most highly prized scenes the lawns are mowed, the edges are clean-cut, and things seem in place. The scene in the lower right in Figure 2 is a case in point, and the fine textures of the top two pictures also exemplify this preference.[3]

Familiarity: Another Factor in Preference

An implicit theme running through this discussion has been the prediction of preference. While the particular studies described have concrete impact in themselves, their usefulness is extended by being related to a larger framework. The particular framework that has guided our work in the general area of environmental preference is informational in orientation. It emphasizes both those environmental elements that facilitate comprehension (or making sense) of the environment and those that provide the opportunity to acquire additional information (S. Kaplan, 1975). The promise of additional information has surfaced several times in these studies, though not as strikingly as in several previous studies. Both mystery and spaciousness are pertinent to this domain. By contrast, the "making-sense" components have been strong, particularly in the drain study, where "order" and "coherence" played a powerful role.

Another predictor of preference that figured importantly in these data is familiarity. Unlike the other predictors identified so far, familiarity sometimes appears to aid the "making-sense" domain while at other times it appears to detract from the "information-promised" domain. Thus it may appear on opposite sides of the ledger. This ambivalence appeared quite clearly in a study of the urban scene (Herzog, Kaplan, and Kaplan, 1976); it shows a similarly fickle character in the studies discussed here.

The sample responding to the roadside study included both "locals" (people residing year round in the region of the pictures) and people who indicated they were spending roughly 5 to 7 days in that area, presumably on a vacation trip. For the sets of pictures as a whole, the locals showed a significantly lower appreciation. Novelty might have served to enhance the visitors' appreciation of the scenes. One might also expect that those who have chosen this area to visit during the summer might view it more favorably because of this context. It was, after all, a long way to come. But the effect of familiarity was not simply to depress the sense of what is scenic.

[3]There is an exception to this finding that would be interesting to study further. The residents of the portion of the drain where it most resembles a stream in the woods, with underbrush and overgrown (not orderly) branches, are also in the highest socioeconomic group. Their preference is strongly in the direction of the most "natural" scenes (e.g., lower left in Figure 2) and their disdain for the large mowed expanses was near-unanimous! If nothing else, such a finding supports the importance of determining the likes and dislikes of the people for whom we plan rather than assuming that a universal solution can work.

For those most familiar with that environment, the preference for the more spacious, more open forest—as compared to the denser, woodland scenes—was strikingly greater, suggesting that the effect of spaciousness on preference does not decline with experience. This result might suggest that the effort to identify the particularly scenic settings in the context of the prevalent scenery is less appropriate for the newcomer, whose criterion may be less rigorous. It is the one who knows the local scene (for whom the scenic designation is not usually offered) who seems to make the subtler differentiation within the everyday natural environment.

In the case of the drain study the role of familiarity seems even more complicated. As has been mentioned before, the residents with the parklike view of the covered drain had a strikingly greater appreciation for pictures of such settings than anyone else. By contrast, in the case of the "backyard creek" (the least desirable of the drain-as-neighbor pictures), there is a hint that those who have the most firsthand experience with such settings have least appreciation for their view, although no one else liked them much either.

The message to the designer here is intricate, at best. Since everyday nature involves the familiar, changes in everyday nature necessarily involve changes in the environment one knows well. When this is a preferred environment, proposals for change are easily threatening. But when it is low on redeeming qualities, familiarity might be an important component in the acceptance of almost any proposed modification.

Some Research Dos

Both case studies I have discussed have generated "useful" data. In a variety of ways, they have shed light on people's preference for the natural environment, on an area of life that is the source of daily gripes and satisfactions. In some cases, the results have pointed to needed changes where the lack of citizens' well-being had not been apparent; in other cases, the results focus on aspects of the natural environment that should not be altered but preserved and maintained. There are also situations in which people's enjoyment of their everyday encounters with nature could be enhanced through modifications suggested by these findings.

The dimensions of landscape preference that have emerged from these and previous studies are not new to landscape designers. In fact, they have had long lists of pertinent factors, including qualities such as spaciousness, unity, diversity, contrast, color, size, and on and on. The research does make it possible, however, both to select some of the most effective among these and to understand their psychological significance. While there is no question that the environmental psychologist has a contribution to make, there is equally little doubt that his efforts will be enhanced by interaction with the people who are in a position to put the results to use.

To make this contribution maximally effective, there are three major areas relating to the researcher's role that I would like to discuss briefly. While they apply to many areas of research, they are particularly important in the context of applied environmental problems. The first two are people-related; they concern the audience for the results and those who are the source of the data. In both cases the issues may be clarified if they are viewed in the context of participation. The third area concerns the measurement of the environment in a way that permits a proper balance between caution and confidence.

Data as a Form of Participation

Citizen participation usually connotes public hearings and other group meetings. To some it suggests an occasion for "the people" to challenge "the experts." Some see it as a one-sided situation in which the few who are articulate dominate. Still, despite their problems, such meetings are preferable to letting the expert—designer, planner, engineer, or whomever—make the decisions without people-input. I would like to suggest that there is an important sense in which the data collected in the studies presented here provide another approach to citizen participation. In a very real sense, the data served as a "voice" for "the people"; they permitted the respondents to be participants in the decision process. The perspective of "data as a form of participation" has important implications for the research process.

For example, it might be argued that a 50% return rate is too low to permit "valid" interpretation of the data. Or that having only a dozen "cases" representing a particular region is as good as useless. Viewed from the perspective of participation, however, these values represent many more people than would otherwise have any input. The two regions with the lowest return rate would have been unlikely to have anyone representing them at a public meeting. The response rate was highest where the folks who are articulate and organized live. They are really not the ones who have trouble being heard. Indeed they are the very ones who are often accused of dominating public meetings. If "participation" is to better reflect a cross-section of the population, there is room to explore other ways to gain access to the less vocal but equally concerned people.

If one takes this perspective seriously, *the researcher's responsibility as communicator of the input becomes even more vital. Not only must he represent even-handedly the data the participants have entrusted in him, but he must do it in such a way that the recipient of the information can process it and act upon it.*

Researchers are often remiss in failing to empathize with the potential consumer of their efforts. The client or user of the research is a human being who is not nearly as interested in the intricacies of the research as is the one who conducted the study. More than likely, the client lacks the training to understand much of what the well-intentioned scientist considers essential. What he does care about, however, is often very difficult to extract from the endless tables, statistics, and technical prose. These concerns include simple questions like "What are the major findings—simply stated?" and "How do I implement these findings?" If the study was worth doing, it is worth the additional thought and effort required to present the material in a coherent, overseeable fashion.

Perhaps the most important implication of viewing empirical efforts as viable sources of input is in the area of what one asks of the person-as-participant. If the respondent is helped to realize the opportunity to have his opinion and perspective heard, he is necessarily treated as a party to the proceedings. If the researcher is concerned to represent the participant accurately, he must be concerned to create a meaningful, interesting, and understandable tool to obtain the information.

Here again it is important to empathize with the human being one is seeking information from. This is an organism with only finite patience, with a propensity to distrust, and a seemingly low threshold for hostility—when treated as a nonperson. Of course the more one views the "subject" as person, the harder it becomes to deceive him, to raise false hopes, or to ask questions that invade his privacy or are unduly frustrating.

A Conceptual Grasp of the Environment

The idea of viewing data as a form of citizen participation provides no shortcuts to the most demanding aspect of the research process. This has to do with achieving a formulation of the particular portion of the environment that is the focus of the study. A clear formulation, in turn, makes the tasks of presenting the results and of gathering the data relatively straightforward. In other words, the initial efforts are devoted not to the technicalities of choosing a sample, nor to getting help putting together a questionnaire, but to figuring out what the major issues are and how one will be able to draw reasonable conclusions about that portion of the environment.

The more one struggles to gain such clarity, the more one realizes how difficult it can be. The portion of the environment under examination inevitably turns out to be a *construct,* a multifaceted entity with unclear boundaries. There is, for example, no operational definition for "everyday nature" that would capture its depth, the diversity of underlying qualities it relates to. All one can hope to accomplish in representing such constructs is that one sample from the range and diversity of the construct's weblike relationships (Cronbach and Meehl, 1955).

The sampling of the environment, then, becomes central to the research process. This forces the researcher to approach the task in a variety of ways, using a variety of measures that complement each other. In this way a "tension" can be created among the measures that permits the "discovery" of interrelations. While it is in some respects safer to avoid the possibility of learning that one's construct is not quite what one thought, from a scientific point of view, a built-in check has certain advantages.

The idea of multiple measures can be realized in a variety of ways. The use of sets of photographs in both the drain and the scenic-route studies is no accident. Many of the questions that are important in the design and planning of the physical environment involve issues that are not experienced in words. By asking verbal questions, one often forces the respondent to provide stereotyped answers, words that are used as a "shorthand" for phenomena that are experienced in visual and spatial ways. Thus the use of both verbal and visual measures provides a check on the interpretations to be made. But the use of a variety of pictures is in itself an important aspect of sampling. It also has the added advantage of making the task potentially more enjoyable. Adequate sampling along these lines is itself a major challenge, often requiring carefully developed criteria, assistance from judges, and a large collection of varied material to select from (cf. R. Kaplan, 1972).

One of the consequences of multiple measures and of using a number of pictures or "items" to measure a construct is that one all too readily ends up with an unmanageable quantity of data. This is where one falls prey to lengthy reports, and even to color coding the sections of the undigested document that is delivered to the potential user of the data. But the whole point of collecting the diversity of material was to get a better handle on those underlying constructs. Thus the data must be "reduced" to determine the coherence of the formulations that absorbed so much of the researcher's initial time. That, of course, is the point of the dimensional analyses described in the contexts of the studies.

The two studies described here are illustrative of a number of the attractions of applied environmental research. They both contribute to knowledge as well as having a bearing on specific practical problems. They both allow the bringing together of a concern for humans and an interest in the physical world. They both utilize photography to take stimuli that are quite obviously "in the field" and place them in a context where there is control more closely approximating that of the laboratory. Both studies employ a methodology that encourages an expansiveness as far as sampling the respective environments is concerned. At the same time, there is an emphasis on achieving the simplicity and coherence so essential if mere humans, limited as they are in capacity, in time, and in patience, are to be able to understand and learn from the results.

References

Burke, H. D., Lewis, G. H., and Orr, H. R. A method for classifying scenes from a roadway. *Park Practice Guideline*, 1968 (March), 125–141.

Cerny, J. W. Scenic analysis and assessment. *CRC (Chemical Rubber Company) Critical Reviews in Environmental Control*, 1974, *4*(2), 221–250.

Craik, K. H. Psychological factors in landscape appraisal. *Environment and Behavior*, 1972, *4*, 255–266.

250   Rachel Kaplan

Cronbach, L. J., and Meehl, P. E. Construct validity in psychological tests. *Psychological Bulletin*, 1955, *52*, 281–302.

Edwards and Kelcey, Inc. Highway Planning Studies (vol. 4: General findings and applications). Minneapolis, 1972.

Fabos, J. G. An analysis of environmental quality ranking systems. In *Recreation Symposium Proceedings*. Upper Darby, Pa.: Northeastern Forest Experiment Station, Forest Service. 1971. Pp. 40–55.

Forest Service, Agricultural Handbook Number 462. *National Forest Landscape Management* (vol. 2, chap. 1: The visual management system). 1974.

Herzog, T. R., Kaplan, S., and Kaplan, R. The prediction of preference for familiar urban places. *Environment and Behavior*, in press.

Kaplan, R. The dimensions of the visual environment: Methodological considerations. In W. J. Mitchell (Ed.), *Environmental design: Research and practice*. Proceedings of the Environmental Design Research Association Conference 3, 1972.

Kaplan, R. Some psychological benefits of gardening. *Environment and Behavior*, 1973, *5*, 145–162.

Kaplan, R. A strategy for dimensional analyses. In D. H. Carson (Ed.), *Man–environment interactions: Evaluations and applications* (part 9). Proceedings of the Environmental Design Research Association Conference 5, 1974. Pp. 66–68.

Kaplan, R. Some methods and strategies in the prediction of preference. In E. H. Zube, R. O. Brush, and J. G. Fabos (Eds.), *Landscape assessment*. Stroudsburg, Pa.: Dowden, Hutchinson & Ross. 1975. Pp. 118–129.

Kaplan, R., and Kaplan, S. Alternative strategies in the study of roadside preference. Unpublished paper, 1973.

Kaplan, S. An informal model for the prediction of preference. In E. H. Zube, R. O. Brush, and J. G. Fabos (Eds.), *Landscape assessment*. Stroudsburg, Pa.: Dowden, Hutchinson & Ross. 1975. Pp. 92–101.

Lewis, C. A. People–plant interaction: A man–environment relationship. Paper presented at Environmental Design Research Association Conference 5, Milwaukee, Wis., 1974.

Polakowski, K. J. Upper Great Lakes Regional Recreation Planning Study, Part 5: Scenic Highway System. Upper Great Lakes Regional Commission. 1974.

Zube, E. H. Scenery as a natural resource. *Landscape Architecture*, 1973, *63*, 127–132. (a)

Zube, E. H. Rating everyday rural landscapes of the Northeastern U.S. *Landscape Architecture*, 1973, *63*, 371–375. (b)

Who Needs What When: Design of Pluralistic Learning Environments

12

MARTIN L. KROVETZ

Throughout the centuries theologians have argued about the one true religion, politicians have argued about the ideal form of government, and educators have argued about the best method of teaching. It is time that we acknowledged that, at least in the last situation, there is no "one best." It seems to this author, as a social psychologist and a high school administrator, that it is just as ridiculous to assume that all students learn best in the same way as to assume that all people will behave in the same manner given a certain set of controlled circumstances. Social psychologists have turned to probability and statistics and hypothesize that more people will behave thusly in one environment than in another environment. In education this is not good enough. We should not say that since a majority of students appear to function adequately in the traditional school environment, we will assume that it is best for everyone. I personally would question the use of the word *majority* in this context, but that is not the point. The point is that schools must begin to offer a plurality of learning environments, allowing teachers and students to function in environments conducive to their personal teaching and learning styles. At the same time, research should be aimed at determining what variables create effective learning environments.

In this chapter, I present psychological theory and research along with architecturally oriented research in order to formulate a model for designing educational settings congruent with students' diverse needs. It is impor-

MARTIN L. KROVETZ ● Carmel High School, Carmel, California. The author served as an assistant professor of psychology at Claremont Men's College, Claremont, California from 1971 to 1974.

tant to note that much of the research to be presented here is preliminary and that therefore many of the conclusions are tentative. The purpose of this chapter, therefore, is to identify potential intervention and evaluation "leverage points" in the educational system. One cannot wait for further data to design better learning environments. It is through the design and study of new environments that worthwhile research and evaluation will occur.

Internal–External Locus of Control

Research related to a personality dimension labelled *locus of control* offers considerable evidence that diverse student needs exist. The concept was defined by Julian Rotter (1966):

> When a reinforcement is perceived by the subject as following some action of his own, but not being entirely contingent upon his action, then, in our culture, it is typically perceived as a result of luck, chance, fate, as under the control of powerful others, or as unpredictable because of the great complexity of the forces surrounding him. When the event is interpreted in this way by an individual we have labeled this a belief in external control. If the person perceives that the event is contingent upon his own behavior or his own relatively permanent characteristics, we have termed this a belief in internal control. (p. 1)

Research has indicated that internal people, people characterized by their internal control, are more active and striving individuals who show resistence to influence and handle success and failure more realistically than externals people (Phares, 1973). Also internals seem to be better adjusted; less angry, hostile, or depressed; and less likely to turn to drinking behavior. Externals seem to be more lacking in interpersonal trust, more suspicious, and lower in self-esteem. Some evidence points to greater suicide proneness in externals, and several studies have pointed out that psychotics and other pathological groups manifest higher external scores than do more normal groups (Phares, 1973).

Before I present some of the research and its relatedness to education, a presentation of social-learning theory (Rotter, 1954) seems important. This theory holds that behavior is determined by both the value of the desired goal and the expectancy that one's behavior will lead to the attainment of that goal. Thus a student will work hard in school in order to learn or in order to earn a good grade only if the student expects that his or her work will lead to learning or to the grade.

Expectancy is determined by expectancies based on past similar situations, expectancies based on previous experience in the specific situation, and the amount of experience in the situation in question. Therefore one's expectation that one's behavior will lead to a reward is dependent on past experience *plus* a general belief in one's ability to control the occurrence of the reward. This latter belief is internal—external locus of control. We should think of this not as an absolute but as a continuum. We should also think of locus of control not as a trait applicable to only one area of one's life but as a general outlook relevant to many areas.

It is important to hypothesize immediately that when an individual believes that he does not control his outcomes, he will not find it useful to generalize from the past and cannot use experiences to generalize to the future. Such a person should learn less than a person who feels that he can control outcomes. Davis and Phares (1967) found, in fact, that in a situation in which the skill–chance component of the task was ambiguous, internals engaged in significantly more information-seeking behavior than externals did.

A more general hypothesis is that internals will be more active in their attempts to control, manipulate, and deal with their environment. Research supports this hypothesis. In a tuberculosis hospital, internals acquired more information about their condition (Seeman and Evans, 1962). In a reformatory, internal inmates knew more about the institution than external inmates did (Seeman, 1963). Black activists have been found to be more internal than the general black population (Gore and Rotter, 1963; Strickland, 1965). Internal college students are more persuasive in changing attitudes of other students regarding campus issues (Phares, 1965). Nonsmokers seem to be more internal than smokers (Straits and Sechrest, 1963).

A third hypothesis is that internals are less susceptible to social influence. Research supports this hypothesis (Gore, 1962; Doctor, 1971). Pines and Julian (1972) found that internals were influenced primarily by informational requirements of a task, while externals were affected by the experimenter's evaluation.

Based on the research reported above one might expect internal people to have a higher need for achievement than externals. This need not be the case. Internals may have a low expectation of success. Also the task might be so highly structured that generalized expectation might not play a role. Yet there are important results in this area. The Coleman Report (Coleman, Campbell, Hobson, McPartland, Mood, Weinfeld, and York, 1966) shows that a belief in personal control of academic rewards was a strong predictor of academic achievement. Other studies indicate that internal schoolchildren as opposed to externals achieve higher grades, do better on achievement tests, and in general display achievement behavior (Crandall, Katkovsky, and Crandall, 1965). Results are usually stronger for males than for females. Research also indicates that internals are better able to delay gratification and show more preference for skill-related tasks than do externals; results in these last two areas are more complex, however, than in some of the other examples. Related to this is Karabanek's research (1972), which showed that internals were more satisfied following a success on a difficult task than were externals. Internals were also more disappointed than externals following failure on an easy task. Results were reversed for success on an easy task and failure on a difficult task. This is, of course, consistent with the image of internals and externals.

Generalizing from all of the results reported above, it seems reasonable to assume that if one is to pursue success one must to some degree attribute responsibility for outcomes to internal factors. It is at this point that the research is most relevent to education. Do internals in actuality attribute success and failure to their own ability, and do externals attribute their success and failures to good and bad luck? If this is true, different teaching strategies may be needed for internal and external students. This author's dissertation (Krovetz, 1974) dealt with this issue. Subjects were college students who scored in the top and bottom one-third on the Rotter I–E (internal–external) scale. They were given a task that asked them to decide which of three African words meant the same as an English word; in fact none of the African words had the same meaning as the English word. The task consisted of 70 pairings. After each pairing, subjects were told if their response was "correct." In actuality, one of five reinforcement conditions was used. All subjects were told that 3 of their first 10 answers were correct, which is consistent with chance. By the seventh block of 10 trials, subjects were told that they were correct on either 1 (10%), 3 (30%), 5 (50%) 7 (70%), or 9 (90%) of the pairings. Attribution of success or failure was determined from answers on a questionnaire. Internal subjects attributed their failures in the 10% and 30% conditions to their own lack of skill in a task that required skill for mastery. Externals attributed their failures to lack of effort and to bad luck. Internals explained their success in the 70% condition to be due to their skill in a difficult task. Externals indicated that they had had good luck on a task requiring little skill for mastery. These results are consistent with the hypotheses of the study.

The results for the 90% condition were different. Internals explained their success as a result of not having much skill in a task that didn't involve much skill for mastery. Externals indicated that they had a lot of skill on a task requiring a lot of skill for mastery; they rated their skill level and the amount of skill necessary for mastery higher than subjects did in any other condition; they also rated their success higher than subjects in any other condition did. It seems that the internals could not accept responsibility for their success in the 90% condition; they had not gathered enough information to accept such a high level of success. Externals, on the other hand, could not use chance to explain such an overwhelming success; here was a case in which they had an *obvious skill*. One last point on this. Instructions for the experiment were pretested on another sample from the same population of students. After reading the instructions, internals expected the task to involve significantly more skill than did externals. This is important; internals and externals began the experimental task with very different expectations.

The following summarizes the results of research on internal–external locus of control reported to this point:

1. Internals seek more information than externals when approaching a task with an ambiguous skill–chance component, and, in fact, they expect the task to require more skill for mastery.
2. Internals are more active than externals in attempts to control their environment.
3. Internals are less suseptible to social influence.
4. Internals in general show more achievement behavior than externals.
5. Internals explain failure on an ambiguous skill–chance task as due to lack of skill; externals report bad luck and little effort.
6. Internals explain success on an ambiguous skill–chance task as due to skill if they feel that they have mastery over the task; externals report good luck.
7. If they do not feel that they have mastered the task, internals explain high success on an ambiguous skill–chance task as due to the task's not requiring much skill for mastery; externals report high personal skill following very high success.

On the basis of these findings, the image of the internal person seems to be the type that education might like to foster. What evidence exists that locus of control can be altered? Research indicates that for school-aged children, internality increases with age (Crandall, Katkovsky, and Crandall, 1965). Results also indicate that externality increases with anxiety (Kiehlbauch, 1967). Average scores for students increased in internality from third grade through tenth grade but decreased for twelfth graders. A curvilinear relationship exists between I–E and inmates in a male reformatory; newcomers and prisoners about to be released are more external than inmates at the midpoint of their stay. It seems likely that a twelfth grader or an inmate about to be paroled faces much uncertainty in his future and thus much anxiety. Research also indicates that patients showing improvement in psychotherapy show greater increases in internality than an untreated group of patients (Gillis and Jessor, 1970). From this, one might conclude that creating an environment that is free of high anxiety, a situation very hard to define, and placing externals in psychotherapy might lead to an increase in internality. Neither of these ides are of real help to the educator, although the author feels that group counseling can be of great value.

Perhaps studying the antecedents of I–E might be helpful. Most relevent research indicates that persons in the lower socioeconomic class are more external than other groups. For the educator, these findings do not offer hope for change. Katkovsky, Crandall, and Good (1967) found that parental behavior that is protective, nurturing, approving, and nonrejecting is associated with a child's belief in internal control. Chance (1965) found a similar relationship between the mother's score on an acceptance–rejection measure and the child's locus of control. These last findings would indicate that students may become more internal if the learning environment is protective, nurturing, approving, and nonrejecting. It would be interesting to study the effects of good open classrooms on external students. This author defines a "good open classroom" to be a learning environment in which the student is *expected* to choose many of his or her own goals, objectives, and learning activities. At the same time, the teacher is an active participant, guiding the student and designing an environment that is very much in touch with both the affective and the cognitive needs of its inhabitants.

At the same time, placing a student in an evnironment that is not consistent with his or her cognitive style may be harmful. Ramirez (1973) feels that this is a major cause for the failure of Mexican-American students in school. His investigations have dealt with field independence–field dependence, but the issue is no less relevent.

Several comments regarding student–teacher matchings should be made. Ramirez's work on field independence–field dependence has led one school at which he is a consultant in Cucamonga, California to pair field-independent teachers with field-independent students and field-dependent teachers with field-dependent students; preliminary results are favorable. Witkens (1972) reported a number of studies in this area, and the results support this concept. Davis and Phares (1969) found that parents whose children have an I–E orientation similar to their own are less disciplinarian and more indulgent in their approach to the child than parents whose children's orientations are discrepant. If a similar pattern of results is true for student–teacher relations, then the development of internal–external screening programs for purposes of matching students and teachers may be worth considering.

It is probably most useful to utilize the research dealing with locus of control to develop appropriate learning strategies for internal and external students. Internal students should thrive in an information-seeking environment. Since this is true both for highly structured and for ambiguous tasks, it would seem advisable to place internals in situations in which they have the control as opposed to the teacher, situations in which the student is responsible for searching actively for information on difficult skill-related tasks, including setting many of his or her own goals and objectives. Internals also need to know that they have mastered the subject matter based on their own information; outside feedback on success will not convince an internal student that he has been successful. Immediate teacher-evaluation is therefore not crucial for internals. This strategy implies that teacher-centered classrooms and self-paced, contingency-based learning may not be the best strategy for internal students. A note of caution: most research is based on the one-third of students who are most internal and is based also on group averages; not all internal students will fit into the strategy being developed.

For external students, the optimal learning environment seems to be different. In the first place, highly structured tasks should overcome the influence of generalized external expectation. In the second place, based on my dissertation and other research on social influence, externals seem to need overwhelming success with immediate and large positive reinforcement from others. It would appear that self-paced, competency-based learning matches both criteria. When tasks are chosen for and by external students, the teacher should make sure that the probability of success is high and that immediate social reinforcement following success will be present. Students should be allowed to choose many of their own activities, since success in meaningful activities will be more meaningful than success in tasks that the student cares little about. Phares (1971) found that externals devalued tasks after failure significantly more than internals did. This implies that if externals fail in school, they will devalue school. We must avoid this, especially until other segments of society are more willing to aid schools in the educational process. The note of caution at the end of the previous paragraph is, of course, relevent here also.

The learning environments being proposed here should not be taken as an argument for homogeneous achievement groupings. The research does seem to support individualized and personalized learning environments, perhaps in a team-taught situation. Students could be tested for I–E, and appropriate learning activities could be prescribed by both teachers and students. One physical environment might consist of several learning environments. More importantly, the research presented here argues strongly for a *pluralistic* approach in the design of learning environments.

Pluralistic schools are in existence.[1] At the present time, Jefferson Primary School in Pasadena, California, and P.S. 1 in Santa Monica are designed around several distinct learning environments. Some classrooms are taught in a very traditional way, others in an open manner, and others in a combination or eclectic style. Students, parents, and teachers work together to decide which learning environment is most appropriate for the student. Research results utilizing students at Jefferson Primary School show that playground aggression is much lower at a pluralistic school as compared to a control traditional school (Johnston and Krovetz, 1976). It is also of importance that during the several years that Jefferson has been pluralistic, achievement-test scores have risen significantly.

In Quincy, Illinois, there is a high school utilizing the schools-within-a-school model. Quincy II, as the program is called, consists of eight schools all existing on the same campus. One of them is for all freshmen and

---

[1]The reader is referred to Fantini (1974) for a more thorough philosophical discussion of pluralism in education.

sophomores. The other seven are open to juniors and seniors. Extensive guidance is given to students to help them make choices. Students can choose an open-classroom environment, a highly structured traditional option, or a flexible program. Options include a fine arts program and a career school. John Adams High School in Portland, Oregon, is organized similarly. The author has worked with Claremont High School personnel in Claremont, California, on evolving a similar model and is now employed as a high-school administrator in Carmel, California, for the same purpose.

The Relevance of Architecturally Oriented Research

To this point the discussion has centered totally on social-learning theory, which is a psychological theory, and its relationship to the design of learning environments. Next we need to consider ways in which architectural-design factors can be meshed with social intervention. This will be at best speculative since very little useful research has been done to date regarding the ways in which architectural design and school programs interact and complement each other.

Proshansky and Wolfe (1974) have pointed out that there are two major ways in which the design and arrangement of space and furniture are factors in implementing educational goals: "First, physical and spatial aspects of a learning environment communicate a *symbolic* message of what one expects to happen in a particular place. . . . Second, physical and spatial factors play a pragmatic role in the learning situation" (pp. 558–559). For example, desks in rows imply that a student is expected to sit quietly and take notes, and in fact such an arrangement will inhibit discussion other than teacher to student or student to teacher.

Recently ERIC published a review of research dealing with open-space schools (Cockburn, 1974). Results are inconclusive and vary from school to school. This should not be surprising since *utilization* of space is more important than the design itself. An open-space school, as differentiated from an open classroom, can be defined as a school plant designed to have a minimal number of interior walls, thus creating a relatively large open space. How this space is used is determined by the people, especially the teachers, who use it. This author has been an observer in several open-space schools in which teachers have placed bookcases in such a way that walls are formed. The bookcases are short enough to give an illusion of open space to an adult, but they are taller than the students. Gump and James (1973) reported that at one open-space school, teachers, in order to prevent noise, took one or more of the following precautions: "They admonished children not to express enthusiasm too vigorously, they avoided use of learning aides like record players except at certain times and places, they were 'careful' about use of outside speakers, and they limited vigorous physical and vocal activity to recess and to assigned times" (p.

D-10). Thus Gump and James concluded that it is foolish to look for achievement-test differences based on architectural consideration until it has been determined that these considerations influence curriculum, staff-relations, instructional strategies, etc.

Gump and James have made coments very relevant to this discussion. They have distinguished between milieu (space) and program. Thus an educational environment may appear to be very inviting for self-teaching activities because of centrally located supply sites well furnished with self-teaching devices; the program may or may not allow for use of this milieu. They also reported from Brunetti's research (1971, 1972) that:

1. Noise bothers teachers much more than pupils—if we accept their self-reports.
2. Noise distracts depending upon the subject's activity; a high noise level in a laboratory activity is not nearly so distracting as similar noise in a study session.
3. Noise distracts depending upon its content, its message value. Students report much higher distraction from overheard social conversations than from subject matter talk.
4. Noise distracts more when conditions are crowded. (pp. D-5-6)

Reflection on these findings indicates that noise cannot be equated with annoyance or distraction; noise abatement is necessary or not, depending upon who the inhabitants are, their current activity, and conditions within and around the noise. This discussion is very consistent with the idea of pluralism; different learning environments have different requirements.

Some additional research does exist that may help in the designing of a milieu useful for a pluralistic school. As the results of each study are reviewed below note (a) the implications of the findings for a traditional program and (b) how these findings would be useful in the designing of a pluralistic school.

1. Rolfe (1961) found that when the storage-free area of a classroom was increased by 18–30% and when movable furniture was placed in the classroom, teacher satisfaction increased but no noticeable changes occurred in teaching methods.
   a. This is consistent with the observations of open-space schools.
   b. A pluralistic school will not evolve without the support and understanding of the staff. Staff inservice training is crucial.
2. Barker and Gump (1964) reported that students in small-enrollment high schools as compared to students in large-enrollment high schools were involved in more activities and were more satisfied with their school.
   a. The large size of many high schools has been a major complaint in recent years.
   b. A pluralistic high school would break the school into smaller schools-within-a-school. A good school plant would allow for

this to happen easily, with, for example, a number of buildings being located on the campus. Many facilities, such as the library, the gymnasium, and the science-lab facilities, would be shared, but a sense of community within a program could be fostered.

It is important to mention that Barker and Gump also found a larger percentage of students who felt alienated at small schools as compared to large schools. Counseling by teachers, peers, and professionals is a necessary part of the program.

3. Festinger, Pepitone, and Newcomb (1952), in their classic study, reported the well-known consequences of deindividualization.
   a. Deindividualization has been a major and perhaps the major complaint against the traditional education system. Students oftentimes complain that the large number of students in a school and in each class, desks in rows, and the highly competitive nature of grading cause students to feel like numbers. In addition, teacher-centered classes leave little time for students and teachers to interact in small groups or on a one-to-one basis. The sense of community found at school, although perhaps greater than 5 years ago, is still not very evident.
   b. The pluralistic schook, by definition, would stress the importance of the individual. Programs would be designed to meet the needs of relatively small groups of students. The individual student must receive increased guidance and counseling in order to be helped to choose the best learning environment for him or her. Counselors would not have offices located in an administration building. They would instead have space allocated within each school. Ideally the role of the guidance counselor would be assumed largely by teachers and trained community-resource people. In addition, students would be choosing to learn in an environment in which they felt that they could be a members of the community.
4. Sommer and Becker (1971) found that the larger the number of students in a classroom, the more complaints aired about ventilation, room size, and overall satisfaction.
   a. A common complaint against traditional education programs is the large size of classes.
   b. Given that a pluralistic school must exist on available and often limited resources, the student–teacher ratio would not differ from that in a traditional school. However, and this is very important, many students in a pluralistic school would choose learning environments that require a substantial time commitment away from the classroom. Schools must be integrated with the community if quality education is to occur. On one hand, this means opening the school for evening and weekend

usage so that adults can participate with high-school students as co-learners; as much as possible all programs would be open to all interested persons. On the other hand, the community would be expected to open its doors to high-school students so that knowledge and skills available away from the school would be available; the use of community resources for instruction, apprenticeships, junior-executive programs, work experience, etc., would characterize one or more of the school's programs.

5. Griffitt and Veitch (1971) found that high density and high temperature lower attraction between individuals. Wilkinson (1969) found that high temperature and noise over an extended period of time affect performance.

   a. Many schools report that heating systems work better in the spring than in the winter. Teachers commonly complain about high noise levels in the corridors and in other classrooms.

   b. Good heating and cooling is important for any educational facility. Proper accoustical equipment is also important. However, based on Brunetti's research reported earlier and on the needs of a pluralistic school, noise in a school environment that stresses projects, laboratories, and/or student involvement can be higher and more distracting than the noise level in other programs. Care must be taken to make sure that programs do not interfere with each other. As stated in 2b above, ideally, different schools would utilize different buildings on campus. At a minimum, programs that are inherently associated with noise should be separated physically from programs that discourage noise.

6. Schwebel and Cherlin (1972) reported that students sitting in the front of the class as compared to students further to the rear are more attentive and are rated more favorably by teachers, peers, and themselves. Whether these results are due to student selection or environmental factors is not known.

   a. A common complaint regarding the traditional teacher-centered classroom is that a student can sit off to the side and "tune out" the class.

   b. A pluralistic school ideally would reduce the number of bored students. Students who learn best in a teacher-centered classroom would choose to do so. Students who learn best when able to move into the community would do so. In many programs, student involvement would be a vital component. In all cases, students would be in a program by choice.

7. Valins and Baum (1973) found that, in comparing the experiences and attitudes of college students living in dorms with long corridors to those of students living in suites, students living in suites felt less crowded, had a higher threshold for crowding across dif-

ferent settings, performed better in cooperative situations, and reported fewer undesirable encounters.

a. Most schools today are characterised by their long corridors and masses of students moving from class to class.

b. In a pluralistic school, this movement from class to class would not occur for many students. Students would be able to choose programs that limited movement to a certain location in school for long periods or that allowed them to enter and leave campus for much of their study. By choosing to be part of a particular learning environment, a student would, in a way, be choosing to live in a corridor environment or a suite.

8. Sommer (1969) defined *personal space* as the spatial area around each individual over which that individual wishes to maintain authority regarding who is allowed to share it and when. Newman and Pollack (1973) reported that deviant as opposed to normal high-school students, both groups of whom were enrolled in special classes, required more personal space. Rothenberg (1972) found in interviews that children in open-space schools yearned to get away from the flux, flow, and stimulation of others for part of the day.

a. Whereas most schools do provide small class size and adequate space for special-education students, little consideration is given to individual differences among students regarding personal-space needs. A traditional school program also does not take into account the effects of masses of people invading each others' personal space while moving from classroom to classroom, waiting in lunch lines, eating lunch, and sitting crowded in a classroom.

b. If a pluralistic school is being built, or in fact any school is being built, special consideration should be given to providing special areas for individuals to work alone or in small groups. Some programs would need this by design, and such spaces could be built within the existing structure by the students. In fact, towers, domes, refrigerator boxes, and quiet areas are being seen more and more in elementary-school classrooms. Allowing students to be off campus for part of their learning experience or at least at lunchtime would reduce some congestion and permit a more flexible regulation of privacy needs on the part of students.

9. Along the same lines, Rogers (1972) reported that students prefer more personal space in the morning than in the afternoon.

a. Typically, little consideration is given to the organization of activities along this dimension.

b. In a pluralistic school, or in fact in any school, Rogers's results imply that individual work should be stressed in the morning.

Physical education, laboratories, many community-based activities, and other learning experiences requiring close interpersonal contact should come later in the day.

10. Maslow and Mintz (1956) found that the aesthetic beauty of rooms influenced the type of response people made to pictures of people. The more beautiful the room, the more positive the response.
    a. Rooms in most schools, and oftentimes the schools themselves, are not very pleasing aesthetically.
    b. Any school facility should be made to look attractive through proper gardening, painting, and upkeep. Rooms also should be made attractive with displays on the walls, drapes if possible, and proper upkeep.

11. Desor (1972) hypothesized that any architectural feature of a space that reduces interpersonal perception within that space should reduce the level of crowding there. Her research shows that partitions of a space reduce perception of crowding; that a door in a partition increases perception of crowding; that rectangular rooms are perceived as less crowded than square rooms; and that interactive activities are perceived as less crowding than coactive activities.
    a. In a traditional learning environment, one-door, self-enclosed, rectangular classrooms should reduce the perception of crowding and serve to insulate students in the classroom. The use of windows in such rooms is questionable; research needs to be done regarding this variable.
    b. A pluralistic school needs to utilize the implications of this research for designing environments with various design needs. This point is discussed more in the following sections.

The research by Desor is based on projective measures of crowding and is, therefore, probably more speculative than the other research presented here. In this study, subjects were asked to place stick figures in various small, scale-model rooms.

Designing for Environment–Behavioral Congruence in the Classroom

It would seem that whereas open-space schools attempt to provide infinitely flexible space, a better strategy would be to provide facilities with many different sorts of space so that new and varied activities could be accommodated in the setting. Space that is too flexible may not do the job well; for example, a facility designed to be both a gymnasium and an auditorium is usually not ideal for either.

The users of a school should be involved in the planning of the physical plant for a pluralistic school. The users are defined not only as administrators and teachers but also as students, parents, and community members. These people should interact with the architect, and the architect should be involved in the evaluation process and the subsequent change process. Thomas David (1974), James Holt (1974), and Robert Sommer (1969) have written persuasive presentations arguing for wide participation in the planning process.

At the same time, it seems that the present discussion would benefit from an example of what a pluralistic school might look like from an architectural perspective. Figures 1–4 are included here to stimulate the reader's thoughts. Such a plant does not exist to this author's knowledge but is solely the dream of several individuals.

For the sake of discussion and the ease of using round numbers, assume that the plant is that of a high school of 1,000 students. Figures are not drawn to scale.

1. Figure 1 represents the building utilized by students and teachers choosing a teacher-centered learning environment. *Teacher-centered* implies that the primary mode of learning is from the teacher's lectures and assignments and teacher-to-student and/or student-to-teacher discussion,

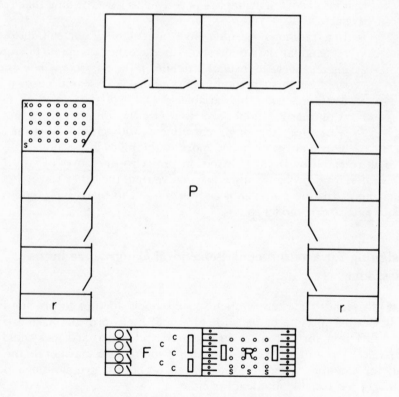

Figure 1. Teacher-centered learning environment.

Table 1. Symbol Key

o	Student desk	S	Storage
×	Teacher desk	r	Restroom
☐	Rectangular table	F	Faculty room
O	Round table	R	Resource room
C	Comfortable chair or couch	P	Patio
⟩	Door		

that is, large-group instruction. Other modes of learning may occur but to a substantially lesser degree. It is expected that about 40% of the students would choose this option. Note that each classroom would be characterized by desks in rows, a teacher's desk in front or back, and an individual storage unit in each room. Several rooms should have movable walls in order to allow for occasional smaller or larger class meetings. Sound-absorbing materials for walls and ceiling, light colors, and nicely decorated rooms should serve to reduce the perception of crowding and increase student satisfaction. The resource room would be basically a study area in which students could work individually. Cubicles would be present to allow for some privacy. The teachers' room would also offer small offices for private meetings or work. The patio area, if nicely landscaped, would allow for an area more pleasant than long corridors for movement between classes; if weather is a problem, some sort of corridor or covering would be necessary. Note that the square shape of this facility would allow it to serve as a self-contained unit, so that leaving one classroom, in fact, would lead one to another classroom.

2. Figure 2 represents the individualized self-paced learning environment. Such an environment would be characterized by students' working individually at their own speed on various learning activities, with teachers readily available to answer questions. About 20% of the students would be expected to choose this environment, which is the learning environment recommended for the external-control students in the earlier discussion. The tasks would be highly structured and teachers would be readily available to offer immediate reinforcement. Peer teaching would also occur, and therefore large round and rectangular tables are recommended. In addition, tables of this kind would allow for small-group instruction, playing of simulation games, and other activities that help to individualize learning. The individual desks at one end of the room would be for test taking. A number of small study rooms would be provided for students who wished privacy or for conferences and small-group work. Note that storage would be readily available to the students, as would the

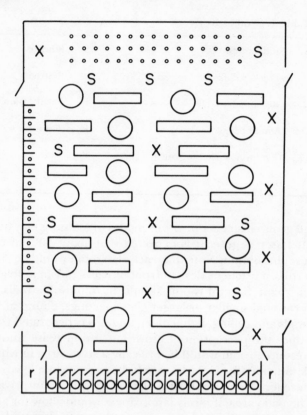

Figure 2. Individualized self-paced learning environment.

teachers' desks. Storage would consist of file cabinets (where student folders and tests would be kept) and shelves (where reference books, simulation games, and similar materials would be readily available). Storage facilities should not be movable, since students must be able to locate needed materials easily and rapidly. They must also be abundant, since individualization requires that many kinds of materials be available for student use. Carpeting and acoustical equipment would be important to this facility; the noise level must be kept low since students would be working while conversations occurred between students and teachers and students and students. Note that the building in Figure 2 would be equivalent in square footage to seven classrooms in Figure 1.

3. Figure 3 represents one of the two or three project-oriented learning environments that would exist in our proposed educational facility. It is expected that 30% of the students would choose these options, but none of the programs should exceed 100–150 students. A project-oriented learning environment would be characterized by students' spending a substantial portion of their time working on individual and/or group projects of a primarily interdisciplinary nature. Large-group, small-group, and indi-

vidual instruction would also occur, since the programs would probably be seminar-oriented, with projects relating to a central focus. Internal- and external-control students would function well in this environment as long as the teachers and students realized that some of the students need more structure and supervision than others. The facility would contain two seminar rooms to accommodate up to 25 students each and four small seminar–conference rooms. Walls would be movable to allow for large-group presentations and other flexible needs. The remaining 50% of the area would be left for students and teachers to design their own study–work areas plus storage areas; these would be very flexible so that changes could be made as the need arose. Some students would design spaces using individual desks, others might use couches, and others might design domes or towers to work in. Note the large number of doors and windows. Students must feel free to move between this environment and the community at large. It is expected that certain project-oriented programs would require students to spend a substantial part of their time in community-based learning activities, such as in the study of civics. Other programs might use

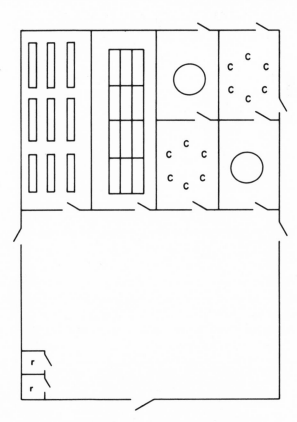

Figure 3. Project-oriented learning environment.

the "Ascent of Man" film series as an interdisciplinary focus or the future as a focus, with Toffler's *Future Shock* (1970) as a starting point. Good acoustical equipment and carpeting would be important here again, since the noise level would vary from location to location within the facility. The partitioning of the building and the interactive nature of the projects should reduce the perception of crowding. Note that the building in Figure 3 would be equivalent in square footage to five classrooms in Figure 1.

4. Figure 4 represents the independent-study facility. About 10% of the students would be expected to enroll in this program. As indicated earlier, internal-control students, given the proper circumstances, should do well in this type of environment. An independent-study learning environment would be characterized by students investigating topics of interest to themselves, which would also meet the graduation requirements of the school. The teachers' responsibility would be to act as facilitator, helping the student locate resources, fulfill commitments, and at the same time obtain the skills that the student needs to graduate and to function in society. The facility would consist of one conference room, one quiet room,

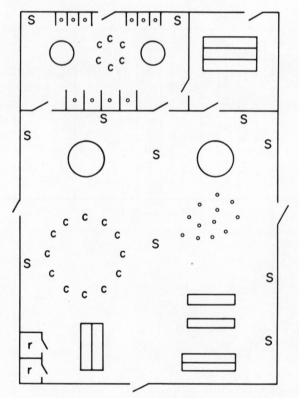

Figure 4. Independent-study learning environment.

and a large core room. The core room must be flexible enough to be utilized by students working on all types of projects. Much movable storage, especially shelving, is recommended. So are tables of various sizes and a workbench. Accoustical equipment would be crucial here. Students would use this facility primarily as a home base, with a majority of their time being spent with the necessary resources. It is important to add that independent-study projects would oftentimes involve more than one student. Note that the building in Figure 4 would be equivalent in square footage to four classrooms in Figure 1.

A number of additional comments are needed for clarification. First, the plan presented here is for a secondary school. At the elementary-school level, pluralism can be handled within self-contained classrooms, depending on the style of the teachers; other designs are, of course, also possible. The reader is referred to Leitman and Churchill (1971) for one example of these alterations. Second, the number of square feet per student would be somewhat greater for students choosing options 3 and 4 than for options 1 and 2 because of the greater amount of flexibility and movement required in the former two learning environments. Third, considerable guidance would be a major component of this program. Students must have information about the environments available and about themselves. Fourth, the library, the science laboratory, the gymnasium, the auditorium, the basic vocational laboratories, the cafeteria, etc., would exist in separate buildings to be shared by all programs. Fifth, when a student enrolled in a particular learning environment, he or she would be committed to spending a major part of the school day assigned to this program. This is very important. A project-oriented curriculum or an independent-study curriculum cannot function in 50-minute time blocks. Time must be flexible for students in both of these learning environments. The teacher-centered learning option may offer some classes in modules other than 50 minutes, as in the case of a 90-minute chemistry lab, but the inflexible time blocks are important to the coordination of activities in such a program. At the same time, a student in any program would have the option of enrolling part time in a different option. A student enrolled in the independent study option might wish to learn math in a teacher-centered environment. This would decrease the flexibility of that student's schedule, but the option would be available. Many students might choose to enroll part time in the individualized, self-paced option to meet some graduation requirements. Flexibility need not be affected. These are solely problems of coordination and tolerance.

Sixth, the figures are obviously for a new school. An existing facility could be adapted to meet many of the needs mentioned here. Seventh, at this time of economic woe and decreasing school enrollment, a pluralistic school must operate with existing resources. A pluralistic school does not need a new plant, and, in fact, John Adams High School utilized the existing plant when its program evolved into a schools-within-a-school model.

Start-up costs for planning, inservice training, and some plant alteration are necessary, but further expenditures must and can come from the existing budget.

In closing, I ask the reader to consider the following thoughts. If one is designing a physical setting with some purpose in mind, then assumptions about what man is like and how he will react to and feel about this environment must be clearly specified. Getzels (1974) pointed out that it is crucial to understand the visions of the child as a learner. We cannot utilize the same learning environment if we assume that the child is a receptical of learning as we would use if we assumed that the child is an active seeker of knowledge. This author contends that each child is an individual possessing a personal learning style. Although all children are seekers, they seek different things and in different ways. Each has his or her own personal needs. Given these assumptions, no one educational environment can meet the needs of students. This author agrees with Chase (1972):

> Would it not be more constructive to build new environments, designed on the basis of realistic appraisals of behavioral abilities and deficits? Such environments could provide support of potential adaptive behavioral growth and would not make demands that clearly cannot possibly be met. The design of environments that are modifiable and responsive not only to individual patterns of behavioral competence, but also to individual styles of behavioral expression, provides excellent opportunities to support available behavioral competence and to learn with greater precision just what an individual is and is not capable of. (p. 184)

References

Barker, R. G., and Gump, P. *Big school, small school.* Stanford, Calif.: Stanford University Press, 1964.

Brunetti, F. A. Open space: A status report. *School environment study.* Stanford, Calif.: School Planning Laboratory, School of Education, Stanford University, 1971.

Brunetti, F. A. Noise, distraction, and privacy in conventional and open school environments. In W. Mitchell (Ed.), *Environmental design: Research and practice. Proceedings of EDRA Conference,* January 1972. Pp. 12-2-1–12-2-6.

Chance, J. E. Internal control of reinforcements and the school learning process. Paper read at the Biennial Meeting of the Society for Research in Child Development, Minneapolis, Minn., 1965.

Chase, R. A. Behavioral biology and environmental design. In M. Hammer, K. Salzinger, and S. Sutton (Eds.), *Psychopathology.* New York: Wiley, 1972. Pp. 175–191.

Cockburn, I. The open school: An annotated bibliography. *ERIC,* February, 1974, ED 082 292.

Coleman, J. S., Campbell, E. Q., Hobson, C. J., McPartland, J., Mood, A. M., Weinfeld, R. D., and York, R. L. *Equality of educational opportunity.* Superintendent of Documents Catalog No. FS 5.238:38001, Washington, D.C.: U.S. Government Printing Office, 1966.

Crandall, V. D., Katkovsky, W., and Crandall, V. J. Children's beliefs in their control of reinforcements in intellectual–academic achievement situations. *Child Development,* 1965, *36,* 91–109.

David, T. G. Environmental literacy. *School Review,* 1974, *82,* 687–706.

Davis, W. L., and Phares, E. J. Internal–external control as a determinant of information-seeking in a social influence situation. *Journal of Personality*, 1967, *35*, 547–561.

Davis, W. L., and Phares, E. J. Parental antecedents of internal–external control of reinforcement. *Psychological Reports*, 1969, *24*, 427–436.

Desor, J. S. Toward a psychological theory of crowding. *Journal of Personality and Social Psychology*, 1972, *21*, 79–83.

Doctor, R. M. Locus of control of reinforcement and responsiveness to social influence. *Journal of Personality*, 1971, *39*, 542–551.

Fantini, M. *Public schools of choice.* New York: Simon and Schuster, 1974.

Festinger, L., Pepitone, A., and Newcomb, T. Some consequences of deindividualization in a group. *Journal of Abnormal and Social Psychology*, 1952, *47*, 382–389.

Getzels, J. W. Images of the classroom and visions of the learner. *School Review*, 1974, *84*, 527–540.

Gillis, J. S., and Jessor, R. Effects of brief psychotherapy on belief in internal control: An exploratory study. *Psychotherapy: Theory, Research and Practice*, 1970, *7*, 135–137.

Gore, P. Individual differences in the prediction of subject compliance to experimenter bias. Unpublished doctoral dissertation, Ohio State University, 1962.

Gore, P., and Rotter, J. B. A personality correlate of social action. *Journal of Personality*, 1963, *31*, 58–64.

Griffitt, W., and Veitch, R. Hot and crowded: Influences of population density and temperature on interpersonal affective behavior. *Journal of Personality and Social Psychology*, 1971, *17*, 92–98.

Gump, P., and James, E. Child development and the man-made environment: A literature review and commentary. Department of Psychology, University of Kansas, 1973.

Holt, J. Involving the user in school planning. *School Review*, 1974, *82*, 707–730.

Johnston, K. D., and Krovetz, M. L. Levels of aggression in a traditional and pluralistic school. *Educational Research*, 1976, *18*, 146–151.

Karabanek, S. A. Balance of success and failure as a function of achievement motives and locus of control. *Journal of Personality and Social Psychology*, 1972, *21*, 101–110.

Katkovsky, W., Crandall, V. D., and Good, S. Parental antecedents of children's beliefs in internal-external control of reinforcements in intellectual achievement situations. *Child Development*, 1967, *38*, 765–776.

Kiehlbauch, J. B. Selected changes over time in internal-external control expectancies in a reformatory population. Unpublished doctoral dissertation, Kansas State University, 1967.

Krovetz, M. L. Explaining success and failure as a function of one's locus of control. *Journal of Personality*, 1974, *42*, 175–189.

Leitman, A., and Churchill, E. H. A classroom for young children: Approximation No. 1. In C. H. Rathbone (Ed.), *Open Education: The Informal Classroom*, New York: Citation Press, 1971, Pp. 168–184.

Maslow, A. H., and Mintz, L. Effects of esthetic surroundings: 1. Initial short-term effects of three esthetic conditions upon perceiving "energy" and "well-being" in faces. *Journal of Psychology*, 1956, *41*, 247–254.

Newman, R., and Pollack, D. Proxemies in deviant adolescents. *Journal of Consulting and Clinical Psychology*, 1973, *40*, 6–8.

Phares, E. J. Internal-external control as a determinent of amount of social influence exerted. *Journal of Personality and Social Psychology*, 1965, *2*, 642–647.

Phares, E. J. Internal-external control and the reduction of reinforcement value after failure. *Journal of Consulting and Clinical Psychology*, 1971, *37*, 386–390.

Phares, E. J. *Locus of control: A personality determinant.* General Learning Press, 1973.

Pines, H. A., and Julian, J. W. Effects of task and social demands on locus of control differences in information processing. *Journal of Personality*, 1972, *40*, 407–416.

Proshansky, E., and Wolfe, M. The physical setting of open education. *School Review*, 1974, *82*, 557–574.

Ramirez, M. Cognitive styles and cultural democracy in education. *Social Science Quarterly*, March, 1973, 895–904.

Rogers, J. A. Relationships between sociability and personal space preference at two different times of day. *Perceptual and Motor Skills*, 1972, *35*, 519–526.

Rolfe, H. C. Differences in space use of learning situations in small and large classrooms. Unpublished dissertation, University of California at Berkeley, 1961.

Rothenberg, M., and the children of P.S. 3. Planning at P.S. 3. Unpublished manuscript, City University of New York, 1972.

Rotter, J. B. *Social learning and clinical psychology*. Englewood Cliffs, N.J.: Prentice-Hall, 1954.

Rotter, J. B. Generalized expectancies for internal versus external control of reinforcement. *Psychological Monographs*, 1966, *80* (Whole No. 609).

Schwebel, A. I., and Cherlin, D. L. Physical and social distancing in teacher–pupil relationships. *Journal of Educational Psychology*, 1972, *63*, 543–550.

Seeman, M. Alienation and social learning in a reformatory. *American Journal of Sociology*, 1963, *69*, 270–284.

Seeman, M., and Evans, J. W. Alienation and learning in a hospital setting. *American Sociological Review*, 1962, *27*, 772–783.

Sommer, R. *Personal space: The behavioral basis of design*. Englewood Cliffs, N.J.: Prentice-Hall, 1969.

Sommer, R., and Becker, K. D. Room density and user satisfaction. *Environment and Behavior*, 1971, *3*, 412–417.

Straits, B. C., and Sechrest, L. Further support of some findings about characteristics of smokers and non-smokers. *Journal of Consulting Psychology*, 1963, *27*, 282.

Strickland, B. R. The prediction of social action from a dimension of internal–external control. *Journal of Social Psychology*, 1965, *66*, 353–358.

Toffler, A. *Future Shock*. New York: Random House, 1970.

Valins, S., and Baum, A. Residential group size, social interaction and crowding. *Environment and Behavior*, 1973, *5*, 421–439.

Wilkinson, R. Some factors influencing the effect of environmental stressors upon performance. *Psychological Bulletin*, 1969, *72*, 260–272.

Witkens, H. A. The role of cognitive style in academic performance and in teacher–student relations. Educational Testing Service, February, 1972.

The Relevance of Crowding Experiments to Urban Studies

13

MARK BALDASSARE
AND CLAUDE S. FISCHER

The experimental study of human crowding is one of the behavioral sciences' fastest-growing areas of research. We come to this forum with two major interests. As social psychologists who have engaged in experimental work on crowding, we are concerned with the conduct and evaluation of these laboratory studies. As urban sociologists, we have noted with dismay the poverty of theory in this young research tradition. As our contribution, we hope to offer a constructive critique drawn largely from the vantage point of over 50 years of urban theory and research. Our main focus will concern the following question: *What do the experimental studies of crowding have to do with the understanding of the social-psychological nature of urban life?* Our proposition is that thus far experimentalists have ignored the central issues in urbanism and have given inadequate answers to this question.

There are a wide variety of reasons for studying the effects of crowding, such as an interest in territorial behavior, the designing of optimal environments, or an interest in cultural kinesic styles. But clearly one of the greatest motivating forces in initiating these experiments has been the concern over urban livability. Similarly many of the lessons drawn from them have been applied to the experience of the individual in dense urban environments. Freedman and Ehrlich (1972) have probably provided the best example of a tendency in this field to extrapolate unconditionally from the laboratory to the city. In their article for the *New York Times*, they began by discussing ecological research on density and pathology in New

MARK BALDASSARE • University of California at Los Angeles. CLAUDE S. FISCHER • University of California at Berkeley. An earlier version of this paper was presented to a symposium on "Theoretical Developments Pertaining to Personal Space and Human Crowding," at the Western Psychological Association meetings in San Francisco, April 27, 1974.

York City. Then they leaped into a summary of their crowding experiments without attempting to explain the connections between the two types of analyses. Finally, they concluded the article with a discussion of the implications of these joint findings for urban life; again we are left with no indication as to the specific relationship between experiments on human crowding and urban issues. This is not an isolated case, for in many other reports of experiments, researchers have made vague and unexplained references to urban problems and to ecological studies of density (e.g., Baum and Valins, 1973; Desor, 1972; Freedman, Klevansky, and Ehrlich, 1971; Freedman, Levy, Buchanan, and Price, 1972; Griffitt and Veitch, 1971; Ross, Layton, Erickson, and Schopler, 1973).

Thus our major criticism of crowding experiments is not that the theoretical links have not been made well but that with rare exception (Stokols, 1972b, 1973; Stokols, Rall, Pinner, and Schopler, 1973) they have not been made at all.

The standard organization of papers written in this field has generally involved the discussion of animal studies in an introductory section, followed by a review of urban-crowding research, and then the reporting of the experiment. Following in the footsteps of Calhoun (1962) and to some extent Hall (1966), the researchers later lead the reader into loosely generalizing their findings to city life.[1] Of course, this sort of *post hoc* theorizing reverses the proper roles of theory and research (unfortunately an all too common practice in social psychology).

This paper will primarily address itself to this issue: since the kinds of extrapolations being made in crowding research seem to us not legitate, how might they be made so and with what implications? We will not, however, discuss each specific experiment nor research efforts in macro-crowding (i.e., urban ecological surveys), since our present concerns are with the theoretical connections between urbanism and crowding experiments.[2]

Before we proceed, it should be emphasized that we are not arguing that the crowding literature is irrelevant to any urban issues. It may, for example, inform architects and planners about the design of certain microenvironments (e.g., housing and public places). However, we care that the experiments have alluded to but not contributed to the "cities-are-teeming-behavioral-sinks" debate. In other words, they have not provided theoretically linked evidence as to what characteristically dense urban living creates (for example) high stress, conflict, social alienation, or aggression.

Just as there are a large number of reasons for studying crowding, so

---

[1]For instance, Freedman, Levy, Buchanan, and Price (1972, p. 546) discuss in their concluding remarks some implications of their findings for behavior in urban settings (i.e., subways, crowded streets, and elevators).

[2]These issues are dealt with in another paper (Fischer, Baldassare, and Ofshe, 1975).

there are a variety of theoretical approaches that could be used for deriving testable hypotheses on this subject. For instance, we can choose to understand crowding phenomena from the viewpoints of ethology, social learning, or systems theory. In this paper, we are solely concerned with the derivation of crowding hypotheses from theories related to *urbanism.* In other words, we believe that if one wishes to draw conclusions about city life from experimental research, one should begin by examining theories of city life—before the design and analysis of the experiment. There are several theories that are concerned with the social-psychological consequences of urban life that provide potential bases for crowding research. We shall examine these theories below.

Why Experimentation?

Before we do so, however, a more fundamental metatheoretical question must be addressed: If the research is interested in people's reactions to dense city life, why do experiments at all?[3] Freedman (1973), Freedman, Klevansky, and Ehrlich (1971), and Ross, Layton, Erickson, and Schopler (1973) all have mentioned that they used experiments to overcome the problems of confounding variables that are associated with population density in ecological studies (e.g., socioeconomic status, noise, and pollution). Although it is perfectly correct to use experiments to assess the effects of density *per se,* these authors still give us no indication of the logical links between the laboratory and the urban environment. Other than these half-hearted attempts, we have yet to find more than two justifications for the relevance of an experimental procedure (Stokols, 1972b, 1973).

In our reading of the literature, there seem to emerge two implicit rationales for performing experimental research on human crowding. One is the argument by analogy: dense rooms are "like" dense settlements; what is true of the former is true of the latter. This is about as valid, to use our own analogy, as stating that the behavior of chimpanzees in a zoo is "like" their behavior in forests. Yet this sort of thinking is blatant in Calhoun (1962) and Hall (1966) and is a hidden assumption in much of the experimental work. Argument by analogy, which is usually a weak forensic procedure anyway, is even more so in this case.[4] Even on the simple basis of formal spatial patterns, the structured environment of seated individuals in a laboratory is not equivalent to the largely nonstatic world of urban individuals (cf. Loo, 1973). A legitimate parallelism between the laboratory

[3]We will not introduce the standard arguments against the validity of experimentation (e.g., artificiality, characteristics of the subject pool, and demand characteristics of the situation). As experimenters, we do not believe that they outweigh the benefits of laboratory studies.

[4]Not only is it logically incorrect, but in an empirical test of this proposition it was found that "crowding effects" in the laboratory (i.e., decreased social behavior) could not be found among residents of city neighborhoods (Baldassare, 1975).

and the city can be made only by a careful explication of their common systemic properties. This is an effort that has not been made by crowding experimentalists as yet—and one that may be extremely complex.[5]

A second, and more legitimate justification of experimental studies is that urban life is composed of a number of crowding incidents. Thus to understand the effects of crowding is to comprehend the effects of urban living. More specifically, this argument states that the average density of urban experiences is greater than the average density of nonurban experiences. Therefore if greater total density is more detrimental to individuals in one instance (i.e., the laboratory), then urbanites must suffer greater total detriment than others. This sort of analysis is suggested by Stokols (1972b), though he rejects the notion that the effects of urban crowding can be assessed as merely an aggregation of microcrowding phenomena (Stokols, 1973).

An illustration of this argument would be the following naturally occurring situation: if crowding on city buses is greater than crowding on rural buses, then the cumulation of such instances would mean greater total crowding and greater total consequences for urbanites. However, the truth is that we do not know how dense the average experiences of average city dwellers are as compared to others. While common sense and personal experience suggest that there are differences, we do not yet have empirical evidence on how much of a difference there actually is.[6]

There is one further comment to be made on this type of a justification. A plausible argument could also be raised that urban life is distinguished from rural life by the greater *frequency* of crowding instances (even at the same levels of density). However, the experimental work to date has not tested that proposition, which would require comparing the amount of time spent in high densities rather than comparing different room densities. In summary, one can make the argument that urban life is an aggregation of microcrowding incidents, but only with full recognition of the weakness of the connection.

The two justifications of crowding experiments offered thus far are either invalid or at best tenuous. One technique that offers a way out of this difficulty is direct field-experimentation. An interest in apartment-building density, for example (Newman, 1973; Bickman, Teger, and Gab-

---

[5]An area in which this has been done somewhat successfully is in the simulation of conflict. Major efforts have been made to establish the parallelism of its systemic properties: party, resources, conflict of interest, negotiation norms, etc. However, doing this for crowding studies would be much more problematic. For instance, urban residents do not reside within the corporal presence of others, nor do they co-act with the masses of the urban scene. Rather they live in adjacent dominciles and interact with select subsets of the population. These and many other problems would perplex an attempt at establishing a laboratory–city isomorphism.

[6]Furthermore data on within-dwelling density even suggests that there are slight trends for rural households to be more crowded than urban households (Fischer, 1976, Chapter 3).

riele, 1973; Gillis, 1974), can be pursued by systematic field studies in apartment settings. The drawback, however, is that, while these studies can provide rich data on social life within the buildings, they will usually not be relevant to the more general issues of urbanism (nor, for that matter, will they usually inform us about the effects of within-room densities). Field experiments can be an optimal technique for crowding research, but their findings are largely specific to the setting. Unless researchers examine the interaction of multiple densities impinging upon individuals *in situ* (e.g., room, household, building, and neighborhood—cf. Michelson and Garland, 1974; Booth, 1974), such studies will have only limited applications to the study of urbanism. For these reasons, and others related to the difficulty of conducting naturalistic studies, this type of experiment has thus far played a minor role in the crowding field.

A fourth possibility exists—one that is more difficult to delineate and that requires more forethought. Experimental work can usefully inform the evaluation of sociological theories of urbanism by testing and identifying critical psychological assumptions in these models. Theories about the social consequences of urbanization are by definition sociological, yet like most sociological theories, they rest on a set of psychological assumptions. Unfortunately these assumptions (e.g., perceptual, cognitive, and behavioral processes of individuals) are generally left untested and are seldom examined by sociologists. Here, then, is the proper connection between urban theories and social-psychological experimentation on crowding: to test the psychological assumptions upon which urban theory rests.

To further elaborate our meaning, we shall provide several examples of the procedure that we are suggesting. They will serve to illustrate what social psychologists recognize as the most fundamental role of the experiment: not to replicate in miniature general social life, but to test under controlled conditions the psychological assumptions in theories of social life. This seems to be the best though hardest way of making the connection between urban studies and experimental work. It raises a new and central point in experimental research on crowding: the primacy of theory. If the relevance of experimental work is to test theoretical propositions of city life, then it can be relevant only when conducted in the context of theories of urbanism.

Theories of Urbanism

We have argued that a researcher who intends to establish the link between crowding experiments and urbanism must start with the urbanism issues first and not address them in a *post hoc* fashion. In this regard, social psychologists have been as derelict in making the connection from data to theory as sociologists have been in making the connection from theory to data.

In this section, we will briefly review five theoretical approaches to the nature of urbanism and attempt to pinpoint their critical psychological presumptions. Later we will suggest the role that experimental work might play in testing these models. This list of theories is by no means a complete one, nor shall we go into great detail at this time (cf. Fischer, 1972, 1976; Sjoberg, 1970); a taste is all we offer.

1. *Psychic overload.* This urban theory was first presented by Georg Simmel in the early 1900's (Simmel, 1969). Recently, it has been modernized in terminology by Meier (1962) and Milgram (1970). It seems to be an assumed model in animal studies such as Calhoun (1962), as well as in the ecological research of Galle, Gove, and McPherson (1972). Furthermore, it is briefly alluded to in the experimental studies of Desor (1972), Baum and Valins (1973), Sherrod (1974), and Griffitt and Veitch (1971).

The theory begins with the assumption that residence in a densely rather than a sparsely populated area leads to more perceptual stimulation from exposure to other humans and their by-products (e.g., noise, pollution, buildings, and information). The large number of stimuli that compete for attention, evaluation, and response tax the limited "channel capacities" of the human mind. Either or both of two consequences may then follow: a series of adaptations by the organism to "screen out" less desirable inputs, and/or psychic stress from the costs of these efforts and from stimuli that leak in because of incomplete adaptation. The results at the social level are high levels of pathology, while at the individual level a cultural life-style develops that serves to isolate the individual from unwanted inputs (e.g., aloofness, blaséness, and dehumanization).

2. *Territoriality.* While some adherents to this view might be reluctant to admit it, this perspective seems to lie behind Hall's (1966, pp. 165–168, 172–173) discussion of cities and the personal-space research of those such as Sommer (1969) and Evans and Howard (1973).

This thesis states that people "naturally" need personal territories and that frustration of these spatial "urges" is anxiety-creating. Residence in highly dense areas means that there will be more such frustrations, due both to more frequent physical intrusions and to people's subjective sense of shared territories. Consequently city life leads to stress, which in turn produces a mélange of aggression, withdrawal, and psychic disorder. Additionally various groups in dense areas are forced to compete for the use of space. To resolve these often-conflicting demands, dominance hierarchies, spatial boundaries, and the control and defense of certain neighborhood areas by groups develop within cities (Suttles, 1968; Hall, 1966; Sommer, 1969).

3. *Structural differentiation.* We are dealing here with a significant part of mainstream sociological thought about the consequences of urbanism. These ideas were first expressed by Park (1916/1967) and were later fully

elaborated by Wirth (1938).[7] Winsborough (1965), for one, has applied this model in his study of the effects of population density.

For reasons explicated in greater detail elsewhere (Durkheim, 1964; Hawley, 1950, 1972), communities that are densely populated are more structurlaly differentiated than less dense communities; that is, social institutions are more specialized in their functions and distinct in their characteristics.[8] On the individual level, the differentiation of social roles and groups causes the individual to develop single-function relationships with others. Thus interactions that in smaller societies occur in primary groups (*Gemeinschafts*) are now replaced by a wide variety of secondary relationships (*Gesellschafts*). The resultant personality differentiation creates problems of social and psychological (identity) management, and the consequences may include stress and related effects, as well as "urban" styles of interaction (e.g., superficiality and exploitativeness).

One of the authors (Fischer, 1975) has presented a variation on this theory by suggesting that the structural differentiation results in specialized but highly supportive subcultures. One could also argue that "single-plex" relationships are less stressful than "multiplex" ones because they avoid conflicting obligations and commitments (for instance, the problems involved in sharing a business with a brother-in-law). Similarly Hawley (1972) states that high physical density and its concomitant structural differentiation may have positive effects, including the easy availability of like-minded individuals, opportunity for selective association, mutual assistance in achieving access to scarce facilities, and exposure to innovative ideas (Hawley, 1972, p. 526).

4. *Social-psychological theory.* There is as yet no integrated social-psychological approach to the study of urban crowding, at least none comparable to the other theories that we are reviewing. However, several promising lines of analysis have been opened up that may promote a better understanding of both the physical and the social components of crowding effects in urban areas.

For instance, Mitchell (1971, p. 23) has found that the specific *combinations* of physical features and social compositions can have ill effects (e.g., crowded dwellings shared by nonrelatives produce stress). In other cases, certain social arrangements may alleviate problems related to density (see Mitchell, 1975). This work suggests that other settings in the city (e.g., parks and public facilities) might be also constructed or used in such ways as to enhance or reduce the sensation of crowding and the responses to it.

Stokols (1972a,b, 1974) has suggested other possibilities. He has con-

---

[7]Also see the discussions by Fischer (1972, 1976).
[8]A common example is the family. In small-scale societies, the family is the emotional, economic, educational, recreational, and security unit for the individual. In large-scale societies, other specialized institutions arise and usurp these functions (e.g., schools, businesses, police, theater).

tinually argued that physical density is in itself an insufficient determinant of crowding perceptions and reactions. He has sought to distinguish the features of the setting, the people, and the ongoing activities that produce the sensation on the part of individuals that they are "crowded." Clearly the distinction between "primary" and "secondary" environments (Stokols, 1974) has important implications for the study of density, for it suggests where in the urban setting (homes or streets, for example) one will find which particular reactions to density.

5. *Nonecological theory, or the null hypothesis.* This perspective on the consequences of urban life has been most forcefully expressed by Herbert Gans (1962a,b, 1967) and Oscar Lewis (1952, 1965). It must be attended to because it is probably the dominant one in urban sociology today. The argument states that ecology is essentially unimportant, since both rural and urban people conduct their lives in small social circles. Thus urbanism has no substantial impact on social life or personality.

However, to the degree that the *experience* of the environment differs substantially by size and density of community (this, as stated earlier, is only an assumption and not yet a fact), a nonecological approach must incorporate some mechanism by which these differences are equalized or neutralized (e.g., the development and isolation of distinct subcultures in cities [Gans, 1962a]). Also, there seems to be implicit a notion that there are adjustments of cultural standards concerning what levels of environmental density are expected and accepted. Thus individuals come to take their respective environments (urban or rural, dense or spacious) as "normal" and hence neutral (cf. Helson, 1948)—either facilely or perhaps gradually over time.

The Role of Crowding Experiments

How can experimental work on crowding be used to test hypotheses derived from these urban theories? The following are a few examples.

1. *Psychic overload.* This model predicts that the evidence of stress will increase as a function of the number of people and products that "input" stimuli to an individual. The stimuli in turn will lead to the uses of adaptive avoidance or screening mechanisms. A laboratory setting could allow for a controlled manipulation of input level. Thus we could test the assumption that other people raise stimulus levels, or we could explore whether certain kinds of people or certain social activities cause this to occur. We could standardize the induction of strain and measure the form and consequences of adaptation. Also we could use the laboratory setting to test the proposition that various living arrangements cause different degrees of stress (cf. Baum and Valins, 1973) or, better yet, that actual urban and rural dwellers differ on these tested dimensions. Some of the studies done to date can be interpreted in this framework, but most on only a *post hoc*

basis. The noise research of Glass and Singer (1972) should provide researchers with a fairly good notion of how to conduct an urban-related experimental study of stress.

2. *Territoriality.* These notions would make predictions similar to psychic-overload theory, although a crucial distinction follows from the fact that most sensory stimulation is independent of distance. Aside from olfactory stimulation, the sights and sounds of other people and their products would be about the same from 5 feet as at 1 foot. However, at the latter proximity, territoriality is infringed upon. Thus we could examine the stress consequences from this invasion (cf. Edney, 1974; Evans and Howard, 1973). Are there aggression–dominance reactions and adaptations? When and to what extent are such reactions erasable because of the "definition of the situation," cultural differences, or an urban socialization?

3. *Structural differentiation.* These theories are macrosociological in nature but do rest upon a few social-psychological assumptions. For instance, to what extent will group size, density, and heterogeneity affect crowding responses and perceptions? Will size and proximity lead to a division of labor? Will relations become "single-plex" in dense situations? Are a number of single-plex roles more or less stressful than one or two multiplex ones, and will these factors generate behavioral styles that are unique? These and similar questions related to density and structural differentiation have been largely untouched by experimentalists.

The experimental work that this theory suggests is not confined to the single variable of density. Rather this framework implies that a *multivariate* experimental design may be needed. For instance, one could set up task groups varying in specialization, density, numbers, and heterogeniety (cf. Wicker, 1974; Wicker and Kirmeyer, Chapter 3).

4. *Social-psychological theory.* Although we still await a complete social-psychological theory of crowding, several social-psychological assumptions in various theories need testing under controlled, laboratory conditions. Stokols's (1972a) analysis of the determinants of perceptions of crowding should be examined. In particular, the contingent effects of activities, goals, and levels of intimacy on crowding responses should be investigated. The association between perceived freedom of choice (Stokols, 1974; cf. Proshansky, Ittelson, and Rivlin, 1970) has undergone preliminary testing (cf. Sherrod, 1974), but other social and psychological conditions should also be manipulated. Following Mitchell's (1971, 1975) lead, we should also consider several aspects of the social setting. For instance, how does the introduction of "strangers" into ongoing groups affect perceptions of and responses to crowding? What is the relationship of the nature of the group task to the spatial arrangements that evolve and the reactions to density? And how do cooperation, competition, interference, and forced interaction affect the performance and satisfaction of people in crowded situations?

5. *Nonecological theory*. This would call for a close analysis of the effects of individual expectations on crowding behavior, involving both general cultural standards and situation-specific standards. The propositions presented here would refer to the variability of crowding as a subjective sensation. One could manipulate subjects, expectations of crowding, and the "definition of the situation" or use naturally varying standards in cross-cultural comparisons. Experiments performed over lage periods of time would allow us to examine adjustments to density and individuals' attempts to "normalize" their social relations under crowded conditions.

Concluding Remarks

There are a number of ways that crowding studies can and have been useful: they have instructed us about classroom sizes (Hutt and Vaizey, 1966; Loo, 1972), the consequences of family size on parents and children (Clausen and Clausen, 1973), and the behavior of isolated groups in confinement (Smith and Haythorn, 1972). There is no lack of interesting and useful implications. However, our concern in this paper has been with one global and very important implication: What do crowding experiments have to offer to urban studies? In what ways do human crowding experiments enlighten our understanding of the social-psychological nature of urban life?

The conclusion that we have been forced to draw is that thus far crowding experiments have had very little relevance to the study of urban life. This is because few efforts have been made by experimentalists to establish the logical connections between the two. More fundamentally, experiments on crowding have been performed with only vague notions about urbanism itself, that is, without seriously considering the theoretical reasons for the research. The simple analogies that have been drawn from the rat studies, to the lab, and then to the city will not suffice if we hope to answer questions about urban life and hope to use experimentation to do so. There can be no substitute for using urban theories in the planning, design, and evaluation of crowding studies.

From a broader perspective, we suggest that crowding be studied at densities appropriate to the problem of interest (see discussion in Fischer, Baldassare, and Ofshe, 1975). The social psychologist interested in how astronauts might cope with crowding in a spacecraft can well use the laboratory: his unit of study parallels his unit of interest. However, the laboratory cannot in the same way serve the experimenter whose concern is social problems associated with urban density. In this case, he or she must specify the theoretical linkages between the experimental manipulations and the operation of the "real-world" phenomena. This is a more difficult process, but, as we sought to illustrate with our examples, one that is feasible. In the long run, it will be worth the trouble, since the research that ensues will directly benefit both urban studies and social psychology.

Unfortunately, the problems of theoretical connection are familiar ones in social psychology: the rush to experiment and the resort to *post hoc* relevance. We hope that this paper will contribute to a sensitization, at least in this field, to the importance of *a priori* theory—so that crowding experiments can become relevant and contribute usefully to our understanding of the urban world.

Acknowledgments

The second author's contribution to this paper was supported in part by the Institute of Urban and Regional Development, University of California, Berkeley. We were helped by discussions with Richard J. Ofshe. The paper was prepared while the first author held an NIMH traineeship under training grant number 5-TOI-MH 08268.

References

Baldassare, M. Residential density, local ties and neighborhood attitudes: Are the findings of microstudies relevant to urban areas? Sociological Symposium, 1975, *14*, 93–102.

Baum, A. and Valins, S. Residential environments, group size, and crowding. Proceedings, 81st Annual Convention, APA, 1973, pp. 211–212.

Bickman, L., Teger, A., and Gabriele, T. Dormitory density and helping behavior. *Environment and Behavior*, 1973, *5*, 465–490.

Booth, A. Preliminary report: Urban crowding project. Canadian Ministry of State for Urban Affairs. Mimeograph 1974.

Calhoun, J. B. Population density and social pathology. *Scientific American*, 1962, *206*, 139–148.

Clausen, J. A., and Clausen, S. The effects of family size on parents and children. In J. Fawcett (Ed.), *Psychological perspectives on population*. New York: Basic Books, 1973. Pp. 185–208.

Desor, J. A. Toward a psychological theory of crowding. *Journal of Personality and Social Psychology*, 1972, *21*, 79–83.

Durkheim, E. *The division of labor in society*. New York: Free Press, 1964.

Edney, J. Human territoriality. *Psychological Bulletin*, 1974, *8*(112), 959–975.

Evans, G. W., and Howard, R. B. Personal space. *Psychological Bulletin*, 1973, *80*, 334–344.

Fischer, C. S. Urbanism as a way of life: A review and an agenda. *Sociological Methods and Research*, 1972, *1*, 187–242.

Fischer, C. S. Toward a subcultural theory of urbanism. *American Journal of Sociology*, 1975, *80*, 1319–1341.

Fischer, C. S. *The urban experience*. New York: Harcourt Brace Jovanovich, 1966.

Fischer, C. S., Baldassare, M., and Ofshe, R. J. Crowding studies and urban life: A critical review. *Journal of the American Institute of Planners*. 1975, *41*, 406–418.

Freedman, J. L. The effects of population density on humans. In J. Fawcett (Ed.), *Psychological perspectives on population*. New York: Basic Books, 1973. Pp. 209–238.

Freedman, J. L., and Ehrlich, P. The impact of crowding on human behavior. *The New York Times*, September 11, 1971, 27.

Freedman, J. L., Klevansky, L., and Ehrlich, P. The effects of crowding on human task performance. *Journal of Applied Social Psychology*, 1971, *1*, 7–25.

Freedman, J. L., Levy, A. S., Buchanan, R. W., and Price, J. Crowding and human aggressiveness. *Journal of Experimental Social Psychology*, 1972, *8*, 528–548.

Galle, O. R., Gove, W. R., and McPherson, J. M. Population density and pathology: What are the relations for man? *Science*, 1972, *176*, 23–30.

Gans, H. Urbanism and suburbanism as ways of life: A re-evaluation of definitions. In A. Rose (Ed.), *Human behavior and social processes*. Boston: Houghton Mifflin, 1962. Pp. 625–648. (a)

Gans, H. *The urban villagers*. New York: Free Press, 1962. (b)

Gans, H. *The Levittowners*. New York: Free Press, 1967.

Gillis, A. R. Population density and social pathology: The case of building type, social allowance, and juvenile delinquency. *Social Forces*, 1974, *53*(2), 306–314.

Glass, D., and Singer, J. *Urban stress: Experiments on noise and social stressors*. New York: Academic Press, 1972.

Griffitt, W., and Veitch, R. Hot and crowded: Influences of population density and temperature on interpersonal affective behavior. *Journal of Personality and Social Psychology*, 1971, *17*, 92–98.

Hall, E. T. *The hidden dimension*. New York: Doubleday, 1966.

Hawley, A. *Human ecology*. New York: Ronald Press, 1950.

Hawley, A. Population density and the city. *Demography*, 1972, *9*, 521–529.

Helson, H. Adaptation level as a basis for a qualitative theory of frames of reference. *Psychological Review*, 1948, *55*, 297–313.

Hutt, C., and Vaizey, M. Differential effects of group density on social behavior. *Nature*, 1966, *209*, 1371–1372.

Lewis, O. Urbanization without breakdown: A case study. *Scientific Monthly*, 1952, *75*, 31–41.

Lewis, O. Further observations on the folk–urban continuum with special reference to Mexico City. In P. Hauser and L. Schnore (Eds.), *The study of urbanization*. New York: Wiley, 1965. Pp. 491–503.

Loo, C. The effects of spatial density on the social behavior of children. *Journal of Applied Social Psychology*, 1972, *2*, 4, 372–381.

Loo, C. Deriving hypotheses for researching the effects of crowding in experimental settings. Paper presented to the American Psychological Association Meetings, Montreal, 1973.

Meier, R. *A communications theory of urban growth*. Cambridge, Mass.: M.I.T. Press, 1962.

Michelson, W., and Garland, K. The differential role of crowded homes and dense residential areas in the incidence of selected symptoms of human pathology. Research Paper No. 67, Centre for Urban and Community Studies, University of Toronto, 1974.

Milgram, S. The experience of living in cities. *Science*, 1970, *167*, 1461–1468.

Mitchell, R. E. Some social implications of high density housing. *American Sociological Review*, 1971, *36*, 18–29.

Mitchell, R. E. Ethnographic and historical perspectives on relationships between physical and socio-spatial environments. Sociological Symposium, 1975, *14*, 25–40.

Newman, O. *Defensible space*. New York: Collier, 1973.

Park, R. The city: Suggestions for the investigation of human behavior in the urban environment. (First published, 1916.) In R. Sennet (Ed.), *Classic essays on the culture of cities*. New York: Appleton-Century-Crofts, 1967.

Proshansky, H., Ittelson, W., and Rivlin, L. Freedom of choice and behavior in a physical setting. In H. Proshansky, W. Ittelson, and L. Rivlin (Eds.). *Environmental psychology*. New York: Holt, Rinehart and Winston, 1970. Pp. 173–183.

Ross, M., Layton, B., Erickson, B., and Schopler, J. Affect, facial regard, and reactions to crowding. *Journal of Personality and Social Psychology*, 1973, *28*(1), 69–76.

Sherrod, D. R. Crowding, perceived control, and behavioral after effects. *Journal of Applied Social Psychology*, 1974, *4*(2), 171–186.

Simmel, G. The metropolis and mental life. In R. Sennett (Ed.), *Classic essays on the culture of .cities*. New York: Appleton-Century-Crofts, 1969. Pp. 47–60.

Sjoberg, G. Theory and research in urban sociology. In R. Guttman and D. Popenoe (Eds.), *Neighborhood, city, and metropolis*. New York: Random House, 1970. Pp. 85–108.

Smith, S., and Haythorn, W. Effects of compatability, crowding, group size, and leadership seniority on stress, anxiety, hostility, and annoyance in isolated groups. *Journal of Personality and Social Psychology*, 1972, *22*(1), 67–79.

Sommer, R. *Personal space: The behavioral basis for design*. Englewood Cliffs, N.J.: Prentice-Hall, 1969.

Stokols, D. On the distinction between density and crowding: Some implications for future research. *Psychological Review*, 1972, *79*(3), 275–277. (a)

Stokols, D. A social–psychological model of human crowding phenomena. *Journal of the American Institute of Planners*, 1972, *38*, 72–83. (b)

Stokols, D. The relation between micro and macro crowding phenomena: Some implications for environmental research and design. *Man–Environment Systems*, 1973, *3*(3), 139, 149.

Stokols, D. The experience of crowding in primary and secondary environments. Paper presented to the American Psychological Association Meetings, New Orleans, 1974.

Stokols, D., Rall, M., Pinner, B., and Schopler, J. Physical, social, and personal determinants of the perception of crowding. *Environment and Behavior*, 1973, *5*, 87–115.

Suttles, G. *The social order of the slum*. Chicago: University of Chicago Press, 1968.

Wicker, A. Theoretical developments pertaining to personal space and crowding: Comments. Paper presented to the Western Psychological Meetings, San Francisco, 1974.

Winsborough, H. The social consequences of high population density. *Law and Contemporary Problems*, 1965, *30*(1), 120–126.

Wirth, L. Urbanism as a way of life. *American Journal of Sociology*, 1938, *44*, 1–24.

Zlutnick, S., and Altmann, I. Crowding and human behavior. In J. Wohlwill and D. Carson (Eds.), *Environment and the social sciences*. Washington, D.C.: American Psychological Association, 1972. Pp. 44–58.

SECTION V
Directions of Research on □ Environment and Behavior

The chapters in this section examine current trends and future directions of environment–behavioral research. The chapter by Brewster Smith traces the intellectual roots of ecological and environmental psychology and links the recent expansion of these areas to the environmentalist movement (cf. Sills, 1975) of the late 1960's and early 1970's.

According to Smith, it is unlikely that environment–behavioral research will emerge as either a theoretically-focused or a problem-oriented field. On the one hand, the environmental context of behavior is viewed as too all-pervasive to permit the delineation of a theoretically focused field. On the other hand, the collaboration of psychologists with academics and professionals from other disciplines is, as yet, too recent and limited to warrant a problem-specific representation of research on environment and behavior.

As for future directions of this research, Smith advocates the continued development of working relationships among psychologists, architects, and planners and an increasing emphasis on descriptive studies for the purposes of discovering the ways in which people actively utilize the environment in various kinds of settings.

An alternative characterization of the environment-and-behavior field is presented by Irwin Altman. A general strategy for research on human–environment transactions is outlined that emphasizes social units, rather than single behaviors, as the basic elements of study. Several distinguishing features of social units are identified, including their incorporation of multiple behavioral levels and the systemic, patterned, and dynamic organization of these levels.

Although social-unit analysis does not constitute a theory of human–environment relations, it does provide a possible basis for distinguishing research on environment and behavior from traditional areas of psychological research (e.g., social psychology). Specifically the social-unit orientation suggests a number of directions and questions for future research that may prompt a more coherent conceptualization of the environment-and-behavior field. For example: What are the crucial personal needs and collective goals that serve to organize complex patterns of behavior within individuals, groups, and communities? Under what environmental conditions will the relative weightings and salience of these behavior-guiding goals shift? These questions suggest the interesting possibility of extending strategies of social-unit analysis to a systematic assessment of the person–environment and group–environment optimization process (cf. Stokols, Chapter 1).

The final chapter, by Arthur Patterson, provides an overview of methodological developments in environment–behavioral research. The experimental, quasi-experimental, and descriptive research designs most commonly used in the environment-and-behavior field are discussed, and an analysis of the respective weaknesses of these designs is presented in relation to the criteria of internal and external validity (Campbell and Stanley, 1966). Also the usage of multiple or convergent measurement-strategies (Campbell and Fiske, 1959) and other techniques for reducing sources of invalidity in environment–behavioral research are specified.

In conclusion, it should be noted that the chapters in this volume reflect not only some common substantive and procedural emphases but also certain differences of opinion among researchers in the field. Whereas some authors emphasize the barriers to developing a theoretically focused field of environment and behavior (cf. Proshansky and O'Hanlon, Chapter 4; Smith, Chapter 14), others point toward emerging themes and strategies that eventually may contribute to a more coherent conceptualization of the field (cf. Stokols, Chapter 1; Altman, Chapter 15; Patterson, Chapter 16). The relative utility of these orientations toward the field should become clearer during the next decade of environment–behavioral research.

References

Campbell, D., and Fiske, D. Convergent and discriminant validation by the multitrait–multimethod matrix. *Psychological Bulletin*, 1959, *56*, 81–105.

Campbell, D., and Stanley, J. *Experimental and quasi-experimental design for research*. Chicago: Rand McNally, 1966.

Sills, D. C. The environmental movement and its critics. *Human Ecology*, 1975, *3*, 1–41.

Some Problems of Strategy in Environmental Psychology

14

M. BREWSTER SMITH

In spite of some quite respectable accomplishments, environmental psychology is still just emerging from the state in which it was a label looking for a content or an agenda. Environmental psychology *ought* to exist, and an increasing number of psychologists are trying to provide its substance. But the label gained prominence before consensual content had emerged. The field as we now know it did not arise from intrinsic urgencies in the trajectory of psychological science. This is an inherently embarrassing state of affairs.

The label caught on among psychologists with the initial surge of the environmentalist movement (Sills, 1975), a fad or fashion of the late 1960's and early 1970's that identified problems that will be with us for a long time, if we are to survive as a species. A literal interpretation of *environmental psychology* might include the entire interplay between people and their environments, a two-way street that could encompass most of psychology and the other social and behavioral sciences too. Actually the competing conceptions of environmental psychology as it is developing are more modest and divide roughly into those that are *theoretically focused* and those that are *problem-centered*.

As an *amicus curiae* who has watched the field develop with eager hopefulness stemming from a strong sense of the unique urgencies of our present human predicament (Smith, 1973a), not a specialist or worker in the environmental vineyard, I am not equipped to undertake a general review of progress in environmental psychology. Important comprehensive statements that together gave the field its initial shape would include books by Hall (1966) and by Sommer (1969) on proxemics—the spatial aspect of human interaction, the book of interdisciplinary readings edited

M. BREWSTER SMITH ● University of California at Santa Cruz.

by Proshansky, Ittelson, and Rivlin (1970) that sought through its selections to provide a kind of ostensive definition, the long review article by Craik (1970), and the programmatic essay by Wohlwill (1970). This volume as a whole attempts to display the present state of environmental psychology. My aim in this chapter is modest: to contribute to the resolution of environmental psychology's identity problem by discussing very selectively some representative guiding conceptions, both theoretically focused and problem-centered.

Theoretically Focused Views

Various psychologists have attempted to establish a conceptual framework for psychology that would give proper attention to the environmental determinants of behavior. Among the major theoretical progenitors of environmental psychology, Edward Tolman (1932) is clearly central. In spite of the lack of any continuity provided by disciples, his own theoretical writings, never self-promoted to the status of a "school," contain ideas that remain alive today when those of his contemporaries Hull, Spence, and Guthrie are dead. A holistic cognitive behaviorism such as Tolman's requires—and provided—differentiated concepts for the behavioral environment that the organism "maps" cognitively. Isidor Chein (1954) built directly on Tolman's concepts in his early essay, a particularly incisive statement of the overarching importance of environmental factors in the control of everyday behavior, providing an array of useful conceptual distinctions and an indictment of the wrongheadedness of psychologists in slighting the environment in their preoccupation with inferred inner dispositions and processes. (Chein's analysis should have been influential, but it wasn't; evidently, the time was not yet ripe.)

Apart from attention in his own writings to the problems of conceptualizing the environment from a psychological perspective, Tolman also stood as intellectual and personal sponsor to two major European émigré psychologists of the next generation whose influence on contemporary thinking is more obvious: Egon Brunswik and Kurt Lewin. Like Tolman, Brunswik (1956; Hammond, 1966), who introduced the concept of *ecological validity* and proposed a heuristically suggestive "lens model" of the relationship between gross environmental facts and their cognitive equivalents as mediated by sensory–perceptual processes, had no talent for organizing movements or founding schools. But his ideas have a continuing life, in their own right and through the work of his students, especially D. T. Campbell and K. Hammond. Lewin (1946), who *was* a founder and a charismatic leader, gave impetus to the emergence of experimental social psychology after World War II. His emphasis on the psychological analysis of the actor's total situation, "life space," or behavioral environment (Koffka, 1935) is an acknowledged influence on the work of Roger Barker (see immediately below). But in retrospect, Lewin's legacy is anamalous. His quasi-topological "mathematics" for the representation of psychological situations and forces now looks like an irrelevant curiosity; his "field theoretical" program for psychology remains unrealized, an interesting perspective left stranded by the moving front of controversy; some of his experimentally based concepts (level of aspiration, Zeigarnik effects, and autocratic versus democratic leadership styles, among them) have been absorbed into general psychology; but the experimental social psychology that he and his students had so much to do with launching has turned in directions that show little continuity with his concerns. And with special respect to psychological formulations about the environment of behavior, Lewin never came to a satisfactory resolution of the relationship between Koffka's geographical and behavioral environments (Murray's [1938] alpha and beta press)—the environment as it exists independently and the psychological environment or life space as we infer it to exist for the behaving person.

The only theoretically focused approach to environmental psychology that has been pursued far enough to allow us to take stock of its accomplishments is the ecological psychology of Roger Barker and his colleagues.[1] As a stream of scientific development, ecological psychology Barker-style is remarkably self-contained. Its most recent and ambitious product, a volume (Barker and Schoggen, 1973) reporting the detailed comparison of the behavioral environments provided by two small rural towns in Kansas and Yorkshire and their changes over a decade, concludes with a brief bibliography that lists virtually all of the publications that fall within the tradition—and very few others. Barker and Schoggen pay no heed to other relevant streams in psychology or—what is more serious—to the relation of their own concepts and methods to ones customarily employed by sociologists and anthropologists sharing much the same concerns.

Over the years, Barker has argued persuasively that a very high proportion of everyday behavior is appropriate to and in some sense under the control of the settings in which it occurs. Baseball playing occurs at baseball games, not in church; the buying and selling of particular products take place in the appropriate offices and stores, much less frequently elsewhere. If psychologists really aspire to give an orderly account of behavior, let alone to predict or control it, they should attend as closely to the structure of the human environment as to the properties and predispositions of the behaving person. To say as much is to belabor the obvious—a realm of the obvious that sociologists and anthropologists acknowledge but that psychologists in the main have trained themselves to ignore.

[1] I draw in the following paragraphs on Smith (1974c). An ambitious attempt to provide a coherent theoretical formulation of human spatial behavior (privacy, territoriality, personal space, and crowding) has recently been published by Altman (1975).

Barker and his colleagues have developed criteria and rating methods according to which the term *behavior setting* acquires a stable technical meaning (see Barker, 1968). The core of their conception is a fusion of physical and cultural criteria (annoyingly, they do not use the term *culture*): an identifiable physical milieu to which is linked a specifiable "standing pattern" or program for behavior. It then becomes possible to catalog the entire array of behavior settings that occur in a particular community or social institution (schools were productively studied in this vein by Barker and Gump, 1964); to identify similar settings or "genotypes" (for example, bowling alley, drug store); and to classify the behavior settings on a variety of dimensions: their "action-pattern" qualities (aesthetics, business, education, government, nutrition, personal appearance, physical health, professional involvement, recreation, and social contact); "behavior-mechanism" qualities (affective behavior, gross motor activity, manipulation, and talking); "attendance attributes" (by age group); "beneficence attributes" (the age group benefited); "local-autonomy" qualities (is the setting under local control?); "authority-system" qualities (private enterprises, government agencies, churches, schools, and voluntary associations); and "inhabitant attributes" (age, sex, social class, and race). Measures or estimates of "behavior output" can then be linked to the characterizations of behavior settings or "habitat." Barker and Schoggen (1973) used five quantitative measures: person-hours of behavior; inhabitant–setting intersections (in which each encounter of person with setting counts as a unit); "claim operations" (in effect, the number of identified individuals performing roles essential to the operation of the setting or class of settings, though the sociological term *role* is not mentioned); leader acts (inhabitant–setting intersections in a leader or executive capacity); and number of leaders (correspondingly identified).

The point of all the detailed description and comparison (the task was immense, and the mind boggles that it was done) eludes the reader until rather late in the Barker–Schoggen volume. There it is brought to bear on a genuinely interesting cluster of predictions, having to do with the ratio of the number of inhabitants to the "size" of their habitat and particularly to the number of jobs that have to be done if the various behavior settings that comprise the habitat are to be operated and maintained. The inhabitants of "Midwest" (the Kansas town) are fewer than those of "Yoredale" the Yorkshire town) but have about as rich a human habitat, one that requires the inhabitants to man more "slots" to keep it going. So the Midwesterners, like the students in the small school studied by Barker and Gump (1964), are busier, more involved, and more important—seemingly a good state of affairs from an American perspective.

The attractiveness, but also the limitations, of this "undermanning hypothesis" are apparent in Barker and Schoggen's analysis of the contrasting systems of child rearing in Midwest and Yoredale. Midwest has a "melting pot" approach:

> Children are best prepared for adulthood by participating in a wide variety of the town's settings. (p. 405)

According to the contrasting "enlightened colonial" approach attributed to Yoredale,

> children are best prepared for adulthood by removing them from the general, public settings and placing them in specially arranged and reserved children's settings under the direction of experts who, over a period of time, are able to prepare the children for entrance into the life of the community. (p. 405)

And these differences, in turn, are traced to the fact that Midwest, but not Yoredale, has bitten off more than its adults can manage unaided.

> The behavior-generating system of Yoredale could probably be maintained and operated by its adults alone, but it is clear that the habitat-claims [jobs to be done] of Midwest are far beyond the capacity of its adult inhabitants. . . . *The Midwest system requires the responsible participation of other than its most able class of human components.* (p. 407—italics are the authors)

There is an element of circularity here that is characteristic of Barker's theory: settings requiring the central participation of children and youth, which would not exist and would not need to exist without them, are differentially characteristic of Midwest and contribute to its quantitatively richer human habitat. Think, for example, of school plays, present in Midwest but not in Yoredale.

As an example of ecological psychology, the Midwest–Yoredale comparison leaves my ambivalence unresolved. Barker and Schoggen tell us more about Midwest and Yoredale than we would ever think to ask, as if they were providing a detailed ethnography for deposit in a time capsule. In quantification and in behaviorally relevant description, their work is obviously an improvement on the less formal methods to which anthropologists are accustomed in the description of even smaller communities. But the cost and the labor are really too great for the result, except to show, once and for all, that the task can actually be accomplished. What took decades to complete with Midwest and Yoredale, moreover, could hardly be done at all with Lawrence, Kansas—or Kansas City, much less Chicago or London. Although it is important to show that the analysis can be carried out in the simpler case, I do not expect to see the study repeated, and I certainly do not expect its methods to be extended to the entire texture of modern metropolitan life. Rather, the concepts and methods and the simple theory that goes with them can be drawn upon selectively and adapted for use in other, more complex settings. While Barker and his students have contributed notably to the naturalistic characterization of the "stream of behavior" (Barker, 1963), the main thrust of their ecological psychology amounts to careful descriptive sociology and anthropology done by psychologists, unfortunately without reference to relevant overlapping concepts pertaining to roles, statuses, norms, and situations, as developed in these sister social sciences.

All the same, there is merit in their coherent paradigm—and in the area under review, Barker has been virtually unique in having such a paradigm. The concept of behavior setting as embracing *both* milieu and behavior pattern, both physical and cultural environment, is useful. If we take it seriously, we are forewarned of the dangers in naïvely trying to relate physical milieu to behavioral consequences without the mediation of culture. Theorizing about the popular topic of *crowding* has only recently overcome this naïveté. Crowding in the traditional Pueblo, in the East Indian extended-family compound, and in central Harlem (a ghetto chaos populated by relatively recent rural migrants) does not, of course, present a single psychological phenomenon. Exclusive attention to the physical dimension of density can lead to absurdities if the culturally provided "programs for behavior" associated with the physical settings are ignored. We cannot wisely apply Calhoun's (1962) "behavioral sink" of mice directly to men.

Problem-Centered Views

There is no end to the conceivable problems with which a problem-focused environmental psychology might be concerned. The most obvious, important, and promising problems have to do with (1) how to understand and cope with the human ingredient in the present crisis in our larger ecosystems, that is, how to contribute to the objectives of the environmentalist movement; and (2) how to contribute to the development of a more humanly advantageous man-made or built environment. By far the greater effort in environmental psychology has been devoted to the second class of problems.

Psychology and the Environmentalist Movement

By now, the educated public is fully aware of the problem context of environmental disruption, although there are deep controversies about priorities among competing interests and values (especially those of the middle-class Sierra Club versus those of blue-collar businessmen in the AFL–CIO, who want an expanding economy with more jobs *now*, versus those of the urban poor; between the interests of the industrialized and the "developing" countries); about particular causal models or interpretations; and about time schedules. The frontiers of planet Earth are closing or are closed. Current worldwide trends of population, food consumption, pollution, and energy and resource depletion lead to absurdity or catastrophe if they are extrapolated very far—and we are compelled to extrapolate many of them an uncomfortable distance by the ballisticlike trajectories (see Platt, 1971) in which they are set for at least the near future. In this sense, the grim forecast of the Club of Rome simulation model (Meadows, Randers, and Behrens, 1972) cannot be dismissed, even if its simplifications and omissions fault it in detail and in time schedule. Even with the addition of damping factors and feedback loops, growth curves cannot be extrapolated indefinitely without breakdown in the ecological system. The succession of energy and food "crises" that have followed the generally critical reception of the book suggests that we should not allow the critics to lull us into complacency. Whether population (Ehrlich and Ehrlich, 1972) or technology (Commoner, 1971) is the more strategic factor in our predicament is a nice point, an important one, yet one that does not make the general warning less cogent. (See Sills [1975] for a scholarly review of the issues dividing the environmentalists and their critics, with a full bibliography.)

The most mind-gripping psychological conceptualization of the predicament underlying our difficulties with the global ecosystem was made not by a psychologist but by the biologist Garrett Hardin (1968) in his classic essay on "The Tragedy of the Commons." According to Hardin's parable, the immediate utility or gain to each sheep-owner of adding one more sheep to the flock grazing on the commons exceeds his share in the loss to all caused by that sheep's contribution to overgrazing. The pursuit of individual gain leads to disastrous loss for all. The earth is a semicommons in regard to food and population (but we are putting up fences); the water and air are commons for the disposal of pollutants; freeways are commons where drivers in cars are substituted for sheep. (The difference is not big!) This is essentially an economist's way of thinking, in terms of rational action to maximize utility. At the origins of economic theory, Adam Smith thought that an Unseen Hand somehow produced the common good out of the sum of self-interested actions. In the Tragedy of the Commons, no such Unseen Hand is evident.

Another nonpsychologist, the biophysicist–futurologist John Platt (1973), generalized Hardin's model in more explicitly psychological terms in his valuable conception of *social traps:* "situations in society that contain traps formally like a fish trap, where men or organizations or whole societies get themselves started in some direction or some set of relationships that later prove to be unpleasant or lethal and that they see no easy way to back out of or to avoid" (p. 641). Platt employed Skinnerian terminology to identify generic cases in which behavior that is rewarding or reinforcing to each individual in the short run is catastrophic to all in the long run. The concept as he developed it helps to clarify many of our most difficult social problems, from armament races (where nation-states stand in for individuals) to the environmental problems of concern to Hardin. Human motivational structure tends to lock us into these traps, as the smoker or the drug addict is locked into his habit. Though his terminology is Skinnerian, Platt's analysis is equally compatible with a more human psychology of beliefs, desires, and incentives, including Lewin's (1964) old analysis of reward and punishment; that is, it is compatible with the common-sense psychology to which any more ambitious scientific system has to accommodate because it is obviously right in broad outlines.

Whether we are Skinnerians, humanistic psychologists, or simply common-sense psychologists, the Hardin–Platt economic model suggests two strategic questions as challenges to conceptually guided, applied research: *How good is its fit* to any particular ecological problem? And to the extent that it fits, *how can we modify the incentive structure so that individual incentives motivate behavior toward the common good?* How, in effect, do we engineer situations of *synergy,*—the term for a man-made Unseen Hand that Maslow (1971) adopted from Ruth Benedict (Maslow and Honigman, 1970).

How good is the fit? In the Skinnerian version, the model is dependably mechanistic; in the economic version, just as dependably rationalistic. For most practical purposes, they amount to the same thing. But the fit to a particular environmental problem may be good, approximate, or very poor indeed. I have suggested (Smith, 1973b), in regard to population issues, that we badly need systematic research to determine the extent to which planful choice (or reinforcement-maximizing behavior) *is* involved in human fertility—for what kinds of people, in what circumstances. Before we can afford to let ourselves be guided by the model, we need to know in much more detail the terms of choice, the time perspective within which it is made, and what is taken for granted as outside the framework of choice. Similar considerations will arise in the case of each serious application of the model.

And how can we *modify the incentive structure?* There are incentives that follow from changing features of social structure, as, for example, the presumed effect on the value of children attendant on modernization and on changing women's roles. Direct economic incentives can be brought to bear, as in the Oregon law forbidding "no deposit–no return" bottles. Economists speak in this connection of "internalizing the externalities," for example, charging industrial firms the equivalent of the actual social costs incurred as a result of the pollutants that they release upon the "commons," thus converting what had been "external" costs (that did not figure in the firm's profit-and-loss balance) into "internal" costs (that do). Psychologists could advantageously—I was about to say, profitably—participate with economists in analyzing the incentive patterns that maintain a particular status quo in designing new incentive schemes, and in evaluating their effectiveness so as to guide their modification or redesign. Given the economists' typical fascination with abstract models, psychologists may be expected to add a needed component of pragmatic realism to the collaboration.

The incentives that enter the analysis of social traps involve human preferences within a scheme of *cultural values.* These can change, and there are indications of a substantial change afoot, especially among the educated young in Western industrialized societies (see Yankelovich, Inc., 1972). Not only in the marginal "counterculture" is there questioning of our pre-viously taken-for-granted values: the bigger the better, economic growth as a criterion of national health, etc. Psychologists ought to be monitoring what could be a very important adaptive change in cultural values, one that Reich (1970) romantically evoked in his *Greening of America,* which was being read by our students only a few years ago. If we gain more self-conscious understanding of cultural changes that psychologists too partici-pate in but (fortunately) cannot direct, our collective ability to guide our future in humanly and ecologically desirable directions should be en-hanced.

Psychology and the Man-Made Environment

The second problem-centered theme to which I call attention in this ven-ture at agenda setting arises in the context of the "urban crisis," though its scope is broader. Though the urban crisis went out of style before the environmentalist movement emerged, the crisis is still with us. And since the two foci of concern are often seen as competitive, they unfortunately *become* competitive in fact, although in the longer run they cannot be neatly separated. As ecological problems close in on us, we all live in the same world.

The urban environment, which is now the environment of most of us, is a man-made environment. Part of the urban problem follows from the fact that most of us—not just the ex-southern blacks and Appalachian poor whites—are newly urban over a generation or so. We haven't had time to shape a viable urban culture by the usual slow process of cultural trial-and-error. Our urban man-made environment is jerry-built, and it would be miraculous were it to turn out to fit human needs. Clearly it does not.

My awareness of the difficulties in bringing the resources of psychol-ogy and the other behavioral sciences to bear in improving the design of man-made environments was sensitized and heightened by the hap-penstance of participating in two conferences organized since 1971 by the National Institute of Child Health and Human Development. The NICHD staff had the reasonable idea that if they could bring psychologists, psychia-trists, and social scientists, on the one hand, together with architects and planners, on the other, wisdom could be collated, or at least a communica-tive social process catalyzed, that would further the objective of designing man-made environments more conducive to optimal child development. It didn't work out that simply. On both occasions, the parties to the discussion—well-chosen persons of competence and goodwill, who were strongly in sympathy with the NICHD objective—found themselves in bad communication and at cross-purposes.

The difficulty was easy to identify but hard to overcome. Psychologists and designers approached the problem from radically different perspec-tives. As men of action committed to the building of man-made environments one way or another, regardless of the adequacy of information and theory about human behavior that may be available, the designers wanted integrated wisdom from psychologists to help them do better a job that they would do in some fashion anyway. They wanted lists of developmental human needs that buildings and neighborhoods and cities ought to satisfy, and priorities among them. The research-oriented psychologists, on their part, valiantly resisted most attempts to extract such wisdom. In their critical awareness of the insecure status and uncertain relevance of psychological knowledge, they found themselves too tongue-tied to express even their latent consensuses, where professional wisdom may indeed surpass common sense. While the thoughtful, avant-garde designers assembled for the conferences necessarily thought in *systems* terms, the psychologists tended to be fixated on *variables* by their professional training. The psychiatrists present, to be sure, moved in more confidently with "wisdom" where the angel–psychologists feared to tread: like designers, psychiatrists too are committed to action in the face of uncertainty. Of course, the psychologists were happy neither with the quality of the psychiatrists' wisdom nor with the fact that it was the psychiatrists who were offering it. The psychologists fell readily into their familiar critical role, emphasizing how little is known. Distrust arising from inappropriate expectations of one another created large barriers.

Even under the pressures of such conferences, it is not hard to identify features of the man-made environment that are clearly bad. On anyone's list might be the slum; the high-rise buildings in urban redevelopment projects that have become cesspools of crime; the single-family home of the suburban ideal, which is becoming a wasteful luxury that cannot conceivably be extended to all with equity. Less obviously bad, but in serious doubt, are residential segregation by age, class, and ethnic groups and the functional segregation of work, family, and recreation.

When it comes to advising designers about good features that they should seek to realize, the fact becomes inescapable that we are dealing with controversial human preferences and values that elude consensus. Rather quickly discussion polarizes between those who would seek better facts to buttress an expert role aimed at serving human *needs* and those who despair of such expertise and seek instead a collaborative relationship responsive to human *wants* with flexibility, openness, and participation. (The latter perspective has radical implications for the design of environments that get frozen in concrete, to serve the diverse purposes of different users, over long periods of time.)

If psychologists could learn to work with architects and planners, they might put their technical skill to use in eliciting and elucidating people's preferences. In spite of the pitfalls (after all, the extinct Edsel was designed according to specifications set by market surveys), this ancillary role could help. More important, we have to study in much more detail how people actually use their environment. It is not enough to stay on the safer and easier ground of studying how they perceive their environment or wish it to be. Still further from what is easy is the task of assessing how they are affected by it, which must come to terms with the wide range of human adaptability and also with consideration that there are some adaptations that may be dehumanizing to make!

My limited exposure as a psychologist to problems in this area (we share a common exposure as thoughtful persons-in-the-street) suggests several challenges to which psychologists might be preparing themselves to respond.

First is the need for psychologists to develop close working relationships with designers and planners, to penetrate the barriers just noted and readjust mutual expectations to a point where real collaboration becomes possible. This is really a prerequisite for any contributions from psychology that stand a chance of being useful. We have very little experience with such a complementary interdisciplinary relationship between dissimilars: most of our discouraging lore of interdisciplinary involvement has come from our dealings with sister disciplines and professions, all in competition for the same ecological niche.

Then, assuming that interprofessional communication has been established, I think we can go further than our cautious scientific habits usually let us in collating professional wisdom about human requirements that bear on planning and design. A good man-made environment for children would certainly provide for safety; for opportunity and challenge for physical activity, exploration, play, and games appropriate to age; for ready retreat to home and comfort; and for progressively wider spheres of social contact with age. Further specifications of such a list could readily emerge from collaboration between designers and developmental psychologists. A new kind of "human-factors" enterprise could emerge in which the *human* factor is criterial.

Descriptive ecological research, guided by the experience and concepts of the Barker group, could provide close-grained information about how people use their man-made environments, as an aid to the architect and planner. Such research could merge into evaluative studies of particular buildings, projects, or new towns, the most ambitious involving the kind of social experimentation that Campbell (1971) has advocated.

Concluding Comments

In these selective remarks about some problems of strategy in environmental psychology, I have obviously ignored many lines of activity in which psychologists are productively involved: studies of personal space, crowding, and privacy; studies of restricted environments in outer space, the Arctic, or underseas; studies of the comparative psychological quality of cities—and so on for a growing list. I will nevertheless venture some tentative judgments about the shape of the environmental psychology that is emerging.

Theoretically focused environmental psychology is not yet a subdiscipline, and I see no good reason for expecting it to become one. The environmental context of human behavior is too all-pervasive to warrant the segregation of a theoretically oriented environmental psychology from the rest of the field. The Barker tradition of "ecological psychology" has made interesting contributions and has developed concepts and methods that could be applied to a wider range of problems than the self-contained group has taken on. The future, I hope, will break down its isolation and also make explicit the relationship of the Barker kitbag to the corresponding tools of sociology and anthropology. Meanwhile this tradition has most usefully kept before psychologists the task of relevantly describing the environments of behavior. Particular subareas, such as the spatial behavior dealt with by Altman (1975), may lend themselves to coherent theoretical treatment.

Neither is problem-focused environmental psychology well conceived as a discipline. It is one facet of an interdiscipline. Psychologists need to learn how to work with others who know about different pieces of the problems at hand: for the environmentalist issues, with biologists, chemists, demographers, geographers, economists, and political scientists; for the ones concerning the man-made environment, with architects, designers, and planners. We have had little experience with such collaboration with specialists whose competences are far removed from our own. Unfortunately university organization typically hampers it.

In our emerging problem-centered roles, I hope that psychologists can aspire to become collaborators, consultants, and resources to people to enhance their ability to use their environments in ways that suit them, rather than technocratic experts who plan for instead of with people. Here I only repeat in a new context Leona Tyler's (1973) eloquent plea in her presidential address to the American Psychological Association.

There may be no discipline of environmental psychology, but people's interrelations with their natural and man-made environment pose exceptionally interesting and important challenges to psychologists.

References

Altman, I. *The environment and social behavior.* Belmont, Calif.: Brooks/Cole, 1975.

Barker, R. G. (Ed.). *The stream of behavior.* New York: Appleton-Century-Crofts, 1963.

Barker, R. G. *Ecological psychology: Concepts and methods for studying the environment of human behavior.* Stanford, Calif.: Stanford University Press, 1968.

Barker, R. G., and Gump, P. *Big school, small school.* Stanford, Calif.: Stanford University Press, 1964.

Barker, R. G., and Schoggen, P. *Qualities of community life.* San Francisco: Jossey-Bass, 1973.

Brunswik, E. *Perception and the representative design of psychological experiments.* Berkeley and Los Angeles: University of California Press, 1956.

Calhoun, J. B. Population density and social pathology. *Scientific American,* 1962, *206,* 139–146.

Campbell, D. T. Methods for the experimenting society. Distinguished Scientific Contribution Address, American Psychological Association, Washington, D.C., September, 1971.

Chein, I. The environment as a determinant of behavior. *The Journal of Social Psychology,* 1954, *39,* 115–127.

Commoner, B. *The closing circle.* New York: Knopf, 1971.

Craik, K. H. Environmental psychology. In K. H. Craik, B. Kleinmuntz, R. Rosnow, R. Rosenthal, J. A. Cheyne, and R. H. Walters (Eds.), *New directions in psychology* (Vol. 4). New York: Holt, Rinehart and Winston, 1970. Pp. 1–121.

Ehrlich, P., and Ehrlich, A. H. *Population, resources, environment: Issues in human ecology.* San Francisco: Freeman, 1972.

Hall, E. T. *The hidden dimension.* Garden City, N.Y.: Doubleday, 1966.

Hammond, K. R. (Ed.). *The psychology of Egon Brunswik.* New York: Holt, Rinehart and Winston, 1966.

Hardin, G. The tragedy of the commons. *Science,* 1968, *162,* 1243–1248.

Koffka, K. *Principles of Gestalt psychology.* New York: Harcourt Brace, 1935.

Lewin, K. Behavior and development as a function of the total situation. In L. Carmichael (Ed.), *Manual of child psychology.* New York: Wiley, 1946.

Maslow, A. H. *The farther reaches of human nature.* New York: Viking, 1971.

Maslow, A. H., and Honigman, J. J. Synergy: Some notes of Ruth Benedict. *American Anthropologist,* 1970, *72,* 320–333.

Meadows, D. H., Meadows, D. L., Randers, J., and Behrens, W. W. *The limits to growth.* New York: Universe Books, 1972.

Murray, H. A. *Explorations in personality.* New York: Oxford University Press, 1938.

Platt, J. How men can shape their future. *Futures,* 1971, *3*(1), 32–47.

Platt, J. Social traps. *American Psychologist,* 1973, *28,* 641–651.

Proshansky, H. M., Ittelson, W. H., and Rivlin, L. G. (Eds.). *Environmental psychology: Man and his physical setting.* New York: Holt, Rinehart and Winston, 1970.

Reich, C. *The greening of America.* New York: Random House, 1970.

Sills, D. L. The environmental movement and its critics. *Human Ecology,* 1975, *3,* 1–41.

Smith, M. B. Is psychology relevant to new priorities? *American Psychologist,* 1973, *28,* 463–471. (Reprinted in M. B. Smith (Ed.), *Humanizing social psychology.* San Francisco: Jossey-Bass, 1974. Pp. 193–208.) (a)

Smith, M. B. A social psychological view of fertility. In J. T. Fawcett (Ed.), *Psychological perspectives on population.* New York: Basic Books, 1973. Pp. 3–18. (Reprinted in M. B. Smith (Ed.), *Humanizing social psychology.* San Francisco: Jossey-Bass, 1974. Pp. 95–113.) (b)

Smith, M. B. Psychology in two small towns. Review of R. G. Barker and P. Schoggen, *Qualities of community life. Science,* 1974, *184,* 671–673.

Sommer, R. *Personal space.* Englewood Cliffs, N.J.: Prentice-Hall, 1969.

Tolman, E. C. *Purposive behavior in animals and men.* New York: Appleton-Century-Crofts, 1932.

Tyler, L. Design for a hopeful psychology. *American Psychologist,* 1973, *28,* 1021–1029.

Wohlwill, J. F. The emerging discipline of environmental psychology. *American Psychologist,* 1970, *25,* 303–312.

Yankelovich, D., Inc. *The changing values on campus: Political and personal attitudes of today's college students.* New York: Pocket Books, Washington Square Press, 1972.

Research on Environment and Behavior: A Personal Statement of Strategy

15

IRWIN ALTMAN

Introduction

This chapter describes an approach to research on environment and behavior that also has implications for social-psychological research in general. I will not offer a "theory," in terms of hypotheses and testable propositions, nor will I present a "methodology," in the sense of procedures or techniques. Rather I will set forth a general strategy for research on environmental and social-psychological phenomena, a kind of perspective within which one can pose specific theoretical and methodological questions.

The central feature of the proposal is an emphasis on *social units* as the basic element of study, in addition to the traditional emphasis on *behavior* as the focus of investigation. Put simply, I believe that we should be as interested in understanding "real" social units, such as couples, teams, and families, as we are in understanding single behaviors, such as aggression, territoriality, and performance; that is, we should come away from a piece of research with some understanding of social units—how they are similar or different from one another and how a social group operates or changes over time. My belief is that much research in the environment-and-behavior field, and in social psychology, is primarily *behavior-oriented*, not *social-unit–oriented*. What I propose is that we enlarge the definition of what it is we study to include both an understanding of *behavior* and an understanding of *social entities*, not one or the other alone.

The next section elaborates on the concept of social units and discusses

---

IRWIN ALTMAN ● University of Utah, Salt Lake City.

how they might be studied and how this approach is similar to and different from other ways of studying human functioning. Then some case studies are presented to illustrate how the approach can be applied to a variety of conceptual and empirical issues. The final section of the chapter considers general implications of this approach and guides for its application.

Before the discussion, two caveats are in order. First, I do not intend to offer a "better" way to do research but only a strategy that offers a supplementary view of environmental and social-psychological phenomena. Second, I do not pretend to describe a "new" approach. It is one that is used in some fields in the social and behavioral sciences, such as clinical psychology and anthropology. It is also characteristic of practitioner disciplines, such as architecture, urban planning, and the design fields. What is perhaps unique is the application of social-unit analysis to *research* on environment-and-behavior problems.

The Perspective of Social-Unit Analysis

Social units refer to individuals or groups of people who exist as intact entities, where group members have some psychological and social relationship to one another. A married couple, a family, a group of children playing together, and members of an office group are examples of such social units. Members of these groups may work on jobs and may engage in social behaviors such as talking, laughing and joking, arguing, and being territorial. They may also have various subjective feelings and attitudes about one another, about the place, and about other groups. Furthermore any or all of these behaviors may change over time and with circumstances. Thus people in social units exhibit single behaviors and patterns of behavior that differentiate one group from another and that reflect changes in group functioning.

My belief is that research in the social and behavioral sciences has focused primarily on the *behavior* of social units, and then often on *single* behaviors, with the goals of generalizing and understanding these behaviors as an end in and of themselves; that is, the traditional objective of research has been to understand a given behavior and to see how it shifts with conditions and time. For example, we see separate experiments and experts on performance, nonverbal behavior, environmental perception, territorial behavior, etc. In a sense, we have sliced up social units into layers of behavior with the goal of understanding behavior, not the social entities within which behaviors are embedded. Of course, we state that the long-range objective is to understand social units, but we reason that it is necessary to understand fully the behaviors they exhibit as a preliminary analytic step. While this is certainly a credible position, I believe that it is equally credible to adopt as our goal the *direct description and understanding of social units* and that we should pose such questions as "How is it that family-type A members argue more, show less cooperative behavior, and spend less time together than family-type B members?" or "How is it that this team is more territorial, works less effectively, and has more hostile member relationships than another type of team?" These questions focus on the social unit as the end product of understanding, whereas the behavior-oriented approach emphasizes specific behaviors as the goal of research. I believe that both aims are important to scientific understanding but that the social-unit orientation has been unduly neglected.

One major input to my thinking about social units stemmed from contacts with design professionals, including architects and planners. Over the course of almost a decade, from the middle 1960's to the present time, environmental practitioners and researchers have tried to communicate and work together. But there has always emerged a problem of "miscommunication" and innumerable attempts to "bridge the gap" between research and action. As a participant in many of these dialogues, I wondered why it was that "we" researchers and "they" practitioners could never quite communicate as well as we all hoped to, and some of my observations are described in an earlier article (Altman, 1973). The central feature of that analysis was that practitioners, in their attempt to solve particular problems, focus their energies on understanding a *place*—a home, a community, a city. In so doing they try to learn as much as possible about the place, for example, relevant social phenomena such as the privacy and territorial needs of the users and economic, political, and technological matters. If we conceive of a two-dimensional matrix with rows depicting "places" and columns depicting "behavioral phenomena," then the practitioners can be described as focusing on a place (a row) and scanning across behavioral phenomena (columns). Their goal is to understand a *place*, with knowledge of specific phenomena being instrumental to that goal. On the other hand, the typical social and behavioral researcher tries to understand a *behavior*, such as crowding or territoriality. Place differences only serve as qualifiers of more general principles. Thus the researcher typically fixes on a column, a favorite variable or behavior, and scans across places—for example, experimental and other settings—to determine the generality of a theory about the phenomena.

There are several derivations from this conceptualization, such as the practitioner's being more pragmatic, more concerned with synthesis of information, more problem-solving–oriented, and more holistic in orientation than the researcher. And it is easy to see how miscommunication can occur. For example, a practitioner will ask the researcher such questions as "What privacy needs should I include in the design of urban low-cost housing?" and be quite frustrated when the reply is "I can't say, since I have only looked at privacy in experimental settings with college sophomores as subjects." Furthermore the researcher may add, "If I research the problem I can only tell you about the general relationship between privacy and satisfaction, not about specific groups or places." Needless to say, the ensuing conversation, or lack thereof, will be frustrating to both parties.

Thus the same phenomenon can be approached from different perspectives. Furthermore neither perspective is "correct"; they are simply different and directed toward different ends. My position is that we researchers might well use the practitioner–researcher divergency in orientation to introspect about our own research strategies. What I propose is that we here conceive of a two-dimensional matrix of *social behaviors* × *social units* and ask whether there is some value in conducting more research along the social-unit axis and not just continue to work only along the social-behavior axis. I believe that we typically have emphasized only the understanding of behavioral processes, not social units, and that we have done so in a one-at-a-time fashion, with research specialists in behavior A not concerned with issues related to behavior B and so on. Perhaps we should attempt to understand social units, just as practitioners try to analyze specific places, by scanning across behaviors and phenomena. By so doing, not only may we generate alternative understandings of social processes, but we may also provide a vehicle for better application of research knowledge to the solution of social and environmental problems. The fact is that social problems tend to appear in the form of time/place/group units, for example, a community faces an urban redevelopment upheavel in the next 6 months. Unless our research can be partially translated into such time/place/social-unit terms, it will be difficult to contribute toward the solution of such problems. It is also the case that a social-unit orientation may add new dimensions to our research capabilities by forcing us to synthesize and to look at phenomena such as performance, privacy, and group cohesion in relationship to one another, rather than just treating them as parallel and unrelated processes.

Implementing a Social-Unit Analysis

How can one achieve the goal of understanding social units as the end product of research rather than dealing with behavior alone? Unfortunately there are no specific procedures that can be listed. Rather we need to think in terms of general features of social units, which can be examined at the outset of each study, and to tap into them whenever possible. Following are some of these features.

1. Social units exhibit many levels of behavior. We have stated elsewhere that an understanding of interpersonal relationships (Altman and Taylor, 1973) or privacy regulation (Altman, 1975) requires an analysis of many levels of behavior—verbal, paraverbal, nonverbal, and environmentally oriented behaviors such as those related to personal space and territory. No single level of behavior can completely capture what occurs in social groups and, therefore, research should ideally tap into more than one level to gain a sense of the dynamics of social groups. If we examine more than one behavioral class in the same study, our focus is likely to shift toward a more holistic approach to the group.

2. *Social units display patterns of behavior.* The various levels of behavior described above have a patternlike quality; that is, they occur in coherent sets and lend a quality of wholeness to behavior. For example, Patterson (1973) and others have indicated that eye contact and personal distance, personal distance and postures, and various verbal and nonverbal behaviors sometimes compensate for one another, sometimes substitute for one another, and sometimes amplify one another. Therefore it behooves us to examine the interrelationshiips of different levels of behavior. Too often we are specialists in one class of behaviors and then superspecialists in a particular aspect of a particular class of behavior. What I am calling for is some movement in the opposite direction—toward the study of several levels of behavior and their interrelationship. To the extent that we focus on patterns of simultaneously occurring behaviors, we will have taken an important step toward understanding social units. Much as the clinical psychologist looks simultaneously at many facets of behavior to understand a "whole-person client," or much as the environmental designer examines many features of a "place," so it is that the understanding of a social unit requires an analysis of patterns of several levels of behavior to see how they fit and do not fit with one another. In a sense, the empirical definition of a social unit is the specification of patterns of behavior.

3. *Social units have a dynamic, process-oriented quality.* It is a truism that behavior shifts over time as circumstances change. It is especially important, I believe, to view social units also in a processlike fashion, as internal dynamics and relations with the social and physical environment ebb and flow. A family, for example, has a dynamic quality, as relationships between members change, as it deals with other groups, and as it responds to environmental pressures. While a particular study may call for a cross-sectional slice of a group's life, a programmatic strategy of research on social units necessitates a process-oriented, longitudinal analysis, either across or within studies. By seeing how individual behaviors and patterns of behavior change and cycle over time, we can gradually piece together a holistic sense of social units.

4. *Social units have a systemlike quality.* The concept of *system,* whether referring to hardware and engineering systems or to social systems, is a popular one. Part of the meaning of the term, as we use it, refers to the points mentioned above, that is, many levels of behavior that co-occur in different profiles over time. Another feature of social units as systems is that they include interlaced and multicausation chains of relationship; that is, we are dealing with a system of interrelated parts, with changes in one part of the system potentially reverberating throughout the system. This aspect of a social system speaks to the idea that we are dealing with inter-locked elements and that examining behaviors separately, in an element-

by-element fashion, may obscure the reverberatory quality of events in social units.

Another aspect of a systems orientation relates to concepts of *causation* and to the nature of independent and dependent variables. Most of us who were trained in the traditions of experimental psychology, and with an environmental–deterministic perspective, typically have an input–output, antecedent–consequent, or an implicit "linear-causation" model of scientific analysis. While I do not disagree with this reasoning, I also believe that we have overly reified the process and have neglected the fact that we are probably dealing with many directions of causation, many of which have been ignored because of our methods and their underlying assumptions. For example, it is typical to assume a one-way relationship between environment and behavior to the effect that environments affect behavior in the form of various stimulus conditions and architectural design variables. My view is that we should view envronment–behavior relationships in a bidirectional fashion, with each direction of relationship equally important. Not only does environment affect behavior but so does behavior affect environmental changes. While it is often convenient and necessary to study a particular direction of relationship, it is also important to realize that we are only abstracting segments of the range of relationships between variables. As another example, it is commonly assumed that cultural and/or environmental factors affect (cause) cognitive representations of the environment, which in turn may affect (cause) certain behaviors; that is, culture × environment → cognitions →behaviors, in a linear, chainlike fashion. The systems orientation proposed here argues that almost any variable in this chain probably can affect any other variable. Cognitions of the environment and behavioral outcomes probably can affect one another in a bidirectional sense, as can behavior affect changes in culture and environments, and vice versa. Thus we propose a model with multidirectional causal links between many, if not all, variables.

Now it might appear to be anarchy if almost everything can cause or produce changes in everything else. But such a framework does not rule out research on specific relationships between variables or an understanding of which relationships are more important. It does suggest, however, that an overly narrow conception of causative relationships may not lead to an understanding of the whole system but will subtly direct one toward specific relationships and away from broader social units. If one adopts the understanding of social units as a goal, I believe that one will move toward a systemlike model of the type proposed here, because it will become evident that the social unit is difficult to grasp by a single-variable, linear orientation. On the other hand, if one adopts a classic "behavior-as-end-product" analysis, then one will drift toward a traditional, behavioral mode of analysis. Again I do not suggest that analyses of specific behaviors be ruled out, only that they be cast within a broader perspective.

To reiterate, the social-unit approach is a general orientation, not a procedure or technique. This means that we may have to separate, to some extent, the strategy and the tactics of research. I once heard it said that it is fine to think broadly, and a systems orientation allows one to do so. But it is probably impossible to do broad research. An empirical study must be specific and detailed; it cannot grasp all elements of a systems orientation at once. But small pieces of research can be fitted within a larger framework, and a general model can serve as a guide, not as something one can literally do. So it is with the approach proposed here. One cannot understand a whole social unit from a single study or by means of a single method. It is simply a way of thinking.

The remainder of the chapter presents a number of empirical case studies, drawn from my own work, that illustrate aspects of the social-unit strategy.

Case 1: Social-Isolation Studies[1]

During the 1960's I participated in a research program that examined group functioning under social isolation. Subjects were volunteer sailors who lived in austere settings, in pairs, with group members strangers to one another before the experience. In one study we varied group composition in terms of homogeneity and heterogeneity on needs for dominance, achievement, affiliation, and dogmatism. In a second study we examined the impact of environmental variables, including availability of private living arrangements, level of social stimulation from the outside world, and expectancies about how long the group was to be in isolation.

Because the studies were enormously expensive (subjects had to be brought from distant locations; observation periods lasted up to 10 days, 24 hours a day; a large research and medical staff was required) and because we were interested in group processes, we made a number of decisions that bear on the issues of this chapter. First, we decided to track behavior over several days to see changes that accompanied a group's history. This decision fit well with the principle of studying social units over time. Second, we measured several different facets of group life, including individual and group task-performance, self-reports of stress, emotional symptomatology and self-disclosure, observer ratings of interpersonal processes, territorial behavior (exclusive use of areas and objects), use of beds (on–off and time in and out of beds), social interaction, urine samples to measure stress, tape

[1]Reports of some of this research appear in Altman and Haythorn (1965), Haythorn, Altman, and Myers (1966), Haythorn and Altman (1967), Altman and Haythorn (1967), Taylor, Wheeler, and Altman (1968), Taylor, Altman, Wheeler, and Kushner (1969), and Altman, Taylor, and Wheeler (1971).

recordings of conversations, and work performance. Thus we adopted a second feature of the strategy proposed earlier, namely, measurement of different levels of group functioning.

The data were analyzed according to what was then an appropriate strategy: behavior-by-behavior analyses. But it soon became apparent that more could be learned if the data were examined in terms of general patterns or profiles. Furthermore it also became clear that there were "successful" and "unsuccessful" groups. For example, a number of pairs did not complete the experiment—they quit and left the isolation area before the studies ended. Because of the pressures "to complete the military mission," the decision to abort was not an easy one.

Comparison of completer and noncompleter groups revealed different patterns of behavior, which were time-linked. In general, successful groups seemed to have satisfactorily coped with group organization in the early days of the experiment, may have appropriately estimated the difficulty of the situation, and may have adequately prepared themselves to deal with the stresses of social isolation. For example, successful groups showed a profile of behavior along the following lines. During the early days and immediately prior to isolation they expressed somewhat more anticipatory anxiety and stress than unsuccessful groups. Successful group members also quickly established territories and relatively exclusive space usage. They also exhibited moderate degrees of self-disclosure and social interaction, whereas unsuccessful groups showed either extreme social withdrawal or excessive social interaction. Also, successful groups quickly fell into a pattern of interpersonal synchrony; for example, they moved about together, spent approximately the same times of day in and out of their beds, and performed well on tasks.

The epitome of a successful group was one in which the members, on the first or second day, laid out an eating, exercise, and recreation schedule; constructed a deck of playing cards, a chess set, and a Monopoly game out of paper; and decided how they would structure their lives over the expected lengthy period of isolation. This early pattern of pacing, synchrony, and group organization was a good predictor of success. And later in isolation, the behavior of both types of groups continued to be different. Though psychological stress mounted for everyone, it was particularly evident in subsequent aborter groups. Also, unsuccessful groups rose markedly in territorial behavior and stress reactions, their performance deteriorated, and so on. Successful groups showed a reverse pattern, and it struck us that they reflected a group in which members had initially dealt with one another cautiously and had maintained their separate individuality but had worked out a way of functioning that eventually permitted them to lower their interpersonal boundaries and to perform as an effective team.

This research reflects several features of the social-unit analysis strategy. In retrospect, we had literally tried to understand *both* single behaviors in relationship to social isolation and the interrelationships among these behaviors. We gained some understanding of several behaviors taken singly, but we also began to understand the nature of a particular type of social unit—isolated groups—and by the end of this work, we were able to generate a kind of case study of "groups who succeed" and "groups who fail" in terms of different profiles of behavior. We did this by tracking many levels of behavior over time and piecing together patterns or profiles of behavior. The end result was a better understanding both of specific behavioral phenomena and of "real live groups."

Two other points are worth mentioning in reference to the social-unit strategy. First, traditional notions of linear, chainlike, cause-and-effect relationships do not seem wholly appropriate to these data. One could argue that the experimental conditions and the bases of group composition "caused" what happened. That may be partly correct, but it is also the case that these manipulations probably set in motion a complex series of events that began to assume an independent momentum. Thus it was impossible to determine whether early stress "caused" early territorial behavior, which in turn "caused" certain patterns of disclosure, and so on. In a sense, we had intervened at a particular node in a complex social system, and once events began to unfold, it was impossible to identify exact causal links. While it may be useful to trace such links in the future, it was impossible for us to do so in this research. All we knew was which behaviors came together in meaningful, descriptive patterns. Most likely, subsequent research will demonstrate that particular links and reverberatory relationships are complex and multifaceted, and while they should be researched, one should not expect to find only simple, one-way relationships among variables.

Second, this research was experimental and laboratory-oriented in concept, although we were not able to control the range of factors one normally controls in time-limited laboratory situations. I raise this issue to emphasize the idea that a social-unit approach is not tied to particular methods. Subsequent examples will include a survey study, a field observational analysis, and a role-playing demonstration.

Case 2: An Analysis of Home Environments (Altman, Nelson, and Lett, 1972)

As an outgrowth of earlier work I became interested in how people use the physical environment to manage social relationships. Rather than focusing on how the physical environment operates strictly as a *determinant* of interpersonal events, the goal was to investigate how the environment is actively used in social relationships—an idea compatible with multidirectional relationships between variables. More specifically, I examined how families used home environments on the presumption that family life involves long-term interactions that are reflected in stable patterns of environmental usage. Two general questions were posed: (1) Are there general styles of use of home environments that characterize all families? (2) Are there unique and different family styles in relationship to home environments? The second question is particularly appropriate to the issue of identifying types of family use of homes. A 300-item questionnaire asked about various aspects of homes: geographical location, general features (number and type of rooms), kitchen and eating areas, bedrooms, bathrooms, living and family rooms, special rooms, how and where the family spent its time, and job assignments to children.

The questionnaire was administered to a sample of 150 young men, 17–21 years of age, who were from a "middle-America" sample of families. They were largely high-school graduates, as were their parents. The fathers worked in technical-skill or white-collar positions, and the families consisted of parents and two or three children. The typical family home was in a suburban-type community, on a small lot, and close to neighbors and service facilities. The homes were modest, with 1–1½ bathrooms and 2–3 bedrooms.

Several characteristics of their homes were common to most families. They typically had two or three entrances; the kitchens had similar equipment, such as stoves, refrigerators, etc.; the living rooms were furnished in a relatively consistent way (sofas, coffee tables, end tables). The parents usually shared the same bedroom and bed. The fathers often had "special" rooms, such as shops, dens, or studies. In addition, most of the families ate dinner together, whereas breakfast and lunch were individual affairs. The families differed in whether they had dinnertime meals in the kitchen or the dining area, although breakfast and lunch were usually taken in the kitchen. There were also consistent job assignments concerning meals, with female members of the family usually responsible for food preparation and cleaning up. Also most of the families usually had fixed seating patterns at dinner, with each family member having his or her own location. The children were scattered around the table, at ends, at corners, or in center positions. However, the father was typically seated at the end or head of the table. The mother's position was more varied, equally divided between being at opposite ends to the father, at his adjacent corner, or at some center position. Mealtime seating was not rigid but fluctuated with the situation. Fixed seating patterns were strong when the family ate together as a group but broke down when family members ate alone or when there were guests.

For bathrooms, closing doors and privacy varied as a function of the intimacy of the activity. When the toilet was being used and during showering, the bathroom door was usually closed in most families. For less intimate activities, such as shaving and combing hair, the door was infrequently closed.

In bedrooms, people usually left the door open when the room was not occupied, but there was considerable variation when people were in the bedroom. When bedroom doors were closed and people were inside, it was typical for many family members to knock before entering, especially on parents' and sisters' doors. Thus there were a number of "universal" practices regarding the use of home environments.

In a second type of analysis, we attempted to identify different family styles in the use of environments, which is directly relevant to a social-unit strategy. One family style, Type A, involved an "open" and "informal" pattern of behaviors. Type B families exhibited opposite characteristics, with firmer boundaries between family members, less accessibility to one another's areas and activities, a more formal approach to use of space, and a lesser degree of family interaction. For purposes of discussion, let us consider the Type A or "open" family.

Accessibility between members of the Type A family was apparent in how they used doors. Members of Type A families left bedroom doors open all day for a variety of activities such as entertaining, sleeping, and studying. They also showed accessibility between family members in other parts of the home. If Type A parents had special rooms, they were readily available to others. Type A family members visited one another's bedrooms frequently, and the family engaged in social interaction to a greater extent than Type B families. They also exhibited overlapping role and job responsibilities around the home, shared activities, and seemed to do things with one another to a greater extent than Type B families.

These families were also more informal. They ate dinner in the kitchen and entertained guests in the kitchen, which was used for a variety of purposes beyond eating. In Type B families, eating was done in the dining room, rooms seemed to have specific functions, and there was a greater degree of formality. In addition, informality in Type A families was reflected in the fact that they tended not to knock on closed doors and that they shared news with almost anyone present rather than in some specific order.

Type A families also had parents seated at opposite ends of the table, or mother at the center and father at the end, whereas Type B families typically had fathers at the end of the table and mothers at the adjacent corner. The Type A pattern may reflect greater family inclusiveness, or broadly based family participation in discussions, and less formal role distinctions between parents. Thus consistencies in patterns of use of the home environment seemed to describe different family styles involving many different levels and types of behavior.

Which features of this study fit the social-unit analysis approach? First, we ended up with a description of intact family groups because we had tapped into different levels of behavior and because we attempted to piece together behaviors into coherent patterns. While the data were of a self-report type, they dealt with several facets of family functioning. And by identifying relationships among these different levels of behavior, we were able to shift the focus from single behaviors to patterns or profiles, the latter being empirical indicators of "family types."

It is also important to note that this study viewed environmental behaviors as part of a complex system of variables, with no immediate concern about causation relationships among variables. For our purposes, it was irrelevant whether or not use of one part of a home "caused" behaviors in other parts of the home. While it would be valuable to learn about factors predisposing one family to have a Type A or a Type B style, this study only sought to identify the nature of such family systems without attempting to establish directional links between variables. I presume that such links exist, but I would not anticipate discovery of simple causation chains no matter how much research was conducted.

Two final points. Again, a social-unit strategy is not restricted to particular methods. Here we used a survey technique, whereas the previous study was experimental and employed a variety of measures. Thus the strategy is related more to how one views one's data and the range of data one collects than to a particular design or measurement procedure. Second, the idea is again brought home that one can deal with complex systems at a theoretical or metamethodological level, as we have done in proposing a social-unit analysis, but that a given piece of research must be specific and delimited. Obviously family units can be observed from a number of perspectives, with environmental behaviors being only one such approach. But it is simply not possible to do a single study that totally captures all features of a social unit, and the researcher must be content to chip away, hoping in the long run gradually to achieve a more complete understanding of its qualities.

Case 3: Dominance and Territorial Behavior (Sundstrom and Altman, 1974)

This research adopted a wholly different methodology than the preceding studies in order to deal with the relationship between a group's dominance hierarchy and territorial behavior. It was a 10-week longitudinal analysis of a single group of boys in a residential facility for juvenile offenders. The research was stimulated by inconsistent evidence in the literature: some studies reported a positive relationship between dominance and territoriality (high-dominant people have territories), other studies showed no relationship, and still others showed a negative relationship, (Altman, 1975). Our view was that a longitudinal study might clarify the issue on the assumption that the dominance–territory relationship varied with stages of a group's history, an idea compatible with a social-unit strategy.

In this 10-week observational study, the location of each of 16–23 boys was tabulated on a map of the cottage residence. In addition, the boys were interviewed three times and ranked others on power or influence. They also rated the desirability of different parts of the cottage. Finally, we used supervisor–behavior logs to identify incidents of disruptive behavior. Thus in line with a social-unit strategy, we tapped several aspects of behavior.

As so often happens in field studies, our original plans were disrupted by administrative decisions involving changes in group composition during the study. In the fifth week two high-dominant boys were removed from the group and were replaced by two new boys, who turned out also to be quite dominant. During the seventh week one high- and one medium-dominant boy were taken from the group. The data were analyzed within three time periods bounded by these changes.

The effect of these actions was to create a kind of naturalistic experiment, and the data fell into a coherent package when examined in light of these changes. During the first 5 weeks, in which membership was stable (it had also been stable during the prior 6 weeks when we were doing pilot work), the group showed the following profile. There was a positive relationship between dominance and territoriality, with the more powerful boys having territories to a greater extent than those in the lower part of the hierarchy. And they also had access to the best places in the cottage. Furthermore disruptive behavior was low during this period, all of which suggests a group with a stable social system, with spatial and member relationships reasonably well worked out.

However, with a shift in group composition, the picture altered dramatically. The introduction of two new dominant boys and the removal of two others who had been powerful were associated with a sharp drop in territorial behavior for the whole group. This meant that all boys' use of space was spread among many places—as if they were now wandering about the cottage in a dispersed fashion. And there was no longer a relationship between dominance and territorial behavior; that is, the low-dominant boys were as territorial as the high-dominant boys. Furthermore disruptive behaviors rose sharply. All of this indicated that the introduction of two new highly dominant boys had created an upheaval in the social structure of the group, which was reflected in a breakdown of the stable spatial and interpersonal system of the earlier period. Speculating, it may have been that this was a period in which the new boys attempted to establish their dominance, partly in terms of space usage, and there may well have been intrusions on others' spaces, counterreactions, and a chain of events that upset a previously stable system. Thus by piecing together several levels of behavior over time, we gained a sense of changes in a social group's functioning that might not have been evident from a cross-sectional analysis of a specific behavior.

By the third period, when group composition changed less dramatically, conflict lessened and territorial behavior of the low- and middle-dominant boys rose. However, the high-dominant boys still showed low territorial behavior (resulting in a negative relationship between dominance and territoriality). And the disruptive behavior of the high-dominant boys continued, whereas that of the other boys declined. It was as if this period reflected a partial movement toward a new stable system for most of the group, whereas the highly dominant boys were still struggling with their role.

In regard to the basic questions of this study, we found a shift in relationship between dominance and territorial behavior. Under stable group composition, a positive relationship occurred; under conditions of dramatic change in group composition, no relationship occurred; when a group was moving toward a stable situation, a negative relationship obtained.

Aside from its specific goals, this study is instructive in terms of a social-unit analysis strategy. The group was studied longitudinally, with behavior and events tracked over time. Also, several levels of behavior were investigated: dominance, the desirability of the space, spatial locations, and disruptive behavior. Moreover we attempted to identify patterns of these behaviors rather than look at each one separately. Furthermore we attempted to piece together relationships between variables without searching for specific causal links. While group-composition changes probably set in motion group instabilities, we did not and could not determine antecedent–consequent links between disruption and spatial behaviors and subsequent impacts on group's social structure. In summary, the approach we took permitted treating the *group* as an important end product of the study. While we learned something about the dominance–territoriality relationship, this knowledge was cast within the context of a group's life over time. Thus allowing a social-unit focus to emerge contributed more to our understanding of group processes than had we restricted ourselves to a behavior-as-end-product analysis alone.

A field study like this is instructive in several other respects. One is faced with only a single group, and one has little control over circumstances such as group membership. The effect is to force the researcher to understand the group rather than a single behavior. One must attempt to tap into many parts of a group's life because any single behavior is only part of a complex set of social processes and often cannot be understood in isolation. While there are many difficulties of interpretation, generalization, and control in field studies, I also believe that a social-unit orientation, as described here, can facilitate the absorption of such data into the mainstream of scientific knowledge and can contribute meaningfully to basic theoretical questions.

Case 4: Nonverbal Behavior and Acquaintanceship (Keiser and Altman, 1974)

This study arose from an interest in the social-penetration process, or how social relationships proceed from strangership through acquaintanceship to close friendship (Altman and Taylor, 1973). Our earlier research dealt with verbal aspects of the process: how long people talked to one another, the level of intimacy of self-disclosure, and the areas of personality that people made accessible to one another. One goal of this study was to examine nonverbal features of the social-penetration process, which ties in with that aspect of a social-unit strategy concerning multiple levels of behavior. A second purpose was to identify patterns of nonverbal behavior that occur in face-to-face communication. Traditionally research on nonverbal behavior examines behaviors one at a time, with relatively little attention given to how behaviors occur in patterns. In accord with the research strategy of this chapter, we wished to see how such behaviors form profiles or patterns.

Our approach was to use established findings in the verbal self-disclosure area and to see if they applied to nonverbal behaviors. This was accomplished within a 2 × 2 experimental design, where one variable involved level of acquaintanceship—good friends or casual acquaintances (the literature indicates greater quantity and intimacy of disclosure among friends). A second variable dealt with degree of topical intimacy (research has demonstrated that intimate topics are talked about less often and more reluctantly than nonintimate topics). We used two pairs of actresses as subjects, on the assumption that they were well versed in nonverbal communication. They acted out all combinations of conditions: good friends talking about either intimate or superficial topics and casual acquaintances talking about each type of topic. For each condition, the actresses were given only a general scenario; they were to improvise conversations and did not know that their nonverbal behavior would be analyzed in terms of 24 dimensions on a second-by-second basis. Measures included eye contact, head movements, body positions, leg and arm positions and movements, forward, backward, and sideways leaning, etc. Each actress was analyzed separately and compared across conditions of the design.

A number of patterns of nonverbal behavior were identified and consisted of at least two behaviors that occurred simultaneously in time at a fairly high frequency. The data were voluminous, so let us consider only one actress's behavior. As predicted, she showed the most relaxed behavior in the good-friend–nonintimate condition. One pattern consisted of eye contact, backward leaning, sitting on legs, and side leaning, coupled with talking, gesturing, hands open, foot movements, smiling, and so on. These behaviors, alone and in combination, portray a relatively free-wheeling, active, and vibrant person in contact with the other person in a relatively informal way. Other patterns showed the same quality. It should be noted that the actress also displayed large number of patterns in this condition, each having a variety of behaviors that were occasionally added to main patterns. Thus her overall orientation was one of activity, relaxation, and behavioral variation.

The same actress presented a strikingly different picture in the casual-acquaintance–intimate-topic condition. Here her behavior reflected tension, rigidity, and little variation. Over half of her behavior was characterized by a single pattern consisting of arm symmetry, grasping the arms of the chair, eye contact, legs crossed and oriented toward the other person, and backward–sideways leaning. Except for a few behaviors, this cluster is reflective of tension. And the relaxed behaviors of eye contact and backward–sideways leaning occurred less often in this condition than in the good-friend–nonintimate condition. Other patterns shown by this girl were comparably tense. Thus in terms of rigidity and nature of patterns, our expectations were confirmed, as they generally were for each of the four actresses.

This study illustrates some of the features of a social-unit analysis. First, it demonstrates how the same data can be used to understand either specific behaviors or individuals as the end product of analysis. Not only were patterns of nonverbal behavior searched out, but we also analyzed the data on a behavior-by-behavior basis. In the latter instance, the data confirmed much of the literature in the field, for example, more smiling, eye contact, and so on in positive social climates. But more importantly, we demonstrated that a pattern analysis of behavior yields something additional. For example, there are both commonalities and differences among *people* as the unit of observation. The four actresses did some things in common (smiling, relaxed postures, etc.), but they also exhibited different and unique behavioral patterns. Thus we identified behavioral consistencies among people and also idiosyncratic personal styles. Furthermore the study demonstrated how the same person shifted behavior from situation to situation. In short, by working with patterns of nonverbal behavior, we were able to re-create, in a sense, individual persons and to end up with a description of *both* behaviors and people, each telling something different about the process of interpersonal exchange.

In addition, the study illustrates how one can work with multiple levels of behaviors within a single domain, such as nonverbal behavior. The examples of research presented earlier emphasized cross-level behaviors, for example, verbal, environmental, and performance. Here we worked within one general domain. Naturally it would have been ideal to explore the fit between verbal and nonverbal behaviors, but it was simply not possible to do so. Again, while one can theoretically speak of a multilevel, systems approach, one can only empirically approach the issue on a limited basis.

Summary and Implications

This chapter has presented a statement of research strategy that emphasizes knowledge of *social units* as an important product of research. I have argued that social psychology has historically focused on the study of single behaviors, without any concerted efforts to examine how behaviors fit together to permit understanding of "real" people or groups. Just as the clinical psychologist focuses on a "whole person," just as the cultural anthropologist attempts to capture an integrated understanding of a "society," and the environmental practitioners analyzes "places," so too should we conduct research to understand social units as holistic entities.

How to do this? I proposed several aspects of a research strategy which could lead to a social-unit analysis:

1. A focus on several levels of behavior. An analysis of more than one level of behavior in a single study—including verbal, paraverbal, nonverbal, and environmentally oriented behaviors—facilitates an understanding of social units.

2. A focus on patterns or systems of behavior. The functioning of a social group is characterized by different levels of behavior that fit together into a coherent whole. In essence, a social unit can be represented by systematic *patterns* of behavior. By examining behaviors in relationship to one another, across and within behavior modalities, we can take substantial steps toward understanding whole social groups.

3. A focus on the systemlike quality of social units. As a "system," a social group's functioning can be affected in any of several ways, and there can also be complex reverberations throughout the system. Therefore the search for simple cause–effect links is likely to be unsuccessful, and the simplistic notion of "manipulate a few things and hold everything else constant" as the *sole* methodological paradigm is apt to overly narrow our perspective. A social-unit analysis, assuming complex chains of relationship, also directs one toward an eclectic methodological strategy: description when necessary, observational analyses when necessary, experimentation when necessary.

4. An emphasis on social units as having dynamic, processlike qualities. Social groups shift and change over time. For example, the family unit changes as children are added, as they mature, and as parental relationships shift. Rather than assume that social groups revolve around some fixed equilibrium point, we see it as a growth process, with social units moving to successively different levels of functioning. By tracking time-linked events, we can better understand a social group's general qualities.

What a Social-Unit Analysis Is Not

In illustrating research appropriate to a social-unit strategy, I intended to demonstrate also what I mean by exclusion, that is, by illustrating what is *not* meant by such an approach. Let me briefly highlight some of these points.

1. A social-unit strategy is not a substitute for a behavioral emphasis. Each study presented as a case example demonstrates a dual concern: (a) with specific behavioral events such as territorial behavior, performance, and specific nonverbal behaviors, and (b) with a piecing together of behaviors to capture some feeling for a specific social group. I do not suggest, therefore, that research dealing with individual behaviors or clusters of behavior be scrapped, only that we also expand our focus along the lines suggested.

2. *A social-unit emphasis is not method bound.* As the case examples demonstrate, a social-unit orientation can employ experimental, survey, observational, role-playing, and field methodologies. I do not suggest that any one is inherently superior. Which should be used depends upon the questions of the research, the available resources, and so on. The essence of the social-unit strategy is not in the procedure but in the types of data collected and how those data are viewed. I must say, however, that the traditional laboratory approach coupled with single, dependent-variable, factorial designs predisposes one toward a single-behavior orientation. But as I have demonstrated, it does not have to do so. The attitude and approach of researchers are the issue, not the methodology *per se.*

3. *A social-unit analysis does not rule out dealing with specific cause–effect relationships.* A central point of the discussion has been that the analysis of social units may require an expanded approach to cause–effect issues. While particular studies may focus on antecedent–consequent effects among variables, it is quite likely that, in the long run, we are dealing with complex chains of causation. I do not intend to unravel completely the idea of simple linear causation in the context of particular studies but only wish to emphasize that a particular directional effect is not necessarily a universal one.

4. *A social-unit analysis is neither idiographic nor nomothetic.* The emphasis on social groups may often lead toward a case-study analysis as one tries to gain a handle on many aspects of a particular group's life. But this does not always have to be the case. As illustrated, one can adopt a case-study approach (the boys' cottage group, the actresses' nonverbal behavior) or a more traditional nomothetic orientation (the social-isolation studies, the survey of family home environments). In all instances, the goal was to understand aspects of a social group's functioning, and a nomothetic or idiographic orientation was used depending upon circumstances.

5. *Social-unit analysis is not a matter of applied versus basic research.* I introduced the topic of social-unit analysis from the perspective of the "place" orientation of the environmental designer and the "person–group" orientation of the clinical psychologist. It is true that by the nature of the problems they deal with, practitioners and applied researchers tend to focus on other than single behaviors as their end product. But it does not necessarily follow that basic research must focus primarily on behaviors. Each of the case examples presented here deals with basic theoretical and research questions from a social-unit perspective, and the dichotomy between basic and applied issues simply does not apply to this discussion.

6. *Social-unit analysis does not demand that every piece of research deal with all facets of a social unit's existence.* The strategy proposed must be applied differently at theoretical and pragmatic levels. It is fine to speak of a mul-

tifaceted analysis of social units, a systems orientation, a longitudinal study, etc. But as stated previously, no single study can do it all. Social-unit analysis is a way of thinking, and individual studies must be specific and limited. They simply cannot encompass all features of the strategy at once. Obviously this is no different than what we already know when we test a theory. Therefore one must approach the issue programatically over the course of several studies.

What Social-Unit Analysis Requires by Way of New or Expanded Skills

Adopting a social-unit analysis strategy probably requires a broadening of research skills, a willingness to pursue a problem without always knowing how or whether it will work out. To be more specific, one must be willing to:

1. *Become proficient in dealing with many types of behavior and methods.* If the social-unit strategy is adopted in part or in whole, the researcher must learn to deal with many levels of behavior. For example, if one is a specialist in some facet of verbal behavior, it will be necessary to learn about other levels of behavior as well. The nature of these behaviors, their quantification, the technology associated with their measurement, metric properties for analysis purposes, etc., will have to be learned. This is no simple matter and can consume enormous amounts of energy. Moreover if the methodological eclecticism proposed here is adopted, one must become skilled in a variety of research methods: experimentation, observation, survey techniques, etc. Again, this is not an easy task. It is sufficiently difficult to become proficient in a single method, let alone a range of procedures. Finally, it is likely that one will have to become knowledgeable about a range of analysis procedures. Too often we become specialists in one technique or another partly because it fits a specific methodological strategy. A social-unit approach calls not only for diverse methodologies but for diverse analysis strategies, especially those that have a multivariate logic. How one accomplishes all this is not easy to say. Alternatives include brute learning by a single individual, team efforts bringing together prople with complementary skills, the use of consultants, and the like.

2. *Conduct fewer studies, seeking a higher yield per study.* If the social-unit strategy is adopted, one should expect to conduct relatively fewer studies within a given period of time. The need to gather data from a variety of domains, the requirement for doing data analyses that piece together multiple behaviors, and a longitudinal approach will simply not permit conduct of very many studies. Furthermore one often must spend considerable time in exploratory data-analyses. This is different from traditional research, in which one often develops a particular problem of interest, defines it in a narrow and precise fashion, develops a methodological and statistical strategy that can be repreatedly applied, and "grinds out" study after study in an almost productionlike fashion. Again, I do not suggest that such a

strategy be eliminated, only that those who wish to pursue the approach proposed here realize the implications of so doing. Hopefully, however, the information yield per study will be higher in a social-unit strategy, and this has been the case in my own research. While the sheer number of studies I have conducted recently is smaller than in the past, what I learn per study is quite rich, so that, in my case, the tradeoff is acceptable.

3. *Adopt a different orientation to subjects and settings.* In conducting traditional research, one naturally focuses on a particular behavior of interest. With social entities as the unit of study it is important that the researcher adopt a broader view, focusing on *people* and *groups* and on the total ecology of the setting within which they are embedded. This is especially important in the early stages of research, since one must attempt to gain some understanding of the total setting before homing in on a measurement strategy. I recall an experiment by a student interested in the effects of crowding on stress. He had so locked in on the notion that stress was best measured by self-report techniques that in his pilot work he failed to recognize that his subjects were showing stress reactions in a variety of ways—verbal and nonverbal behaviors and so on. In a sense, he had too quickly narrowed his view to specific behaviors and not to the "people" as intact units. So it is that we should see how a social unit is responding to a setting in a multidimensional sense, at least initially, and not overly tunnel our vision to predetermined behaviors.

This issue is somewhat related to the so-called humanist approach to research, which calls for treating subjects as people, not objects, and which suggests that we become more sensitive to subjects as whole human beings. While I do not wish to deal with the ethical and moral underpinnings of this view, it is important, for research purposes, to do a molar analysis of an ecological setting. Put another way, we should design research from the perspective of what Barker (1968) has termed a *behavior setting:* a combination of people, places, and purposes. Within this context we can then narrow our focus to deal with a particular question. The error is, in my opinion, a premature narrowing of that perspective.

A Capstone Thought

I am reminded of the classic dictum of Kurt Lewin, the intellectual forerunner of present-day social psychology, who stated the formula:

$$B = f(P, E)$$

The left side of the equation, Behavior (B), was to be understood as an interactive function of the needs, values, history, and capabilities of a Person (P) and the Environment (E), which consisted of physical and psychological aspects of the environment that had current psychological meaning for the person.

It is my view that we may have too literally and incorrectly interpreted Lewin's statement by assuming that *all* of our efforts are to be solely devoted to understanding behavior as some specific act and by assuming that the true path to understanding human functioning can proceed only according to the Lewinian formula. As I read Lewin (1964) in the context of the issues raised in this chapter, I discovered that he meant all three terms—*P, B, E*—to be *interchangeable* and that any term could be studied as a function of any combination of the other terms. In this spirit, what I have suggested in this chapter is that we pay as much attention to the logic of:

$$P = f (B,E)$$

as we have to the traditional $B = f (P,E)$ formula. Or to put it another way, perhaps we should redefine the study of human functioning from "the study of behavior" to "the study of behavior *and people*—individuals and social groups."

References

Altman, I. Some perspectives on the study of man–environment phenomena. *Representative Research in Social Psychology*, 1973, *4*(1), 109–126.

Altman, I. *Environment and social behavior: Privacy, personal space, territory and crowding.* Monterey, Calif.: Brooks/Cole, 1975.

Altman, I., and Haythorn, W. W. Interpersonal exchange in isolation. *Sociometry*, 1965, *23*, 411–426.

Altman, I., and Haythorn, W. W. The ecology of isolated groups. *Behavioral Science*, 1967, *12*, 169–182.

Altman, I., Nelson, P. A., and Lett, E. E. The ecology of home environments. *Catalog of Selected Documents in Psychology*. Washington, D.C.: American Psychological Associaton, Spring, 1972.

Altman, I., and Taylor, D. A. *Social penetration: The development of interpersonal relationships.* New York: Holt, Rinehart and Winston, 1973.

Altman, I., Taylor, D. A., and Wheeler, L. Ecological aspects of group behavior in social isolation. *Journal of Applied Social Psychology*, 1971, *1*, 76–100.

Barker, R. G. *Ecological psychology*, Stanford, Calif.: Stanford University Press, 1968.

Haythorn, W. W., and Altman, I. Together in isolation. *Transaction*, 1967, *4*, 18–22.

Haythorn, W. W., Altman, I., and Myers, T. Emotional symptomatology and stress in isolated pairs of men. *Journal of Experimental Research in Personality*, 1966, *1*, 290–305.

Keiser, G., and Altman, I. Nonverbal aspects of the social penetration process. *Catalog of Selected Documents in Psychology*, Winter, 1974.

Lewin, K. *Field theory and social science.* New York: Harper and Row, 1964.

Patterson, M. L. Compensation and nonverbal immediacy behaviors: A review. *Sociometry*, 1973, *36*(2), 237–253.

Sundstrom, E., and Altman, I. Field study of dominance and territorial behavior. *Journal of Personality and Social Psychology*, 1974, *30*(1), 115–125.

Taylor, D. A., Altman, I., Wheeler, L., and Kushner, E. N. Personality factors related to response to social isolation and confinement. *Journal of Consulting and Clinical Psychology*, 1969, *33*, 411–419.

Taylor, D. A., Wheeler, L., and Altman, I. Stress reactions in socially isolated groups. *Journal of Personality and Social Psychology*, 1968, *9*, 369–376.

Methodological Developments in Environment–Behavioral Research

16

ARTHUR H. PATTERSON

This chapter is concerned with research methods in the area of environment and behavior. Specifically it deals with the research methods that have been used, how relevant and valid (in terms of theory, research design, and data collection) these methods have been, and finally, it suggests the kinds of research methods that need to be developed in the area. The chapter is not intended as an overview of the current research literature. For this the reader is directed to any of the numerous recent texts on environmental psychology (e.g., Altman, 1975; Ittelson, Proshansky, Rivlin, and Winkel, 1974; Heimstra and McFarling, 1974). Rather the aim here is to present the most commonly used research designs and data-collection techniques and to evaluate them in terms of their contribution to the theory and problem-oriented nature of the field.

This approach implies an existing definition of environmental–behavioral research. In more established areas of research, the theoretical development of the field tends to define the researchers' questions. However, in emerging areas such as this one, the field tends to be defined by the questions asked by the researchers who identify with the area. Thus this chapter will include research that deals with the wide range of questions that self-identified environmental–behavioral researchers study.

The emerging field of environmental–behavioral research is both theoretically focused and problem-oriented. An interesting discussion of this dichotomy is presented by Smith in Chapter 15. However, the major thrust of the area has been problem-oriented in nature (Proshansky, 1972; Proshansky, Ittelson, and Rivlin, 1970; Rapoport, 1973), and it is that

ARTHUR H. PATTERSON • The Pennsylvania State University, University Park.

orientation that underlies this discussion of research methods. As will be seen below, there is a need for theory and data to support this problem-solving orientation.

This chapter presents some of the methodological threats to both theory-relevant research and problem-applicable data-collection. Theory-relevant research is considered to be that research that can be meaningfully applied to theory, and thus facilitate theory development.

Theory and the Problem-Oriented Nature of the Area

In referring to environmental psychology, Proshansky (1972) has stated that "By problem-oriented, we mean that it addresses a variety of questions posed for and asked by architects, interior designers, physical and social planners, and sometimes by supervising professionals (such as hospital administrators or school principals) concerned with people, their activities, and the physical settings in which human activities take place" (p. 452).

Altman (1973) has pointed out that this problem orientation creates difficulties for the researcher. He states that scientists tend to be analytical and "independent-variable oriented" and are not usually working under pressure to achieve an immediate "real-world product." The researcher's goal is usually a scientific publication, with unknown or little immediate application. The environmental practitioner, on the other hand, is (in Altman's terms) a "doer" whose work is directed toward a specific end-product. Altman has persuasively argued that this difference in orientation can lead to an impasse and impedes progress in the environment-and-behavior area.

The problem-oriented nature of the environment-and-behavior field also has been discussed by Studer (1973). He distinguishes between the "interventionist" orientation of environmental practitioners and the "noninterventionist" orientation of the environmental researcher. Among other differences, the practitioner is concerned with the *design* of man–environment relations, while the researcher is concerned with the *discovery* of man–environment relations. In an effort to balance the emphasis on an interventionist approach, there has been an increasing call among both environmental researchers and practitioners for the development of theory in this area. The call is not so much directed at extending the earlier, foundation-laying psychological research into the effects of environment on behavior (e.g., Tolman, 1932; Lewin, 1946; Brunswick, 1956) but rather to facilitate the design and conduct of research that can contribute to the solution of those problems of current interest within the field.

Rapoport (1973) has presented five arguments in favor of theory development in this area. Briefly summarized, these are:

1. A need exists to make sense of the growing numbers of papers and items of empirical data and thus make some order of the many disparate pieces of work.

2. A framework to reduce such confusion must provide for a wide variety of work on many aspects of man–environment interaction. As much of the work is contradictory, or not comparable, the effect on both theory development and problem solving is detrimental. Thus another reason for theory building is to reveal gaps and inconsistencies, as well as areas of agreement, and to suggest areas needing further work.

3. An important role of theory is to lead from description to explanation and ultimately to prediction (although the latter is a distant goal). At present the field is remarkably weak even in description (cf. Willems, Chapter 2).

4. Theory is badly needed to aid in teaching-environment and behavior studies, for the reasons stated in Number 1 above.

5. Theory will help practitioners apply the body of knowledge now available to solving environmental issues.

It is of interest to note that much recent environmental–behavioral work either has been directed at or has emphasized theory (e.g., Stokols, 1972; Evans and Howard, 1973; Edney, 1974; Altman, 1975; and the present volume). Given the need for the development of theory in this area, the goal here is to present the typical research designs and data-collection techniques now in use and to evaluate them in terms of their relevance to theory and their value for application to the problem-solving nature of the field.

The remainder of this chapter is divided into four parts. The first section presents some of the major methodological threats to theory-relevant research and valid data-collection. The second part provides an overview of the most common research designs used for empirical research in the environmental–behavioral area. These designs will be evaluated in terms of their strengths and weaknesses in relation to the discussion of theory relevance and validity. The third part is parallel to the second, but the topic of discussion is the various methods of data collection used. The final section deals with the design and conduct of future environment-and-behavior research—research that is relevant to theory in the area and provides valid and useful data.

Methodological Threats to Theoretical Development

The theoretical relevance of any given study is affected by the choice of the phenomena studied, the choice of the physical setting in which it is studied, and certain validity issues. This section will discuss how the concepts of internal, statistical-conclusion, construct, and external validity (Campbell and Stanley, 1966; Cook and Campbell, 1975) relate to the relevancy issue. Further it will be shown how the concepts of mundane and experimental realism (Aronson and Carlsmith, 1968), phenomenon legitimacy

(Proshansky, 1972), and what shall be defined here as *experiential realism* can be applied to empirical research on environment and behavior.

Internal Validity

As Campbell and Stanley (1966) and Cook and Campbell (1975) have pointed out, threats to internal validity suggest that a demonstrated relationship between two variables of interest might, in fact, be spurious. Only if there are no other plausible alternative explanations of the results than the stated relationship between the variables can the study be said to be internally valid. Because randomization is the usual eliminator of most threats to internal validity, the environmental–behavioral researchers, who operates in the real world and thus often had to forgo randomization, must be exceedingly careful of these threats.

Among the many threats to internal validity presented by Cook and Campbell, there are several that pertain directly to environmental–behavioral research. These include:

1. *History.* When the observed effects might be due to some event that took place during the testing and is unrelated to the treatment.
2. *Maturation.* Effects due to the development of the subject that are unrelated to the treatment.
3. *Testing.* Effects due to the taking of the test.
4. *Instrumentation.* Effects due to the measuring instrument.
5. *Selection.* Effects due to the different subjects in the experimental groups, as opposed to the different treatments received.

If the researcher cannot confidently rule out these threats to the internal validity of his study, the obtained results may be spurious and thus of dubious value for application to real-world problems, as well as to theory development.

Statistical-Conclusion Validity

Statistical-conclusion validity is concerned with the validity of conclusions drawn about the relationships between variables that are made on the basis of statistical evidence. This is different from the sources of systematic bias, which are presented in the section on threats to internal validity. Rather statistical-conclusion validity has to do with sources of error variance and with the appropriate use of statistics and statistical tests. It is these threats that prevent valid conclusions about the effect of a treatment or about the degree of relationship between variables of interest.

Some of the relevant threats to statistical-conclusion validity offered by Cook and Campbell (1975) are:

1. *Statistical power.* The probability of making a Type I (incorrect difference conclusion) or Type II (incorrect no-difference conclusion)

error because of the *alpha* level chosen, the sample size, and the type of statistic used.

2. *"Fishing" and multiple comparisons.* When multiple comparisons of mean differences are made ("fishing" for significance), the probability is increased that some of the comparisons will be different by chance alone. However, it should be noted that multivariate statistics (cf. Bock, 1975) and other procedures, such as adjustment of the *alpha* level (Ryan, 1959), can deal with this problem.

3. *Measure reliability.* Measures of low reliability inflate error terms, thus potentially providing invalid results.

4. *Treatment-implementation reliability.* Although Cook and Campbell referred to variations in the implementation of a treatment by different people, this threat may also apply to studies in which a naturally occurring treatment over which the researcher does not have control (such as an aspect of the physical environment) is used. When such a treatment is readministered (whether it be later in time to the same subjects or to an entirely new group of subjects), it is important to know that the treatment is reliable, that is, that it has not changed.

5. *Random irrelevancies in the research setting.* Frequently features in the research setting (other than the variables of interest) affect the data collected through increasing the error variance. Again, because it is often conducted in natural settings, environmental–behavioral research would appear to be particularly susceptible to this extraneous variance.

Research that cannot rule out these threats to statistical-conclusion validity may provide spurious data. The value of such data is, at best, difficult to assess.

Construct Validity

According to Cook and Campbell (1975), "construct validity refers to the validity with which cause and effect operations are labeled in theory-relevant and generalizable terms; and external validity refers to the validity with which a causal relationship can be generalized across persons, settings, and times" (p. 223). Although the above definitions refer to attempts to establish causal relationships, for our purposes the concepts of construct and external validity apply equally well to research in which noncausal inferences are made about the nature of relationships between variables. Construct validity deals with the problems of inference that occur when an operational definition can be construed in terms of more than one construct, thus making it difficult (if not impossible) to understand the "true" nature of the relationships among the variables of interest. It should be noted that this is one potential result of a lack of experiential realism (discussed below) where it is not clear to which aspects of a subject's environment he is responding. In a sense, construct validity refers to the experimental problem of "confounding," where it is not possible to tell what variable(s) account for the obtained findings.

In explicating construct validity, Cook and Campbell (1975) used as an example the Hawthorne studies (Roethlisberger and Dickson, 1939), which gave rise to the well-known Hawthorne Effect. As they pointed out, the interpretive problem there was not one of establishing that a treatment had increased the workers' productivity but rather of correctly labeling what it was that had caused the increase. Was the observed effect due to the increased illumination (the operationalized construct) or to some confounding variables, such as the apparent administrative concern for improved working conditions?

As presented by Cook and Campbell, there are numerous threats to construct validity. Those most pertinent to environmental–behavioral research are:

1. *Inadequate preoperational explication of constructs.* This refers to clearly defining and selecting the appropriate construct(s) prior to operationalization.
2. *Mono-operation bias.* Each operation should be multiply operationalized in order to increase validity.
3. *Monomethod bias.* Similar to Number 2 above; treatments and measures should be varied in order to increase validity.
4. *Subject effects and experimenter effects.* There is some literature indicating that artifactual findings may result from the subjects' fear of evaluation (Rosenberg, 1969; Weber and Cook, 1972) and/or the experimenter's expectancies (Rosenthal, 1966). For a review of these and similar threats to validity as they pertain to environmental–behavioral research, the reader is referred to Patterson (1974) and to Rosenthal and Rosnow (1969).
5. *Generalizing across time.* Statements about the relationship between variables should also include statements of the duration of that relationship. Many effects do not persist over time.

If, as stated above, construct validity is concerned with the proper identification of variables in theory-relevant terms, then a study that suffers from a lack of construct validity is of dubious value for the development of theory.

External Validity

As Bracht and Glass (1968) have stated, external validity is concerned with the correspondence between samples, the populations they represent, and the populations to which generalization is required. This can be extended to include generalization across times and, of particular importance for environmental–behavioral research, across settings. A typical way of increasing external validity is to sample randomly from the populations, times, and settings of interest. However, when one is attempting to conduct research in the settings in which the phenomena naturally occur, it is often difficult (if not impossible) to achieve this randomization. A basic difference between external validity and construct validity is that while external validity is concerned with correct sampling of people, places, and times, construct validity is concerned with correct sampling of abstract ideas (constructs) and measures.

Campbell and Stanley (1966) and Cook and Campbell (1975) have presented numerous threats to external validity. Among these are several that are particularly applicable to environmental–behavioral research:

1. *The interaction of multiple treatments.* When subjects are exposed to more than one treatment, it is impossible to generalize the results to other situations in which one or more of those treatments is not present. This is obviously a problem for naturalistic studies of environmental effects.

2. *The interaction of testing and the treatment.* In some cases, the measurement techniques utilized may "sensitize" the subject to the treatment, resulting in findings that are not generalizable.

3. *The interaction of subject selection and the treatment.* This is the most commonly thought of threat to external validity. To what extent are the obtained results due to the characteristics of the subject population involved (age, sex, race, etc.) and therefore not generalizable to people with different characteristics receiving the same treatment?

4. *The interaction of the setting and the treatment.* This refers to the extent to which the obtained relationship between the variables of interest will hold over different settings. This is not often a threat to environmental–behavioral research, where the setting frequently serves as the treatment.

5. *The interaction of history and treatment.* It is possible that the obtained results are to some extent due to some event that has interacted with the treatment. Thus it would be incorrect to generalize those results to some future time when the effects of that event have decayed.

Data that lack external validity, and thus cannot be generalized beyond the research setting in which it was collected, cannot contribute to useful environmental–behavioral theory.

The above threats to theory development are obviously also threats to valid data-collection. However, there are additional methodological weaknesses that can result in spurious data-collection and thus to which this problem-oriented field should be particularly sensitive. These problems include issues of measurement validity, reliability, and measure specificity (scope and sensitivity). For a review of these topics, the reader is directed to Campbell and Fiske (1959), Lindzey and Aronson (1968), Campbell and Stanley (1966), and Cook and Campbell (1975).

Experiential Realism

As stated above, theory-relevant research is considered here to be research that is derived from and applicable to theory and that thus can aid in theory development. In doing research, the scientist is rarely able to deal directly with the conceptual variables with which he is concerned. Thus he is forced to employ some translation ("operationalization") of the conceptual variables in the actual study. This fact of research life has import for the theory relevance of any given study.

Aronson and Carlsmith (1968) have developed the joint concepts of *experimental realism* and *mundane realism* to distinguish two ways in which an experiment involving such operationalizations can be said to be realistic to the subject. Although Aronson and Carlsmith were referring to laboratory experiments in social psychology, their concepts are applicable to both laboratory and field environmental–behavioral research.

A study can be said to have experimental realism if the situation of the experiment involves the subject and creates an impact on him. Mundane realism refers to how likely it is that the events that occur in the experiment will also occur in the real world. Many (perhaps most) events that occur in the real world are quite uninvolving, so a subject can be totally bored and uninterested and yet the experiment has mundane realism.

Thus the necessity to translate conceptual variables into measurable operations can result in research that is weak in either or both experimental and mundane realism. Such a study may provide results that are not relevant to a theory about how people actually behave in the real world. For the environment and behavior area, where the research is primarily problem-oriented, this is a highly salient problem.

In recognizing the problem-oriented approach of environmental psychology, Proshansky (1972) has utilized the term *phenomenon legitimacy* for evaluating research methods in the area. He has stated that the environmental psychologist must conduct his research in the actual physical settings or environments that concern him. Further the research must be carried out in ways that maintain the integrity of those settings, the people who are contained by them, and the activities that take place in them. Although Proshansky uses phenomenon legitimacy specifically for assessing whether the research instruments used are appropriate to the nature of the phenomenon being studied, the concept applies equally well to the relevance of the study for theory. A study that does not have phenomenon legitimacy would be of doubtful value, for the same reasons as stated above, in building a useful theory in this area.

It is apparent that experimental realism, mundane realism, and phenomenon legitimacy speak to the same general threats to theory-relevant research in the area of environment and behavior. That is, considering that the field is oriented toward solving problems that occur at the interface of environment and behavior, the choice of variables to be researched, the environment in which they are studied, and the effects of that examination and/or measurement upon the subjects in the study are crucial to the theory relevance of the research. It is possible to devise a single term for the above considerations: *experiential realism*. *Experiential realism* will be used in this chapter to refer to research that is realistic within the subject's experience and as such maintains fidelity to the variables and settings with which environmental–behavioral research is concerned. Any study, ranging from a laboratory manipulation to unobtrusive field research, in which the subject is asked to respond to variables that have no correspondence with his everyday experience, or that are not congruous with the settings in which the behavior of interest usually occurs, can be said to suffer from a lack of experiential realism. It is apparent that research that is lacking in experiential realism cannot meaningfully contribute to the development of environmental–behavioral theory.

Research Designs

The next section of this chapter examines some of the more typically employed environmental–behavioral research designs and data-collection methods. It is often difficult to separate research designs from the data-collection techniques utilized with those designs. For example, a descriptive-survey design would by nature utilize some type of questionnaire and/or interview. However, because many designs are not bound to any particular measurement techniques, and also because many designs employ more than one measurement technique in a given study, the examples below are arbitrarily divided into separate design and measurement sections.

These research methods will be discussed in terms of their strengths and weaknesses regarding the threats to theory discussed above. In most cases, examples of research that employ the design or data collection method will be cited. This is not intended as either a criticism or an endorsement of any particular study. Rather the examples were selected because they are illustrative of the method being discussed and are readily available to the interested reader in the area of environment and behavior.

Quasi-Experimental Designs

For an extensive review of quasi-experimental designs, the reader is directed to Campbell and Stanley (1966) and Cook and Campbell (1975). The quasi-experimental design used by Newman (1972) will be examined here in some detail, as it provides a good model for illustrating the above threats to theory relevance and validity. It is readily apparent that the lack of randomization that makes an experimental design quasi-experimental results in many threats to the internal validity of such a study. However, by dispensing with the necessity of randomization, the design provides an opportunity for strong experiential realism and external validity.

Newman offers an extensive quasi-experimental study of the relationship between crime rates and building design in a pair of New York City public-housing projects. The design used by Newman is what Campbell and Stanley (1966) call a "static-group" comparison, in which a group that has experienced a treatment is compared with one that has not, for the purpose of establishing the effect of the treatment. For Newman's purpose, the "treatment" was a differing amount of the design characteristic he labeled *defensible space*. One of the projects, a low-rise, was proposed to be high in defensible space, while the other project, a high-rise, was proposed to be low in defensible space. He reported significantly higher crime rates for the high-rise than for the low-rise, and he attributed that difference to the "treatment" (the physical-design differences).

In terms of experiential realism, Newman's quasi-experimental design is an exemplary model. The residents of the project had no idea that they were involved in a study (except for providing questionnaire data after the crime rate [dependent variable] had been established), the behaviors of interest were those that were real to their experience, and they performed those behaviors in their everyday settings.

However, this study suffers from a lack of construct validity. Although this is not necessarily a flaw of quasi-experimental designs, Newman's study yields some examples of the problems that can occur. He offered a theory of territoriality to explain why defensible space results in lower crime rates. His explanatory construct is that the "social fabric" created by spatial arrangements results in the defense of space (territory) against intruders (criminals). However, Hillier (1973) has argued persuasively that the literature does not support Newman's use of territorial theory. Further, Newman presented no data to indicate that the residents of the low-crime-rate project perceived any greater sense of territoriality than did the residents of the high-crime-rate project; that is, there is no evidence to show that he correctly labeled his explanatory construct. Thus the contribution of the study to further theory in this area is severely limited.

A further limitation to this study is due to threats to its external validity. The generalizability of the study is questionable because Newman carefully selected a subject population that embodied the characteristics he needed. No efforts to establish equivalence to other populations were reported. As presented by Kaplan (1973), neighboring projects had vastly differing crime rates. Further Kaplan reported that the experimental projects were apparently safer than most other neighborhoods in New York.

There are also major threats to the internal validity of Newman's study. In this (and most) quasi experiments, it is essential to establish that the groups would have been equivalent had it not been for the treatment. There is no formal means of doing this, other than randomization, which then provides a true rather than a quasi experiment. However, informal evidence can be presented to support the assumption of equivalency between the groups. Newman (1972) presented some data on the size and social characteristics of the families in the two projects in an effort to show that they were "comparitively identical populations" (p. 39). There was no statistical analysis of these data, and as Hillier (1973) has pointed out, even a casual viewing of the data indicates some important differences between the resident populations. Thus it is difficult to make the necessary assumption that the findings of the study are due to the effect of the "treatment" and not due to some difference between the groups.

Although not specific to quasi-experimental designs, this study contained several threats that serve to illustrate statistical-conclusion validity. Newman presented numerous analyses of variance. However, he presented only the total cases, the means, and the standard deviations. He never presented the F's, the degrees of freedom, or the error terms. The reader is left to accept his statement of "significance" and to ignore both the magnitude of the effect and the appropriateness of the test. In addition, a multiple-regression analysis of physical and social variables with indoor robberies is reported. After noting but failing to deal with problems of multicolinearity (cf. Tucker, Cooper, and Meredith, 1972) within the categories of variables, and also problems of small r^2's, Newman reported "significant" findings. However, because of his failure to present a model for his regression analysis, the results are not readily interpretable. There are further statistical-conclusion validity problems with this study that result from Newman's use of archival crime statistics. However, these will be dealt with later when data-collection methods are discussed.

The remaining research designs and data-collection methods are presented in general rather than specific terms. However, the reader is invited to apply the threats to theory development and valid data-collection presented earlier to the examples cited and/or to the reader's own research.

Experimental Designs

Both laboratory and field experiments are common in environmental–behavioral research. Prototypical of the laboratory experiments has been the research on human crowding (e.g., Freedman, Klevansky, and Ehrlich, 1971; Stokols, Rall, Pinner, and Schopler, 1973). These studies are inherently strong on internal validity. However, in terms of experiential realism they have little, if any, correspondence to the subjects' real world (cf. Baldassare and Fischer, Chapter 14). Further, the external validity is usually weak because of the use of subject populations that are easily available for laboratory experiments (typically college students and people who are institutionalized) and the use of the nongeneralizable laboratory setting.

Field experiments have ranged across such topics as invasions of personal space (e.g., the early work of Felipe and Sommer, 1966) and the real-world establishment of territoriality (Edney, 1972). As with laboratory experiments, field experiments can rule out all threats to internal validity. However, unlike laboratory experiments, field experiments can be high on experiential realism and external validity. By conducting the research in the field, diverse populations may be studied while engaging in typical behavior in natural settings. There are, of course, numerous obstacles to conducting true experiments in field settings, but the creative researcher can successfully overcome them.

Exploratory–Descriptive Designs

Much of the extant environmental–behavioral research is exploratory and/or descriptive in nature. Designs used in such studies are not intended to test a hypothesis of a cause-and-effect relationship between variables but are utilized specifically for developing an accurate description and/or exploration of a situation or of an association between variables. For an extensive discussion of exploratory and descriptive studies, the reader is referred to Selltiz, Jahoda, Deutsch, and Cook (1959). As Selltiz *et al.* point out, because these designs are not constrained by requiring a test of causal relationship, they can be extremely flexible in nature. As a result, a great diversity of designs has been used, with the major methodological concerns centering around the data-collection techniques employed. Therefore the threats to theory relevance and validity associated with exploratory descriptive research will be discussed below in the section on data-collection methods.

Simulations

Simulations of "real-world" settings and events for research purposes have included a wide range of situations, among them the use of the arrangement of dolls for measuring personal space (Kuethe, 1962) and crowding (Desor, 1972), the playing of laboratory games for the measurement of multiple types of environmental behavior (House and Patterson, 1972), the use of the computer to simulate human urban movement (Studer and Hobson, 1973), and laboratory visual equipment intended to simulate the entire environment (Craik and Appleyard, 1970; McKechnie, Chapter 8). In all cases, the fact that a simulation is used, as opposed to a measurement of "real-world" phenomena, results in a loss of experiential realism. It should be noted that simulations are used to create artificially either the independent and dependent variables or both of them. However, regardless of what is simulated, the results will have limited applicability to non-simulated, naturally occurring events.

Similarly, external validity must suffer when either setting or behavior is simulated. The obtained findings can be generalized only to similarly simulated conditions. This is indeed ironic, for simulations are often offered as an alternative to the difficulties of actual tests of theory or measurments of phenomena in multiple field settings! Extensive work on validating various simulation techniques is necessary in order to establish their external validity.

Construct validity is a particular problem for simulation research. Although these designs can be very strong on internal validity because of the almost total control of the researcher, the operations necessary to simulate environmental variables are prone to threats to construct validity. That is, when the researcher creates a construct, its relationship to a theory-relevant, real-world referent is often difficult to ascertain.

Mathematical Modeling

Math models have been used in environmental–behavioral research to study such phenomena as human movement in space (King, 1969) and the impact of large-scale built projects (Peterson, Schofer, and Gemmell, 1974). Although not technically a research design, the technique of developing mathematical models to account for observed phenomena is susceptible to the methodological problems discussed above. These models are dependent on the validity of the data used in their construction. It is therefore obvious that threats to statistical-conclusion validity are exceedingly damaging to a math model, for unreliable measures and incorrect statistics could only result in spurious outcomes. Other threats to the validity of math models are related to data-collection methods and will be discussed below.

Cross-Cultural Designs

There has not been a large output of cross-cultural environmental–behavioral research. Examples of what has been done are cross-cultural observations of proxemic behavior (e.g., Hall, 1966) and experiments on cross-cultural environmental perception (Kates, 1970). This relative paucity of research is unfortunate, for as Whiting (1968) points out, one of the great advantages of cross-cultural research is that it ensures results that relate to human behavior in general rather than being bound to a single culture. However, what is gained in external validity is often lost in internal and construct validity. If the researcher is not totally familiar with the culture he is investigating, the study can easily lose internal validity (because of biased subject selection) and lose construct validity (because of misinterpretations of the nature of the treatment variable in that culture).

Data-Collection Methods

Environmental–behavioral researchers have utilized the full range of data-collection methods offered by social scientists, besides having invented a few of their own. For explanatory purposes, the methods are divided here into two major categories: observational methods and self-report methods.

Observational Methods

One observational data-collection method is the obtrusive method, in which the subject is aware that he is being observed. The specific methods used have included research in which the observer is present, such as Barker (1968) and his associates' recording of the ecology of behavior settings, and Ittelson, Rivlin, and Proshansky's (1970) work on behavioral mapping; research on human crowding phenomena in which unmasked filming (the camera and cameraman are openly present in the setting) is employed (Rohe and Patterson, 1974); and research in which behavior in an extreme environment (the Tektite 2 undersea habitat) is recorded, with the subject's knowledge, through continuous video and audio monitoring (Helmreich, 1974). As a group, obtrusive observational methods suffer from the threats to internal and construct validity that arise from the subjects' perception of being "measured." For a review of the potential artifacts resulting from this perception, the reader is directed to Patterson (1974).

With the possible exception of participant observation (which may yield the observer greater insight into the phenomena he is studying), unobtrusive observational methods can yield the same (if not richer) data as obtrusive observations, with fewer threats to validity. The richer data may result from the fact that removing the conspicuous observer results in a study with greater experiential realism. Further many of the threats to internal and construct validity will be alleviated by the nonreactivity resulting from the subjects' lack of awareness of being observed (cf. Webb, Campbell, Schwartz, and Sechrest, 1966). Among the many environmental–behavioral studies that have used unobtrusive measures are studies of physical design and archival crime records (e.g., Galle, Gove, and McPherson, 1972; Newman, 1972); observations of the use of human space (e.g., Reid and Novak, 1975); and a study of density and helping behavior using the lost-letter technique (Bickman, Teger, Gabriele, McLaughlin, Berger, and Sunaday, 1973). Although methods such as using archival records and the lost-letter technique are clearly not observational in nature, they fit the observational category used here more closely than they do the self-report category and serve to illustrate some of the strengths of unobtrusive measures.

However, unobtrusive measures are prone to some threats to construct validity. When one is using unobtrusive measures, it is often difficult, if not impossible, to ascertain what it is that is resulting in the subject's behavior; that is, is the subject responding to what is assumed to be the "treatment" or to some other feature(s) of the research setting? Ironically this threat to construct validity can often be eliminated only through the use of obtrusive measures.

Self-Report Methods

Perhaps the most commonly used environmental–behavioral data-collection methods are those that record the self-reports of the subjects (or respondents, in this case). Of these, interviews and questionnaires that measure some form of the respondent's attitudes have been most popular. Interviews have most typically been employed in the evaluation of buildings and architectural programming studies (cf. Gutman and Westergaard, 1974; Zeisel, 1975). As interviews are subject to the same threats to validity as questionnaires, the discussion below applies as well to them.

The techniques used for questionnaire-type measurement of attitudes have included surveys measuring environmental attitudes (e.g., Canter, 1969; Althoff and Greig, 1974); scales that assess environmental preferences and dispositions (e.g., McKechnie, 1970; Kaplan, 1973); and methods such as the semantic-differential andrepertory-grid technique that measure perceptions of the environment (cf. Bechtel, 1973; Harrison and Sarre, 1975). There are also questionnaire-type measures that are not directed at attitudes. Among these are cognitive mapping methods (Stea and Downs, 1970, 1973) and time-budget research (e.g., Chapin, 1971).

All of these self-report methods threaten the experiential realism of the research. The mere presence of an interviewer or being asked to complete a questionnaire (or draw a map or complete a time budget) changes the features of the natural, everyday settings. Although we are fast approaching it with some overstudied populations, being asked to participate in research is still not part of the typical behavioral experience of the average person.

If the researcher is skillful, he can avoid the threats to internal validity in such designs, but the obtrusive nature of the self-report method results in some threats to construct validity. Largest among these are the possible artifactual findings due to subject and experimenter effects (cf. Patterson, 1974; Rosenthal and Rosnow, 1969). Some of these threats can be reduced through the use of multiple measures. Campbell and Fiske (1959) have suggested this approach in order to gain what they term *convergent validation*. In effect, to the extent that the results obtained from the different methods converge, the more likely it is that those results are valid and are not artifactual. The use of compound methods, in which two or more different measurement techniques are employed, has been advocated for evaluations of buildings by Patterson and Passini (1974). In this case, construct validity can be increased by the measurement of both attitudes *and* behavior. Similarly the crowding research of Stokols *et al.* (1973) utilized a questionnaire, unobtrusive observations of behavior, and the score on a laboratory game as dependent variables.

Environmental–Behavioral Research: The Future

The research designs and data-collection methods discussed above all suffer, in varying degrees, from threats to theory-relevant research and problem-applicable data collection. Perhaps these problems are compounded for the environmental–behavioral researcher because the area is historically and practicably bound to traditional social-science research methods while attempting to study nontraditional phenomena.

However, the researcher is by no means in a state of methodological helplessness. As stated above, each method has its strengths, which can be utilized, and its weaknesses, which can be avoided. We can achieve this by embracing innovative techniques, which are at the forefront of the social sciences today, and/or by developing techniques specifically for environmental–behavioral research.

An example of applying innovative procedures would be the Campbell and Fiske (1959) multiple-methods approach to "convergent validation" discussed above, whereby the strengths of the various methods can be utilized in compound designs. That is, laboratory experiments can be combined with field experiments, quasi experiments with true experiments, etc., in order to increase the validity of any given set of findings. Similarly (as Campbell and Fiske suggest), data-collection methods can be combined in studies for the same reason. The continuing development of multivariate statistical techniques (cf. Bock, 1975) enables the researcher to analyze and interpret these multiple variables.

Advances in social-science research methods by creative and innovative researchers indicate the nature of other new techniques. Certainly quasi-experimental research designs such as interrupted time-series analysis, regression-discontinuity designs, and cross-lagged panel correlations (Cook and Campbell, 1975) have great potential for use in the real-world settings of environmental–behavioral research.

What of the innovative techniques yet to be developed? These will reflect the needs and the ingenuity of the environmental–behavioral researcher. One example of what has already occurred in this area would be the elaborate observational and recording methods devised by Barker (1968) and his associates to study behavior in its natural setting. It is apparent that in order to avoid being severely constrained by the very environment that they wish to study, environmental–behavioral researchers need to move forward into innovative research methods.

In closing, let us note that the problem-oriented nature of the environmental–behavioral area often results in research that is directed toward some applied goal, such as increasing user satisfaction within a particular setting. In this and similar cases, there is no concern for the development of theory or generalizability to other settings (Sommer, 1973). Here the researcher can ignore many of the threats to theoretical development discussed above and need only be concerned with measurement validity and reliability. The design and data-collection methods utilized can be selected solely on the basis of whether they are effective in achieving the desired goal. Thus the environmental–behavioral researcher can make optimal use of the available research methods by trying to achieve maximum congruence between the particular problem being researched and the design and data-collection method to be utilized.

References

Althoff, P., and Greig, W. Environmental pollution control policy-making. *Environment and Behavior*, 1974, 6(3), 259–288.

Altman, I. Some perspectives on the study of man–environment phenomena. *Representative Research in Social Psychology*, 1973, 4(1), 109–126.

Altman, I. *The environment and social behavior*. Monterey, Calif.: Brooks/Cole, 1975.

Aronson, E., and Carlsmith, J. M. Experimentation in social psychology. In G. Lindsey and E. Aronson (Eds.), *The handbook of social psychology* (vol. 2). Reading, Pa.: Addison-Wesley, 1968.

Baldassare, M., and Fischer, C. The relevance of crowding experiments to urban studies. In D. Stokols (Ed.), *Perspectives on environment and behavior: Conceptual and Empirical Trends*. New York: Plenum Press, 1976.

Barker, R. G. *Ecological psychology: Concepts and methods for studying the environment of human behavior*. Stanford, Calif.: Stanford University Press, 1968.

Bechtel, R. B. Architectural space and semantics: Should the twain try to meet? In W. Preiser (Ed.), *Environmental design research* (vol. 2). Stroudsburg, Pa.: Dowden, Hutchinson, and Ross, 1973.

Bickman, L., Teger, A., Gabriele, T., McLaughlin, C., Berger, M., and Sunaday, E. Dormitory density and helping behavior. *Environment and Behavior*, 1973, 5(4), 465–490.

Bock, R. *Multivariate statistical methods in behavioral research*. New York: McGraw-Hill, 1975.

Bracht, G., and Glass, G. The external validity of experiments. *American Educational Research Journal*, 1968, 5, 437–474.

Brunswik, E. *Perception and the representative design of psychological experiments*. Berkeley: University of California Press, 1956.

Campbell, D., and Fiske, D. Convergent and discriminant validation by the multitrait–multimethod matrix. *Psychological Bulletin*, 1959, 56, 81–105.

Campbell, D., and Stanley, J. *Experimental and quasi-experimental designs for research*. Chicago: Rand McNally, 1966.

Canter, D. V. The subjective assessment of the environment. *Building performance research unit*. Glasgow: University of Strathclyde, 1969.

Chapin, F. S., Jr. Free time activities and the quality of urban life. *Journal of the American Institute of Planners*, 1971, 37, 411–416.

Cook, T., and Campbell, D. The design and conduct of quasi-experiments and true experiments in field settings. In M. Dunnette (Ed.), *Handbook of industrial and organizational research*. New York: Rand McNally, 1975.

Craik, K., and Appleyard, D. Discussion of the environmental simulator. *Berkeley Catalogue*. Berkeley: University of California, 1970.

Desor, J. A. Toward a psychological theory of crowding. *Journal of Personality and Social Psychology*, 1972, *21*, 79–83.

Edney, J. Property, possession, and permanence: A field study in human territoriality. *Journal of Applied Social Psychology*, 1972, *2*, 275–282.

Edney, J. Human territoriality. *Psychological Bulletin*, 1974, *81*(12), 959–975.

Evans, G., and Howard, R. Personal space. *Psychological Bulletin*, 1973, *80*, 334–344.

Felipe, N., and Sommer, R. Invasions of personal space. *Social Problems*, 1966, *14*(2), 206–214.

Freedman, J., Klevansky, S., and Ehrlich, P. The effect of crowding on human task performance. *Journal of Applied Social Psychology*, 1971, *1*, 7–25.

Galle, O., Gove, W., and McPherson, J. Population pathology and density. *Science*, 1972, *176*, 23–80.

Gutman, R., and Westergaard, B. Building evaluation, user satisfaction, and design. In J. Lang, C. Burnette, W. Moleski, and D. Vachon (Eds.), *Designing for human behavior*. Stroudsburg, Pa.: Dowden, Hutchinson, and Ross, 1974.

Hall, E. T. *The hidden dimension*. Garden City, N.Y.: Doubleday, 1966.

Harrison, J., and Sarre, P. Personal construct theory in the measurement of environmental images. *Environment and Behavior*, 1975, *7*(1), 3–58.

Heimstra, N. W., and McFarling, L. H. *Environmental psychology*. Monterey, Calif.: Brooks/ Cole, 1974.

Helmreich, R. Evaluation of environments: Behavioral observations in an undersea habitat. In J. Lang, C. Burnette, W. Moleski, and D. Vachon (Eds.), *Designing for human behavior*. Stroudsburg, Pa.: Dowden, Hutchinson, and Ross, 1974.

Hillier, W. In defense of space. *RIBA Journal*, 1973 (November), 539–544.

House, P. W., and Patterson, P. D. (Eds.). *An environmental simulation laboratory for the social sciences*. Washington, D.C.: United States Environmental Protection Agency, 1972.

Ittelson, W., Proshansky, H., Rivlin, L., and Winkel, G. *An introduction to environmental psychology*. New York: Holt, Rinehart, and Winston, 1974.

Ittelson, W., Rivlin, L., and Proshansky, H. The use of behavioral maps in environmental psychology. In H. Proshansky, W. I. Ittelson, and L. Rivlin (Eds.), *Environmental psychology*. New York: Holt, Rinehart and Winston, 1970.

Kaplan, R. Some psychological benefits of gardening. *Environment and Behavior*, 1973, *5*(2), 145–162.

Kaplan, S. Defensible space: A review. *Architectural Forum*, 1973 (May) 98.

Kates, R. W. Human perception of the environment. *International Social Science Journal*, 1970, *22*, 648–660.

King, L. J. *Statistical analyses in geography*. Englewood Cliffs, N.J.: Prentice-Hall, 1969.

Kuethe, J. L. The pervasive influence of social schemata. *Journal of Abnormal and Social Psychology*, 1962, *65*, 71–74.

Lewin, K. Behavior and development as a function of the total situation. In L. Carmichael (Ed.), *Manual of child psychology*. New York: Wiley, 1946.

Lindzey, G., and Aronson, E. (Eds.). *The handbook of social psychology* (vol. 2, *Research methods*). Reading, Pa.: Addison-Wesley, 1968.

McKechnie, G. E. Measuring environmental dispositions with the environmental response inventory. In J. Archea and C. Eastman (Eds.), *EDRA Two*. Pittsburgh, Pa.: Carnegie-Mellon University, 1970.

McKechnie, G. E. Simulation techniques in environmental psychology. In D. Stokols (Ed.), *Perspectives on environment and behavior: Conceptual and empirical trends*. New York: Plenum Press, 1976.

Newman, O. *Defensible space*. New York: Macmillan, 1972.

Patterson, A. Unobtrusive measures: Their nature and utility for architects. In J. Lang, C.

Burnette, W. Moleski, and D. Vachon (Eds.), *Designing for human behavior*. Stroudsburg, Pa.: Dowden, Hutchinson, and Ross, 1974.

Patterson, A., and Passini, R. The evaluation of physical settings: To measure attitudes, behavior, or both? In D. Carson (ed.), *EDRA 5*. Stroudsburg, Pa.: Dowden, Hutchinson, and Ross, 1974.

Peterson, G. L., Schofer, J., and Gemmell, R. Multidisciplinary, design-interactive evaluation of large-scale projects. In D. Carson (Ed.), *EDRA 5*. Stroudsburg, Pa.: Dowden, Hutchinson, and Ross, 1974.

Proshansky, H. M. Methodology in environmental psychology: Problems and issues. *Human Factors*, 1972, *14*(5), 451–460.

Proshansky, H. M., Ittelson, W. I., and Rivlin, L. *Environmental psychology*. New York: Holt, Rinehart and Winston, 1970.

Rapoport, A. An approach to the construction of man–environment theory. In W. Preiser (Ed.), *Environmental design research* (vol. 2. Stroudsburg, Pa.: Dowden, Hutchinson, and Ross, 1973.

Reid, E., and Novak, P. Personal space: An unobtrusive measures study. *Bulletin of the Psychonomic Society*, 1975, *5*, 265–266.

Roethlisberger, F., and Dickson, W. *Management and the worker*. Cambridge, Mass.: Harvard University Press, 1939.

Rohe, W., and Patterson, A. The effects of varied levels of resources and density of behavior in a day care center. In D. Carson (Ed.), *EDRA 5*. Stroudsburg, Pa.: Dowden, Hutchinson, and Ross, 1974.

Rosenberg, M. The conditions and consequences of evaluation apprehension. In R. Rosenthal and R. Rosnow (Eds.), *Artifacts in behavioral research*. New York: Academic, 1969.

Rosenthal, R. *Experimenter effects in behavioral research*. New York: Appleton-Century-Crofts, 1966.

Rosenthal, R., and Rosnow, R. (Eds.). *Artifacts in behavioral research*. New York: Academic, 1969.

Ryan, T. Multiple comparisons in psychological research. *Psychological Bulletin*, 1959, *56*, 26–47.

Selltiz, C., Jahoda, M., Deutsch, M., and Cook, S. *Research methods in social relations*. New York: Holt, Rinehart and Winston, 1959.

Smith, M. B. Some problems of strategy in environmental psychology. In D. Stokols (Ed.), *Perspectives on environment and behavior*. New York: Plenum, 1976.

Sommer, R. Evaluation, yes; research, maybe. *Representative Research in Social Psychology*, 1973, *4*, 127–133.

Stea, D., and Downs, R. (Eds.). Cognitive representations of man's spatial environment. *Environment and Behavior*, 1970, *2*(1) (entire issue).

Stea, D., and Downs, R. *Image and environment*. Chicago: Aldine, 1973.

Stokols, D. A social–psychological model of human crowding phenomena. *Journal of the American Institute of Planners*, 1972 (March), 72–83.

Stokols, D., Rall, M., Pinner, B., and Schopler, J. Physical, social, and personal determinants of the perception of crowding. *Environment and Behavior*, 1973, *5*(1), 87–113.

Studer, R. G. Man–environment relations: Discovery or design. In W. Preiser (Ed.), *Environmental design research* (vol. 2). Stroudsburg, Pa.: Dowden, Hutchinson, and Ross, 1973.

Studer, R. G., and Hobson, R. J. Simulation of human learning in urban movement systems. In W. Preiser (Ed.), *Environmental design research* (vol. 2). Stroudsburg, Pa.: Dowden, Hutchinson, and Ross, 1973.

Tolman, E. *Purposive behavior in animals and men*. New York: Appleton-Century-Crofts, 1932.

Tucker, L., Cooper, L., and Meredith, W. Obtaining squared multiple correlations from a correlation matrix which may be singular. *Psychometrika*, 1972, *37*, 143–148.

Webb, E., Campbell, D., Schwartz, R., and Sechrest, L. *Unobtrusive measures*. Chicago: Rand McNally, 1966.

Weber, S., and Cook, T. Subject effects in laboratory research. *Psychological Bulletin,* 1972, 77, 273–295.

Whiting, J. W. M. Methods and problems in cross-cultural research. In G. Lindzey and E. Aronson (Eds.), *The handbook of social psychology* (vol. 2). Reading, Pa.: Addison-Wesley, 1968.

Willems, E. Development of the ecological perspective in psychology. In D. Stokols (Ed.), *Perspectives on environment and behavior: Conceptual and empirical trends.* New York: Plenum Press, 1976.

Zeisel, J. *Sociology and architectural design.* New York: Russell Sage, 1975.

Author Index

Subject Index